Muhammad, the Qur'an & Islam

by N. A. Newman

Interdisciplinary Biblical Research Institute
P.O. Box 4253
Hatfield, PA 19440 USA

Muhammad, the Qur'an & Islam
Copyright 1996 by N. A. Newman

Published by the
Interdisciplinary Biblical Research Institute
P.O. Box 423, Hatfield, PA 19440-0423 USA
Phone (215) 368-5000x153 (voice mail)
Fax (215) 368-7002

Library of Congress Catalog Card Number 96-78495

hardcover ISBN 0-944788-85-8
paperback ISBN 0-944788-86-6

Cover design by James I. Newman

Table of Contents

Introduction   vii

Pre-Islamic Arabia   1

The Sources for Muhammad's Biography   15

Muhammad: Birth to Ministry   25

Muhammad: His Call   39

Muhammad: Meccan Opposition   77

Muhammad: The Hijra   139

Muhammad: Break with the Jews   187

Muhammad: Victory and Death   245

The Qur'an   311

Islamic Tradition   323

Appendix A: *Sira* Traditions   329

Appendix B: Sura Orderings   349

Appendix C: Qur'anic Time Chart   357

Appendix D: Qur'anic Narratives   363

Appendix E: Qur'anic Prophets and Persons   391

Appendix F: Verse Source Information   409

Bibliography   419

Table of Contents

vii

1

13

25

35

77

171

187

245

311

327

339

349

Appendix ... Uniform Case Chart ... 357

363

Appendix E: ... Preface and Glossary ... 391

Appendix F: Verse Source Information ... 409

Bibliography ... 419

Key to Abbreviations
for works referenced

ECMD	*The Early Christian-Muslim Dialogue*
EI²	*Encyclopaedia of Islam* (2nd edition)
GQ	*Geschichte des Qorans*
JRAS	*Journal of the Royal Asiatic Society*
JSAI	*Jerusalem Studies in Arabic and Islam*
MW	*The Moslem World*
SEI	*Shorter Encyclopaedia of Islam*
WMJA	*Was hat Mohammed aus dem Judenthume aufgenommen?*
ZDMG	*Zeitschrift der deutschen morgenländischen Gesellschaft*

Key to Abbreviations

for works referenced

Introduction

Over the centuries, much research has been done on the life of Muhammad, the text of the Qur'an and the development of Islam. Almost no works, however, have sought to systematically integrate the various results of the research in these areas. The discrepancies, for instance, between the biographical (*Sira*) traditions about Muhammad and the inherent witness of the Qur'an have certainly been known to those familiar with both of these sciences. What is not well known, though, is why no one has tried to generally reconcile these discrepancies.

One prominent Western biographer of Muhammad, for instance, has openly defended his own neglect[1] of research into the direct "sources" of the Qur'an by appealing to the example of Shakespeare's work *Hamlet* and reasoning that:[2]

> 1) "the study of sources does not explain away the ideas whose sources are found, nor does it detract from their truth and validity."
>
> 2) "Shakespeare's play of *Hamlet* remains a very great play even after we have found the 'source' from which Shakespeare derived the outline of the story."
>
> 3) "No more does our knowledge of the source tell us anything of importance about the creative processes in Shakespeare's mind."

These arguments appear to be unjustified, however, since:

> 1) The proper study of sources is not to "explain away the ideas whose sources are found," but rather to aid in better understanding the text at hand. The choice of *Hamlet* as a comparison for the Qur'an was inadequate, since Shakespeare claims neither truthfulness (historicity) nor

validity for *Hamlet*, and his audience certainly expects neither of these.

2) As a piece of entertainment, Shakespeare's *Hamlet* remains a great play in the opinion of many, even after the sources of its plot have been found.

3) With respect to *Hamlet*, "the creative processes in Shakespeare's mind" can *only* be realized by comparing the sources to his production and then noting all of the modifications which Shakespeare himself made.

As opposed to Shakespeare's *Hamlet*, the Qur'an not only claims historicity and validity, but it also professes to be God's Word. It is indeed the magnitude of these claims which warrants serious investigation of both the text of the Qur'an and its *possible* sources. Furthermore, as the development of Islamic tradition indicates, one's knowledge of Muhammad's life and the earliest stages of Islam is greatly enhanced by practically any aspect of Qur'anic research.

This present work discusses and references the findings and theories of many generations of scholars concerning the *possible* sources of the Qur'an. Nevertheless, the conclusive evaluation of these materials is left to each individual reader.

One non-Qur'anic illustration of how source information *can* be employed in a theological sense, may be found in the development of traditions surrounding the Old Testament priest Zachariah, the son of Jehoiada: In II Chr. 24:21f the priest Zachariah is shown as having been murdered in the court of the Temple at Jerusalem as he called for the Lord's vengeance. This request of Zachariah was then at least partially fulfilled when Joash, the king who had ordered Zachariah's killing, was murdered by his own servants (II Chr. 24:25). As an apparent exegetical elaboration on Ezek. 24:7f,[3] Jewish rabbis claimed that Zachariah's death was avenged by the Babylonian Nebuzaradan during the destruction of Jerusalem in the time of Nebuchadnezzar.[4] The apocryphal Protevangelion, which was used by sects that had broken off from Christianity, seems to have confused Zachariah, the son of Jehoiada, with Zacharias, the father of John the Baptist in a story similar to the Jewish legends.[5] The Islamic accounts, whose plots are even more dependent on the Jewish traditions about vengeance for Zachariah, not only exchange John the Baptist for Zachariah, but they also maintain that the Babylonians invaded Jerusalem after John had been executed.[6] Clearly, II Chr. 24:21f is the ultimate source of these traditions,[7] which was subsequently modified and changed in the accounts mentioned above. Jewish traditions seem to have wanted Ezek. 24:7f to have been fulfilled by the Babylonians as a vengeance for Zachariah's death, and the writers of the Protevangelion may have simply desired to depict Zacharias as a martyr (Prot. 16:14). None of the Islamic traditions about the vengeance for John the Baptist's execution are said to have originated with Muhammad, but the "corrected" version of the story (where Nebuzaradan appears in place of Nebuchadnezzar)[8] strongly suggests that a non-Christian exegesis of Qur'an 17:4-8 may have been the main motive for modifying the earlier accounts.[9]

Although some sources can be traced with relative certainty, such as in the previous example, others are more indefinite. For example, the "wife of the Pharaoh" (in the time of Moses), who is depicted as having been a "believer" in Qur'an 66:11, was named "Asiya" by later Muslim authorities. One Western scholar[10] thinks that "Asiya" was probably derived from "Asenath," the wife of Joseph (cf. Gen. 41:45), but this name could rather have come from a 4th century AD Coptic work, in which Monophysites claim that "Assia" was one of the daughters of Joseph the carpenter from a previous marriage.[11]

Similar to the examples discussed above, the Qur'an often makes allusion to narratives which ultimately came from the Bible. Although Muslims of later generations have charged that the Bible was corrupted by its transmitters (e.g. in passages portraying Jesus as the Son of God), it can rather easily be shown that the Bible manuscripts pre-, ante- and postdating Muhammad bear none of the changes which Muslims purport. Moreover, throughout the centuries Muslims exegetes have often availed themselves of information from the Bible in order to either fill in a Qur'anic narrative, or simply to better understand the text of the Qur'an. As an additional form of source research, Muslim scholars tried to find the etymologies for foreign vocabulary in the Qur'an and attempted to trace the lives of persons named or mentioned in the Qur'an. Later, this science attracted scholars from Judaism and Christianity, who though less familiar with the Qur'an, were more acquainted with the non-Arabic languages of the Middle East, the Bible and Judeo-Christian traditions.

Whereas biographers of Muhammad's life have generally favored the *Sira* traditions at the expense of Qur'anic research, scholars of the Qur'an have pretty much done the opposite in favoring Qur'anic research over Islamic tradition. Early Muslim scholars were the first to try to arrange the Qur'an's suras chronologically,[12] and although this established the broadest link to the *Sira* traditions, the results of this research were not implemented in conjunction with them. Later, Western sura orderings were also constructed, which were more or less "chronological" by virtue of their dependence on the chronological Islamic orderings.[13] Nevertheless, Western scholars also did not attempt to integrate these findings generally with the *Sira* traditions.

It is the view of the present author that the most accurate understanding of the Qur'an, the biography of Muhammad and the earliest developments in Islam is obtained by attempting to reconcile the widest spectrum of information about them.

Unfortunately, modern Western research of Islam seems to be approaching the limit of historical skepticism. Many of the critics of Islamic tradition, for example, have concluded that there is practically nothing reliable to be found in tradition, and some have maintained that the most trustworthy Islamic source is the Qur'an.[14] In the field of Qur'anic research, however, the notion of "chronological sura orderings" has been abandoned,[15] and the Qur'an is said to have been revealed in passages from indefinite time periods.[16] At least one Western scholar claims that the "standard text" of the Qur'an "as implied in the `Uthman recension traditions"[17] could hardly have predated the 3rd century AH.[18]

As will be shown in the pages that follow, there is rather solid evidence which shows that the Qur'an has not been preserved to our generation without modifications or loss. At the same time, *some* of the "hadith" (in the broadest sense of "Islamic traditions," whether they come from the *Sira* or later canonical collections) can be shown to have been at least "improvements" of later Islamic theologians. Nevertheless, as one of the tenets of source research implies, some parts of the Qur'an appear to have been modified *because* there was earlier something there to modify, some parts of the Qur'an have apparently been lost *because* there must have been something there originally, and some hadith were improved *because* there was previously something there to improve.

A bibliography of the references which were used in this work is provided at the close of this book. Frequently in the notes an editor or translator of a reference is shown in the position of the author simply as a means of briefly identifying the work cited; the abbreviation "f" is also used for "ff" in the interest of saving space. The author apologizes for the (at times) abrupt style of the book, but the transfer of information was deemed to be more important than having a "flowing" literary style which would have significantly lengthened the text.[19] The collections of *Sira* traditions which have been used are given in Appendix A, and the sura orderings of Nöldeke have been employed, with some alterations.[20] The identification of Qur'an passages follows the Cairo system of verse division, and references to the canonical hadith of Bukhari, Muslim and Abu Dawud are from the editions listed in the bibliography.

The author would like to thank IBRI for their willingness to publish and distribute the present work, and gratefully acknowledges the resource assistance of Dr. Robert C. Newman, Peter Reinecke and Eugen Pietras.

Notes:

[1] Watt in *Introduction*, p. vi; cf. Watt, *Muhammad*, p. 46.

[2] Watt, *Introduction*, pp. 184 f.

[3] See Lightfoot in *Lost Books*, p. 36, n. 1, who references Taanit 69 of the Jerusalem Talmud.

[4] Cf. Sanhedrin 96b (Babylonian Talmud); Ginzberg, *Legends*, vol. 4, p. 304; vol. 6, pp. 396 f, or *Legends of the Bible*, p. 610; *SEI*, p. 654.

[5] Protevangelion 16:9f (*Lost Books*), p. 36; cf. *SEI*, p. 654.

[6] Tabari, *History*, vol. 4, pp. 104-111.

[7] II Chr. 24 is certainly the oldest of the works mentioned in this regard.

[8] In Tabari, *History*, vol. 4, pp. 103-107, it is Nebuchadnezzar who avenges John the Baptist's death, but after reasoning that Nebuchadnezzar had fought the Israelites much earlier than this (Ibid., vol. 4, p. 107), Tabari gives a tradition from Ibn Ishaq whereby it is Nebuzaradan (cf. Jer. 39:9f and the Talmudic references in nn. 3 and 4, above), who was sent by the Babylonian king "Khardus" (Herod!) who avenges John's death (Tabari, *History*, vol. 4, pp. 108-111). Cf. *SEI*, p. 640.

[9] Qur'an 17:4-8 appears to refer to the two destructions of the Temple at Jerusalem, and in his *History* (vol. 4, p. 111), Tabari shows that the first destruction of the Temple was in the days of Nebuchadnezzar and that the second was in the time of Nebuzaradan (see n. 8, above). Whereas the Jews do not seem to have had a good "explanation" for the destruction of the second Temple (cf. Josephus, *Wars of the Jews*, 6, 5, 4), Christian doctrine shows that the second Temple was destroyed because of the rejection and execution of Jesus Christ (Dan. 9:25f; Lk. 19:41f; 20:13f). However, since at least the later Muslim Qur'an exegetes did not believe that Jesus was killed, they seem to have claimed that the vengeance for John the Baptist's death was the reason for the second destruction which is mentioned in Qur'an 17:4-8. This passage in the Qur'an is moreover thought to be similar to the works of early Christian writers (see p. 102, n. 263, below).

[10] Horovitz, *Untersuchungen*, p. 86; cf. Brinner in Tabari, *History*, vol. 3, p. 31, n. 167; and p. 393, below.

[11] See *The* (Coptic) *History of Joseph the Carpenter*, chapter 2, as given in *Ante-Nicene Fathers*, vol. 8, p. 388.

[12] See Appendix B. Cf. Watt and Bell, *Introduction*, pp. 108 f; *EI²*, s.v. "Kur'an", pp. 414 f.

[13] See Appendix B. Cf. Watt and Bell, *Introduction*, pp. 109 f; *EI²*, s.v. "Kur'an", pp. 416 f.

[14] See Schwally, *GQ*, vol. 2, pp. 193 f; Watt in Tabari, History, vol. 6, pp. xvii f.

[15] Watt and Bell, *Introduction*, pp. 113 f; *EI²*, s.v. "Kur'an," pp. 417 f.

[16] Partially because of the evidence that some passages of the Qur'an were re-edited after they had been committed to writing, Bell did not attempt to date many parts of the Qur'an; see Bell, *Translation*, passim.

[17] See pp. 312 f, below.

[18] See Wansbrough, *Quranic Studies*, p. 44. Some changes were indeed made to the text of the Qur'an well into the 3rd century AH (see p. 314, below), however, it is generally held that the orthographical variants to the text of the Qur'an ('Uthman's recension) were committed to writing in the 2nd century AH; *GQ*, vol. 3, pp. 9, 20.

[19] Those who have read Nöldeke and Schwally, *GQ*, vol. 1; Horovitz, *Untersuchungen*, or Wansbrough, *Quranic Studies*, to name a few, are no doubt familiar with this problem.

[20] Nöldeke's list of sura orderings was implemented in this work because of its relative accuracy and practicality. Contrary to some generally phrased critiques of these sura orderings, Nöldeke and Schwally did assign the shorter passages of some suras to varying time periods. In some places in the text below, the sura orderings of Blachère were used. The Qur'anic research of Bell is mentioned occasionally, but on the whole, his extreme fragmentation of suras along with his reservations about dating many parts of the

Qur'an, were too impractical for this present work. The recent publishing of Bell's long-awaited notes (as *A Commentary on the Qur'an*) also did little in the way of resolving these difficulties.

Quran Index

Sura	Page	Sura	Page	Sura	Page	Sura	Page
1	51	25	100	$53^{19\text{-}32}$	91	82	46
2	188	26	84	54	78	83	48
$3^{1\text{-}111}$	206	27	103	55	50	84	47
3^{112f}	211	28	150	56	50	85	45
4	213	29	152	57	212	86	44
5	276	30	145	58	251	87	44
$6^{1\text{-}159}$	158	31	153	59	246	88	48
6^{160f}	198	32	139	60	265	89	48
$7^{1\text{-}155,159f}$	156	33	253	61	212	90	43
$7^{156\text{-}58}$	209	34	155	62	200	91	44
8	203	35	155	63	248	92	43
9	271	36	93	64	200	93	43
10	154	37	79	65	216	94	43
11	146	38	92	66	262	95	45
12	148	39	151	67	97	96	40
13	160	40	150	$68^{1,17\text{-}33}$	44	96	47
$14^{1\text{-}37,43f}$	147	41	140	$68^{2\text{-}16,34f}$	79	97	44
$14^{38\text{-}42}$	199	42	153	69	49	98	199
15	85	43	93	70	50	99	46
$16^{1\text{-}110}$	144	44	81	71	80	100	47
$16^{111\text{-}25}$	199	45	140	72	95	101	46
16^{126f}	144	46	157	$73^{1\text{-}19}$	45	102	42
17	102	47	205	73^{20}	198	103	45
18	104	48	260f	$74^{1\text{-}7}$	40	104	42
$19^{1\text{-}34}$	88	49	269	$74^{8\text{-}30,35f}$	49	105	42
$19^{35\text{-}41}$	97	50	82	$74^{31\text{-}34}$	204	106	42
$19^{42\text{-}75}$	88	$51^{1\text{-}23}$	50	75	48	107	42
19^{76f}	97	51^{24f}	77	76	81	108	42
20	82	$52^{1\text{-}20}$	50	77	47	109	51
21	99	52^{21}	79	78	48	110	266
22	258	$52^{22\text{-}28}$	50	79	47	111	42
23	98	$52^{29\text{-}49}$	79	80	44	112	96
24	249	$53^{1\text{-}18,33f}$	46	81	46	113-4	51

Discussions of Qur'an Passages
In Order of Appearance

96^{1-5}, $74^{(1-7)}$, 111, 106, 108, 105, 104, 107, 102, 92, 90, 94, 93, 97, 86, 91, 80, $68^{1,17-33}$, 87, 95, 103, 85, 73^{1-19}, 101, 99, 82, 81, $53^{1-18,33f}$, 84, 100, 79, 77, 78, 88, 89, 75, 83, $74^{8-30,35f}$, 69, 51^{1-23}, $52^{1-20,22-28}$, 56, 70, 55, 109, 113, 114, 1, 51^{24f}, 54, $52^{21,29-49}$, $68^{2-16,34f}$, 37, 71, 76, 44, 50, 20, 26, 15, $19^{1-34,42-75}$, 53^{19-32}, 38, 36, 43, 72, 112, $19^{35-41,76f}$, 67, 23, 21, 25, 17, 27, 18, 32, 41, 45, $16^{1-110,126f}$, 30, 11, $14^{1-37,43f}$, 12, 40, 28, 39, 29, 31, 42, 10, 34, 35, $7^{1-155,159f}$, 46, 6^{1-159}, 13, 2, 6^{160f}, 73^{20}, $16^{111-125}$, 14^{38-42}, 98, 64, 62, 8, 74^{31-34}, 47, 3^{1-111}, $7^{156-158}$, 3^{112f}, 61, 57, 4, 65, 59, 63, 24, 58, 33, 22, 48, 66, 60, 110, 49, 9, 5.

Pre-Islamic Arabia

Compared with the lands in the fertile crescent, the Arabian peninsula was deficient in agricultural and usable natural resources. Consequently, it was not coveted by many of the renowned empires of the past and was thus spared much of the warfare and domination which was so characteristic of the pre-Islamic Middle East. This general neglect of Arabia also made it a relatively safe haven for those fleeing persecution and oppression in neighboring lands.

The Jews

One of the earliest known groups of refugees to Arabia were the Jews. As a result of the countless invasions of Israel over the course of centuries, Jews had become quite numerous in Yemen[1] and also had settlements in Medina (Yathrib), Khaybar, Fadak, Wadi al-Qura and Tayma', which were along the trade routes to Syria. Together with these, there were substantial numbers of Jews at Maqna, near the Gulf of Aqaba, and in Bahrain.[2] The Jews were prosperous merchants, who aside from their agricultural achievements, were also famous as manufacturers of ironware and weapons.[3] Although they remained a minority on the peninsula,[4] they appear to have been active in proselytizing some of the Arab tribes.[5] The Jews of Medina reportedly possessed copies of the Torah[6] and their rabbis evidently also taught them from the Talmud and Jewish legends.[7] Nevertheless, the Jews had not translated their scriptures into Arabic in written form before the advent of Islam.[8]

Other Early Refugees

Although there is little direct evidence for their presence, it is relatively certain that Ebionites, Elkasaites, Gnostics, Manichaeans, Arians or their sympathizers were in Arabia, living dispersed among the general populace, rather than in settlements of their own.[9]

The Christians

The intermittent persecutions of Nestorians and Monophysites, resulting from the Councils of Ephesus (431 AD) and Chalcedon (451 AD), not only brought refugees to, but also seem to have spawned new missionary activities on the Arabian peninsula. In the 6th century, Christianity was slowly making its way to central Arabia and the Hijaz (which is roughly composed of the area around Mecca and Medina). There were Arab Christians among the Taghlib, Bakr and `Ijl (near Mesopotamia),[10] among the Tayy, Tha`laba and Quda`a (in the center of Arabia),[11] among the Hanifa (in Yamama),[12] the Kinda (in Duma; i.e. Dumat al-Jandal),[13] and among the Judham and `Udhra (who had settled along the trade routes from Wadi al-Qura to Syria).[14] Christian bishops were known to have been at Tayma', Duma and Ayla (which is near Elat).[15]

Christianity among the Arabs in the north and west was best established in the tribes of the Ghassanids and the Lakhmids. The Ghassanids originally came from Yemen, had settled near Damascus and accepted Christianity in about 490 AD.[16] They were predominantly Monophysite and generally allies with Byzantium. The Lakhmids dwelt in al-Hira, which was not far from Kufa in southern Iraq. Politically, they were vassals of the Persians and as such were in almost constant armed conflict with the Ghassanids throughout the 6th century. The Nestorians had a monastery and a bishop in al-Hira as early as 410 AD[17] and seem to have remained more influential there than the Monophysites.[18] Although the Persians favored Zoroastrianism and persecuted the Nestorians, these, nevertheless, were able to propagate Christianity within the Persian sphere of influence to Oman, Bahrain,[19] and Yemen.[20] The last Lakhmid king Nu`man III was converted in about 593 AD by a Nestorian bishop.[21] Al-Hira had developed into an Arabic literary center in the 6th century[22] and was probably at least instrumental in introducing the art of writing to the Arab tribes of the peninsula.[23] For at least some syncretistic Arab Christians of southern Iraq, it seems that Allah of the Ka`ba in Mecca was held on equal terms with Jesus.[24]

It appears that Christianity was first established in Yemen sometime between the 5th and 6th centuries[25] and was then spread to the Hadramawt along the southern coast. Owing to its proximity to Abyssinia and trade with al-Hira,

Yemenite Christianity, whose centers were in Najran and San`a' came under the influence of both Monophysites and Nestorians. Groups of Christian pilgrims from Yemen on their way to Jerusalem and Sinai must have been a common sight for the Arabs of the Hijaz and particularly for those of al-Ta'if and Medina.[26]

For the most part, the level of Christianity practiced among the Arab tribes of the peninsula was not, and perhaps could not have been very high during the 6th century.[27] Similar to their Jewish counterparts, none of the churches of the East appears to have even started to systematically translate the scriptures into Arabic,[28] and thus, except for those Arabs who knew Greek, Syriac or Ethiopic, the Bible remained a closed book, and the worship services of Christianity remained a ritualistic mystery. The little understandable information about Christianity available to those who only spoke Arabic may have come through the preaching of Syrian and Abyssinian missionaries,[29] or the works of pre-Islamic Arab Christian poets.[30]

Arabian Idolatry

Whereas paganism had been in rapid decline for hundreds of years in lands with a Christian majority, it was still the predominant faith of most of the Arab tribes in the 6th century. As opposed to traditional idolatry,[31] Arabs generally worshiped stones[32] and trees[33] as the habitations of gods and spirits.[34] The sanctuaries of their gods[35] became popular pilgrimage sites,[36] whose associated markets brought regional economic prosperity.[37]

Again, owing primarily to the influence of Christianity, the paganism of Arabia was slowly disappearing. Together with some of the Arab poets of the day, the inhabitants of Mecca (and with them no doubt those of other pilgrimage towns) had begun to realize the inferiority of their native religions; and this even though pride and the fear of financial loss at the markets tended to deter such notions.[38] Later Islamic legends report at least four Meccan Arabs who had abandoned paganism in the search for true religion.[39]

Perhaps the greatest phenomenon of religious development in pre-Islamic Arabia, was the idea of contemporary nationalistic prophethood. Although the evidence is by no means overwhelming, there are traditions which show

3

that two Arabs had aspired to be prophets before Muhammad.[40] The little information which seems to have survived regarding them, definitely points to Christian or later sectarian sources for this doctrine, as both prophets appear to have assimilated some Christian practices or terms.[41]

Government

By comparison to the older empires to the north and west, 6th century Arabia was politically underdeveloped. With the exception of the rather centralized governments of the Ghassanids, Lakhmids and for a time the Kinda,[42] most of the Arabs on the peninsula were still under tribal rule. Moreover, due to the deficiency of arable land, periodic migrations were often the only means by which a tribe could insure its survival. However, these migrations also caused petty wars between various tribes (or even among the separate clans of a single tribe), raiding and blood feuds; all of which appear to have been the norm for Arabs of the time period.[43]

Political Wars

The century before Muhammad's birth found the empires of Byzantium and Persia in frequent wars with each other. Those who in general sided with the Byzantines were the Abyssinians and several Arab tribes in the northwest. The most influential of Byzantium's Christian Arab allies were the Ghassanids, and the most powerful Arab allies of the Persians were the Lakhmids, both of whom have been mentioned above. Although they were political enemies, who often warred against each other, both the Ghassanids and Lakhmids suffered at the hands of their respective overlords. The Persians had the Lakhmid king Nu`man III murdered in 601-602 AD, and this provoked the rebellion of the eastern Arabs, who consequently defeated the Persians at Dhu Qar.[44] As Monophysite converts, the Ghassanids became the target of Melkite persecution resulting from the Council of Chalcedon in 451 AD. Although the Ghassanids had, in general, served the Byzantines faithfully, the latter betrayed them and sent the last two Ghassanid rulers into exile in Sicily. This action did much to create a deep sense of mistrust in and resentment of Byzantium among the Arab tribes of the west, some of whom became loyal to Persia as a result.[45] The Persians then defeated the Byzantines near Damascus in 614 AD and got control of Syria.[46] The Byzantines later fended off a Persian attack on Constantinople and won Syria back in about 626 AD, only to lose it in 636 AD to Arab Muslims.[47] The treacherous Arabian policies of the Byzantines and Persians brought about the disintegration of the Ghassanid-Lakhmid buffer between these empires, incited the enmity of the Arab tribes and paved the way for the massive defections of Arabs to the Muslim cause in the early Islamic expansions.[48]

Abyssinia

In the south, the Abyssinians were allied with Byzantium. Early in the 6th century, the Christian Abyssinian king Ella Asbaha invaded Yemen and left an occupational force there. In 523 AD the Jewish leader Dhu Nuwas came to power in Yemen, attacked the Abyssinians and got control of Najran for a time. He is said to have burned down the church there, killing those who had gathered in it. Dhu Nuwas then had some Christians executed in another public burning.[49] The Abyssinians returned and defeated the Yemenites again and killed Dhu Nuwas in battle.[50] Ella Asbaha then appointed a ruler for Yemen, who was later overthrown by the former slave Abraha.[51] Ella Asbaha's successor accepted Abraha as the viceroy of Yemen.[52] Abraha built the famous church at San'a', and after a small provocation, decided to destroy the Ka'ba in Mecca, so that the Arabs would make their pilgrimage to his church instead.[53] Abraha assembled an army, which also had at least one elephant, and set off for Mecca.[54] After defeating several groups of Arabs, who had become incensed on hearing that Abraha wanted to destroy the Ka'ba, the Abyssinians arrived at Ta'if.[55] According to Islamic accounts, Abraha's army was either stoned by birds, or contracted the measles and smallpox.[56] In any event, the Abyssinians returned to Yemen before 570 AD[57] without having destroyed the Ka'ba.[58] Aided by disgruntled Yemenites, the Persians later succeeded in driving out the Abyssinians and made Yemen a province of their empire in about 597 AD.[59] Consequently, the Arab Christians of Yemen came under the influence of the Nestorian church by virtue of the Persian conquest.[60]

Notes:

[1] A Jewish king appears to have reigned in Yemen in the middle of the 5th century; and at the beginning of the 6th century Yemen was ruled by the well-known Jewish leader Dhu Nuwas; see Andrae, *Ursprung*, pp. 9 f. The probable presence and influence of Abyssinian Jews should also not be overlooked, as even Ethiopian Christianity maintained many Jewish characteristics, such as the observance of the Sabbath, the practice of circumcision and the abstention from unclean meats; cf. *The Oxford Dictionary of the Christian Church*, s.v. "Ethiopian Church," p. 474.

[2] Buhl, *Muhammad*, pp. 18, 71.

[3] Guillaume, *Islam*, p. 12. For more information on Jewish trade in Arabia, see Crone, *Trade*, pp. 140 f.

[4] See Jahiz in *ECMD*, pp. 702 f.

[5] Guillaume, with others before him, noted the lack of distinctly Jewish names among the various lists given in Muslim sources on Jews in Arabia; see *Muhammad*, p. 240, n. 2; Buhl, *Muhammad*, pp. 18 f.

[6] *Sahih Bukhari*, vol. 8, pp. 529 f. The Jews may also have had copies of the Psalms and some other books of the Old Testament, but, aside from the narration of Jonah, neither the Qur'an, nor early Islamic tradition betray any acquaintance with the books of the Prophets.

[7] See Geiger, *WMJA* and Ginzburg, *Legends* for Talmudic information and legends which made their way into the Qur'an and Islamic hadith.

[8] *Sahih Bukhari*, vol. 6, p. 13. The best known early translation of the Old Testament by Jewish scholarship dates from the 10th century; see Würthwein, *The Text of the Old Testament*, p. 100.

[9] Practically the only traces which confirm the existence of these groups in Arabia are the narrations about Zacharias, Mary and Jesus found in the

Qur'an (3:30f; 19:48f, etc.). See Andrae, *Ursprung*, p. 204; *Mohammed*, pp. 105 f; Bell, *Origin*, p. 20.

[10] *Enzyklopedia des Islams*, s.v. "Nasara"; Buhl, *Muhammad*, p. 64; Jahiz in *ECMD*, p. 702.

[11] *Enzyklopedia des Islams*, s.v. "Nasara"; Jahiz in *ECMD*, p. 702.

[12] *Enzyklopedia des Islams*, s.v. "Nasara"; Buhl, *Muhammad*, p. 64.

[13] Andrae, *Ursprung*, p. 31; Guillaume, *Muhammad*, p. 607.

[14] Shahid, *Byzantium and the Arabs of the Fifth Century*, p. 359; Guillaume, *Islam*, p. 13; *Enzyklopedia des Islams*, s.v. "Nasara".

[15] *SEI*, p. 440.

[16] *EI²*, s.v. "Ghassan".

[17] *SEI*, p. 440; Bell *Origin*, p. 26.

[18] Andrae, *Ursprung*, p. 25.

[19] *SEI*, p. 440.

[20] Some think that Christianity was brought to Yemen through its commercial ties with al-Hira before Persian control. Others maintain that Yemen came under Christian influence from Abyssinia; see Andrae, *Ursprung*, p. 8.

[21] This is also reported by the pre-Islamic Lakhmid Christian poet `Adi b. Zayd (c. 587 AD). Buhl, *Muhammad*, p. 6; Andrae, *Ursprung*, p. 26; *SEI*, p. 440; Margoliouth, *Relations*, p. 73.

[22] Jeffery, *Vocabulary*, p. 21.

[23] Ibid. p. 14.

[24] An oath of `Adi b. Zayd is quoted by Andrae as containing the phrase: "Mecca's lord and the Crucified," see Andrae, *Mohammed*, p. 25.

[25] Andrae, *Ursprung*, p. 9. See n. 19 above.

[26] Cf. Nau in *ECMD*, p. 18. Buhl, (*Muhammad*, p. 64) shows that there probably were some nominal Christians in Mecca from other lands, who, however, do not appear to have been very good representatives of Christ. For a brief discussion of Byzantine and Syrian trade with Mecca, see Crone, *Trade*, pp. 139 f.

[27] Polygamy was practiced by both the dynasties of the Ghassanids and Lakhmids (Buhl, *Muhammad*, pp. 6, 66). A quote attributed to `Ali reports that the only thing the Taghlibs retained (knew) of Christianity was the drinking of wine (Buhl, *Muhammad*, p. 66; *SEI*, p. 440). Arab Christians even attended the pagan Hajj to Mecca (Buhl, *Muhammad*, p. 66; Andrae, *Ursprung*, p. 39; *Mohammed*, p. 25. Cf. also Rafi` b. `Umayra in Guillaume, *Muhammad*, p. 668.

[28] Cf. Bell, *Origin*, p. 17. It appears that the Gospel, or perhaps more appropriately Diatessaron, was first translated for `Amr al-`As in the course of the first Islamic expansions by the Jacobite Patriarch John I in 639 AD; see *ECMD* pp. 7, 17.

[29] There are traditions which report that Muhammad heard Quss the (Nestorian) bishop of Najran preach at the market of `Ukaz, which same traditions appear to have been suppressed by the earliest Islamic historians; see Jeffery, *Vocabulary*, Andrae *Ursprung*, pp. 201 f; *Mohammed*, p. 92.

[30] Cf. Jeffery, *Vocabulary*, pp. 20 f.

[31] Only Hubal, who was worshiped by the Quraysh in Mecca, is thought to have been an idol in the normal sense. See note 35 below for references.

[32] Wellhausen in *Reste*, p. 101, quotes Clement of Alexandria as saying (trans.): "The Arabs revere (the) stone," to which Wellhausen adds (trans.):

"Stone is the necessary and most characteristic symbol of Arabian sanctuaries." The worshipers tried to touch or kiss stones and circumambulated them (Buhl, *Muhammad*, pp. 74 f, 82). The milk of sheep or the blood of a sacrificial animal was poured over the stone, and in the case of the victim, its flesh was eaten by participants; see Buhl, *Muhammad*, pp. 84 f. Cf. *Sahih Bukhari*, vol. 5, p. 467, for a brief description of stone worship and circumambulation.

[33] "Clothing, weapons or jewelry" were often hung on trees and sacrifices were offered; Buhl, *Muhammad*, pp. 78 f; Wellhausen, *Reste*, p. 104. This is still practiced in some regions; Guillaume, *Islam*, p. 9; *Muhammad*, pp. 568 f.

[34] Guillaume also shows that there were (and still are) cults related to water wells and springs; *Islam*, pp. 8 f; which along with stones and trees, are somewhat of a rarity in some desert areas.

[35] There were many Arab gods and goddesses, the evidences of whose worship were rather systematically destroyed by the first generations of Arab Muslims. Those listed here are mentioned in the Qur'an and major Islamic traditions:

Wadd - ("Love," "Friendship") was worshiped by tribes in central and northern Arabia, but especially by the Kalb at Duma. Wellhausen, *Reste*, pp. 17 f; Buhl, *Muhammad*, p. 74; *Sahih Bukhari*, vol. 6, p. 414; Rudolph, *Koran*, p. 527, n. 4.

Suwa'- (meaning disputed) was a goddess worshiped by the Hudhayl near Mecca or Yanbu`. Wellhausen, *Reste*, pp. 18-19; *Sahih Bukhari*, vol. 6, p. 414; Rudolph, *Koran*, p. 527, n. 4.

Yaghuth - ("He helps") was worshiped by the Murad and then the Banu Ghutayf near Yemen. Wellhausen, *Reste*, pp. 19 f, *Sahih Bukhari*, vol. 6, p. 414; Rudolph, *Koran*, p. 527, n. 4.

Ya`ug - ("He hinders" or "He preserves") was a god of the Yemeni Hamdan, whose main place of worship was near San`a. Wellhausen, *Reste*, p. 22; *Sahih Bukhari*, vol. 6, p. 414; Rudolph, *Koran*, p. 527, n. 4.

Nasr - ("Eagle" or "Vulture") a god of the Himyar in southern Arabia, who was also worshiped in the north. Wellhausen, *Reste*, p. 23; Buhl, *Muhammad*, p. 74; *Sahih Bukhari*, vol. 6, p. 414; Rudolph, *Koran*, p. 527, n. 4.

Al-Lat - ("The goddess") was a sun goddess worshiped by many Arab tribes; a stone was made sacred to her in Ta'if. Wellhausen, *Reste*, pp. 29 f; Buhl, *Muhammad*, pp. 74 f; Rudolph, *Koran*, p. 479, n. 12.

Al-`Uzza - ("The most powerful") was a goddess worshiped as the morning star (Venus) in northern Arabia. Three trees and a stone formed a sanctuary for her in Nakhla near Mecca. A Lakhmid king (Mundhir III) once offered 400 Christian nuns to her. Wellhausen, *Reste*, pp. 34 f; Buhl, *Muhammad*, pp. 76 f, 84; Rudolph, *Koran*, p. 479, n. 12; *SEI*, p. 617; Guillaume, *Muhammad*, p. 38.

Manat - ("Fate") was a goddess whose sanctuary at Qudayd consisted of a black stone. Wellhausen, *Reste*, pp. 25 f; Rudolph, *Koran*, p. 479, n. 12; *SEI*, p. 325; Guillaume, *Muhammad*, p. 38.

Hubal - (meaning uncertain) was a man-like idol worshiped in Mecca, who was also consulted by the casting of arrows. He was allegedly the greatest idol of the Quraysh or Mecca itself. Wellhausen, *Reste*, p. 75; Buhl, *Muhammad*, p. 79; *SEI*, p. 140; Tabari, *History*, vol. 6, pp. 3-5; Guillaume, *New Light*, p. 19.

[36] There were many pilgrimage sites; see Wellhausen *Reste*, pp. 84 f.

[37] There were many seasonal markets on the Arabian peninsula; see Wellhausen, *Reste*, p. 246.

[38] Buhl, *Muhammad*, pp. 92 f.

[39] It is interesting to note that each of these four men came into contact with Christianity: Waraqa b. Naufal supposedly researched the scriptures and became a Christian; ʿUbaydullah b. Jahsh fled to Abyssinia with other early Muslims, but became a Christian and died there; ʿUthman b. al-Huwayrith went to the Byzantine Emperor and became a Christian; Zayd b.ʾAmr allegedly asked a monk about Hanifiyya (a term which came to mean "Islam" in the late Meccan suras), but died neither a Jew nor a Christian; Guillaume, *Muhammad*, pp. 99 f.

[40] Umayya b. Abu al-Salt was a poet of Ta'if, who dressed as a monk and sought prophethood for himself; Buhl, *Muhammad*, p. 97; Andrae, *Ursprung*, pp. 48 ff. Musaylima was a prophet of Yamama, who was allegedly called "Rahman" and whose teachings appear to have been heavily influenced by Christian doctrine; Buhl, *Muhammad*, p. 99; *SEI*, p. 416 (cf. *EI²*, s.v. "Musaylima").

[41] The Jewish expectations of the future Messianic advent may also have played a limited role with respect to the idea of contemporary prophethood. One serious problem with this view is that neither Muhammad nor his rivals seem to have known or used the Hebrew "Messiah" as applying to themselves. The Qur'anic "Masih" appears to have come from Syriac and was only used of Muhammad for Jesus. According to certain late Islamic traditions, Muhammad was claimed to be the future prophet whom the Jews were awaiting; cf. Guillaume, *Muhammad*, pp. 197 f, 240 f. The understanding of a national prophethood may well have come from any of the Christians of the east; whose language divisions and political bonds appear to have influenced the Arabs in this direction. Another possible source for this idea may have been the followers of Elxai; see Bell, *Origins*, pp. 59 f; Andrae, *Mohammed*, p. 101.

[42] Buhl, *Muhammad*, pp. 6, 16, 28.

[43] Ibid., pp. 28 ff.

[44] Tabari, *History*, vol. 2, p. 324; Buhl, *Muhammad*, p. 6; Guillaume, *Islam*, pp. 15 f.

[45] Guillaume, *Islam*, pp. 16 f.

[46] Ibid., p. 19.

[47] Savas, *John of Damascus*, p. 19.

[48] cf. Nau in *ECMD*, pp. 12 f, 19 f.

[49] Andrae, *Ursprung*, pp. 10 f, updated by *EI²*, s.v. "Dhu Nuwas." This event of Christian martyrdom is thought by many western scholars to have been alluded to in Qur'an 85:4-7; See Ahrens, "Christliches," *ZDMG*, vol. 84 (1930), pp. 148 f.

[50] Andrae, *Ursprung*, p. 13; *EI²*, s.v. "Dhu Nuwas."

[51] Tabari, *History*, vol. 2, p. 269; Guillaume, *Muhammad*, p. 20.

[52] Tabari, *History*, vol. 2, p. 270; Guillaume, *Muhammad*, p. 21; Andrae, *Ursprung*, p. 13.

[53] Tabari, *History*, vol. 2, pp. 271 f; Nöldeke, *Perser*, pp. 205 f, Guillaume, *Muhammad*, pp. 21 f; Andrae, *Ursprung*, p. 13.

[54] Tabari, *History*, vol. 2, pp. 273 f; Guillaume, *Muhammad*, p. 23.

[55] Guillaume, *Muhammad*, p. 23.

[56] This event is mentioned in Qur'an 105; cf. Tabari, *History*, vol. 2, p. 277; Guillaume, *Muhammad*, p. 26 f; Buhl, *Muhammad*, p. 12.

[57] The events surrounding Abraha's campaign to Mecca are placed in the year 570 AD by Muslims, as this is generally thought to be the year of Muhammad's birth. However, Buhl, (*Muhammad*, pp. 12 f) shows that Nöldeke thought Abraha's offensive to be a part of the larger Byzantine-Persian war which began in 540 AD (cf. Crone, *Trade*, pp. 142 f). Buhl, moreover, shows that Abraha and two sons after him reigned in Yemen (cf. Tabari, *History*, vol. 2, pp. 282 f; Guillaume, *Muhammad*, pp. 30 f) before

it came under Persian control ca. 570 AD (Buhl, *Muhammad*, p. 14, n. 41; cf. Andrae, *Mohammed*, p. 31).

[58] Tabari, *History*, vol. 2, p. 277; Guillaume, *Muhammad*, p. 27.

[59] Andrae, *Ursprung*, p. 16; Tabari, *History*, vol. 2, pp. 286 f.

[60] Andrae, *Ursprung*, pp. 17 f, 21.

The Sources for Muhammad's Biography

In that the Qur'an does not contain sufficient information regarding subjects of Islamic rituals, jurisprudence, early history or even the biography (*Sira*) of Muhammad, some early Muslim scholars began to collect and transmit traditions to fill these deficits. Generally, an Islamic tradition (hadith) is preceded by a chain of names (isnad), which is to represent the transmitters of a hadith,[1] originating with a witness and concluding with someone contemporary with the respective writer of the tradition. Very often, the value attached to a certain tradition by Muslim scholars is relative to the trustworthiness of those mentioned in the isnad of that hadith.[2]

It appears that the first collections of Islamic historical traditions, known as "maghazi" books, gave the reports of the raids and expeditions, which took place during Muhammad's lifetime.[3] There were at least nine early maghazi books,[4] of which only parts of two seem to have survived to the present.

The biography of Muhammad, composed by Muhammad b. Ishaq (d. 151 AH - c. 767 AD),[6] is the earliest of which major portions are still available. Although Ibn Ishaq's text as a whole appears to be lost,[7] the extensive quotations of those who copied out his lectures,[8] can be found in the works of later Islamic scholars.[9] Of the sources used in this present book, the traditions collected by Ibn Ishaq are quoted extensively in the *Sira* of Ibn Hisham (d. 218 AH),[10] the *Kitab al-Tabaqat al-Kabir* of Ibn Sa`d (d. 230 AH),[11] the *Ta'rikh* of Tabari (d. 310 AH),[12] and a manuscript of a shaykh al-Bazzaz (d. 400 ? AH).[13] Another work, which may contain parts of Ibn Ishaq's traditions, is the *Maghazi* of al-Waqidi (d. 207 AH).[14]

One of the features of Ibn Ishaq's work is that he was not very careful about recording the isnads for his traditions.[15] However, none of the early Islamic historians appear to have attached much importance to this science,[16] which first became rather developed in the 3rd Islamic century, when both the historical and canonical collections[17] of traditions began to take their present form.[18] In his biography of Muhammad, Ibn Ishaq, as other early Muslim historians also, quotes a fair number of poems, which were generally said to have been composed by Muhammad's contemporaries during or after major events. In the judgment of many Islamic[19] and Western scholars,[20] however, many of the poems cited by Ibn Ishaq are obvious forgeries, which possess little historical value.

With the exception of Ibn Hisham's *Sira*,[21] other early Islamic works containing information on Muhammad's biography also bring together a vast collection of traditions from sources other than Ibn Ishaq. Waqidi may have quoted Ibn Ishaq occasionally,[22] however, much of the text of his *Maghazi* appears to have come to him through other narrators.[23] Among Western scholars of Islam, Waqidi's *Maghazi* is generally held in almost equal esteem with Ibn Ishaq's *Sira*,[24] and Waqidi's use of isnads[25] and his chronology[26] are often regarded as superior to Ibn Ishaq's.[27] The *Kitab al-Tabaqat*, consisting of traditions collected by Waqidi's former secretary Ibn Sa`d, not only relies on the *Maghazi* of Waqidi and several recensions of Ibn Ishaq[28] in relating Muhammad's biography, but it generally presents more developed forms of isnads than either Waqidi or Ibn Ishaq.[29] Islamic scholars are usually hesitant to accept some of Ibn Sa`d's traditions, although they frequently view Ibn Sa`d as being more trustworthy than Waqidi.[30] Western scholars, however, often consider his work with respect to Muhammad's biography to be dependent on and yet practically as valuable as Waqidi's.[31] The *Ta'rikh* of Tabari is also based on a few recensions of Ibn Ishaq,[32] as well as the works of Waqidi and Ibn Sa`d.[33] In contrast to other early Islamic works, Tabari not only gives the texts of traditions which others omitted, but he often presents narrations which contradict one another.[34] Tabari is generally regarded by Muslims as being trustworthy, although they often maintain that his *Ta'rikh* contains unreliable traditions.[35]

In the mid-19th century, Western scholars began writing biographies of Muhammad based on a critical analysis of Islamic traditions.[36] With the works of R. Dozy[37] and I. Goldziher[38] a great deal of skepticism developed regarding the truthfulness and authenticity of Islamic hadith; finally H. Lammens claimed that the only historical foundation for Muhammad's biography is the Qur'an itself.[39] As some scholars have since pointed out, there are problems with Lammens' assumptions:[40] the chronology of Muhammad's biography cannot be determined from the Qur'an without the aid of traditions,[41] there are Qur'anic passages which are explained only by historical hadith,[42] and many of the earliest sources for traditions were also the transmitters of the Qur'an,[43] etc.

It cannot be denied that there are many fallacious hadith in both the *Sira* and other early Islamic works, and even Muslims recognize this.[44] On the other hand, there are traditions which are probably true, but which are condemned by some Muslims on theological grounds.[45] In the end, the authenticity and witness of Islamic hadith cannot be rejected out of hand; rather each tradition must be examined on an individual basis.

The biography of Muhammad, which follows, is primarily structured on Ibn Hisham's *Sira* as given in *The Life of Muhammad* (ed. and trans. Guillaume), Ibn Bukayr's recension of Ibn Ishaq's *Sira* as given in *New Light* (ed. Guillaume), Ibn Sa`d's *Kitab al-Tabaqat* (trans. Haq), Tabari's *Ta'rikh* as given in *The History of al-Tabari* (ed. and trans. YarShater et al.) and Waqidi's *Maghazi* (abridged, ed. and trans. Wellhausen). The English translation of *Kitab al-Tabaqat* is referred to as *Classes*, and that of the *Ta'rikh* of Tabari is referred to by the title *History*. A general outline of the early traditions on Muhammad's biography can be found in Appendix A.

Notes:

[1] Unfortunately, there are very many traditions, whose isnads have been falsified or corrupted over the centuries. The following pages also provide an ample number of cases where the isnads of various traditions have been tampered with.

[2] There are many istances, however, where even traditions with "sound" chains of transmitters have been rejected by Muslim authorities as they do not conform to one's theological views. See Juynboll, *Authenticity*, p. 139; Jeffery, *Materials*, p. viii; Ibn Hisham's note in Guillaume, *Muhammad*, p. 691, n. 10. Numerous examples of this sort can also be found in the following pages. See p. 326, n. 11.

[3] Schwally, *GQ*, vol. 2, p. 129; Guillaume, *Muhammad*, p. xiv.

[4] Guillaume, in *Muhammad*, pp. xiv f, gives a brief description of these collections and biographical information regarding the editors, who were:

Aban b. 'Uthman b. 'Affan	(d. ca. 100 AH)
'Urwa b. Zubayr	(d. 94 AH)
Shurahbil b. Sa'd	(d. 123 AH)
Wahb b. Munabbih	(d. 110 AH)
'Asim b. 'Umar b. Qatada	(d. ca. 120 AH)
Muhammad b. Muslim	(d. 124 AH)
'Abdullah b. Abu Bakr	(d. 130 or 135 AH)
b. Muhammad b. 'Amr	
Abu'l-Aswad Muhammad	(d. 131 or 137 AH)
Musa b. 'Uqba	(d. 141)

[5] Guillaume was not certain of the genuiness of a fragment of Wahb b. Munabbih's *Maghazi* (*Muhammad*, p. xvii); but he gives the translation of the fragments of Musa b. 'Uqba's work, which follow the edition of Sachau; see Guillaume, *Muhammad*, pp. xvi, xlii f. The *Sira* of Musa b. 'Uqba also contained biographical traditions about Muhammad's life and was once seen as a rival to Ibn Ishaq's works; some of his traditions can be found in the canonical traditions.

[6] Ibn Ishaq was the grandson of a manumitted slave, whose father was also a Muslim traditionist. Ibn Ishaq was raised in Medina, where he began collecting traditions. Although it appears that his (now lost) work on the practice of Muhammad (*Sunan*) was disliked by some, he was generally held in high regard as a traditionist; Guillaume, *Muhammad*, pp. xiii, xxxiv f. For more biographical information, see the first references given in n. 7, below.

[7] Guillaume, *Muhammad*, pp. xvii f; Sezgin, *Schrifttums*, vol. 1, pp. 288 f; *SEI* and *EI²*, s.v. "Ibn Ishak, Abu 'Abd Allah Muhammad." Ibn Ishaq's work originally contained not only the biography of Muhammad, but also a history of the prophets up until his time; (Guillaume, *Muhammad*, pp. xvii f.) Barring any new manuscript discoveries, it has been hoped that someday the original text of Ibn Ishaq may be able to be reconstructed from all of the secondary sources where it has been cited.

[8] There were at least fifteen direct recensions of Ibn Ishaq's biography of Muhammad, a list of which Guillaume quotes from Fueck in *Muhammad*, p. xxx:

1) Ibrahim b. Sa`d [b. Abu Waqqas]	(d. 184 AH)
2) Ziyad b. `Abdullah al-Bakka'i	(d. 183 AH)
3) `Abdullah b. Idris al-Audi	(d. 192 AH)
4) Yunus b. Bukayr	(d. 199 AH)
5) `Abda b. Sulayman	(d. 187-8 AH)
6) `Abdullah b. Numayr	(d. 199 AH)
7) Yahya b. Sa`id al-Umawi	(d. 194 AH)
8) Jarir b. Hazim	(d. 170 AH)
9) Harun b. Abu `Isa	
10) Salama b. al-Fadl al-Abrash	(d. 191 AH)
11) `Ali b. Mujahid	(d. ca. 180 AH)
12) Ibrahim b. al-Mukhtar	
13) Sa`id b. Bazi`	
14) `Uthman b. Saj	
15) Muhammad b. Salama al-Harrani	(d. 191 AH)

[9] See nn. 10-13, below, and Guillaume, *Muhammad*, pp. xxxi f.

[10] Ibn Hisham used the Ibn Ishaq recension of Ziyad b. `Abdullah al-Bakka'i, which he rather heavily edited, omitting: parts not mentioning Muhammad, parts not supported by the Qur'an, some poetry, matters which were "disgraceful to discuss," material "which would distress certain people" and "reports" which al-Bakka'i himself "could not accept as trustworthy" (see Ibn Hisham's note in Guillaume, *Muhammad*, p. 691, n. 10).

[11] According to *Kitab al-Tabaqat* (see Sachau's edition III, 1, p. xxv and III, 2, p. 51, ll. 17-19), which was composed by some of his students, Ibn Sa`d made use of the Ibn Ishaq recensions of Ibrahim b. Sa`d b. Abu Waqqas and Harun b. Abu `Isa. Guillaume mistakenly gives Yunus b. Bukayr (*Muhammad*, p. xvii), in which he appears to have exchanged Ibrahim b. Sa`d (whom Sachau describes as Ibn Sa`d's *fourth* narrator) with Yunus b. Bukayr (whom Fueck describes as being Ibn Sa`d's *fourth* narrator). However, even Schwally must have noticed (*GQ*, vol. 2, p. 135,

nn. 4-5), that in the text of *Kitab al-Tabaqat* dealing with Muhammad's biography (vols. I and II of Sachau's edition), Ibrahim b. Sa`d b. Abu Waqqas is not referred to, and that the recension of Harun b. Abu `Isa is indirect (it is traced through Ruwaym b. Yazid; cf. Haq's translation I, 1, pp. 44 and 52, II, 1, p. 1). Direct quotations of Ibn Ishaq by his narrators as given in n. 7, above, are:

		Haq's translation
3) `Abdullah b. Idris		II, 1, pp. 66, 68, 98.
6) `Abdullah b. Numayr		II, 1, p. 141.
		II, 2, p. 299, 317.
11) `Ali b. Mujahid		I, 2, pp. 361, 409.
(also indirectly)		I, 1, pp. 188, 191.

Indirect quotes are additionally given from:

10) Salama b. al-Fadl	I, 1, p. 194.

Other narrators, not found in Fueck's list (n. 7, above) also quote Ibn Ishaq directly: Isma`il b. Ibrahim al-Asadi (II, 1, p. 232), Ya`la b. `Ubayd (II, 2, p. 243), Muhammad b. `Umar (II, 2, p. 380), Muhammad b. `Ubayd al-Tanafisi (II, 1, p. 170), Yazid b. Harun (II, 1, p. 103; and indirectly: Hushaym [b. Bishr] (I, 2, p. 105), Shu`ba [al-Hajjaj b. al-Ward] (II, 2, p. 437), `Abdul-Warith b. Sa`id (II, 1, pp. 154, 156), Mandal (I, 2, p. 575).

[12] In the sections of *Ta'rikh* relating Muhammad's biography, Tabari only appears to use the Ibn Ishaq recension of `Ali b. Mujahid directly (*History*, vol. 6, p. 159), whom he also quotes indirectly (*History*, vol. 6, pp. 66, 82). Other narrations are indirect:

	History
4) Yunus b. Bukayr	vol. 6, p. 82.
7) Yahya b. Sa`id	vol. 6, 134.
10) Salama b. al-Fadl	passim
i5) Muhammad b. Salama	vol. 7, 16.
Yunus b. Ibrahim	vol. 6, 107.

[13] As found in Guillaume, *New Light*. The manuscript gives an indirect Ibn Ishaq recension of Yunus b. Bukayr; see *New Light*, p. 5.

[14] Since Waqidi never makes mention of Ibn Ishaq, it is difficult to determine whether or not he used him as a source. Schwally, *GQ*, vol. 2, pp. 133, was of the opinion that some passages in Waqidi appear to be abbreviated versions of Ibn Ishaq. Guillaume, *Muhammad*, pp. xxxi f. is a little more apprehensive, but shows Tabari (iii, 2512) as saying that Waqidi regarded Ibn Ishaq as "a man to be trusted."

[15] Cf. Schwally, *GQ*, vol. 2, pp. 130 f.

[16] See Guillaume, *Muhammad*, pp. xv f.

[17] The first collections of canonical traditions were those of Bukhari (d. 256 AH) and Muslim (d. 261 AH); cf. *SEI*, p. 119.

[18] Guillaume, in *Traditions*, p. 19, rejects a hadith mentioned by Muir, which states that the first collections of Islamic traditions were made during the reign of 'Umar II (d. 720 AD), on the grounds that no such collections are referred to in the works of later Muslims.

[19] See Guillaume, *Muhammad*, p. xxv, for references to the remarks of Ibn Hisham, al-Jumahi and Ibn al-Nadim. See also p. xxviii of the same book for the summaries of the theses of 'Azzam and 'Arafat.

[20] Schwally, in *GQ*, vol. 2, p. 132, thought that much of the poetry may have been geniune, owing to the charges which were levelled against Muhammad in them. Wellhausen, *Medina*, p. 15, and Guillaume, (*Muhammad*, p. xxx), as most other Western scholars, were of the opinion that most of the poems are later fabrications.

[21] See n. 10, above. Ibn Hisham also cites other sources occasionally, but his main text is the Ibn Ishaq recension of al-Bakka'i

[22] See n. 14, above.

[23] Schwally, *GQ*, vol. 2, p. 133; Guillaume, *Muhammad*, p. xxxii; *SEI*, p. 548. Watt, in Tabari, *History*, vol. 6, p. xv, shows that among others, Waqidi studied under Ibn Ishaq's rival Musa b. `Uqba, see n. 5, above.

[24] See the first three references in n. 23, above. Muslim scholars, in general, view Waqidi as a source of fallacious traditions; see the remarks of Islamic authorities on Tabari's Qur'an Commentary (*Tafsir*) as quoted by Rosenthal in Tabari, *History*, vol. 1, p. 110; see also Haq and Ghazanfar, in Ibn Sa`d, *Classes*, p. xxi.

[25] Schwally, in *GQ*, p. 133.

[26] Wellhausen, *Medina*, p. 15; Watt in Tabari, *History*, p. xv. For a critique of Waqidi's chronology, see Crone, *Trade*, pp. 223 f.

[27] After examining a text of Yunus b. Bukayr's recension of Ibn Ishaq's *Sira* materials, Guillaume thought that Ibn Ishaq may not have arranged his traditions chronologically at all, and that Ibn Hisham may have personally arranged these in his *Sira* of Muhammad.

[28] See n. 11, above.

[29] The traditions of Ibn Sa`d were collected from a rather wide range of sources.

[30] Haq and Ghazanfar, in Ibn Sa`d, *Classes*, p. xxi.

[31] Nöldeke and Schwally, *GQ*, vol. 2, p. 136.

[32] See n. 12, above.

[33] Schwally, *GQ*, vol. 2, p. 139, shows that in relating the Medinan portion of Muhammad's biography, Tabari cites the traditions of Ibn Ishaq 200 times, Waqidi 47 times and Ibn Sa`d 15 times. Tabari also quotes other traditions in addition to these. In his work *Tafsir*, Tabari did not make use of Waqidi's traditions; see the the statements of Muslim scholars in Tabari, *History*, vol. 1, p. 110.

[34] The variety of opposing traditions given in Tabari's *Ta'rikh*, provides valuable insight into the development of Islamic narrations; see Schwally, *GQ*, vol. 2, p. 140. Watt in Tabari, *History*, vol. 6, p. xix, contends that Tabari may have cited contradictory traditions, because he was not sure which was correct.

[35] The historical event of the "Satanic verses" is well documented in Tabari, *History*, vol. 6, pp. 107 f; and traditions such as those relating the circumstances of Muhammad's marriage to Zaynab b. Jahsh (Tabari, *Ta'rikh*, 1460 f.) are also not appreciated by many Muslim theologians; see *SEI*, p. 653. Cf. nn. 24 and 33, above. The popular Turkish version of Tabari's *Ta'rikh* (*Tarih-i Taberi*), for example, has edited out not only practically all of the isnads, but also traditions which are generally contrary to modern Islamic theological opinion.

[36] Sprenger had portions of his work published in various magazines in 1856, and the first volume of Muir's *Life of Mohamet* appeared in 1858; see Schwally, *GQ*, vol. 2, pp. 193 f.

[37] See Schwally, *GQ*, vol. 2, p. 194.

[38] Goldziher, *Muhammedanischen Studien*, vol 2, published in 1890. See Schwally, *GQ*, vol. 2, p. 194; Watt, in Tabari's *History*, vol. 6, pp. xvii f.

[39] Lammens, *Qoran et Tradition...*, published in 1910. See Schwally, *GQ*, vol. 2, p. 197. Watt in Tabari's *History*, vol. 6, pp. xvii f, shows that the tendency among some scholars to reject practically all Islamic traditions reached a high with a book by Wansborough (*Qur'an Studies...*) in 1977 and another by some of the latter's students (Crone and Cook, *Hagarism...*) in the same year.

[40] Schwally, *GQ*, vol. 2, pp. 197 f; Watt, in Tabari, *History*, vol. 6, pp. xviii f.

[41] Watt, in Tabari, *History*, vol. 6, p. xviii, appears to be referring to canonical hadith in his statement: "...there are no chronological Hadith." (see Ibid., p. xix.) The *Maghazi* of Waqidi, as one late example, is essentially

a collection of "chronological" hadith. Without even a skeleton of chronology provided by Islamic tradition: Muhammad's calling - opposition Hijra - raids - conquest, sorting out the chronology of Muhammad's *Sira* would be purely guesswork.

[42] Schwally, *GQ*, vol. 2, p. 157 f, gives as examples:`A'isha - Qur'an 24:11f; Zaynab's marriage to Muhammad - Qur'an 37:33f and Muhammad and the slave Mary (the Copt) being in Hafsa's apartment Qur'an 66:1f. There are many other such passages also: e.g. without the aid of hadith, one might think that Abu Lahab (Qur'an 111:1f) was actually Satan or some other supernatural figure.

[43] Ibn Mas`ud, `Ali, Ibn `Abbas, Abu Musa, `Umar, `A'isha, etc. who are sources for many traditions, are also said to have had Qur'an codices; see Jeffery, *Materials*, p. 14.

[44] E.g., see n. 23, above, for general Islamic opinion on Waqidi as a source.

[45] E.g., see Ibn Hisham's editorial remarks referred to in n. 10, above.

Muhammad
From His Birth to Ministry

Muhammad is said to have been a descendant of Ishmael,[1] even though early Muslim traditionalists express their reservations regarding the authenticity of such genealogies.[2] Muhammad was the son `Abdullah b. `Abdu'l-Muttalib and Amina bt. Wahb, whose marriage is only briefly related in tradition.[3] `Abdullah died before his son's birth,[4] which is said to have been accompanied with miracles[5] and to have occurred in the Year of the Elephant.[6] As a small child, Muhammad's heart was said to have been cleansed by two men in white,[7] but the narration of this tradition is thought to have been based on a misunderstanding of Qur'an 94:1-3.[8] Muhammad's mother Amina died when he was six years-old, and he then passed into the custody of his grandfather `Abdu'l-Muttalib.[9] Muhammad's being raised as an orphan is confirmed by the Qur'an (93:6). `Abdu'l-Muttalib died when Muhammad was eight, and he was then taken in by his uncle Abu Talib.[10]

It is said that when Muhammad was twelve years old, Abu Talib decided to take him on a trading journey to Syria.[11] At Bostra they met a monk,[12] who after recognizing that Muhammad would be a prophet, warned Abu Talib to protect his nephew from the Jews.[13] When he was a youth, Muhammad tended the goats of his relatives,[14] and as a young man, is said to have been protected from participating in pagan practices.[15]

Muhammad is reported to have been 20 years old at the time of the battle of al-Fijar[16] which he witnessed with his relatives and at which he is said to have shot some arrows.[17] After this battle, the oath of al-Fudul was drawn up.[18]

Economically, neither Abu Talib and his family,[19] nor Muhammad (Qur'an 93:8a) were wealthy. It is reported that Abu Talib once heard that a wealthy woman of the Quraysh named Khadija was preparing to send a trading caravan to Syria. Muhammad was encouraged by his uncle to ask if he could work for her,[20] and Khadija, after hearing of Muhammad's virtues, called for him and offered him employment.[21] When the caravan reached Bostra, a monk confirmed that Muhammad would be a prophet.[22] Upon returning from the journey, one of Khadija's slaves told her about the monk and how the slave had seen two angels shade Muhammad.[23]

A hadith shows that the pagans of Mecca boasted of their high rank,[24] and the Qur'an (43:30) indicates that Muhammad was not among these.[25] From what is known of Khadija, she was indeed a wealthy widow, whom many other Meccans desired to marry.[26] At 25 years, Muhammad was probably older than most unmarried men in his culture,[27] and Khadija's real reasons for choosing Muhammad, who was reportedly 15 years younger, appear to be unknown.[28] Early Islamic traditions are at variance with each other regarding the details of how Khadija married Muhammad,[29] but probably the most reliable version relates that Khadija had her father get drunk so that he would give his approval for the wedding.[30] After coming to himself and realizing what had happened, Khadija's father was said to have been angry. He implied that he would not have given his consent to the marriage, as he had rejected even prominent suitors from the Quraysh.[31]

By virtue of his marriage to Khadija, Muhammad seems to have become wealthy (Qur'an 93:8b), and for the duration of her life, he married no one else. Khadija bore Muhammad six children,[32] whose names are given as: al-Qasim, Zaynab, Ruqayya, Umm Kulthum, Fatima and `Abdullah, the last of whom may have been born after Muhammad's call and was given the epithets al-Tayyib and al-Tahir.[33] In a tradition accepted as authentic by some, `Abdullah's real name is said to have been the pagan `Abd Manaf.[34] Both al-Qasim and `Abdullah are reported to have died early in life.[35]

Based partially on the use of merchant terms in the Qur'an, Muhammad is presumed to have been a businessman after his marriage to Khadija,[36] and, in that bills of lading must have been read, some scholars are even of the opinion that Muhammad, as a tradesman, must have been literate.[37] However, as commerce was the primary occupation of the Meccans (cf. Qur'an 106:1-2), the knowledge of business terminology on the part of Muhammad should not be viewed as having been uncommon,[38] and in the Middle East of today, where the use of commercial documents is more widespread than in the past, there are still unlearned merchants, who rely on their relatives or friends to read for them.[39]

The rebuilding of the Ka`ba, which was said to have taken place when Muhammad was 35,[40] is generally thought to have been the innovation of Muslim historians, who aside from other discrepancies, have Muhammad walk through a gate to the Ka`ba,[41] which did not even exist during his lifetime.[42]

Narrations about soothsayers and fortune-tellers,[43] who allegedly foretold Muhammad's advent, are also unreliable (since Muhammad would have no doubt referred to such testimonies later) and one would expect the mention of such in the Qur'an, had they really taken place.[44]

With respect to the various versions of traditions relating to supposed Jewish prophecies concerning Muhammad, it is obvious that Messianic predictions were applied to Muhammad by Muslims in some,[45] and that others were simply invented.[46] With the respect to the books of the Old Testament, the Qur'an (7:156) claims that the Torah mentions the coming of an unlearned (or heathen) prophet,[47] in which Muhammad is meant (Qur'an (7:158), Nevertheless, none of the early Islamic sources attempt to produce any evidence for this claim,[48] but rather try to show that it is Muhammad who is referred to in a distorted Islamic version of Is. 42:1-7.[49]

The Qur'anic verse (7:156), moreover, maintains that the unlearned (or heathen) prophet and his message are mentioned in the Gospel, but instead of pursuing this, the earliest Muslim scholars tried to find a confirmation for Qur'an 61:6, in which Jesus is said to have proclaimed the coming of Ahmad (Muhammad).[50] Generally, Islamic sources claim that Jesus' statements regarding the Paraclete[51] are the evidences of this,[52] but such notions are not very credible.[53]

Other alleged Christian testimonies to Muhammad's advent, including those where a physical description of him was said to have been given in certain books,[54] also seem to be later Islamic additions, in that the Qur'an makes no allusions to them.

Although the stories about Salman al-Farisi and the four non-polytheists may contain some authentic materials,[55] their general credibility is doubtful, since references to "the religion of Abraham,"[56] which are at times crucial to the plot of the narration, are most probably anachronisms.[57]

Nevertheless, in one of the traditions about the four non-polytheists, there is a curious account of Zayd b. `Amr scolding the younger Muhammad for eating the meat of sacrifices, which he (Muhammad) had offered to idols.[58] Other Islamic sources also relate versions of this narration,[59] which at least one Western scholar of Islam has described as "the only authentic story of Muhammad's early years."[60] In addition to these, there is a tradition quoting Muhammad as saying he once offered a white sheep to the goddess al-`Uzza.[61] The content of both of these narrations not only concurs with the witness of Qur'an 93:7[62] ("did He [Allah] not find you [Muhammad] erring and guide you?"),[63] but also with Qur'an 74:5, in which even some Islamic translations of this verse depict Muhammad as being commanded by God to "flee the idols."[64] The intense desire of Islamic scholars to later absolve Muhammad from any involvement with idolatry is apparent in the works of the early historians,[65] theologians[66] and commentators.[67]

Notes:

[1] See Guillaume, *Muhammad*, p. 3; Ibn Sa`d *Classes*, vol. 1, 1, p. 50; Tabari, *History*, vol. 6, pp. 38f.

[2] Ibn Sa`d quotes Ibn `Abbas as saying that the genealogy narrators were liars, see *Classes*, vol. 1, 1, 50. Tabari (*History*, vol. 6, pp. 38f) gives seven different versions of the genealogy. The development of Ishmael in the Qur'anic accounts also reveals that Muhammad only came to know of Ishmael through outside sources and that he did not claim to be his descendant. See n. 56, below.

[3] The somewhat discrepant narrations, whose progressions can be traced through Ibn Hisham (Guillaume, *Muhammad*, pp. 68f) to Tabari, *History*, vol. 6, pp. 38 f. to Ibn Sa`d, *Classes*, vol. 1, 1, pp. 101 f. appear to have led early Christian polemicists to make unjust accusations; see Jahiz in *ECMD*, p. 705. The charge seems to have evoked as a response the Muslim traditions found in Ibn Sa`d, *Classes*, vol. 1, 1, pp. 55 f. For the accounts of

the legendary miracles surrounding Amina's pregnancy, see Guillaume, *Muhammad*, p. 69, cf. *New Light*, p. 19.

[4] Other versions also state that 'Abdullah lived until Muhammad was either 7 months or 28 months old; see Ibn Sa'd, *Classes*, vol. 1, 1, p. 108. General opinion is that 'Abdullah died before Muhammad's birth.

[5] For the alleged miracles surrounding Muhammad's birth and suckling, see Guillaume, *Muhammad*, pp. 69 f; Ibn Sa'd, *Classes*, vol. 1, 1, pp. 111 f, 121 f, 170 f. The Qur'an makes no mention of such miracles and in the earliest traditions, Muhammad never refers to such as a confirmation of his calling. The development of Islamic hadith ascribing miracles to Muhammad appears to have been a reaction to the later polemic of Jews and Christians; see *ECMD*, p. 724.

[6] Guillaume, *Muhammad*, p. 69; Ibn Sa'd, *Classes*, vol. 1, 1, p. 110. According to Islamic tradition, this year is thought to have been 570 AD. Western scholars, although maintaining that Muhammad was born c. 570 AD, have shown that the Year of the Elephant must have occurred earlier than this date. See p. 12, n. 57 above.

[7] Guillaume, *Muhammad*, p. 72; Ibn Sa'd, *Classes*, I, 1, pp. 123 f, 170 f. The historian Tabari places this event after Muhammad's call; see *History*, vol. 6, p. 75.

[8] Buhl, *Muhammad*, p. 117; *EI²*, s.v. "Muhammad," p. 362.

[9] Guillaume, *Muhammad*, p. 73; Ibn Sa'd, *Classes*, vol. 1, 1, p. 129.

[10] Guillaume, *Muhammad*, pp. 73 f, 79; Ibn Sa'd, *Classes*, vol. 1, 1, p. 132.

[11] For the various Islamic narrations of the following meeting with the monk, see Guillaume, *Muhammad*, pp. 79 f; Ibn Sa'd, *Classes*, vol. 1, 1, p. 134; Tabari, *History*, vol. 6, pp. 44 f. See n. 22, below.

[12] In some traditions the monk is unnamed, in others he is called "Bahira," which is not really a name, but rather Syriac epithet meaning "proven;" see Nau in *ECMD*, p. 38, n. 37.

[13] Tabari's account (*History*, vol. 6, p. 46), not only depicts stones and trees as bowing to Muhammad, but shows Bahira as also warning Abu Talib not to take Muhammad to the lands of the Byzantines, because they would kill the child.

[14] Ibn Sa'd, *Classes*, vol. 1, 1, 140f, in which Muhammad is quoted as saying that all prophets grazed goats; cf. *Sahih Bukhari*, vol. 4, p. 408; vol. 7, p. 264; *Sahih Muslim*, vol. 3, p. 1130, where Muhammad says in effect that all prophets were shepherds.

[15] Tabari, *History*, vol. 6, pp. 46 f; Guillaume, *Muhammad*, p. 81, n. 2; and a version of Ibn Ishaq given in Guillaume, *New Light*, p. 20. Muhammad is said to have been protected from the sin of fornication.

[16] The causes of the battle are discussed briefly in Guillaume, *Muhammad*, p. 82; Watt, *Muhammad*, pp. 8 f, and the reference in n. 17, below.

[17] Ibn Sa'd, *Classes*, vol. 1, 1, pp. 141 f.

[18] Ibid. p. 144.

[19] Ibid. p. 145.

[20] Ibid.

[21] Ibid.; Guillaume, *Muhammad*, p. 82; Tabari, *History*, vol. 6, pp. 47 f.

[22] Guillaume, *Muhammad*, p. 82; Tabari, *History*, vol. 6, pp. 48. Ibn Sa'd, *Classes*, vol. 1, 1, pp. 146 f. gives the monk's name as Nastur, which no doubt comes from "Nestorius." Andrae (*Mohammed*, p. 38) expresses serious doubts that Muhammad ever visited Syria or any other "Christian" country, as the Qur'an reveals no familiarity on Muhammad's part with the

institutions and rituals of Christians. Muhammad's alleged trips to Syria are generally regarded as later literary productions by Western scholars; see *SEI*, p. 391 and *EI²*, s.v. "Muhammad," p. 362.

[23] Guillaume, *Muhammad*, p. 82; Tabari, *History*, vol. 6, p. 82. Ibn Sa`d, *Classes*, I, 1, pp. 146 f. depicts Khadija as seeing the two angels herself when Muhammad returned to Mecca. Again, there is no mention of these events in the Qur'an.

[24] *Sahih Muslim*, vol. 2, p. 444.

[25] *SEI*, p. 391; Guillaume, *Islam*, p. 24.

[26] Guillaume, *Muhammad*, p. 82; Tabari, *History*, vol. 6, p. 48.

[27] Buhl, *Muhammad*, p. 119, n. 30, also sees Muhammad's age at marriage as another indication of his financial poverty.

[28] The traditional accounts described in n. 23 above, imply that Khadija chose Muhammad based on the witness of her slave, who told her about seeing the two angels and about what the monk in Bostra had said. Ibn Hisham adds a tradition (mistakenly placed after Khadija's wedding), which claims that Khadija went to her cousin Waraqa to ask about the things her slave had witnessed concerning Muhammad; (Guillaume, *Muhammad*, p. 83). Another version of Ibn Ishaq's narrations does not contain this tradition; see Guillaume, *New Light*, p. 21. According to tradition, Khadija had been married twice before; see *SEI*, p. 231.

[29] Ibn Sa`d, *Classes*, vol. 1, 1, pp. 147 f; Tabari, *History*, vol. 6, pp. 49 f.

[30] This tradition is given through various chains of narrators. Oddly enough, the versions of this tradition allegedly traced through Ibn `Umar (Ibn Sa`d, *Classes*, vol. 1, 1, p. 149) and Waqidi (Tabari, *History*, vol. 6, p. 49) are deemed to be false by both. The reason for this contradictory rejection given by both transmitters is that both maintain Khadija's father had died before the battle of al-Fijar, and that she was married off by an uncle. Buhl,

Muhammad, p. 119, counters Sprenger's notion that the later rejection of this tradition was motivated by the desire to hide anything scandalous, by claiming that 1) Khadija, as wealthy and independent, could have married whom she pleased and 2) that the literary device of having someone get drunk to approve a marriage is known from other Arabic works. In Middle Eastern culture, however, women, irrespective of their rank or personal wealth, generally must be given in marriage by a male relative. The identification of literary devices, moreover, does not preclude historicity, as later generations are often inspired to action by deeds described in earlier works. Based on the information provided in the Qur'an (93:68a), that Muhammad was an orphan deprived of wealth and high social rank (43:30), there must have been resistance within the family of Khadija against such a marriage. Furthermore, it is well documented that Muslim traditionalists often suppressed information which they regarded as being negative (Ibn Hisham chose not to mention how Khadija married). One must question also the possible motivation for Muslims to have invented and propagated the tradition about the role of Khadija's father at her marriage, if it were not true. Andrae, *Mohammed*, p. 41, gives the tradition of the drunkeness of Khadija's father without making further comment on variant accounts.

[31] This remark also implicitly concurs with the testimony of Qur'an 43:30, that Muhammad was not a notable person among the Quraysh.

[32] In Tabari, *History*, vol. 6, p. 49, n. 60, Watt and McDonald state that Muslim sources appear to have had no problems with Khadija being 40 and bearing seven children. Buhl, *Muhammad*, p. 119, n. 33, gives, among others, Ibn Sa`d, *Tabaqat*, vol. 8, 10, p. 2, as showing Khadija to have been 28 years old when she married Muhammad.

[33] Guillaume, *Muhammad*, p. 83; Ibn Sa`d, *Classes*, vol. 1, 1, p. 150; Tabari, *History*, vol. 6, pp. 48 f. Only Ibn Sa`d shows `Abdullah as having been born after Muhammad's call.

[34] This view was held by Sprenger and others; see Buhl in *SEI*, p. 391. Buhl, *Muhammad*, p. 120, n. 36, gives Halabi, III, 335, 17 as an example of an Islamic source. The reasons for accepting this tradition as historical are that Muslims would have no logical reason for inventing this, and yet a great

number of reasons for later trying to suppress this information. See nn. 64-66, below.

[35] See the references in n. 33, above. Ibn Hisham and Tabari show that all of Muhammad's sons died before his call.

[36] Buhl, *Muhammad*, p. 121.

[37] Nöldeke and Schwally, *GQ*, vol. 1, pp. 15 f; Buhl, *Muhammad*, p. 120; *SEI*, p. 392; Guillaume, *Islam*, p. 57.

[38] Andrae, *Mohammed*, p. 42, reiterates that in Islamic traditions there is no further information regarding other trading journeys of Muhammad or Khadija, and that the trade vocabulary found in the Qur'an is related to religious terminology.

[39] The Qur'anic regulation of business transactions in 2:282 is very revealing on this point. Each party is to agree on a scribe who is to write the transaction, if one is unable to dictate, then his representative (waliy) is to do this for him. Moreover, *every* transaction is to be witnessed by the equivalent of two male witnesses (i.e. two females for one male). Such a regulation, which may have been relatively standard anyway for that time, only requires that the scribe (who is to write as God has taught him) be literate.

[40] Guillaume, *Muhammad*, pp. 84 f; Ibn Sa`d, *Classes*, vol. 1, 1, pp. 164 f; Tabari, *History*, vol. 6, pp. 51 f. A strange hadith in Guillaume, *New Light*, p. 24, places this event much earlier, and depicts `Abdu'l-Muttalib as the one who put the black stone in place.

[41] Guillaume, *Muhammad*, p. 86; Tabari, *History*, vol. 6, p. 58; Ibn Sa`d, *Classes*, vol. 1, 1, 166 (gives the gate of the Banu Shayba).

[42] See Buhl, *Muhammad*, p. 122. Cf. *Sahih Bukhari*, vol. 5, p. 109, in which it is reported that the wall around the Ka`ba was first built during the reign of `Umar.

[43] Guillaume, *Muhammad*, pp. 90 f; Ibn Sa`d, *Classes*, vol. 1, 1, pp. 172 f.

[44] The fabulous events of a speaking calf (Ibn Sa`d, *Classes*, vol. 1, 1, p. 180), or the carcass of a calf (Guillaume, *Muhammad*, p. 93) are also the sort of things the Qur'an would have made mention of had they really occurred. Tabari, *History*, vol. 6, p. 66, adds to the story of the the speaking calf's carcass, the speaking of a slaughtered camel.

[45] Guillaume, *Muhammad*, pp. 93 f; Ibn Sa`d, *Classes*, vol. 1, 1, pp. 181 f. Jewish Messianic expectations, of course, are for a Jewish Messiah.

[46] The story about Ibn al-Hayyaban, for example, (Guillaume, *Muhammad*, p. 94; Ibn Sa`d, *Classes*, vol. 1, 1, pp. 183 f) not only contains the flaw that the main character, himself a Jew, addresses his religious colleagues as "O Jews," but also that this narration is used to explain how some Jews (contrary to Ibn al-Hayyaban's reported message) became Muslims.

[47] It is relatively clear from Qur'anic passages (2:73; 3:69; 62:2) and early Muslim works, that the word "ummi" was understood by Muhammad to mean "unlearned" or "heathen." According to Qur'an 7:156, the Torah and Gospel say this prophet will: "enjoin on them which is right and forbid them that which is wrong. He will make lawful for them all good things and prohibit for them only the foul; and he will relieve them of their burden and the fetters that they used to wear. Then those who believe in him, and honor him, and help him and follow the light which is sent down with him: they are the successful." (Pickthall). Western scholars of Islam generally consider the Arabic "ummi" to have been derived from a Jewish term for gentiles, and thus tend to translate it as "heathen"; cf. Nöldeke and Schwally, *GQ*, vol. 1, pp. 14 f; Watt and Bell, *Introduction*, pp. 33 f. See also p. 209.

[48] In general, the Old Testament passages used by early Muslim polemicists to strengthen the Islamic claim for Muhammad's prophethood are Deuteronomy 18:18 and Is. 21:7 (Peshitta). See *ECMD*, p. 734, for references to early Muslim works.

[49] Guillaume, *New Light*, p. 32; Ibn Sa`d, *Classes*, I, 2, pp. 422 f. *Sahih Bukhari*, vol. 6, pp. 345 f, gives this passage as a parallel to Qur'an 48:8.

[50] The names "Muhammad" and "Ahmad" come from the same Arabic root.

[51] John 14:26; 15:26; 16:7.

[52] See *ECMD*, p. 734, for references to early Islamic polemical works. In Guillaume, *Muhammad*, p. 103 f, Ibn Hisham gives a corrupted reading of John 15:23f, which is from the Palestinian Syriac Lectionary. In the text, the name "Munahhemana" has been exchanged for "Paraclete." According to Guillaume (p. 104, n. 1) the Syriac "menahhemana" means "life-giver." Probably since "Munahhemana" phonetically resembles "Muhammad," Ibn Hisham chose to insert it into the text (see also Schwally in *GQ*, vol. 1, p. 9, n. 1). By including this in his work, however, Ibn Hisham seems to have forgotten that Qur'an 61:6 refers to the title "Ahmad" and not the name "Muhammad."

[53] It is obvious from the accounts in the Gospel of John that the Paraclete was to be sent in the lifetimes of the disciples of Jesus. In John 14:26, Jesus identifies the Paraclete as the Holy Spirit (in 15:26 and 16:13 as the "spirit of truth"), who according to Acts 1:8 and 2:1f. came upon the disciples at Pentecost.

[54] Guillaume, *Muhammad*, p. 103; Ibn Sa`d, *Classes*, vol. 1, 2, p. 426; Tabari, *History*, vol. 6, p. 64 f.

[55] Guillaume, *Muhammad*, pp. 95 f.

[56] Guillaume, *Muhammad*, pp. 96, 99; Tabari, *History*, vol. 6, p. 64.

[57] The phrase "religion of Abraham" (Qur'an 2:124, etc.) and the Qur'anic Abraham legend (2:118 f) are distinctly Medinan; see Appendix D, p. 385. This anachronism also appears in the account of the rebuilding of the Ka`ba in Ibn Hisham (Guillaume, *Muhammad*, p. 85), in the story of the

Hums (Ibid., p. 87) and in essentially every attempt of later Muslim scholars to present Muhammad as a descendant of Ishmael and Abraham.

[58] Guillaume, *New Light*, pp. 27 f.

[59] Guillaume (Ibid.) cites *Sahih Bukhari* (vol. 5, p. 106), Suhayli (*Al-Raud al-Unuf*, p. 146) and Ibn Kathir (*Al-Bidaya wa al-Nihaya*, p. 239) as giving various versions of this tradition, in which attempts to cover up its scandalous nature are evident.

[60] Guillaume, in his book *Islam*, p. 26.

[61] Ibn Kalbi on "al-`Uzza" in Wellhausen, *Reste*, p. 34.

[62] The Christian apologist Kindi used this verse as proof that Muhammad was idolatrous, and claimed that Muhammad worshipped the idols al-Lat and al-`Uzza just as his relatives did. See al-Kindi in *ECMD*, p. 426.

[63] Translation of Arberry.

[64] See the translations of Kahn in *Sahih Bukhari*, vol. 1, p. 5; vol. 6, pp. 420 f, Siddiqi in *Sahih Muslim*, vol. 1, pp. 98 f, and Gölpinarli in *Kur'an*, p. 361. For a discussion of this text, see p. 41, below.

[65] See Ibn Hisham in Guillaume, *Muhammad*, p. 80, where Muhammad is reported to have said that nothing was more hateful to him than al-Lat and al-`Uzza (cf. Ibn Sa`d, *Classes*, vol. 1, 1, pp. 146, 176, 178). See also Guillaume, *Muhammad*, p. 81, in which it is said that God protected Muhammad and kept him from the vileness of heathenism, because He wanted to honor him with apostleship. An interesting, but contradictory addition to this statement appears in Guillaume, *New Light*, p. 20, and a similar one in Ibn Sa`d, *Classes*, I, 1, p. 134, to the effect that God protected Muhammad... because He wanted to honor him with apostleship: "(while) he followed the religion (creed) of his people... " Cf. reference in n. 61, above.

[66] See the *Fikh Akbar II*, (c. 10th century AD), article 9, as given in Wensinck, *Creed*, p. 192 : "...He [Muhammad] did not serve idols, nor was

36

he at any time a polytheist, even for a single moment. And he never committed a light or a grave sin." For the role of early Christian polemicists in the development of this doctrine, see *ECMD*, pp. 723 f.

[67] E.g. Tabari, *Tefsir*, vol. 6, p. 2826, n. 1; Ali, *Qur'an*, vol. 1, p. 1752, n. 6183 (comment to Qur'an 93:7), etc.

Muhammad
His Call

According to the majority witness of early Islamic tradition, when Muhammad was about 40 years old, the first part of the Qur'an revealed to him was sura 96:1f.[1] The circumstances of this revelation are said to have been that Muhammad was in the cave at Hira' near Mecca performing his monthly devotions,[2] when the angel Gabriel appeared to him,[3] commanding him to "recite" (or "read"). Muhammad then recited Qur'an 96:1f and the angel vanished. Believing himself to have become a "poet" or "possessed," both of which he despised, Muhammad thought of jumping off the mountain.[4] Gabriel then called from heaven saying that Muhammad was the apostle of Allah. Muhammad either went to or was found by Khadija and told her what had happened. Khadija then decided to take her husband to her cousin Waraqa b. Naufal, who had become a Christian and was even said to have read and translated the scriptures.[5] After hearing Muhammad's story, Waraqa said that the angel was the Namus[6] who had come to Moses. Waraqa also warned Muhammad that he would experience opposition.

One Muslim historian shows Qur'an 68:1f; 74:1f and 93:1f as being the next suras to have been revealed,[7] and most Islamic sura orderings also place Qur'an 68 immediately after Qur'an 96.[8] Major Islamic histories report that after the first revelations, there was a period during which Gabriel did not appear to Muhammad, and the revelations ceased.[9] The reason for this interruption (fatra) in revelations is not explained at all in the earliest accounts of Muhammad's biography, but is rather strongly implied in some canonical hadith.[10] According to one collection of *Sira* traditions, Khadija told Muhammad she thought his Lord "must have come to hate" him during the fatra, but then Qur'an 93:1-3 was revealed to Muhammad as a reassurance that Allah had not forsaken him, and the resumption of revelation is then inferred.[11]

Western scholars of Islam have very many reservations about the authenticity of these traditions. `A'isha, one of the original narrators, could not have been an eyewitness of these events, as she was not yet born,[12] the alleged name of the angel, "Gabriel", first appears in suras which were undoubtedly revealed in Medina,[13] the notion of Qur'an 96:1f (or 74:1f) as being the first parts of the Qur'anic revelation are doubtful,[14] the accusation of Muhammad being a "poet" or "possessed" was made by Meccans who later opposed him,[15] the word "apostle" was probably first used in Qur'an 73:15,[16] the name "Namus" never appears in the Qur'an or in other *Sira* hadith[17] and the "fatra" is generally viewed as being a later innovation.[18]

Nevertheless, the majority of Western Islam scholars do follow the Muslim accounts in maintaining that Qur'an 96:1f was probably the first revelation.[19] The reasons for this opinion are that based on the internal evidence of the Qur'an alone, it is impossible to determine which of the existing passages were revealed first, and the majority of the only early external evidences (Islamic traditions) show Qur'an 96:1f as the first part of the Qur'an to have been revealed. The view of most Islamic authorities that Qur'an 68 was the second revelation is justifiably rejected by Western scholars,[20] but even some Western listings place this sura earlier than it probably should be.[21] Muslim views regarding Qur'an 74:1f and 93:1f as being the next Qur'anic revelations are closely related to the traditions about the fatra,[22] and as such these evidently did not carry much weight with the scholars who constructed the various Islamic sura orderings.[23] For the Meccan periods at least, Muslims seem to have been more influenced by Qur'anic exegesis than the traditions of Muhammad's *Sira* in composing the chronological sura orderings.[24]

In what appear to be the earliest suras, Muhammad does not seem to have had a following. The openings of the passages Qur'an 96, 74 and 107, for example, are in the imperative and are addressed to a singular person, who is generally thought to be Muhammad. Qur'an 93 and 94 are also suras which appear to have been "private" communications to Muhammad.[25]

On closer examination of **Qur'an 96:1-5** and **74:1-7**, the influences of the pagan soothsayers and Syrian Christianity are obvious. The general style of the Qur'an was so similar to the loosely rhymed "poetry" (saj`) of the soothsayers,[26] that Muhammad's contemporaries even accused him of being a "poet," "kahin" or "possessed."[27] In 74:1 Muhammad is called "the enshrouded" (cf. 73:1) and the custom of wrapping oneself up during supernatural inspiration, appears to have been pagan.[28] The word "Qur'an" seems to have been related to the Syriac "qeryana" used in conjunction with "reading" or "reciting" a lesson from the scriptures.[29] In 74:5, the word usually translated "abomination" or "defilement," seems to be the Syriac "rujza" (="wrath"),[30] and 74:4-7 contains Biblical phrases which could hardly have been coincidental.[31]

One might suppose Muhammad received his initial information from a variety of sources, were it not for a lesser-known tradition which can be found in later Islamic works. Accordingly, Muhammad is said to have heard the preaching of Quss the bishop of Najran at the market of `Ukaz. Quss, who was most probably Nestorian, reportedly gave his "recitations" about the vanity of life and the imminence of the Judgment in the form of saj`.[32] The general (but very rare) agreement between Islamic traditionists and Christian polemicists that Muhammad at least had some form of fleeting contact with a monk[33] also seem to concur with the background evidence found in the earliest suras of the Qur'an which show Syrian Christian influence.

Islamic traditions show the institution of the ritual prayers (salat) and ablution (wudu') as being taught to Muhammad by the angel Gabriel, and that Muhammad then instructed Khadija.[34] According to the most popular accounts, the ritual prayers were originally to be performed five times daily, and the direction of prayer (qibla) was initially the Ka`ba.[35] The Qur'an also testifies to the early development of at least some form of the ritual prayers,[36] but that the introduction of ablutions and the qibla[37] must have been much later; probably in Medina.[38] The ritual prayers were first performed only twice daily (Qur'an 17:80), and it appears that the night prayer was added later (Qur'an 20:130; 11:116). The "middle" prayer was added at Medina (Qur'an 2:239).[39] The five daily prayer times, as they stand today, are not mentioned in the Qur'an, but occupy a very important place in the canonical hadith. Muhammad's form of early "devotions" may have been influenced by a Christian practice,[40] and the basic genuflexions of the ritual prayer appear to have been borrowed from Syrian Christians.[41] The original two daily times of prayer follow the rule of the Nestorians which prescribes two prayer times for their laity.[42] The night prayer may have later taken the place of the vigils Muhammad used to hold.[43] The introduction of the "middle" prayer was probably influenced by the Jews,[44] who generally prayed three times a day.[45]

Islamic *Sira* traditions contradict one another concerning who became Muhammad's first male follower, and these hadith appear to have been colored by the various political and theological persuasions of the narrators.[46] Some traditions depict Muhammad and two of his followers as praying the ritual prayers together rather early on,[47] and almost all of the *Sira* accounts report that three years after Muhammad had his first revelation, he received the command to preach publicly in Qur'an 15:94 and 26:214.[48]

Some traditions then show that **Qur'an 111** was revealed after Muhammad's uncle Abu Lahab (`Abd al-`Uzza) ridiculed Muhammad's message.[49]

Interestingly enough, both Islamic and Western sura orderings have Qur'an 111 appear very early, whereas the suras 15 and 26 are generally placed about 50 positions later.[50] Indeed, the texts of Qur'an 15:94 and 26:214 do not necessarily imply that Muhammad only then began to preach openly, and the definitely earlier suras 102 and 92, for example, imply that Muhammad was preaching to others at that point in time.

Another Islamic *Sira* tradition associates Qur'an 111 with the boycott against the Hashimites,[51] and some Western scholars even think this sura was revealed after the death of Abu Talib.[52]

The **suras 106, 108**[53] and **105** appear to be based on mainly Arabian sources. Muhammad held to the supremacy of his tribe the Quraysh (106:1), retained the cult of the Ka`ba (106:3)[54] with pagan sacrifice (108:2) and used a legendary narration of Abraha's unsuccessful attack on Mecca as an example of God's punishment (105).

The texts of the **suras 104, 107** and **102**, however, reveal the influence of Christianity. The similarities between 104:2-4 and Luke 12:16-20 together with that of Qur'an 107:4f and Matthew 6:5 are more than coincidental, the notion of a burning Hell (104:4-6; also 111) and Judgment (107:1) are Biblical ideas, and definitely not pagan Arab.[55] The condemnation of the coveteous (102:1f) seems to follow a hymn of the Syrian Church.[56] Already in these few suras a pattern of preaching can be seen, which is not only reminiscent of Christian sermons to pagans,[57] but which was to influence the structure of Muhammad's message. At this stage Muhammad appears to have begun preaching to others (102:1f): that man should recognize God's goodness (96:3; 106:3f); he should pray (108:2), sacrifice (108:2) and give alms (74:6); those who are coveteous and hoard wealth will be punished (104:1f; 102:1f); God, who is mentioned in the first person plural (108:1), has punished others in the past (105:1f).[58]

Another distinguishing feature in many of the earliest suras of the Qur'an is that they often begin with or contain the pagan oaths of soothsayers,[59] and it seems that Muhammad used these in the saj` form[60] to increase the credibility of his message.[61]

Perhaps the earliest of the suras to b˄gin with such oaths are **Qur'an 92** and **90**. Aside from the well-known discrepancy in the oath of 92:3 among pre-`Uthmanic codices,[62] this sura as a whole represents a further development of doctrines influenced by Christianity (92:5) and may contain an early reference to Paradise (92:5,9). Sura 90 also begins with oaths, but alludes to various Biblical illustrations.[63] An early usage of the word for "believe" is found in 90:17, and although belief in God's signs seems to be inferred (cf. 90:19), the object of believe is not specifically defined. This borrowing was probably from Christian sources;[64] just as the heavy dependence of 90:18-20 on Mt. 25:33, 34, 41 was. Sura 90 contains perhaps the earliest usage of the phrases "companions of the right" and "companions of the left."

The **suras 94** and **93** appear to have been addressed to Muhammad personally. Islamic exegetes and traditionists generally interpret 94:1 as having to do with Muhammad's heart being washed by angels,[65] but the word for "breast" is also an idiom for "mind"[66] Since the end of this sura deals with Muhammad reciting the Qur'an, v. 1 may simply mean that Muhammad's memory was being expanded to retain the suras which had been revealed up until that point. In the sense of 94:2-4, however, the word "breast" (v. 1) could have been meant physically, referring to Muhammad having been freed from manual labor by virtue of his marriage to Khadija. Sura 93 begins with two oaths and much of its contents have already been elaborated upon above.[67] As with Qur'an 108:1, sura 93 (cf. v. 8) must have also been revealed when Muhammad was still prosperous, and thus before any of the hardships which later followed.

The beginning of **sura 97** is thought to be missing.[68] Muslim scholars see 97:1-3 as referring to the night (of al-Qadr) when the first parts of the Qur'an were revealed.[69] This sura contains perhaps the earliest mention of angels or spirit (v. 4).

Qur'an 86 is composed of two fragments, each beginning with oaths;[70] the vv. 15-17 appear to be an early allusion to opposition against Muhammad's message.

Sura 91 also begins with a long list of oaths, which is followed (vv. 11f) with the punishment narrative of Thamud. This story was also used by Christian and pagan Arab poets[71] whose works were probably at least an indirect source.

Sura 80, which appears to be composed of three fragments,[72] begins with what is usually regarded as Muhammad being rebuked (vv. 1-10),[73] the vv. 11-15 seem to describe the Qur'an as a heavenly writing and the vv. 33-42 give an early allusion to the coming Judgment, which is very similar to some works of the Syrian Church.[74]

Qur'an 68, although containing apparently old fragments, was probably updated or added to later.[75] However, vv. 2-14 resemble later suras, where Muhammad was accused of having been possessed (cf. v. 51),[76] the vv. 15-16 must have been revealed after suras with narratives,[77] the parable of vv. 17f is probably from a Syrian work,[78] and the foreign vocabulary of vv. 37 and 39 also indicate a later time period.[79] The reference to Jonah in vv. 48f must be old, as his name is not used ("companion of the fish"), and may well imply that it dates from a time when Muhammad's own situation with respect to the Meccans had deteriorated (v. 48a).

Sura 87 begins with a phrase which is definitely Biblical ("Praise the name of your Lord..."); vv. 12f concur with the message of Mk. 9:48 and Is. 66:24 and v. 6 seems to show that no part of the Qur'an had yet been committed to writing. Prayer is again presented as the only ritual (v. 15) and the cryptic reference to the scrolls of Abraham and Moses (v. 19) implies that Muhammad had contact with heretical groups which had broken off from Christianity.[80]

The **suras 95** and **103** are thought to be incomplete as they stand,[81] and both begin with with at least one oath. The nouns in the oaths of 95:1f appear to be Christian in nature,[82] and v. 5 is similar to a hymn of Ephraem the Syrian.[83] The oath in Qur'an 103:1 probably does not refer to the afternoon prayer, but rather to "fate."[84]

Qur'an 85 begins with several oaths and then (vv. 4f) seems to relate the story of the execution of Christians by the Jewish Yemenite leader Dhu Nuwas.[85] It is clear from v. 7 that Muhammad considered those who were executed as having been "believers." The vv. 10-11 are thought to be later additions.[86] Muhammad has learned the stories of the hosts of Pharaoh[87] and Thamud (vv. 17-18), which stories are said to have been lies by Muhammad's opponents (v. 19). The v. 21 contains perhaps one of the first direct references to the "Qur-'an."

Doctrinally, Qur'an 103:2 may be related to the New Testament idea of "the lost" and although 95:6; 103:3 and 85:11 are thought to be later additions to these suras,[88] the phrase "those who believe and do righteous works" cannot have been too much later.[89] The coupling of belief and good works is somewhat common in pre-Reformation Christianity, nevertheless, some Western scholars maintain that the Syrian Church was Muhammad's most probable source for such teachings.[90]

Sura 73 presents Muhammad as being cloaked, holding vigils and "chanting" (the Qur'an),[91] which is somewhat reminiscent of the practices of Christian monks.[92] Qur'an 73:7 seems to imply that because of his work during the day, Muhammad did not have enough time to devote to the revelation until evening. The vv. 9f imply Muhammad's need for protection and speak of opposition to his message. The description of the end of the world being preceded by an earthquake (73:14),[93] as well as the sky being split apart (73:18)[94] appear to have come from Christian sources. The vv. 15f give perhaps the earliest instance of Muhammad being compared with a Biblical prophet (in this case Moses, who is unnamed); and this idea became even more developed later on.[95] The mention of gray-haired children appears to have come from Jewish sources.[96] The verse 73:20 is certainly Medinan and seems to have been added to this sura by either Muhammad himself or later editors, due to the similarity between v. 20a and 73:2f.[97]

Qur'an 73:9f definitely indicate that the rejection of Muhammad's message had begun, and the *Sira* traditions also have much to say about the various forms of rejection and persecution which Muhammad and his early followers faced. After relating that Muhammad publicly began preaching three years after receiving his first revelations,[98] traditions relate how Abu Lahab opposed him[99] and even threw excrement in front of Muhammad's door.[100] At least one tradition shows that the first Muslims sat around the Ka`ba,[101] although they probably prayed secretly in glens.[102] Muhammad appears to have still practiced the pagan rites at the Ka`ba[103] and even kissed the stone[104] as the Ka`ba was still filled with idols.

The **suras 101, 99, 82** and **81** generally describe the coming Judgment and the end of the world. The origin of the similes in 101:3-4 does not appear to be known, but idea of scales being used in the Judgment seems to come from Jewish or Christian apocalyptic literature.[105] Qur'an 101:6 contains a peculiar word from Ethiopic.[106] The opening verses of the suras 99, 82 and 81 are weak modulates of Rev. 6:12-14 and must have come from Christian sources. The notion of the sun being folded (81:1) may have been due to a misunderstanding,[107] and 81:10 is similar to Rev. 20:12. Qur'an 81:8 is a reference to the old Arab practice of burying infant girls alive, but their giving testimony at the Judgment appears to be based on ideas from Jewish and Christian eschatology[108] The oaths of Qur'an 81 are positioned in the middle of the sura rather than at the beginning. Muhammad again denies being possessed (v. 21) and briefly mentions an encounter (vv. 22-24), on which he appears to elaborate later in 53:2-18. In 81:25, not only does the word for "Satan" seem to be a loan from Ethiopic which predates Muhammad[109] but the word usually translated as "stoned" in this verse is also from the same language and actually means "cursed."[110]

Qur'an 53 begins with an oath, and since the vv. 2-18 are very similar to 81:22-24 in describing what appears to be how Muhammad was shown a sign and given revelation, both Muslim and Western scholars[111] place this sura earlier than it probably should be. Although 53:1-18 may be early, traditions surrounding the background of vv. 19f and the context of these verses, that Muhammad had begun openly attacking the pagan deities of the Meccans, can hardly be reconciled with the evidence from the other suras of this period.[112]

Actually two distinct events are related in the beginning of this sura; one (vv. 5-12) is the improved description of 81:22-24; the other (vv. 12-18), which refers to a covered lote tree, seems to contain a reference to a pagan practice,[113] rather than implying that Muhammad had been in Paradise as some Muslim scholars hold.[114] The mention of these events in both of the suras 81 and 53, was probably to counter the accusation that Muhammad had been "possessed" or in error (cf. 81:22; 53:2). Qur'an 53:34f also appear to be older than vv. 19-32. The verses about the scrolls of Moses and Abraham (vv. 37f) are similar to 87:19; and aside from the mention of God as the "Lord of Sirius" (v. 50), most of the phrases used are typical of an early Meccan period. Of the early passages in this sura, a few of them are similar to Biblical verses.[115] The verse 53:53 represents one of the first references to the prophet Noah and the `Ad, who together with the Thamud, appear in Qur'anic stories of God's punishment.[116] At least two additional verses of sura 53 are said to have existed according to information on pre-`Uthmanic Qur'an codices.[117]

One Western Qur'an scholar maintains that the remainder of **sura 96 (vv. 6-19)** should be placed sometime after Qur'an 53.[118] These verses show that Muhammad's message was being opposed (vv. 9f) and rejected (vv. 13f - cf. 53:34f). The description of punishment (vv. 18f) is similar to some of the works of Ephraem the Syrian.[119]

The **suras 84, 100, 79** and **77** all speak of the coming Judgment and the Resurrection. Qur'an 84 begins with a phrase based on Rev. 6:14a, and this is later followed by a depiction of the Judgment in which books are given in the right or left hands (vv. 7f). It is thought that Muhammad also received this from Christian sources,[120] and the notion of "those who believe and do righteousness" being well rewarded (v. 25) parallels the doctrines of the Eastern churches, as far as the content of belief is left undefined as here.[121] The oaths of vv. 16f seem to be used as a confirmation of the Resurrection. Sura 100 also begins with oaths, reiterates the ingratitude of mankind (v. 6) and warns of the Resurrection and Judgment. The opening oaths of Qur'an 79 are followed by the apparent rejection of the Resurrection by the Meccans (vv. 10-14). The story ("hadith") of Moses has come to Muhammad (v. 15), but the name "valley of Tuwa" was probably confused with some other location and then committed to Arabic,[122] The idea of

Moses asking Pharaoh if he wanted to become purified (vv. 18f), although alien to the much older Biblical narrations, appears to have much in common with the preaching style of Muhammad,[123] who often substituted himself in the role of the Biblical prophets and then modified their histories.[124] The vv. 6f seem to follow another work of Ephraem the Syrian,[125] and one pre-'Uthmanic codex contained an extra verse between vv. 5-6.[126] Sura 77 also begins with oaths and contains parallels to the Biblical signs of the Judgment.[127] A peculiar feature of this sura is that it gives series of short verses on the Judgment, the Resurrection and an early description of Paradise, which are each followed by a sort of chorus: "Woe on that day to those who cry it lies." Clearly the Meccans must have already begun to reject Muhammad's message about the Resurrection when these suras were first composed, and some *Sira* traditions reveal the problems the Meccans had with this doctrine.[128] The usage of the term "sinner" in vv. 18, 46 is no doubt based on a Biblical source.

The **suras 78, 88, 89, 75** and **83** not only continue the theme of the Resurrection, but also generally relate something about Paradise. Qur'an 78 is one of the first suras (v. 21) to mention "jahannam," which word for hell Muhammad seems to have gotten from Ethiopic.[129] The description of a trumpet being sounded before the coming of a host (v. 18) is from the Bible (cf. Mt. 24: 31), and some of the details of the sensual Paradise (vv. 31f) appear to be based on a misuderstanding of a text of Ephraem the Syrian.[130] Some Western scholars place the vv. 37f in the second Meccan period "because of their style,"[131] and no doubt also because v. 37 contains the word "Rahman." Nevertheless, certain *Sira* traditions also show that the Meccans also had their reservations about this word fairly early on.[132] In sura 88 Muhammad has again received a story (v. 1), Hell (vv. 2f) and Paradise (vv. 8f) are contrasted, and the wisdom and power of God in Creation are alluded to (vv. 17f). Qur'an 89 begins with oaths, one of which (v. 1) may be a reference to the first 10 days of the pagan Hajj.[133] The 'Ad is mentioned (v. 5) along with Iram (v. 6).[134] A peculiar description of the Thamud is given v. 8), in which Wadi al-Qura may be meant,[135] and the brief narration about Pharaoh (vv. 9f) shows that Muhammad was relatively unacquainted with the Biblical history of Moses up to that point in time.[136] The vv. 13f contain a warning of Judgment and an instruction to help orphans and the poor. The vv. 27-30 run somewhat parallel to Mt. 25:21,23. Sura 75 begins with an oath by the Day of Resurrection and an oath by the self-accusing soul. The vv. 3-4 show again that Muhammad's message regarding the Resurrection was being rejected. The vv. 13-14 reiterate the idea of being accused by one's own self at the Judgment, and Jewish eschatology may have been the source for this.[137] The vv. 16-19 were probably interpolated,[138] and the vv. 20f may have also been added later due to v. 40 again mentioning the Resurrection. In the vv. 31f one doomed for Hell is described as having neither believed, nor prayed, and as having accused (the message) of lies and then turning away. The opening verses of Qur'an 83 betray Jewish influence,[139] as well as the use of the word "'Illiyun" (vv. 18f).[140] The usage "the pious" (or "just") (vv. 18, 22) indicates a Biblical source, and the words "Sijjin" (vv. 7f) and "Tasnim" (v. 27) appear to have been invented by Muhammad.[141] Opposition to Muhammad's doctrine on the Day of Judgment is again evident (vv. 10f) and v. 13 contains an early reference to the accusation of the Qur'an being the "tales of the ancients."[142]

One Western Qur'an scholar places the rest of **sura 74** (vv. 8f) after sura 83.[143] These verses were probably composed earlier than this, however, as it is clear that they give a description of Hell (as the suras 73, 101 and 82), but are deficient of any mention of Paradise (which the suras 88, 89, and 83 do give). The verses 83:11-16 and 74:16-26 are very similar, but it appears that 74:16-26 are older as they are more specific,[144] and 83:16 seems to be an improvement on 74:26-27. The verse 74:30 may have been influenced by Gnostic teachings,[145] and the vocabulary of the vv. 31-34 reveal that these verses were probably Medinan additions to the sura,[146] inasmuch as the "nineteen" (v. 30) were identified as angels (v. 31). The oaths beginning in v. 35 may have marked what was earlier a separate sura (vv. 35-55). The verses 74:44-47 are related to, but more detailed than 75:31-32.[147] The verse 74:49 represents an early example of the use of the term "intercessor," and 74:55 is perhaps one of the earliest passages in which the notion of "forgiveness" appears.

Qur'an 69:4-10 relates the stories of the Thamud, the 'Ad and Pharaoh briefly, after which an abrupt change in person (vv. 11f) ushers in what may refer to Noah.[148] The vv. 13-17 describe the end of the world (where Muhammad is said to have arrived at the number of "eight" angels, v. 17, because it fit the rhyme so well),[149] the vv. 18-24 relate the situation of those who receive their books in the right hand, and the vv. 25-37 explain the fate of those who receive their books in the left hand.[150] The belief in Allah and the feeding of the poor are listed as the duties which were neglected by those sent to Hell. In the vv. 38f an oath is given that Muhammad's message is from God, and that were his message against God('s), he would have been killed (vv. 44-46).

In **sura 51**, which begins with oaths, only the vv. 1-23 are thought to belong to the first Meccan period,[151] and they do not appear to contain much new material.

Qur'an 52 also begins with oaths, and only the vv. 1-20 and 22-28, which again describe Hell and Paradise are regarded as early.[152]

Sura 56 begins with oaths, and then explains the destiny of those who will go to Paradise (vv. 10-25), the future of those who will be the "companions of the right" (vv. 26-39) and those who will be the "companions of the left" (vv. 40-56).[153] The vv. 57-73 form an appeal for man to believe after realizing the magnificence of God's creation, and the vv. 74-96 give an oath as a guarantee for the truthfulness of Muhammad's message. The verse 56:52 seems to be similar to a Jewish tradition (Sukkah 32), and an early Qur'an codex is said to have contained a short extra verse after 56:50.[154]

Sura 70 also contains little that is new for the early Meccan period of the Qur'an. Verse 8 is similar to the Bible reference II Pet. 3:12, and the vv. 22f describe those who will go to Paradise as those who pray, give to the poor, believe there will a day of Judgment, etc.

Qur'an 55 contains perhaps the earliest usage of the term "Rahman," which Muhammad probably borrowed from Jews or Christians.[155] This sura is most famous for its refrain which begins in v. 12 and is repeated inconsistently for the remainder of the sura. The v. 33 is thought to have been a later modification, because of its comparatively unusual length.[156] The dual plural form was employed frequently in this sura ("two Easts", v. 16; "two Wests," v. 17; "two waters," v. 19; later - "two gardens, " v. 46; with "two springs," v. 50; "two kinds of fruits," v. 52; etc.) to conform with the rhyme scheme.[157]

The *Sira* traditions are generally in agreement that the Meccans did not really reject or oppose Muhammad until he denounced their deities[158] and said that their forefathers were in Hell.[159] According to these hadith, some of the Quraysh came to Abu Talib to persuade him to give up his support of Muhammad and some spoke of wanting to kill the latter, because he had reviled their gods, derided their customs and caused disunity in the tribe.[160] Abu Talib, however, continued to protect and support Muhammad. Occasionally, Muhammad was insulted or even threatened while at the Ka`ba,[161] and although Muhammad was accused of having been a kahin, poet or possessed,[162] others of his relatives also began following him.[163] The Quraysh later tried to dissuade Muhammad from continuing to preach his message,[164] while others charged him with being taught by others.[165] The first public recitation of the Qur'an by Ibn Mas`ud did not go well,[166] and his being from the lower classes, as many of Muhammad's early followers were,[167] may have also negatively affected the already meager chances of being heard.

The most obvious Qur'anic evidences for Muhammad's rejecting the Meccan deities are the **suras 112** and **109**, which although not easy to date, are generally considered to have been early Meccan.[168] Some Western Qur'an scholars regard the **suras 113** and **114** as having been magical formulae, which may have been intended to seal and protect the Qur'an.[169]

One of the main texts for the Islamic ritual prayers, **Qur'an 1**, also remains a chronological enigma for most Qur'an scholars, even though practically every phrase and idea of this sura appears to have its source in Judaism or Christianity.[170] At least one pre-`Uthmanic Qur'an codex contained none of the suras 1, 113 or 114, and one reason for this may have been that these were considered to have been liturgical, and thus not part of the Qur'an.[171]

Two additional "prayer" suras were found in another famous pre-`Uthmanic Qur'an codex.[172]

Conclusions

The Qur'anic evidence from what are generally held to be the earliest suras presents prayers and vigils as having been the primal rituals of Islam. Noteworthy doctrines of this period seem to have been belief, which was not always well defined, the performing of good deeds (including almsgiving) the reality of the coming Judgment, the punishments of Hell and the rewards of Paradise. Later, the first half of the Islamic creed (shahada) may have been added to these.[173] Of the narratives, none of which are very complete, those of the Thamud, the `Ad, Pharaoh and Noah are the most developed. Although Abraham, Moses and Jonah are mentioned or alluded to, not very much information is related about them.

From Arab paganism, Muhammad had already retained the "sanctity" of the Ka`ba (Qur'an 106:3) and some form of pagan sacrifice (Qur'an 108:2), as well as saj` verse.[174] The stories of the Thamud, the `Ad and Noah appear to have come from the works of Arab poets predating Muhammad.[175] The influence of Jewish or Christian sects seems to have been relatively limited in this period,[176] and the amount of foreign vocabulary borrowed from Ethiopic[177] or Hebrew[178] is also minimal.

By far the major source for the early suras of the Qur'an appears to have been the Eastern, or perhaps more specifically, Syrian Church. The early Qur'anic regulations of prayer follow Nestorian practice,[179] and the vigils described in sura 73 appear to be patterned on those of the Eastern monks.[180] In that Muhammad's general style of proclamation is reminiscent of Christian missions' liturgies,[181] it is also possible, if not probable, that the first part of the Islamic creed (shahada) was adapted from a Christian message to polytheists. The usage of the term "belief" or "believer" as well as the mention of good works are probably of Christian origin,[182] and the Qur'anic doctrine of almsgiving, as a means of "purifying" oneself was indeed a precept of Eastern Christianity.[183]

Early Qur'anic passages reveal their closest ties to the Syrian Church in their eschatological descriptions. These not only frequently follow certain works of Ephraem the Syrian (d. 373 AD),[184] but they even resemble more mundane communications of that Church, such as this excerpt from a letter of a monk, which was written in 535 AD:[185]

> "May he (the Archimandrite Yohannan)... on that Day,
> a dreadful and great Day (cf. Qur'an 83:5), when the
> callers shout (cf. Qur'an 54:6), the graves split open
> (cf. Qur'an 82:4), the dead arise (cf. Qur'an 75:1-4)
> and praise, when the throne is set up (cf. Qur'an 69:17),
> the Judge sits down, the books are opened (cf. Qur'an
> 69:19f, 25f), and each receives what he has done (cf.
> Qur'an 82:5; 74:41) from the just Judge (cf. Qur'an
> 95:8), in whose Judgment is no respect of persons (cf.
> Qur'an 74:49; 26:88)... [then later] "... on that Day,
> when the good are separated from the bad, the goats
> from the sheep, the tares from the wheat..." (cf. Qur'an
> 90:18-20) [186]

In addition to these similarities, early verses of the Qur'an also contain foreign words from Syriac.[187] Although it is obvious that Muhammad must have had some sort of contact with a Syrian Christian, it would be inaccurate to suppose that Muhammad had any first-hand knowledge of either the Bible, the works of Ephraem or institutional Christianity. In the earliest passages of the Qur'an Muhammad seems to have been oblivious to any differences between Judaism and Christianity; and even in the latest Qur'anic passages he shows no intimate knowledge of either the Christian sacraments or the Gospel. Muhammad may have heard some of the messages of trained Syrian missionaries early on,[188] but those with whom he is generally said to have had more than intermittent contact were Christian slaves.[189]

For the most part, the *Sira* traditions provide little or no information on many of the suras of this period, and although the canonical hadith may at times preserve earlier versions of some traditions,[190] it is obvious that a great portion of Muhammad's early biography was irretrievably lost with the deaths of the first generation of Muslims.[191] In addition to this, the texts of many *Sira* traditions have been edited, censored and even corrupted over the centuries.[192] Not infrequently, the extant biographical hadith contradict Qur'anic evidences, as has been shown above in the section on Muhammad's life before ministry. For this period, it appears that the Meccans' rejection of and opposition to Muhammad's message actually began before he started to revile their gods, and not afterwards as the *Sira* traditions maintain.[193] The pagan Arabs, for example, did not believe in the Resurrection, much less in a Judgment, Paradise or Hell,[194] and the suras which contain such descriptions seem to predate Qur'anic passages proclaiming Monotheism.

Notes:

[1] Guillaume, *Muhammad*, pp. 104 f; Ibn Sa'd, *Classes*, vol. 1, 1, pp. 219 f; Tabari, *History*, vol. 6, pp. 68, 70 f. Other traditions give Qur'an 74:1f, (Tabari, *History*, vol. 6, pp. 73 f; *Sahih Bukhari*, vol. 6, pp. 417 f) Qur'an 1 or Qur'an 68 (Sell, *Development*, p. 3) as having been revealed initially.

[2] It is said that this was a pagan practice among the Arabs in Muhammad's time; see the editors in Tabari, *History*, vol. 6, p. 67, n. 95, however, others view this as a pagan adaptation of a Syrian Christian practice; see n. 40, below.

[3] The account in Ibn Hisham indicates that Muhammad was asleep, so that Gabriel's coming to him must have been a dream.

[4] A tradition found in the Ibn Ishaq recension of Yunus b. Bukayr also reports that Muhammad suffered from the evil eye before and after the first parts of the Qur'an were revealed; see Guillaume, *New Light*, p. 29.

[5] Guillaume, *Muhammad*, p. 107; Ibn Sa'd, *Classes*, vol. 1, 1, pp. 225 f; Tabari, *History*, vol. 6, pp. 68, 72. *Sahih Bukhari* (vol. 1, p. 4) erroneously presents Waraqa as being a Christian who wrote out passages of the Gospel in Hebrew. *Sahih Muslim* (vol. 1, p. 98) gives Waraqa as writing out passages of the Gospel in Arabic. Neither of these canonical traditions mention that Waraqa may have known the Torah.

[6] "Namus" is said to have been Gabriel by practically all Islamic historians. Western scholars of Islam rather early on recognized that the narrators

of this tradition confused "Namus" with the Greek νομος = "Law," which was indeed given to Moses.

[7] Tabari, *History*, vol. 6, p. 69.

[8] See Appendix B, below.

[9] Ibn Hisham (*Muhammad*, p. 155) and Tabari (*History*, vol. 6, p. 70 do not specify the length of this period; Ibn Sa`d (*Classes*, vol. 1, 1, p. 227) gives "a few days." Later Islamic scholars contend that this "fatra," or period of cessation, lasted three years; see Nöldeke and Schwally, *GQ*,   vol. 1, p. 85; *EI²*, s.v. "Muhammad."

[10] In *Sahih Bukhari* (vol. 1, p. 5; vol. 6, pp. 420 f) three hadith of Jabir b. `Abdullah show that Muhammad was commanded to "desert the idols" in Qur'an 74:5, after which revelations came uninhibited (cf. *Sahih Muslim*, vol. 1, pp. 98 f). These accounts also appear to give a different (and perhaps older) version of Muhammad's seeing "the angel" who called to him from the sky; cf. Ibn Sa`d, *Classes*, vol. 1, 1, p. 227.

[11] Tabari, *History*, vol. 6, p. 70. *Sahih Bukhari*, vol. 6, pp. 447 f, gives "a lady" instead of Khadija, whom Khan indentifies as Abu Lahab's wife. The Ibn Ishaq recension of Ibn Bukayr shows Muhammad thought that his companion hated him and had forsaken him; Guillaume, *New Light*, p. 30.

[12] Nöldeke and Schwally, *GQ*, vol. 1, p. 78. There were also other original narrators of these traditions; cf. *GQ*, vol. 1, p. 79; Buhl, *Muhammad*, p. 134; Tabari, *History*, vol. 6, pp. 67 f.

[13] Qur'an 2:92. If Gabriel had really been the angel, one would expect this to have been mentioned in the early Qur'anic passages regarding the signs or visions which Muhammad reportedly saw: e.g. Qur'an 81:23f and 53:6f. Even the tradition about Waraqa appears to show that Muhammad did not know who or what he had seen, since Waraqa had to tell him it was "Namus." The attempt to connect Gabriel with the first Qur'anic revelations is definitely an early interpolation (it may have originated with Muhammad), which aims to make Muhammad a "Biblical" prophet.

[14] Muir viewed 18 suras as predating Muhammad's call (see *EI²*, s.v. "Kur'an," p. 417. Buhl (*Muhammad*, p. 136) felt that it is quite possible that the first revelations were lost. Watt (*Religionen*, pp. 187 f) thinks the traditions about Qur'an 96: 1f (or 74:1f) being the first Qur'anic revelation were developed later, based on exegetical interpretations of their texts (cf. Is. 40:6 also); i.e. the phrases "Recite!..." (96:1) and "Arise and warn!... (74:2) generally lend themselves to being considered as primary. Cf. Welch, in *EI²*, s.v. "Muhammad," p. 363.

[15] Open opposition to Muhammad's message could have only begun after he made it public; cf. Guillaume, *Muhammad*, pp. 121, 135 f; Tabari, *History*, vol. 6, p. 101.

[16] In Qur'an 73:15f Muhammad is likened to the apostle (or messenger) sent to Pharaoh, but in 69:40f Muhammad's being an apostle is used to confront the charges of him being a poet or soothsayer.

[17] The traditions regarding Muhammad's visit to Waraqa (who is said to have become a Christian) are suspect, because of the mention of Namus (see n. 4, above) and Moses, but not the Gospel and Jesus. The name Moses also appears in later Qur'anic suras (e.g. Qur'an 87:19; 53:37) and Muhammad's knowledge of him develops only gradually (cf. Qur'an 79:15f).

[18] Nöldeke and Schwally, *GQ*, vol. 1, p. 85; Watt, *Muhammad*, p. 20; Welch, *EI²*, s.v. "Muhammad," p. 363. In general, there is a three year discrepancy in the various traditional accounts of Muhammad's age and the Meccan period of his ministry, see: Tabari, *History*, vol. 6, pp. 60 f.

[19] See the sura orderings of Weil, Nöldeke and Blachère as given by Welch in *EI²*, s.v. "Kur'an," pp. 416 f. Bell, in that he viewed many suras as composite texts modified over time, did not arrange the suras in any particular order. He did, however, regard the texts of Qur'an 96:1f and 74:1f as being early. Watt (*Muhammad*, p. 23; *Introduction*, p. 198, n. 9; *Religionen*, p. 206) has put together a list (according to Nöldeke's sura orderings) of those portions of the Qur'an which Bell considered as having been early. See also n. 12, above.

[20] Nöldeke and Schwally, *GQ*, vol. 1, p. 96, show that mention of opposition to Muhammad (68:1-16) could not have been so early. See also the editorial remark in Tabari, *History*, vol. 6, p. 69, n. 102, where it is pointed out that the accusation of Muhammad being possessed (68:2) was not made at the beginning of his ministry.

[21] In Qur'an 68:15-16 one is quoted as having regarded the "signs" of the Qur'an as "fables of the ancients." What appears to have been meant are the narrations of the Qur'anic "messengers," and this would presuppose their having already been revealed. However, Weil and Nöldeke list Qur'an 68:1-16 before practically all of the suras containing such narratives. Blachère wisely places sura 68 in the second Meccan period (see Appendix B), but Bell (*Qur'an*, vol. 2, p. 597) maintains that Qur'an 68:10-16 is Medinan, and gives no reason for this in his notes, which were published by Bosworth and Richardson; cf. Watt (*Introduction*, p. 190, n. 1). Others are most probably correct in disagreeing with Bell, as the phrase "fables of the ancients" appears to have been a Meccan accusation and not a Medinan one; see the references in n. 15, above. The similarity between Qur'an 96:4 and 68:1 may have led Islamic authorities to believe sura 68 was the second Qur'anic revelation; see Nöldeke and Schwally, *GQ*, vol. 1, p. 96.

[22] For the source on Qur'an 74:1f, see n. 9, above. For sources on Qur'an 93:1f, see the references in n. 11, above.

[23] Most Islamic sura orderings give Qur'an 73, 74, and 111 after the suras 96 and 68; Qur'an 93 is usually placed a little later in the listings; see Appendix B. The positioning of the suras 73 and 74 together seems to have been influenced by the similarity of 73:1 to 74:1; cf. Nöldeke and Schwally, *GQ*, vol. 1, p. 98.

[24] As has been seen in some of the examples above (nn. 13, 21; the relationship between Qur'an 96:4 to 68:1 and the roles of 74:1f and 93:1f in the fatra traditions), Qur'anic exegesis even appears to have been the basis for some *Sira* traditions, rather than vice versa. This phenomenon also provides another reason for doubting the reliability and authenticity of some of the *Sira* accounts. Cf. Nöldeke and Schwally, *GQ*, vol. 1, p. 91, concerning sura 111: trans.- "One gets the impression that already very early on no

trustworthy traditions were available, (and) that what we have [before us] are rather the productions of the exegetes."

[25] Blachère considered these two suras as having been early; see Appendix B.

[26] See Watt and Bell, *Introduction*, pp. 77, 79; Andrae, *Mohammed*, p. 30. Cf. *Sahih Muslim*, vol. 3, p. 905.

[27] See Qur'an 68:2, 69:40f, 81:22, etc.

[28] Wellhausen, *Reste*, p. 135; Nöldeke and Schwally, *GQ*, vol. 1, pp. 87 f; Welch, *EI²*, s.v. "Muhammad," p. 363. Another more remote possibility may have been that Muhammad clothed himself as a monk when practising his devotions; see Bell, *Origins*, p. 88; Andrae, *Mohammed*, p. 43.

[29] The word اقرا (Qur'an 96:1) is based on the same Arabic root as "Qur'an." See Bell, *Origins*, pp. 90 f; Watt, *Muhammad*, pp. 20 f; Welch, *EI²*, s.v. "Kur'an," p. 400.

[30] Muslims generally equate رِجْز with رِجْز = "abomination" (e.g. Qur'an 2:56); (see Jeffery, *Vocabulary*, p. 139) and four canonical traditions say that "rujz" meant "idols;" see the reference given in n. 10, above. Most Western scholars follow Bell (*Origins*, pp. 88 f) in viewing this as a word which Muhammad borrowed from Syrian Christians (cf. Matt. 3:7); without perhaps knowing what it meant.

[31] "Purifying garments" (74:4 - cf. Rev. 7:14); "fleeing the wrath" (74:5 - cf. Mt. 3:7); "not giving in order to receive more" (74:6 cf. Lk. 6:30,35) and "being patient for the Lord" (74:7 - cf. Ja. 5:7) all reveal that Muhammad had been influenced by Christian sources. See Appendix F, p. 409.

[32] Andrae, *Ursprung*, pp. 201 f, references the fourth century (AH) Abu-Faraj al-'Ishbahani, Mas'udi and the theologian Abu Nu'aim. The traditions of the first two of these is traced through Muhammad b. Sa'ib al-Kalbi, whose son many Muslim authorities regard as untrustworthy; cf.

Haq and Ghazanfar, in Ibn Sa`d, *Classes*, p. xxi; Andrae, Mohammed, p. 92. Jeffery, in *Vocabulary*, p. 22, also makes mention of Quss. In Wellhausen, *Reste*, p. 250 (additional n. to p. 239), Nöldeke is cited as saying that the word "qass" is a technical expression for Christian clergy. See n. 188, below.

[33] See p. 29, n. 11 and p. 32, n. 22, above, for the Muslim sources; see *ECMD*, p. 732, for the Christian sources. Christians later distorted these traditions to present Muhammad as killing the monk, who had helped him, in a well; see Gerard Salinger, "A Christian Muhammad Legend, etc." *ZDMG*, 117 (1967), pp. 328 f.

[34] Guillaume, *Muhammad*, pp. 112 f; Tabari, *History*, vol. 6, p. 77. Cf. the canonical traditions in *Sahih Bukhari*, vol. 1, p. 297; *Sunan Abu Dawud*, vol. 1, pp. 102 f.

[35] Guillaume, *Muhammad*, pp. 112 f. Tabari (*History*, vol. 6, pp. 78 f) gives the hadith about the famous "night journey," in which five daily times for prayer are said to have been made obligatory, immediately following Muhammad's teaching Khadija the ritual prayers. Guillaume, *New Light*, pp. 30 f, and Tabari, *History*, vol. 6, p. 81, show the Ka`ba as being the first qibla.

[36] Qur'an 108:2; 107:5; and later 96:10; 74:44. Some canonical hadith indicate that the regulation of ritual prayers was not very strict at first, as one was permitted to talk to someone while he performed his prayers; see *Sahih Bukhari*, vol. 5, p. 137; *Sahih Muslim*, vol. 1, p. 272; *Sunan Abu Dawud*, vol. 1, p. 235. Muslims returning from Abyssinian asylum then noticed that conversation was no longer allowed during prayers.

[37] The earliest Qur'anic evidence is probably 10:87, where the Jewish anachronism of the institution of synagogues in the time of Moses is most likely being referred to; see p. 154, below. The first mention of a qibla as clearly being used by Muslims is in Qur'an 2:136f. Aside from the Ka`ba, it has been speculated that the first qibla of the Muslims may have been Jerusalem; based on Qur'an 2:136f or, following Eastern Christian practice, the East; cf. *SEI*, p. 240.

[38] Cf. Qur'an 5:8-9; which regulation was borrowed from the Jews (Talmud, Berakhot 15a, 46) and not pagan sources. Cf. *SEI*, p. 635.

[39] The meaning of the text of Qur'an 20:130 is disputed by Muslim theologians, some of whom try to find in it Qur'anic authority for the five daily prayer times. The texts of Qur'an 20:130f and 30:17-18 are generally regarded as having been later interpolations.

[40] Andrae, (*Mohammed*, pp. 42 f) thinks this practice was an adaptation from Syrian Christianity.

[41] See Andrae, *Mohammed*, p. 89.

[42] See Andrae, *Ursprung*, p. 37.

[43] Qur'an 73:1f; 17:81. These vigils also seem to have Syrian Christian practices as their models; see Andrae, *Mohammed*, pp. 88 f; *Ursprung*, pp. 191 f.

[44] Buhl, in *SEI*, p. 398

[45] See Berakhot, 31a, as related to Dan. 6:10 and Ps. 55:17.

[46] Ibn Hisham (Guillaume, *Muhammad*, p. 114) and some traditions in Tabari (*History*, vol. 6, pp. 80 f) show `Ali as the first male follower at 10 years old. Tabari (*History*, vol. 6) also presents hadith which report that Abu Bakr (pp. 84 f) or Zayd b. Haritha (p. 86) were the first male followers. The Ibn Ishaq recension of Yunus b. Bukayr (Guillaume, *New Light*, p. 32) gives `Ali as first, Zayd as second and Abu Bakr as third. Sunnis usually try to discount `Ali's being the first follower (he was a child) and maintain that Abu Bakr was the first adult male. Shiites tend to use such hadith to show `Ali's preeminence over Abu Bakr.

[47] Tabari, *History*, vol. 6, pp. 88 f. The two followers were said to have been Khadija and `Ali.

[48] Guillaume, *Muhammad*, p. 117; Ibn Sa`d, *Classes*, vol. 1, 1,

pp. 230 f (gives Qur'an 26:214 but not 15:94); Tabari, *History*, vol. 6, p. 88.

[49] Ibn Sa`d, *Classes*, vol. 1, 1, p. 230; Tabari, *History*, vol. 6, p. 89. For more information on Abu Lahab, see *SEI*, p. 11; *EI²*, s.v. "Abu Lahab."

[50] See Appendix B. Bell did not try to date Qur'an 111; see *EI²*, p. 418.

[51] Ibn Hisham in Guillaume, *Muhammad*, pp. 159 f.

[52] Watt, *Muhammad*, p. 80; Watt and Bell, *Introduction*, p. 11, maintain that Qur'an 111 was revealed after Abu Lahab refused to offer Muhammad protection; cf. Ibn Sa`d, *Classes*, vol. 1, 1, p. 244. Barth, in *SEI*, p. 11, holds that the use of the perfect tense in Qur'an 111:2 presupposes Abu Lahab's death, and thus that this sura must have been revealed after the battle of Badr.

[53] Some *Sira* traditions date Qur'an 108 much later; cf. Guillaume, *Muhammad*, p. 180.

[54] At least some Arab Christians contemporary with Muhammad also regarded the Ka`ba as holy; see p. 8, n. 24.

[55] The Qur'an indicates that the belief in the Judgment and Resurrection were alien to Arab paganism; cf. 82:9; 75:3; etc. The works of the pre-Islamic poets also reveal practically no acquaintance with the doctrines of Judgment and Resurrection; cf. Andrae, *Ursprung*, pp. 43 f.

[56] Cf. Qur'an 102:1f and Carmina Nisibena 74:97-98 (Ephraem the Syrian) - "The foolish worldly man divides and covets to receive more, and death extinguishes him and gives him three cubits (of) room in the grave.'" Trans. from Andrae, *Ursprung*, p. 130.

[57] Cf. Andrae, *Mohammed*, p. 54; Ahrens, "Christliches," *ZDMG*, 84 (1930), p. 58.

[58] Similar but more general schemes are given in Watt and Bell, *Introduction*, p. 116; Watt, *Muhammad*, pp. 23 f; Guillaume, *Islam*, p. 29.

[59] This characteristic is discussed in Nöldeke and Schwally, *GQ*, vol. 1, pp. 75 f; Watt and Bell, *Introduction*, pp. 79, 110, 154. In the Bible God does not swear by created things, but only by Himself. Swearing is generally forbidden Christians (Mt. 5:33-37).

[60] See the apparently unique testimony to the alleged effectiveness of incantations given in the saj` style, as found in the Ibn Ishaq recension of Yunus b. Bukayr; Guillaume, *New Light*, p. 15.

[61] See Andrae, *Mohammed*, p. 30. For examples of the oaths of pagan soothsayers in the style of saj`, see the replies of Satih and Shiqq to the king of Yemen in Ibn Hisham (Guillaume, *Muhammad*, pp. 5 f). The relative strength of oaths and their alleged power in persuading one to believe are alluded to in Qur'an 89:4 and 56:75.

[62] Muslims in Iraq and Damascus apparently disputed this verse. Ibn Mas`ud is said to have read: "by the male and the female" rather than: "by that which created the male and female" (*Sahih Muslim*, vol. 2, pp. 393 f. Although the Qur'an codices of `Ali and Ibn `Abbas seem to have agreed with Ibn Mas`ud's (Jeffery, *Materials*, pp. 109, 192, 208), it is the reading of the Syrians which prevails even today.

[63] Cf. 90:10 with Mt. 7:13f; 90:12f with Is. 58:6f; 90:18 with Mt. 25:34 (see also the *Testament of Ephraem* in *Nicene and Post-Nicene Fathers*, vol. 13, p. 134); cf. 90:20 with Mt. 25:41. See Appendix F, p. 409.

[64] The phrases "those who believe" (90:17) or "believer" are often used by Christians and sects which broke off from Christianity, rather than Jewish or pagan groups. Cf. Ahrens, "Christliches," *ZDMG*, 84 (1930), pp. 37 f; Horovitz, *Untersuchungen*, pp. 55 f.

[65] See p. 25, above.

[66] Cf. Qur'an 64:4; 67:13; 28:69; etc.

[67] See pp. 25 f, above.

[68] See Rudolph in *Koran*, p. 565, n. 1.

[69] Canonical traditions report that Muhammad himself forgot when the night of Qadr was, but said it should be sought in the last 7 or 10 days of the month of Ramadan; see *Sahih Bukhari*, vol. 3, p. 140; *Sahih Muslim*, vol. 2, pp. 570 f. The mention of this night being better than 1000 (months) in 97:3 is not only remotely similar to Ps. 84:10, but is seen as a special night to receive forgiveness by some Muslims; see *Sahih Bukhari*, vol. 3, p. 129.

[70] See Rudolph in *Koran*, p. 553, n. 9.

[71] Imru'ul-Qays (Andrae, *Ursprung*, p. 47) as well as al-Afwa al-Audi (c. 570 AD) and the Lakhmid ʿAdi b. Zayd (c. 587 AD) all mention the Thamud (Margoliouth, *Relations*, p. 73).

[72] See Rudolph in *Koran*, p. 544, n. 1; the fragments are given as vv. 1-10; 11-15; 16-42.

[73] Nöldeke and Schwally, *GQ*, vol. 1, pp. 95 f. Western scholars of Islam generally see in this criticism of Muhammad evidence for his having been sincere and honest in his early ministry; see Buhl, *Muhammad*, p. 141; Andrae, *Mohammed*, p. 117;

[74] The "deafening noise" of v. 33 is generally thought to refer to a clap of thunder or a trumpet blast announcing the Judgment; cf. Andrae, *Ursprung*, p. 64. Ephraem the Syrian also described the Judgment as being preceded by a clap of thunder; Ibid. p. 141. That even nearest relatives will stand alone in the Judgment is also found in the works of Ephraem (*Op. Gr.*, I, 29; cf. II, 201 - as cited by Andrae in *Ursprung*, pp. 143 f). The joyful faces of the just and the darkened faces of the unjust at the Judgment are also referred to in Jewish and Christian apocalyptic literature; see Andrae, *Ursprung*, p. 69.

[75] This sura was perhaps one of the first to have the mysterious letters, and also begins with an oath. Nöldeke and Schwally, *GQ*, vol. 1, p. 96, felt

that vv. 17-33 and vv. 48-60 were probably added in the second Meccan period, whereas Bell, following others, held vv. 17f for Medinan.

[76] Cf. Qur'an 81:22; 53:1; 51:39,42; 52:29; 54:9; 37:35; 26:26; 15:6; etc.

[77] See n. 21, above.

[78] See Andrae, *Ursprung*, p. 133, and Appendix D, p 363.

[79] The use of درس (v. 37) from Aramaic and قيامة (v. 39) from the Christian-Palestinian dialect of Syriac (Jeffery, *Vocabulary*, pp. 128, 244) imply closer contact with those who "studied" books or had contact with Palestine; both of which circumstances seem to agree better with Muhammad's ministry in Medina.

[80] The description of the alleged contents of these scrolls (87:16f) seems to indicate apocryphal works such as the Apocalypse of Abraham and the Apocalypse of Moses; see the references in Appendix D, p. 363. Another mystery regrarding this verse (87:19) is that the Qur'anic names for Abraham and Moses do not appear to have predated Muhammad, and there are very many theories as to how Muhammad may have arrived at such adaptations; (see Jeffery, *Vocabulary*, pp. 44f, 274f.)

[81] See Nöldeke and Schwally, *GQ*, vol. 1, p. 97.

[82] Fig and olive trees are common Biblical metaphors. An oath by Mount Sinai also appears in the Testament of Ephraem the Syrian (*Nicene and Post-Nicene Fathers*, vol. 13, p. 134). The word used in 95:2 for "Sinai" seems to come from the Christian-Palestinian dialect of Syriac (Jeffery, *Vocabulary*, p. 184), but here (95:2) Muhammad has changed the word to "Sinin" (cf. Qur'an 23:20 were the word is given correctly) in order to fit the rhyme scheme of the sura; see Nöldeke and Schwally, *GQ*, vol. 1, p. 40, n. 2.

[83] Carm. Nisib. 74:1-4; see Rudolph, *Koran*, p. 563, n. 5.

[84] Rudolph, *Koran*, p. 569, n. 6, agrees with Blachère.

[85] See Appendix D, pp. 363 f, for the references.

[86] Nöldeke and Schwally, *GQ*, vol. 1, pp. 97f, argue that the verse length, style and rhyme does not match those in the rest of the sura.

[87] The Qur'anic name for Pharaoh is not Arabic and probably comes from Syriac; it does not seem to predate Muhammad (Jeffery, *Vocabulary*, p. 225. For "Thamud," see n. 71, above.

[88] See the reference in n. 86, above.

[89] The object(s) of belief are not given, or explained as in later passages, and it appears that Muhammad simply used the term he had heard from Christian sources; see n. 64, above.

[90] Ahrens, "Christliches," *ZDMG*, 84 (1930), pp. 63 f; cf. Andrae, *Ursprung*, pp. 180 f.

[91] Although most English translations of the Qur'an give "chant" or "recite," Bell, following Lane's definition (cf. 73:4) as "arrange a sentence well so that it is clear," thought that v. 4 was actually referring to the "composition of the Qur'an" and so contended that this verse must be from his "Qur'an period." (*Commentary*, vol. 2, p. 444; *Origin*, vol. 2, p. 613.

[92] Andrae, *Ursprung*, pp. 191 f; *Mohammed*, pp. 88 f. In the latter of these works Andrae shows that Pachomius and Macarius commanded their monks to keep a vigil for half of the night, cf. Qur'an 73:3.

[93] Cf. Rev. 6:12a; 16:18.

[94] Cf. Rev. 6:14a.

[95] Muhammad often saw himself in the roles of the Biblical prophets, and at times appears to have changed their biographies to fit his own circumstances; cf. Horovitz, *Untersuchungen*, pp. 9, 18 f.

[96] Andrae, *Ursprung*, p. 70 : the Jewish apoclayptic works Sibyll. II, 155 and Jub. 23, 25 state that children will be born gray-headed in the end times.

[97] Nöldeke and Schwally, *GQ*, vol. 1, p. 98.

[98] Guillaume, *Muhammad*, p. 117; Ibn Sa`d, *Classes*, vol. 1, 1, p. 230; Tabari, *History*, vol. 6, p. 88.

[99] Guillaume, *Muhammad*, p. 159 f; Ibn Sa`d, *Classes*, vol. 1, 1, p. 231; Tabari, *History*, vol. 6, p. 89.

[100] Ibn Sa`d, *Classes*, vol. 1, 1, p. 230.

[101] Ibn Sa`d, *Classes*, vol. 1, 1, p. 233.

[102] Guillaume, *Muhammad*, p. 118.

[103] Muhammad circumambulated the Ka`ba; Guillaume, *Muhammad*, p. 105; Tabari, *History*, vol. 6, p. 70.

[104] Guillaume, *Muhammad*, p. 131; Tabari, *History*, vol. 6, p. 101.

[105] IV Ezra; see *Apokalypse*, p. 144; see also Andrae, *Ursprung*, p. 69.

[106] Although the meaning of the word هاوية is disputed by some, Jeffery seems to be correct in seeing it as another name for Hell based on an Ethiopic word for "fire"; see *Vocabulary*, pp. 285 f. Jeffery translates the verses 101:6-8 as follows: "And as for him whose balances are light, "hawiya" is his mother. And who shall teach you what that is? It is a raging fire."

[107] Baumstark thought this was due to Muhammad having misunderstood a Christian picture which he had seen; *ZDMG*, 82 (Neue Folge 7), LXVIII as referred to in Ahrens, "Christliches," *ZDMG*, 84 (1930), p. 51, n. 1.

[108] Andrae, *Ursprung*, p. 66.

[109] Ahrens, "Christliches," *ZDMG*, 84, (1930), p. 23; Jeffery, *Vocabulary*, pp. 187 f.

[110] Muhammad apparently thought the Ethiopic "regum" ("cursed") was the same as the Arabic رجـيـم ("stoned"); see Ahrens, "Christliches," *ZDMG*, 84, (1930), p. 39; Jeffery, *Vocabulary*, pp. 139 f.

[111] See Appendix B p. 351.

[112] Nöldeke and Schwally (*GQ*, vol. 1, p. 103), in noticing the chronological contradicition of placing sura 53 so early, while tradition gives a later date, mention the possibility that vv. 19f was a later addition, even though there is no stylistic evidence to support this. They do maintain that the vv. 23, 26-33 are certainly later, however, the verses dealing with angelic intercession fit the traditions about vv. 19f very well. See p. 91, in the text below.

[113] See p. 9, n. 33. It should also be added that these passages do not explicitly say that Muhammad saw an angel.

[114] Cf. Nöldeke and Schwally, *GQ*, vol. 1, p. 100.

[115] 53:39 - cf. Gal. 6:5; 53:45 - cf. I. Sa. 2:6 and the Jewish Tefillah; 53:46 - cf. Gen. 1:27. See Appendix F, p. 410.

[116] The Arabic name for Noah seems to come from Syriac and predates Muhammad; Jeffery, *Vocabulary*, p. 282. Along with the Thamud, the names of the `Ad and Noah were known to pre-Islamic poets; Margoliouth, *Relations*, p. 73; see also n. 71, above.

[117] The codex of Ibn Mas`ud contained an additional verse near 53:60; the codex of Ubayy b. Ka`b had one near 53:58; Jeffery, *Materials*, pp. 95, 167.

[118] See Blachère's listing in Appendix B. His ordering differs somewhat from Nöldeke's and he places the suras 51 and 68 in the second Meccan period, whereas Nöldeke has them in the first. Nevertheless Nöldeke and

Schwally offer no suggestion as to where the remaining verses of sura 96 should be placed.

[119] 96:18 - cf. Op. Syr. III, 237, 244, 624 (Ephraem); the word زبانية also comes from Ephraem (Op. Syr. III, 237, 244); see Jeffery, *Vocabulary*, p. 148. See Appendix F, p. 410.

[120] Ahrens ("Christliches," *ZDMG*, 84 (1930), p. 55) thinks this came from Christianity and cites Baumstark as maintaining Muhammad had seen something about this in a Christian picture. Cf. Andrae, *Ursprung*, p. 68.

[121] Andrae, *Ursprung*, pp. 181 f; Ahrens, "Christliches," *ZDMG*, 84 (1930), pp. 63 f.

[122] See Appendix D, p. 364.

[123] Cf. 80:3,7; 87:14; and especially 2:123,146; 3:158; etc. See also n. 183, below.

[124] See n. 95, above.

[125] See Appendix F, p. 410.

[126] The codex of Ibn Mas'ud; see Jeffery, *Materials*, p. 107.

[127] Cf. 77:8-10 with Rev. 6:12-14; 77:46 - cf. Lk. 12:19f. See Appendix F, p. 410.

[128] Guillaume, *Muhammad*, pp. 143, 165.

[129] The original source for this word was, of course, the Hebrew; see Jeffery, *Vocabulary*, pp. 105 f.

[130] (*Op. Syr.* III, 563 f; Ephraem): "Whoever has held himself from wine until his departure will be awaited by the grapevines of Paradise with longing. Each of them extends its hanging grapes out to him. And if someone had lived in virginity, they (fem.) receive him into their pure bosoms,

because he as a monk did not fall into the bed and bosom of earthly love." (trans. from Andrae, *Ursprung*, p. 148); cf. Andrae, *Mohammed*, p. 88.

[131] Nöldeke and Schwally, *GQ*, vol. 1, p. 104.

[132] According to Guillaume, *Muhammad*, p. 134, the word "Rahman" was a title for Musaylima, and Muhammad was accused of having been his student. It is clear from the Qur'an, however, that Muhammad used "Rahman" for God, and that the Meccans did not accept "Rahman" (cf. Qur'an 25:61; Buhl, *Muhammad*, p. 166.

[133] See Rudolph, *Koran*, p. 556, n. 2.

[134] Iram was probably a city in South Arabia; Jeffery, *Vocabulary*, p. 53.

[135] Rudolph, *Koran*, p. 557, n. 6.

[136] The various explanations of the Muslim and Western commentators for "he of the pegs (stakes)" are not very satisfactory. It is also clear from the verses following v. 9, that Muhammad did not know the story about Pharaoh very well at the time of this sura. Cf. Qur'an 38:11; Horovitz, *Untersuchungen*, p. 130; *SEI*, p. 107.

[137] See Andrae, *Ursprung*, p. 69, where he cites Volz, *Judische Eschatologie*, p. 266 and Taanit 2a.

[138] Nöldeke and Schwally, *GQ*, vol. 1, p. 105.

[139] Cf. Amos 8:4f; Deut. 25:13f; Prov. 11:1. Many Muslim scholars consider this sura to have been one of the last Meccan suras; see Appendix B, p. 353; cf. Nöldeke and Schwally, *GQ*, vol. 1, p. 105.

[140] The word probably came from the Hebrew "Elyon" = "The most High," which was another term for God, and not the name of a book; Nöldeke, "Qur'an," p. 14; Jeffery, *Vocabulary*, pp. 215 f. Margoliouth,

"Additions," *JRAS*, (1939), pp. 57 f, thinks that the Arabic may have been misspelled and may have come from Syriac, based on Is. 8:1f.

[141] Nöldeke, "Qur'an," p. 15; Jeffery, *Vocabulary*, p. 165 (Sijjin), p. 91 (Tasnim). Margoliouth, "Additions," *JRAS*, (1939), p. 58, suggests that the word "sijjil" was actually meant here, but that "sijjin" was used to conform with the rhyme. Margoliouth thinks that the Rabbinic "gillayon" (for "unwritten writing material") may have been the source.

[142] See n. 21, above.

[143] See Blachère's listing in Appendix B. Nöldeke and Schwally give no ordering for these verses.

[144] A *Sira* tradition of Ibn Hisham (Guillaume, *Muhammad*, p. 122) shows Al-Walid b. al-Mughira as the one who was meant in these verses.

[145] Rudolph, *Koran*, p. 533, n. 8, supposes the number 19 to represent the 12 signs of the zodiac and the seven planets, which the Gnostics regarded as demons who torment the rising souls of the dead.

[146] Nöldeke and Schwally, *GQ*, vol. 1, p. 88.

[147] Cf. Abu Jahl's accusation against Muhammad in Ibn Hisham (Guillaume, *Muhammad*, p. 141): "Muhammad pretends that God's troops who will punish you in Hell and imprison you there, are nineteen only, while you have a large population..." See n. 51, above. Muslims have attempted to make all sorts of claims regarding Qur'an 74:30 (cf. Ali, *Qur'an*, vol. 2, p. 1643, n. 5793; Deedat, *Al-Qur'an: The Ultimate Miracle*, pp. 27 f; etc.), most of which have been proven to be false (cf. Campbell, *The Qur'an and the Bible*, pp. 250 f).

[148] See Ali, in *Qur'an*, vol. 2, p. 1597.

[149] Nöldeke and Schwally, *GQ*, vol. 1, p. 40; Nöldeke, "Qur'an," p. 12.

[150] See n. 120, above. Nöldeke was of the opinion that Muhammad invented the word "ghisilin" in 69:36; "Qur'an," p. 15.

[151] Nöldeke and Schwally, *GQ*, vol. 1, p. 105.

[152] Ibid.

[153] Cf. Qur'an 90:18-20. Among some Western scholars of the Qur'an attempts have been made to show that at least some suras were written in stanzas. Nöldeke and Schwally (*GQ*, vol. 1, pp. 43 f) mention the work of D.H. Müller in this area, and hold that his theories regarding the "stanza-construction" of the Qur'an best apply to the suras 56 and 26. In more recent times, G. Lüling has also tried to show that suras were originally constructed in stanzas, based on Christian hymns; see his dissertation: *Kritisch-exegetische Untersuchung des Qur'antextes*, or its revision: *Über den Ur-Qur'an*. These works have generally found little acceptance among other Western Qur'an scholars.

[154] The codex of Talha b. Musarrif; see Jeffery, *Materials*, p. 264.

[155] The word was not originally Arabic; see Jeffery, *Vocabulary*, pp. 140 f. Ibn Mas'ud is said to have begun a public recitation of this sura before he was stopped by the Meccans; see p. 51, above.

[156] Nöldeke and Schwally, *GQ*, vol. 1, p. 107.

[157] Cf. Nöldeke and Schwally, *GQ*, vol. 1, p. 40.

[158] Guillaume, *Muhammad*, p. 118; Tabari, *History*, vol. 6, p. 93. Both of these traditions, apparently from Ibn Ishaq, are qualified by the phrase "as far as I know." See also n. 159, below.

[159] Ibn Sa'd, *Classes*, vol. 1, 1, pp. 230 f, contains this addition. Cf. Qur'an 37:64-72, for example. Qur'anic evidence seems to indicate that the rejection of and opposition to Muhammad's message began prior to Muhammad's reviling the Meccan gods; see pp. 53 f, above.

[160] Guillaume, *Muhammad*, pp. 118 f; Ibn Sa`d, Classes, vol. 1, 1, pp. 233 f; Tabari, *History*, vol. 6, pp. 93 f.

[161] Abu Jahl once persuaded someone to place camel intestines (or a foetus) on Muhammad's back as he prayed at the Ka`ba, which Fatima removed; *Sahih Bukhari*, vol. 1, p. 151; vol. 2, p. 295; vol. 5, p. 122; *Sahih Muslim*, vol. 3, p. 986. In another tradition, Abu Bakr protects Muhammad from a death threat in the Ka`ba; Guillaume, *Muhammad*, p. 131; Tabari, *History*, vol. 6, p. 102; *Sahih Bukhari*, vol. 5, pp. 123 f; etc.

[162] Guillaume, *Muhammad*, pp. 121, 135 f; Tabari, *History*, vol. 6, p. 101. See also n. 27, above.

[163] E.g. Hamza, see Guillaume, *Muhammad*, pp. 131 f; Tabari, *History*, vol. 6, pp. 103 f.

[164] Guillaume, *Muhammad*, pp. 133 f; Tabari, *History*, vol. 6, p. 106 f.

[165] He was accused of being taught by Musaylima; Guillaume, *Muhammad*, p. 134; see also p. 11, n. 40; but this tradition may just have been an exegetical innovation on the word الرحمن= "Rahman." For Muhammad's later reply to this alleged charge (Qur'an 13:29), see Guillaume, *Muhammad*, p. 140.

[166] Guillaume, *Muhammad*, pp. 141 f; Tabari, *History*, vol. 6, pp. 104 f. It is reported that Ibn Mas`ud began reciting Qur'an 55:1.

[167] Guillaume, *Muhammad*, pp. 143 f; Abu Bakr also purchased the freedom of several slaves, including Bilal; see Guillaume, *Muhammad*, p. 144.

[168] Nöldeke and Schwally, *GQ*, vol. 1, pp. 107 f. Blachère also considered both suras to be early Meccan; Bell, however, thought sura 112 to be Medinan and refused to date Qur'an 109; see *EI²*, s.v. "Kur'an," pp. 416 f. One interesting feature of sura 112 in the pre-`Uthmanic codices is that those of Ibn Mas`ud and Ubayy b. Ka`b do not seem to have had the opening

word "say;" see Jeffery, *Materials*, pp. 113, 180. It is also probable that sura 112 was composed after the Sonship of Christ had been rejected; see p. 96, below.

[169] Nöldeke and Schwally, *GQ*, vol. 1, pp. 109 f; Nöldeke, "Qur'an," p. 8. These suras may also have been composed later; cf. Qur'an 44: 19a.

[170] Nöldeke and Schwally, *GQ*, vol. 1, pp. 112 f, n. 1, I-IV. Nöldeke, "Qur'an," pp. 18 f. Cf. Qur'an 1:5 with Ps. 27:11. It is also possible that this sura was composed later; cf. Qur'an 1:1 with Qur'an 26:46 (& passim); 37:182; and 1:6 with 20:135.

[171] Jeffery, *Materials*, p. 21.

[172] Dodge, in Ibn an-Nadim, *Fihrist*, vol. 1, p. 61, nn. 44, 45, erroneously interpreted the sura names al-Khal` and al-Hafd; see Jeffery, *Materials*, pp. 180-1; Suyuti, *El-Itkan*, vol. 2, pp. 153 f; Nöldeke and Schwally, *GQ*, vol. 2, pp. 34 f; Watt and Bell, *Introduction*, p. 46; *SEI*, p. 208; *EI²*, s.v. "Kur'an," p. 407. Cf. *ECMD*, Al-Kindi, p. 458.

[173] The dating for development of the first part of the creed is heavily dependent on the chronology of Qur'an 112 and similar passages.

[174] See nn. 26 and 60, above. This style could have also come from Syrian missionaries; cf. p. 53, above.

[175] See nn. 71 and 116, above.

[176] See nn. 74, 105 and 145, above.

[177] See nn. 106, 110 and 129, above.

[178] See nn. 130 and 140, above.

[179] See Andrae, *Mohammed*, p. 89, and n. 42, above.

[180] See nn. 43 and 92, above.

[181] Andrae, *Ursprung*, p. 173.

[182] See nn. 64 and 90, above.

[183] Cf. Qur'an 92:18; 80:1-7; Andrae, *Ursprung*, pp. 181 f; *Mohammed*, p. 89. For similar Jewish doctrines, see Cook, *Muhammad*, pp. 78 f, 92.

[184] See nn. 56, 63, 74, 82, 83, 119, 125 and 130, above.

[185] This similarity was first noticed by Ahrens in "Christliches," *ZDMG*, 84 (1930), p. 55, who found the text of this letter in "Verhandlungen der Kirchenversammlung zu Ephesus, 22 Aug. 449 (AD)," trans. by Dr. Georg Hoffmann (Kiel, 1873), p. 80. The text as presented here was translated from the German.

[186] Many of the Qur'an references provided by Ahrens in "Christliches," *ZDMG*, 84 (1930), p. 55, have been changed to correspond with early Qur'an passages which present basically the same material. Ahrens often used later sura references for comparison.

[187] See nn. 30, 79, 82 and 87.

[188] See nn. 32 and 33, above. By far the most Qur'an passages which seem to be based on the works of Ephraem the Syrian fall in the first Meccan period (Cf. Appendix F, pp. 409 f), and this may indicate that at least one of Muhammad's sources was an educated Christian, such as Quss may have been.

[189] See Guillaume, *Muhammad*, pp. 180, 193; Wellhausen, *Medina*, pp. 42, 55; *Sunan Abu Dawud*, vol. 2, p. 829; and Ahrens in "Christliches," *ZDMG*, 84 (1930), p. 187.

[190] E.g. see n. 10, above.

[191] See nn. 14, 24 and 165, above. It should perhaps also be noted that many of the first Muslims were involved in military exploits and/or often pre-occupied with the subjugation of conquered lands; see Nöldeke and

Schwally, *GQ*, vol. 2, pp. 7 f, where the knowledge of the Qur'an among Muslim soldiers is discussed, and the following statement of `Amr b. Ma`di-karib is given: "I converted to Islam in Yemen, but I was always in battle later and therefore did not have time to memorize the Qur'an." (trans.)

[192] See pp. 35 f, nn. 57 and 58; pp. 39 f; the nn. 13, 15, 17 and 18, above for examples. Muhammad probably did not consider himself to be a "prophet" until the second Meccan period, since this term does not appear in any of the earliest suras. Muhammad is generally described as having been a "messenger" or "apostle" (رسول) in the oldest suras of the Qur'an. Bell, rather unjustifiably, seems to have considered all verses containing the word for "prophet" (نبي) as having been Medinan, simply because he thought Muhammad must have gotten the term from the Jews, and the Jews were in Medina (Watt and Bell, *Introduction*, p. 28). Similarly, Bell assumed that if the word "mathani" (Qur'an 15:87) came from "mishnah" as Geiger maintained, the word must have come from the Jews, and thus the passage must have been Medinan; Bell, *Commentary*, vol. 1, pp. 428 f.

[193] E.g. Qur'an 73:8f. See also nn. 158 and 159, above together with the references in n. 194, below.

[194] Cf. Qur'an 79:10-14; 75:3-4.

Muhammad
Meccan Opposition

The extant major collections of *Sira* traditions are almost unanimous in presenting the first emigration to Abyssinia and the boycott of the Hashimites as being directly a result of the Meccan opposition to Muhammad's message. However, as with many other developments in Muhammad's Meccan ministry before the Hijra, the chronology of these events is still a matter of discussion among Islamic and Western scholars.

As opposed to the witness of the *Sira* traditions, Qur'anic evidence not only seems to shed more light on the circumstances regarding the Meccans' increased opposition, but it also implies that at least some of the events of this period probably did not take place in the manner which many traditions relate.

Although Qur'an 54 is generally thought to be the first sura of what is known as the second Meccan period, it seems that the passage 51:24f preceded it.[1]

Qur'an 51:24f gives the narrations about certain prophets, who were either warned of punishments, or were warners themselves (vv. 24-49), and Muhammad is later compared with them (vv. 50-55). The narrative of Abraham's guests is said to have come to Muhammad (v. 24), and the notion that the angels did not eat the food offered them by Abraham (vv. 26-28), not only contradicts the Biblical account,[2] but seems to have Jewish legends as its ultimate source.[3] The description of the punishment of the "sinful people" (v. 32, i.e. of Sodom and Gomorrah) in which only one house of "Muslims" (Lot's house) was spared (v. 36), parallels the implied judgment of the Meccans and the deliverance of Muhammad's followers. The usage of the term "Muslim" here is, of course, an anachronism, and the narration of Lot's having left the city could have served as an example for the early Muslims from the lower classes to emigrate to Abyssinia. The brief story of Moses and Pharaoh (vv. 38f) contains an obvious allusion to Muhammad's own circumstances in that Pharaoh says Moses is a "magician" or "possessed."[4] The narrations of the ʿAd, Thamud and Noah then follow (vv. 41f), and for the Biblical figures at least, a chronological sequence was not followed. In v. 51 an early statement for Monotheism can be found, and v. 52 replies to the accusation that Muhammad was either a magician or insane. Although 51:57 is similar to later verses in which Muhammad denies asking for a wage (cf. 52:40; 68:46; 38:86), it is probably actually related to Ps. 50:12.

The beginning verse of **sura 54** mentions the splitting of the moon, and later Muslim exegetes interpreted this to mean that the moon was miraculously split in the days of Muhammad (cf. v. 2).[5] However, the first phrase of this sura ("The hour has drawn nigh...") indicates that the reference to the moon was as a sign of the coming Judgment (cf. Qur'an 81:1f; 82:1; 84:1), and not as a miracle of Muhammad.[6] The Qur'an rather openly admits that Muhammad could perform no miracles (cf. 25:8; 17:61, 92-98; 29:49; 10:21; 6:35-37; 13: 27-32; etc.), thus traditions attributing miracles to Muhammad were later innovations of Muslim exegetes.[7] In 54:9-17, a distorted version of Noah's story is related, in which Noah is rejected by his people after being accused of lying and being possessed. He then cries to his Lord for help and the flood is sent.[8] It is obvious that Muhammad exchanged himself for Noah in this narration in order to make parallels to his own ministry. It was Muhammad who was accused of being possessed, and it was he who expected God's judgment against the Meccans. The `Ad also made the accusation of lying and were punished (vv. 18f). The Thamud considered the warning to be a lie (v. 23), and the phrase about not wanting to follow one of their own people who was alone and said to have received the warning (vv. 24-25), must likewise have been an accusation leveled against Muhammad by the Meccans. The people of Lot[9] are also said to have accused the warning of being a lie (v. 33). Each of these punishment stories is concluded with a rhetorical question comparing the Qur'an (as an admonition) with the mentioned warnings (vv. 17, 22, 32 and 40). The house of Pharaoh is said to have been warned,[10] but that they thought all the signs to have been lies (vv. 41-42). In 54:43f[11] Muhammad concludes the Meccans of his day are no better than the punished peoples of the past, and in so doing threatens the Meccans with a temporal judgment, which has been fused together with the Last Judgment (vv. 46f). Thus, the general warning of the coming of a universal Judgment, as seen so often in the earlier suras, has been modified to be a warning for the Meccans of a specific judgment which they would experience for rejecting Muhammad and his message.

The remainder of **sura 52 (vv. 21, 29-49)** may have been composed in about this time period. Not only was Muhammad accused of having been a sooth-sayer or being possessed, but the charge of being a poet has been added (vv. 29-30). The v. 31 contains one of the earliest usages of the phrase "قل" = "say," and this shows that Muhammad felt he had begun receiving direct answers to immediate problems or questions by way of revelation. The v. 39 is similar to 53:21 and v. 43 is a statement against polytheism. One early Qur'an codex is said to have contained an extra verse near 52:43.[12] The vv. 48f show the original two daily prayer times and may also refer to vigils.[13]

One Western Qur'an scholar places **sura 68** just after Qur'an 54,[14] and al-though the whole sura may not have been composed so late (i.e. vv. 1, 17-33), many of the verses in this sura (**vv. 2-16, 34f**) have much more in common with the suras of this period than with earlier sections of the Qur'an.[15] Qur'an 68:45 is similar to 52: 42, 46; the vv. 68:46-47 are the same as 52:40-41.

The first verses of **Qur'an 37** present a spiritual interpretation of the celestial[16] and combine elements in defense of the Resurrection (vv. 12f; 51) with narratives warning of the Judgment and proclaiming Monotheism (vv. 70f). That these themes (i.e. the Resurrection, the Judgment and Monotheism) presented major problems for the Meccans is also made manifest in several sections of this sura. Of special note is the alleged reply to a statement of Monotheism, in which the Meccans rhetorically asked if they should give up their gods on the account of a "possessed poet" (vv. 34f). Paradise is described in vv. 39f, and Hell is depicted in vv. 59f. The influence of Jewish or Christian ideas can be found in the doctrine of the gathering in for the Judgment (vv. 22f),[17] reward according to works (v. 38),[18] the oath "by Allah" (v. 54)[19] and the implication of a second death (vv. 56f).[20] The greetings given in the narratives of this sura (vv. 77, 109, 120, etc.) may also have come from similar sources.[21] The story of Noah (vv. 73f) is based on the account of Qur'an 54:9f,[22] and that of Abraham (vv. 81f) appears to have been based on Jewish traditions, at least ultimately.[23] The description of Abraham's attempt to sacrifice his son is also related to Jewish and Christian sources[24]; nevertheless the ambiguity of this Qur'anic passage has led both Islamic and Western scholars to speculate as to whether Isaac or Ishmael was actually meant.[25] In v.

112 Isaac is introduced as having been a prophet, and this is probably one of the earliest appearances of this term نبي = "prophet," in the Qur'an.[26] Aaron is mentioned with Moses (v. 110)[27] as having received the Book (v. 117). The narrative of Elias and Baal is very abbreviated (vv. 123f), and most Western scholars are of the opinion that this story came from Ethiopian sources.[28] The narrative of Lot (vv. 133f) seems to show that at least until this time Muhammad did not know that the "old woman" who was not saved was really Lot's wife.[29] The story of Jonah (vv. 139f) is thought to have come from Christian sources, although one Western scholar thinks the strange Arabic word for "gourd" (v. 146) was "garbled" from Hebrew.[30] Qur'an 37:149f is related to 52:39, where only "daughters" are mentioned as being attributed to Allah. The v. 157 contains an early challenge to prove one's claims by showing the book from which they came. The commands for Muhammad to turn away from the unbelievers in 37:174, 178 is similar to 51:54, and 37:182 parallels Qur'an 1:1. The subject of Monotheism is particularly emphasized in the narratives of Abraham and Elias in this sura.

Sura 71 is primarily a narrative about Noah, in which the Biblical information has been radically changed. The vv. 1-2 present Noah as having been sent to his people as a warner, who proclaimed obedience to Allah and himself (v. 3). It is, however, Muhammad who saw himself in the role of a warner (e.g. 51:50f; 53:57), and the novel idea that a messenger (prophet) should be obeyed rather than God alone, also seems to have Muhammad as its source (cf. 3:29, 126; 4:62, etc.). Noah is portrayed as a preacher of forgiveness (vv. 4, 9), who complains of how his people turn away from his message (vv. 6), which he shared with others publicly and privately (v. 7-8). None of this information is found in the Biblical accounts, but all of these circumstances fit Muhammad conveniently.[31] After making an allusion to Creation (vv. 12f), Noah is dismayed that his people have rebelled against *himself* and that they have schemed (v. 21) to undermine his implied Monotheistic message (vv. 22-23). It is Muhammad, however, who frequently appealed to the wonder of God's Creation (e.g. 88:17f; 56:57-73), who was wary of the Meccans designs against him (e.g. 86:15-16; 77:39; 52:42, 46; etc.), and who was preaching Monotheism. Another feature of the vv. 22-23 is that the Qur'an has Noah anachronistically mention the names of the gods and goddesses of the Arab tribes contemporary with Muhammad.[32] The prayer attributed to Noah in this sura (particularly v. 29) was most probably a prayer of Muhammad instead.[33] Some Western Qur'an scholars consider this sura to be an incomplete fragment.[34]

According to some *Sira* traditions, the Meccan al-Nadr b. al-Harith had learned pagan stories during his visits to al-Hira and boasted of being able to tell better stories than Muhammad.[35] Later Ibn `Abbas also credited al-Nadr with having been the originator of the phrase "fairy tales of the ancients," which appears several times in the Qur'an.[36] Indeed, the opportunistic corruptions of Jewish and Christian narratives which are found in the Qur'an have induced the critical comments of Western and Islamic authorities alike.[37]

In **sura 76** almsgiving is mentioned again (vv. 8f) along with a description of Paradise (vv. 11f). The v. 24 shows that Muhammad was not to obey pagans, and vv. 25f present the ritual prayers as being prayed twice a day together with a form of vigil. Muhammad seems to have invented the word "salsabil" in v. 18,[38] and 76:13 is similar to Rev. 7:16.

Qur'an 44 begins with mysterious letters and v. 2 is usually connected with the idea of the "Night of Qadr." 44:7 gives a Monotheistic statement, and 44:13 contains one of the earliest accusations against Muhammad that he had learned from others, to which only the threat of judgment is given as a reply.[39] The vv. 16f relate briefly about Moses before Pharaoh and the exodus, in which the word for "tranquil" (v. 23) probably came from Ethiopic.[40] One of the earliest appearances of the word "Israel" occurs (v. 29). The v. 19 is not only similar to Qur'an 113:1 and 114:1, but the threat of Moses being stoned (cf. Ex. 14:10) seems to have been employed by Muhammad, as he himself was probably threatened with stoning (cf. also Shu`ayb in Qur'an 11:93). There is at least a faint parallel between the exodus of the children of Israel from Egypt and the first emigration of Muslims to Abyssinia; Muhammad's apparent interest in this particular narrative at this point in time may have somehow been related to the idea of sending the early Muslims away for protection. The vv. 34f seem to present a reaction of the Meccans, and the vv. 34 and 56 appear to be based on Rev. 2:11 and 20:14. The destruction of the people of Tubba` is mentioned in vv. 36f, and the source of this legend is not well known.[41]

Sura 50 begins with a mysterious letter, and the vv. 2f deal with the apparently Meccan rejection of the Resurrection. The following verses (vv. 6f) describe the wonder of God's creation and include an agricultural parable which is used to support the Qur'anic doctrine of Resurrection. The vv. 12f briefly refer to the punishment narratives of the people of Noah, those of al-Rass,[42] the Thamud, the `Ad, Pharaoh, the brothers (?) of Lot, those of the Thicket[43] and the people of Tubba`.[44] The Judgment is spoken of in vv. 16f, in which the sin of polytheism is mentioned (v. 25). The v. 37 alludes to the six-day creation and the day of rest, for which it was thought by some to have been revealed in Medina.[45] The two prayer times are referred to in vv. 38f, and it appears that the night vigils were slowly becoming an additional prayer time.[46] The themes of the Judgment and Resurrection are returned to in vv. 40f, and v. 44 again shows that Muhammad's message was being opposed by the Meccans. Qur'an 50:2 is remotely related to Dt. 18:15; and 50:29 is similar to Prov. 30:15f.[47]

In some of the *Sira* traditions, `Umar is said to have become a Muslim after reading a page of the first 14 or so verses of Qur'an 20.[48] Accordingly, this does not mean that `Umar would have been converted when this sura was revealed, but that this sura would have already been committed to writing at the time.[49] Apparently, because of traditions connecting sura 19 to the emigration to Abyssinia, which event must have preceded `Umar's conversion, most Islamic sura orderings position Qur'an 20 after Qur'an 19.[50]

Sura 20 begins with mysterious letters[51] and the first verse indicates that Muhammad may have been suffering financially from Meccan opposition (cf. v. 132).[52] The v. 7 is a statement of Monotheism, followed by the story of Moses, which Muhammad received (vv. 8f).[53] The Qur'an seems to have the incident at the burning bush take place at night (vv. 9f),[54] and the valley of Tuwa is mentioned again (v. 12).[55] Moses is said to have been told by God to perform the (ritual) prayer (v. 14), and is told of the coming "hour" (v. 15) in which everyone will be rewarded according to his works (v. 16).[56] None of these items are mentioned in the Biblical account,[57] yet all of these are familiar to Muhammad and the Qur'an.[58] Verse 26 is also similar to Qur'an 94:1. In v. 30, it is Moses who asks for a "wazir" (in this sense "helper"), and in the canonical hadith Muhammad is reported to have said that `Ali was to him as Aaron was to Moses.[59] In v. 39 Moses' basket (tabut)[60] is said to have washed ashore, contrary to the Biblical witness and Jewish lore.[61] Moses refers to a book previous to his time (v. 54), and some parts of his speech to Pharaoh seem to have come from Jewish sources.[62] Stylistically, the vv. 12f not only present Allah as speaking in first person singular (e.g. vv. 12-15, 43f) and plural (e.g. vv. 37f),[63] but they also contain the inconsistency of having Allah speak of himself in third person singular (e.g. vv. 20a, 22a, 36a, 48a). For some reason Pharaoh (v. 59) and his people (v. 66) think that Moses has come to drive them out of the land. The notion of Pharaoh being a magician (v. 74) seems to come from Jewish sources,[64] and the threatened punishment of crucifixion is no doubt an anachronism.[65] The vv. 75-78 also reveal the doctrines of forgiveness of sins, the neither life nor death existence in Hell and the Qur'anic view of Paradise; all of which seem to be out of place in this narrative. The words used for "manna" and "quail" in 20:82 are of foreign origin.[66] The mention of al-Samiri in the vv. 87f is also an anachronism, and a direct source for this narrative, in which a Samaritan poses as Moses' antago- nist, is still lacking.[67] In v. 99 Allah is said to have given Muhammad the narratives and the admonition, and the following verses (vv. 100f) describe the Resurrection. The v. 102 has been translated in various ways, but it seems to show that sinners are to be resurrected with blue eyes (vv. 125f has "blind"). The v. 108 relates of intercession, and v. 112 appears to give an early state- ment of the "sending down" of an "Arabic Qur'an." The vv. 114f present a narrative of Adam, which is generally considered to have come from Christian sources.[68] One of the many peculiarities of this story, is the usage of the word for "unprosperous" (vv. 115, 122),[69] which was also used in 20:1. Adam and his wife[70] are said to beware that they should not be driven out of Paradise (v. 115) and this passage is remotely similar to Qur'an 17:78, where Muhammad is said to have almost been scared from the land. In v. 118 Muhammad seems to have confused the Tree of Life for the Tree of the Knowledge of Good and Evil,[71] and the names "Adam," "Iblis" and "Eden" are all of foreign origin.[72] Verse 130 again describes the times for the ritual prayers, and in v. 132 Muhammad is to enjoin his family to pray. The vv. 130f show that Muhammad was asked why a sign (miracle) did not accompany him. This question evi- dently was not answered, since only an appeal to wait for the Judgment is given (v. 135).

Qur'an 26 also begins with mysterious letters, which are said to be the "signs"[73] of the clear book.[74] After showing Muhammad's desire for his countrymen (v. 2), this rather "structured" sura gives the narratives of seven prophet figures. The story of Moses (vv. 9f) roughly follows the scheme of his narrative in Qur'an 20, and emphasizes his Monotheistic message. The v. 26:12 is also similar to 20:26f, and the often-repeated description of Allah as the "Lord of the worlds" (vv. 15, 22, 46, 77, 98, 109, 127, 164, 179, 192) also appears in Qur'an 1:1. Qur'an 26:21 seems to have the enslavement of the Israelites take place while Moses was away in Midian, contrary to the Biblical account,[75] but it may be that Muhammad was referring to his own situation.[76] Moses is charged with being possessed (v. 26),[77] and the description of Pharaoh considering himself to be God (v. 28) seems to come from Jewish sources.[78] Moses is again accused of wanting to drive the Egyptians from their land (v. 34; cf. 20:59, 66), and Pharaoh is portrayed as having been a magician (cf. 20:74).[79] The vv. 69f give a narrative of Abraham in which his Monotheistic preaching is not only related, but is also anachronistically Muhammad's style.[80] In the vv. 105f the story of Noah is told, and in keeping with earlier Noah narratives (cf. 54:9f; 37:73f; 71), the flood is sent because Noah has been accused of lying and then calls to God for deliverance (vv. 117f). In the vv. 108 and 110 the idea of obedience to God and a messenger are reiterated,[81] and the statement that (only) the vilest follow Noah (v. 111), must have actually been a remark of the Meccans about Muhammad,[82] since Noah was only "followed" by his own household.[83] In v. 116 Noah is threatened with being stoned, and Muhammad also seems to have been threatened in a similar manner.[84] The vv. 123f relate the stories of the `Ad, to whom the messenger Hud[85] is now sent, the Thamud, to whom Salih[86] is now sent, Lot, and the people of the Thicket, to whom Shu`ayb[87] is now sent. Hud, Salih, Lot and Shu`ayb also appear as the advocates of Monotheism. The doctrine of obedience to God and messenger is stated again (vv. 126, 131, 144, 150, 163, 179). Hud, Salih, Lot and Shu`ayb say they do not expect a wage from their respective peoples (vv. 127, 145, 164, 180), and Muhammad also made this disclaimer (cf. 52:40; 68:46).[88] The voice of the Meccans resounds from the various peoples (vv. 136f, 153f, 167, 185f)[89] all of whom reject their messengers and are consequently severely punished. Together with Noah - Hud, Salih and Lot are said to have been the brethren of those to whom they were sent, and Abraham is also shown as having preached to his father and people.[90]

Later, Muhammad is also called upon to warn his relatives (v. 214). In the vv. 192f the Qur'an is said to be a "sending down" of the "Lord of the worlds," and Muhammad is compared to the messengers of past. The v. 193 shows how the doctrine of revelation was moved away from pagan Arab descriptions (cf. 81:23f; 53:5f)[91] toward a more Biblical basis.[92] The v. 195 states that Muhammad warns in clear Arabic, and v. 197 is probably one of the first direct references to the Jews, for which reason some scholars consider this verse to have been Medinan.[93] There is evidence, however, which indicates the presence of Jews in Mecca,[94] and the Arabs of Mecca must have at least had frequent contact with Jews as merchants. The vv. 208f hint that, as a parallel to the punishment narratives of this sura, a punishment for the city of Mecca is to be expected if the Meccans reject Muhammad's message (cf. 15:4f). In the *Sira* traditions v. 214 is usually dated very early,[95] but such a notion has been rejected by most Western scholars on the grounds that the style of the verse indicates a later time period.[96] The vv. 221f refer to the eavesdropping of spirits (cf. 37:10; 72:9; 15:18; etc.), and vv. 224f contain a ridicule of Arab poets,[97] from which this sura derives its name.

Qur'an 15 begins with mysterious letters, and v. 1 parallels 26:1.[98] The vv. 2-5 refer to the now specific judgment of Mecca (cf. 20:208f), v. 6 shows that Muhammad was accused of being possessed,[99] and the vv. 7f reveal that the Meccans asked for a sign (in this case an angel), which was not given because they would still persist in their unbelief (vv. 8, 14f).[100] Qur'an 15:18 is reminiscent of other passages (cf. 37:10; 26:221f; 72:9; etc.), after which a short narrative of Adam and Satan (Iblis) similar to the one in 20:115 is told. The description of Hell as having seven doors (v. 44) seems to have come from Jewish sources.[101] The story of Abraham and his guests (vv. 51f) pretty much follows the account in Qur'an 51:24f, with notable exceptions being that it is now known that it was Lot's household who was to be saved (v. 59),[102] but not his wife (v. 60).[103] In the vv. 78f the people of the Thicket are mentioned briefly, and the story about those of al-Hijr (vv. 80f) is thought to refer to the Thamud (cf. 15:82 with 26:149). The various theories as to what the "seven mathani" (v. 87) could mean are inconclusive, but it seems that the seven punishment narratives of Qur'an 26 may be meant,[104] rather than the typical Muslim view that the "mathani" are the seven verses of Qur'an 1.[105] The vv. 90-91 appear to be missing some text,[106] and the vv. 94f show again that Muhammad was being opposed. As with Qur'an 26:214, the passage 15:94 is often placed much earlier in the *Sira* traditions, however, this idea is again rejected by Western scholars in that the verse betrays a style in keeping with later passages.[107] Some sources claim that this sura originally contained 190 verses, instead of the 99 of today's verses.[108]

One of the distinguishing features of the Qur'an for this (second or middle) Meccan period, is the extensive use of the term "al-Rahman" ("the Compassionate") for Allah.[109] The identification of "Rahman" with God probably came from Jewish or Christian sources,[110] and since it was related to the Arabic رحمة other Arabs had a fair idea of what it meant.[111] However, it appears that this designation also caused some confusion among the Meccans, and may have led them to think Muhammad was referring to two gods.[112] In any event, the term "al-Rahman" generally disappears from the texts of the suras in the third Meccan period.[113]

The suras of this period rather openly show that two daily prayers were the only regular ritual up to this point and that the earlier vigils were slowly becoming a nightly prayer (cf. 52:48f; 76:25f; 50:38f). Several verses of this period also contain phrases very similar to those used in Qur'an 1 (cf. 26:46, & passim; 37:182; 20:135).

The doctrine of the Last Judgment, which appeared so frequently in the earliest suras of the Qur'an, has been extended to include a specific judgment against the Meccans in this period (cf. 51:52f; 54:43f; 26:208f; 15:2f; etc.). This development seems to have been facilitated by prophet narratives and punishment stories, which tell about localized and temporary judgments on various peoples. Muhammad's primary interest in the Biblical and legendary prophet histories appears to have limited itself to "judgment stories." In the progression of the Qur'anic narratives Muhammad gradually *becomes* the messenger of each story; as the plots are changed to conform to his own circumstances. In the suras 51 (vv. 24f), 54 and 37, Muhammad's character is increasingly intertwined with those of the other messengers. In sura 37 it appears that Muhammad discovered the usefulness of Monotheistic narratives; Abraham (vv. 81f) and Elijah (vv. 123f); and from Qur'an 71 through suras 44 and 20 to Qur'an 26, all of the messengers become advocates of Monotheism. Muhammad apparently had no reservations about altering the narratives he had learned; nor does he seem to have appreciated the need for a proper chronology.[114] It is obvious that Muhammad received the original plots for the Biblical narratives from Jews and Christians, and the fact that he was being instructed by others was also known to the Meccans (cf. 44:13). Muhammad was accused by the Meccans of passing off as "revelations" the stories he had heard, and the Qur'anic rebuttals of this repeated charge seem to have done little to alleviate this problem.[115] Indeed, almost in answer to these accusations, the *Sira* and canonical traditions attempt to provide the names for Muhammad's informants, all of whom appear to have been Christians.[116]

Of the Biblical prophets, Muhammad seems to have identified himself best with Noah at first,[117] and the warning of a specific and impending judgment on the Meccans may have played a role in this choice. Many, but certainly not all of the Qur'anic punishments in these narratives are depicted as being natural catastrophes, and the most feared (and recurring) natural disaster of Mecca was flooding.[118] Later, Muhammad begins to appear more and more in the person of Moses,[119] and it may have been that the punishment of the drowning of Pharaoh and his people also played a role in this decision.

Despite the fact that Muhammad develops the stories of Arab prophets somewhat in this section of suras,[120] it is the Old Testament figures of Adam, Noah, Abraham and Moses to which he commits the most text and detail. Oddly, although the Biblical narratives in these suras must have been ultimately Jewish, their Qur'anic versions generally have a Christian coloring.[121] On the one hand, if Muhammad's informants were Jewish, one would expect to find more familiarity with conventional Judaism in these suras; and on the other hand, if Muhammad's instructors were Christians or from heretical sects, an acquaintance with the doctrines regarding the person of Christ would have been evident. As opposed to the first Meccan period, however, Muhammad seems to have been far less interested in the doctrines of Judaism and Christianity; and yet captivated by the utilitarian aspects of certain Biblical histories. Muhammad appears to have been very selective in his choice of narratives, and those which spoke of judgment and Monotheism seem to have gotten the most attention at first. Essentially, Muhammad's ministry had little in common with that of Jesus, and the New Testament narratives on judgment and Monotheism are not as abundant as those of the Old Testament.[122] Whatever contact Muhammad may have had with Jews,

Christians or other groups, it may have simply been used to obtain histories about these two themes.

Muhammad's polemic in this section is decidedly anti-polytheist. Rhetorically Muhammad asked his opponents if it was befitting to attribute daughters to Allah and sons to themselves (cf. 52:39; 37:149-153 and later in 53:21f; 43:15f; 16:59f). This idea must have run aground when Muhammad was confronted by Christians (for it could easily have been used against him), and the last mention of it is made early in the third Meccan period.

According to *Sira* traditions, the Meccans were persecuting lower class Muslims, who were not afforded protection by their clans. Moreover, Muhammad was also in no position to be able to shelter them from persecution.[123] Although many traditions depict Muhammad as saying that Abyssinia was a friendly country, the decision to send his followers to that country may well have been motivated by the fact that the Abyssinians were no doubt viewed as the political enemies of Mecca.[124] The predominantly Christian Abyssinians must have been very interested in the Muslim refugees from Mecca, at least with respect to their general desire to politically influence the Arabs of the Hijaz in the greater Byzantine-Persian power struggles.[125] Naturally, the Abyssinians would have wanted to know what Muhammad believed about Jesus, and the abrupt introduction of Zacharias, John the Baptist, Mary and Jesus to the text of the Qur'an (sura 19) is somewhat suspicious. A *Sira* tradition reports that one of the early Muslims read (or recited) Qur'an 19 to the Abyssinian king.[126] This seems to indicate that this sura was composed before the emigration, and possibly even tailored to suit an audience there.

Based on its style and content, Western scholars view Qur'an 19 as having been composed in at least two stages. The first: **19:1-34, 42-75**, is definitely more pro-Christian than the second (vv. 35-41, 76-98), which appears to have been a later addition.[127] Sura 19 begins with mysterious letters,[128] after which a narrative of Zacharias and John the Baptist are given (vv. 1f). Although this account appears to have had Luke 1 as its source, in Qur'an 19:5 Zacharias asks for an heir for himself and the house of Jacob (?), and v. 11 presents Zacharias' having been unable to speak for just three nights (as purely a sign, rather than also a punishment for his unbelief; cf. Lk. 1:20).

Moreover, no mention of Gabriel is made in this sura, even though one would definitely expect to find it here, if indeed Muhammad was claiming to have received his revelations from Gabriel at this time. Instead, a few verses later (cf. 19:17) Allah's spirit appears in the place of Gabriel, and other Qur'an passages also indicate that Muhammad had been claiming that his revelations had been given him by a "spirit" (cf. Qur'an 26:193).[129] The blessing in 19:15, for John, is basically the same as the one in v. 34, which is given for Jesus.[130] The vv. 16f relate a narrative about Mary, who is said to have had a book named after her,[131] and the birth of Jesus, who remains unnamed until v. 35 (which appears to have been a later addition). Most of the materials for this story seem to have come from apocryphal works of various sects.[132] In v. 16 Mary is said to have withdrawn from her relatives,[133] and again, no mention of Gabriel is made where it should have been (vv. 17, 19), but simply a spirit (v. 19) is referred to.[134] In vv. 23f Mary is said to have given birth under a palm tree, and "her Lord" has a brook flow beneath her (v. 24).[135] Mary is later accused of immorality (vv. 28f),[136] and is addressed as the "sister of Aaron" (v. 29). It is certain that Muhammad confused Miriam the sister of Moses with Mary the mother of Jesus,[137] as this misunderstanding also serves as the basis for other Qur'an passages, where Amram ('Imran) the father of Moses is said to be the father of Mary (cf. 3:30f; 66:12).[138] In v. 30 the infant [Jesus] speaks from the cradle to absolve Mary from the charge of immorality,[139] and v. 34 contains the blessing similar to that of John's in v. 15.[140] Strangely enough, the name of Jesus does not appear in this earlier section, nor does Muhammad reveal any acquaintance with the title Messias ("Masih") until Medinan passages. Since the term "Masih" together with "son of Mary" was used for Jesus among the pre-Islamic Arab poets,[141] it may have been that Muhammad did not yet know of Him from those sources. The vv. 42f give a narrative about Abraham (cf. 87:19), who is said to have a book named after him, whose father is depicted as having been an idolater (vv. 43f),[142] and whose sons were (apparently) Isaac and Jacob (v. 50).[143] A brief narrative about Moses follows (vv. 52f), who is also said to have a book bearing his name (cf. 87:19). In the vv. 55f a story about Ishmael is given, who is also said to have had a book. The fact that he was not mentioned together with Isaac and Jacob indicates that Muhammad must not have known that Ishmael was Abraham's son at the time.[144] The ministry of his prophethood, as described in these verses, was probably an invention of Muhammad, for not only are the doctrines mentioned typically Qur'anic, but later Islamic traditionists were hard put to find any sources for this narrative.[145] In vv. 57f a book is ascribed to Idris, who is briefly described,[146] vv. 61f Paradise is associated with Eden, and the vv. 67f deal with the Resurrection. The Qur'anic names for most of the characters in these sections of this sura, seem to have come from (or have been influenced by) Syriac,[147] and at least three of them: the names for Zacharias, Mary and Idris, do not appear to have existed in Arabic before Muhammad's time.[148] Just how well these early sections of this sura may have been accepted by the Abyssinians can only be inferred from the accounts of the *Sira* traditions and from the apparent fact that the Muslims were granted asylum. Certainly the Abyssinians must have recognized that Muhammad's message was nearer to that of Christianity than to Arab paganism; moreover, their decision to accept the Muslims, as mentioned previously, may have also been politically motivated.

As presented in the *Sira* traditions, the general reason for the emigration to Abyssinia was that Muhammad could not protect Muslims from the lower classes from persecution.[149] At least one set of traditions gives two emigrations to Abyssinia instead of one,[150] but Western scholars usually agree[151] with another set,[152] which presents the flow of emigrants from Mecca as having been intermittent. Concerning the names of those who emigrated and their numbers *Sira* traditions give differing accounts,[153] and one collection of such traditions seems to inadvertently list Ibn Mas'ud as having gone to Abyssinia, only to have him be the first to publicly recite the Qur'an in Mecca a short time later.[154] The Meccans are then said to have sent two or three[155] emissaries to bring the refugees back.[156] According to these accounts, the Meccans wanted to continue their persecution of the Muslims, and it was no doubt also in their interest to try to keep a local problem from becoming an international one. In the end, the Meccan's attempt to bring the Muslims back was a failure, and the evidence of Muhammad's increasing influence must have troubled them all the more.

After the emigration to Abyssinia, *Sira* traditions relate that `Umar became a Muslim.[157] At the time, `Umar is said to have been the most influential Muslims, which is evidenced by his success in securing the right for himself and other Muslims to pray at the then idol-filled Ka`ba.[158] Tradition states that Muhammad also prayed at the Ka`ba, and that his direction of prayer ("qibla") was Syria (or better: Jerusalem),[159] however, this is extremely unlikely, since the word "qibla" first appears in later suras.[160]

According to *Sira* traditions, the Meccans were so disconcerted by the Abyssinian emigration and the conversion of `Umar that they imposed a boycott against the Hashimites and the clan of the Muttalib, to which Muhammad belonged.[161] With the exception of his uncle, Abu Lahab, Muhammad's clan remained loyal to him, even though many of them were not Muslims.[162] The boycott is said to have lasted three years, and probably did much to exhaust the wealth of Abu Talib and Khadija.[163] By virtue of their not belonging to Muhammad's clan, Abu Bakr and `Umar were exempt from this boycott, but to what extent they may have been able to help Muhammad is not clear.[164] The hardships endured during the boycott,[165] as well as the increased opposition of the Meccans[166] in this period are also related in hadith.

Sira traditions describe Muhammad's desire for the conversion of his countrymen as being so great, that he was once seduced by Satan to insert false verses into the Qur'an.[167] Accordingly, Muhammad was in an assembly of the Quraysh[168] when he began reciting Qur'an 53.[169] After Qur'an 53:19-20, Muhammad is reported to have recited a verse describing al-Lat, al-`Uzza and Manat as approved intercessors, and the Quraysh, joyful over this concession, are then said to have prostrated themselves. Some hadith depict Gabriel as having rebuked Muhammad the same evening,[170] but it is much more likely that a longer period of time passed, since the news that the Quraysh had accepted Islam is said to have reached the emigrants in Abyssinia, upon which at least some decided to return to Mecca.[171] Later, Muhammad is reported to have retracted this passage and Qur'an 22:52 is said to have been revealed to him as an assurance that Satan had given him the false text.[172]

The passage **Qur'an 53:19-32,** which is against the pagan goddesses al-Lat, al-`Uzza and Manat, and is also in opposition to the intercession of angels, may have been composed at this time.

Whereas many Muslims have tried to suppress these traditions over the centuries,[173] Western scholars have generally argued over the authenticity of these.[174] Attempts to discredit the chains of transmitters (isnads) as unreliable, together with the presumption that these hadith did not exist in the earliest collections of *Sira* traditions, are certainly unfounded, because these traditions appear in practically all of the earliest major Islamic histories.[175]

Provided that the compromise of the Satanic inspiration was of some duration, the Meccans would have no longer had any reason to maintain their boycott against the Hashimites. The *Sira* traditions generally agree in showing the destitute situation of the Hashimites resultant to the boycott,[176] and that the first impulse to end their suffering was human.[177] Although traditions describing the supernatural destruction of the boycott document report that all but the words "in the name of Allah" were consumed, they contradict one another in the finer points of how this occurred.[178] One of the real reasons for the repeal of the boycott may have actually been the Satanically inspired verses, which would have moved the Quraysh to accommodate this concession.

The news of the Meccans' conversion may well have been sent by Muhammad himself, since the emigrants had now decided to return to Mecca, but had previously refused to return with the envoys of the Quraysh. Although in contradiction of *Sira* traditions, it is, however, possible that the return of the emigrants affected Muhammad's later decision to withdraw the verses of Satanic inspiration, since Muhammad's message of Monotheism was earlier reported to have been the cause of increased Meccan opposition and persecution which drove them to Abyssinia in the first place.[179]

Sura 38 begins with a mysterious letter, following which apparent dialogues with the Meccans are given (vv. 1f). In the vv. 11f Muhammad is compared with the earlier messengers and the vv. 16f are among the earliest passages containing a narrative about David. The descriptions of the mountains praising with David (v. 17), and of birds coming to him (v. 18) seems to have been a distortion of Ps. 148:7-10.[180] Muhammad also appears to have understood the prophet Nathan's parable (cf. II Sam. 12:1-5) as a real event (vv. 20f), in which two men (or angels)[181] brought their case to David for a judgment.[182] In the vv. 30f one of the first narratives about Solomon is given. Solomon is shown as having loved horses (vv. 30f), and as then repenting and asking for a kingdom (v. 34), rather than as having made his original request for wisdom (cf. I Kgs. 3:6f).[183] The notions of a form being seated on Solomon's throne (v. 33) and of the wind and demons being made subservient to Solomon (vv. 35f) appear to have their origins in Jewish traditions.[184] In the vv. 43f one of the first narratives about Job appears, which seems to contain a very disorganized allusion to Job 2:8-10.[185] The awkwardness of v. 45 mentioning Abraham, Isaac and Jacob together, only to have v. 48 later name Ishmael with Elisha and the enigmatic Dhu'l-Kifl,[186] indicates that Muhammad did not know that Ishmael was Abraham's son at the time.[187] Descriptions of Paradise and Hell are given (vv. 49f), and the narrative of Adam and Iblis (vv. 71f) was probably a later addition, since the rhyme scheme of the vv. 67-87 does not match that of the remainder of the sura.[188] In v. 86 Muhammad again shows that he was not asking for a wage from the Meccans.[189] The Arabic names for David, Solomon and Job all seem to predate Muhammad,[190] and it is not known who was meant by Dhu'l-Kifl. In 38:6 the word "milla" was probably borrowed from Syriac.[191] Remote similarities to Bible passages can be found in 38:8 (cf. Ps. 135:7) and 38:40 (cf. Ja. 5:11).[192] Some *Sira* traditions connect the revelation of this sura with the death of Abu Talib.[193]

Qur'an 36 also begins with mysterious letters. Muhammad is presented as a messenger to a people who had not been warned (vv. 1f). The narrative of the envoys and the city appears to come from either Christians or sects having broken off from Christianity,[194] and some wording is thought to be missing between the vv. 24 and 25.[195] The vv. 33f relate the witness of Creation,[196] after which the Meccan objections to almsgiving (v. 47) and questions about the advent of the Judgment are given (vv. 48f). The vv. 63f contain a description of Hell, in which the Jewish idea that body members will testify is given,[197] and the vv. 78f reproduce some of the Meccan's objections to the doctrine of the Resurrection. 36:38 is similar to Eccl. 1:5, and 36:82 is similar to Ps. 33:9. According to some *Sira* traditions, Muhammad recited this sura as his opponents once tried to murder him.[198]

Mysterious letters open **sura 43**, which includes an oath "by the clear book" (v. 1). The vv. 5f contain one of the earliest direct implications that Muhammad considered himself to be a prophet, as opposed to a "messenger," following which Creation is described (vv. 8f). The rhetorical question against the Meccans attributing daughters to Allah is reiterated (v. 15),[199] and the pagan notion that angels were feminine is also mentioned (vv. 18f). The vv. 21f reflect the problems Muhammad had convincing the Meccans, and this leads into a narrative about Abraham, in which Muhammad figures as Abraham and the Meccans as Abraham's pagan audience (vv. 25f). Since no such "two cities" are known from any of the histories or legends of Abraham, v. 30 can not only be seen as a direct allusion to the cities of Mecca and al-Ta'if, (where Muhammad was not among the powerful) but also as a corruption of the story. The v. 35 contains one of the earliest admonitions against apostasy, and may well indicate that some Muslims had ceased being followers of Muhammad. A narrative about Moses and Pharaoh is given in the vv. 45f, and an echo of the Meccans can be heard in Pharaoh's remarks about neither gold nor angels being sent down to Moses, i.e. Muhammad (cf. Qur'an 15:7). In v. 57 Muhammad appears to have told the Meccans of the son of Mary (Jesus), and the strange reply of the pagans: "Are our gods better, or is He?" (v. 58) implies that Jesus must have been presented as divine.[200] The v. 59 contains one of the earliest denials of Jesus' deity, and v. 63 oddly depicts Him as having been sent to resolve disunity (cf. v. 65). In the vv. 67f Paradise and Hell are described, and v. 81 gives the condition, that if the Compassionate had had a Son, then Muhammad would have been the first to worship Him. The v. 86 mentions intercession, and v. 88 is obviously missing enough text to make its intended context incomprehensible.[201] Passages of this sura, which are similar to Bible verses, are: 43:37 (cf. Ps. 103:12), 43:39 (cf. Ex. 4:11), 43:66 (cf. Mk. 13:36) and 43:85 (cf. Mt. 24:36). One of the earliest occurrences of the Arabic name for Jesus can be found in v. 63. Although quite a few legitimate theories exist as to the origins of the Qur'anic name for Jesus (`Isa) in Arabic, it does not appear in pre-Islamic writings, and its exact origin remains somewhat of a enigma.[202]

The emigration of Muslim refugees to Abyssinia not only seems to have awakened Muhammad's interest in the person of Christ, but also resulted in his learning more about Christianity's principal doctrines. As discussed above, the obviously anti-polytheist polemic against pagans ascribing daughters to God but sons to themselves, must have been ineffectual, even detrimental to use against Christians, all of whom believe in the Sonship of Christ. Even heretical sects which had broke off from Christianity, such as the Gnostics and Ebionites,[203] as well as the Manichaeans[204] maintained the

94

Sonship of Jesus. Moreover, Muhammad's motivation to deny Christ's Sonship could also hardly have been the Jews, as they would have rejected any mention of Jesus, much less His prophethood. The Muslims returning from Abyssinia may not only have influenced Muhammad to recant the "Satan inspiration," but they may also have acquainted him with the doctrines of Christ's Sonship and deity. The context of Qur'an 43:57-58 indicates that Muhammad not only knew of the doctrine of the divinity of Christ, but that he may have also presented Jesus as divine at least once. The Meccans also rejected this doctrine (cf. 43:58), and in the end it may have been their perception of "Qur'anic" Monotheism which caused Muhammad to deny both the deity of Christ (43:59) and His Sonship (43:81). Although some Western scholars of Islam give various reasons for why Muhammad did not become a Christian,[205] the real causes should be sought in his decision for these denials, which alienated him from both Christianity and the sects which had broken off from Christianity.

Evidence for the coincidence of the Muslim's returning from Abyssinia and Muhammad's rejection of Christ's Sonship can be found in the composition of **sura 72**. Various Islamic traditions present different settings and times for the revelation of this sura,[206] whose real significance lies in the witness of its internal evidence. The message of 72:3, which denies that Allah had a wife or son, gives one of the earliest Qur'anic indications of familiarity with a Monophysite (Abyssinian?) interpretation of the position of Mary. The vv. 6 and 12 speak of refuge and flight in a strange manner, and as will be shown, the emigration to Abyssinia seems to fit both of these verses. The vv. 14 (for jinn), 16f and 24 (for humans) concern themselves with apostasy, and perhaps the first Muslim to apostatize was `Ubaydullah b. Jahsh, who became a Christian in Abyssinia and had apparently turned against his comrades.[207] Moreover, v. 18 contains the word for "mosques" (plural), as places of prayer, and traditions report that some of the Muslims in Abyssinia had been inside the churches there.[208] The vv. 1-2 of sura 72 present jinn as being of lesser importance than Muhammad, since some of the jinn heard and believed the Qur'an; the context of vv. 3-5 strongly implies that a "foolish" jinn had said that Allah had a son, and v. 6 speaks of humans who had taken refuge among the men of the jinn and thereby increased their folly. Functionally, the passage vv. 1-6 makes jinn (demons),[209] who are inferior to Muhammad, responsible for the doctrine of Christ's Sonship, and the emigrants, who must have been affected by Christian doctrines, had sought refuge among the Abyssinians, who may well have been "the people (men) of the (deviant) jinn" in these verses. In 72:7 this people is said to have denied that God would resurrect the dead, in a manner similar to the Meccans' rejection of this teaching; and it is known that Gnostics[210] and Manichaeans[211] denied the doctrine of a physical Resurrection. Apparently, Muhammad's contact with "Christian" Abyssinians at this time may have been limited to members of one of these sects, since the earliest sections of sura 19[212] and parts of sura 36[213] also seem to have the books of the Gnostics and the Manichaeans as sources. The verses 72:8f explain the eavesdropping of the jinn (cf. 37:10; 15:18, etc.), and 72:10 describes the jinn as not knowing what the Lord will do in the future (cf. v. 26 for the counterpart for Muhammad). 72:12 contains the admission of the jinn, that they never thought they could have frustrated God through flight, and quite possibly this is a reference to the apostasy or doctrinal swaying of some of the emigrants, who had "fled" to Abyssinia. The apostates of the jinn (vv. 14f) and humans (vv. 16f) are to be punished in Hell. The v. 18 claim all places of prayer for Allah and prescribe prayer to Him alone, and the vv. 19f may refer to an occasion at the Ka`ba. The v. 24 is generally thought to be a Medinan addition, in which disobedience to Allah and Muhammad is to be punished in Hell. 72:26f not only shows that future events had not been revealed to Muhammad, but stipulates that God would only share His secrets with Muhammad himself, who was then protected by those guaranteeing that he recited God's revelation.

Since the inferior jinn were now shown to be responsible for the doctrine of Christ's Sonship, early Muslims must reject this Christian influence if they were to remain as followers of Muhammad. Islam had openly parted with Christianity and its related sects, and as an apparent result, the following suras of the Qur'an became increasingly dependent on Jewish sources.

The denial that God should have a Son became an important part of the Qur'anic polemic, and it may have been that **sura 112** was composed at this time.[214]

The *Sira* traditions are in disagreement over the fate of the emigrants who returned to Mecca. One collection of traditions state that they remained in

Mecca,[215] whereas another shows at least some of them as returning to Abyssinia.[216] After the ending of the boycott against the Hashimites, traditions report that Muhammad's uncle Abu Talib became ill to the point of death. Muhammad pleaded with his uncle to repeat the first part of the Islamic creed (shahada), but he refused. Abu Talib is reported to have died a pagan[217] in the tenth year of Muhammad's ministry at the age of more than 80.[218] About one month and five days later, Muhammad's wife Khadija also died,[219] and not long after her death, Muhammad married the widow Sawda bt. Zam`a, whose earlier husband Sakran b. `Amr died after returning from Abyssinia.[220] Muhammad's uncle Abu Lahab then became clan leader and Muhammad's protector, until Muhammad (in answer to a question) said that their ancestor `Abd al-Muttalib was in Hell.[221] Muhammad then appears to have lost the support of his clan,[222] and decided to go to the nearby city of al-Ta'if to find support and protection.[223] Muhammad is said to have met with many in al-Ta'if, but that he was unable to find anyone who would support him.[224] On the way back to Mecca, Muhammad stopped in Nakhla to pray. It is said that some jinn[225] heard his prayer, and that this event is referred to in Qur'an 72.[226]

Upon his return to Mecca, Muhammad secured the protection of Mut`im b. `Adi.[227]

The composition of the remainder of **sura 19 (vv. 35-41, 76-98)** may well have fallen in this period. Jesus is named in v. 35, as opposed to being called simply "son" (cf. 19:19f), and v. 36 denies His Sonship. The v. 38 shows that the sects are in disagreement about Jesus, and in vv. 39f Muhammad is to warn them of the Judgment. The vv. 76f again speak of the Judgment and the future state of unbelievers. The denial that the Compassionate ("Rahman") should have a son is found in the vv. 91f. "Those who believe and do good" are spoken of (v. 96), the Qur'an is said to have been made easy for Muhammad (v. 97) and the doom of earlier generations is mentioned (v. 98).

Qur'an 67 begins by presenting all creation as a kingdom in God's hand (vv. 1f). The notion of seven heavens in v. 3 seems to have Jewish traditions as its ultimate source.[228] The stated purpose of the stars (v. 5) is similar to other Qur'an passages describing the eavesdropping of spirits and jinn (cf. 37:10;

72:9; 15:18, etc.). The vv. 6f relate about the judgment of unbelievers and the vv. 13f present God as Creator, Punisher and Provider.

The first few verses of **sura 23** speak of believers who pray and give alms, after which one of the earliest Qur'anic passages against sexual impurity appears (vv. 5-7). Those who are trustworthy, keep their promises and hold their prayers are spoken well of (vv. 8f), in that they will be the "heirs" of Paradise (cf. Ja. 2:5; Mt. 25:34). The vv. 12f tell of the creation of man, which is compared to the Resurrection in the vv. 15f. Islamic traditions report that the last phrase of v. 14 was actually an exclamatory remark of the scribe, which was then added to the text of this sura on Muhammad's instruction.[229] In the vv. 18f God is presented as the Provider, and in v. 20 Mount Sinai is referred to.[230] The vv. 23f contain a narrative about Noah, in which the comments of an alleged leader of the unbelievers — that God should have sent an angel to Noah, that their ancestors had told them nothing about him, and that Noah was possessed—were more likely the things a Meccan leader said of Muhammad. In v. 26 Noah cries to the Lord for help against the accusation of lying, after which the "warm water" (v. 27)[231] flood is eventually sent to drown the sinners (vv. 28f). Another narrative about a Monotheist messenger, who is probably to be identified with Salih (cf. 11: 64f), is found in vv. 32f. The accusations of the leaders of his people against this messenger, i.e. that he is just a man who eats and drinks (vv. 34f), was a complaint of the Meccans against Muhammad (cf. 21:3, 7-8; 25:8f, 22). The rejection of the message of the Resurrection by the messenger's people (vv. 37f) was also a trait of the Meccans. In the vv. 44f a comparison with later peoples is made. The vv. 47f give a narrative about Moses and Aaron in which Pharaoh rhetorically asks if they are to believe men as themselves, and the Egyptians were then destroyed because they accused Moses and Aaron of lying (v. 50). Naturally, these circumstances fit Muhammad better, who was accused of being simply a man, and who obviously hoped for the specific judgment of those who thought he was lying. In v. 50 a book is said to have been given to Moses, and in v. 52 Jesus and Mary are said to have been made a sign, who were given a dwelling on high. The vv. 55f tell of the disagreements of the sects. The accusation of Muhammad having a jinn is reproduced in v. 72, and the matter of Muhammad not seeking a wage from the Meccans is mentioned again in v. 74. The vv. 80f speak of God's provision, v. 84 mentions the rejection of the teaching of the Resurrection and v. 93 denies that God has either a son or a companion. In the vv. 99f Muhammad is said to seek refuge with God, following which the judgment of unbelievers (vv. 101f) and believers (vv. 111f) is described. Some of the verses of this sura are similar to Bible passages; cf. 23:64 with I Cor. 10:13 and 23:98 with Rom 12:21.[232] The word used for "proof" ("burhan") in 23:117 appears to come from Ethiopic.[233]

The opening verses of **Qur'an 21** give some Meccan reactions to Muhammad's message, where Muhammad is accused of being just a man, and in the vv. 6f a comparison with the earlier messengers is made. The v. 7 is thought by some to have been composed in Medina, due to its mentioning the "people of the Remembrance."[234] 21:8 states that the earlier messengers were also human, and in v. 10 the Qur'an is inferred to have been sent as a warning for the Meccans. A comparison with the fate of other cities is found in the vv. 11f. The question in v. 21, about choosing deities who could raise the dead, seems to have been posed to pagans and not Christians,[235] although hints of v. 22 show up in the later polemic of Muslims against Christianity.[236] The vv. 23f give some arguments against polytheism, and v. 25 states that all previous messengers preached Monotheism.[237] The vv. 26f contain the denial that the Compassionate has children, and the vv. 31f speak of the witness of creation. The v. 37 gives what may have been a Meccan mockery of Muhammad in the aftermath of the Satanic inspiration. The vv. 38f show that Judgment will come, the vv. 42f present some arguments against the Meccans and the vv. 47f speak again of the Judgment. In the vv. 49f Moses and Aaron are said to have received the "furqan,"[238] which is said to have been "sent down" by God as a light and admonition for those who fear God. A narrative about Abraham, which emphasizes Monotheism, is given in the vv. 52f. The v. 71 tells of Abraham and Lot being delivered to a land which was to be a blessing for all, and in v. 72 Isaac and Jacob are said to have been given Abraham.[239] The vv. 74f give a brief narrative about Lot, and more extensive narratives about David and Solomon follow (vv. 78f). In v. 78 David and Solomon are said to have decided a case about sheep who apparently grazed in another's field,[240] v. 79 presents mountains and birds as serving David,[241] v. 80 depicts David as having been instructed in the arts of making armor,[242] and the vv. 81f portray the wind and demons as having been subservient to Solomon.[243] The vv. 83f give a narrative of Job, and in the vv. 85f Ishmael is mentioned with Idris and Dhu'l-Kifl, but again, apart from Isaac and Jacob (cf. Qur'an 38:45, 48).[244] A narrative about Dhu'l-Nun (Jonah) is presented in the vv. 87f, and the vv. 89f give a short narration regarding Zacharias and John the Baptist. In the vv. 91f a strange description of Mary is given, in which the Spirit was said to have been breathed into her; she and "her son" were made a sign for all the world. In the vv. 95f Gog and Magog[245] appear to be mentioned in connection with the end of the world and the Judgment. In v. 107 Muhammad is also said to have been sent as a "mercy" for all (cf. v. 91 and 23:52), and the confession of Muhammad that he did not know when or what will occur concerning punishment is related to Qur'an 72:26. Passages of the sura at least remotely similar to Bible verses are: 21:48 (cf. Mt. 17:20); 21:105 (quotes Ps. 37:29); 21:108 (cf. Dt. 6:4). The Arabic names for Gog and Magog (v. 96) seem to have been modified by Muhammad from the Syriac.[246] This sura appears to give one of the earliest usages of the foreign word "zabur" for the Psalms only (v. 105),[247] and Muhammad seems to have misunderstood the Syriac word "furqan" (v. 49)[248] In v. 104 the strange word سِجِلّ ("sijill") appears, which is thought to have come from Greek or Syriac, and was probably also misunderstood by Muhammad.[249]

The first verse of **Qur'an 25** describes either the "furqan" or Muhammad as a warner for all. In v. 2 the kingdom of heaven and earth is shown to be God's, who is said to have no son. The vv. 5f appear to reproduce Meccan accusations[250] that Muhammad received help from others in composing the Qur'an,[251] which is said to have been "stories of the ancients" he wrote (for himself),[252] having been dictated morning and evening. The denial of the charge of human assistance (but not of his "writing") is found in v. 7. Other Meccan accusations are given in vv. 8f, whereby Muhammad is described as one who eats and goes to markets (cf. 25:22 for the reply). Questions are also asked as to why no angel was sent to him to confirm his warning, why he was not given a treasure or a garden (cf. 25:23f for a reply). In answer to the charge of not having a garden, the garden of Paradise is described in v. 11, following which Judgment and Hell are spoken of. The vv. 32f are concerned with others' rejection of the Qur'an, and in v. 34 the question is posed as to why the Qur'an was not revealed all at one time. In the vv. 37f Moses is again said to have received the Book and Aaron is described as having been his helper (cf. 20:30). In v. 39 a summary of Noah's ministry is given, the 'Ad, Thamud and the inhabitants of al-Rass are mentioned in

v. 40, and these are all to serve as examples to the Meccans (vv. 41f). The vv. 47f depict God as the Provider, who among other things, divided salt and fresh water with a barrier (v. 55)[253] and created man from water (v. 56). The vv. 57f show pagans to be unbelievers. In v. 59 Muhammad reiterates that he is asking for no wage,[254] and the vv. 61f indicate that the name "Compassionate" ("Rahman") for God was alien to the Meccans. In the vv. 62f God is described as the Creator, and the vv. 64f contrast the servants of the Compassionate and the ignorant. A few passages of this sura are similar to Bible passages: 25:28 (cf. Rev. 12:10); 25:46 (cf. I Pet. 2:25; Is. 53:6); 25:64 (cf. Mt. 5: 5), or the Talmud: 25:64 (Avot 4,15).[255]

At least one collection of *Sira* traditions portrays a deputation of Christians from Abyssinia as accepting Islam in Mecca; however, this information is hedged by doubts on the part of Ibn Ishaq.[256] *Sira* traditions relate how Muhammad was allegedly transported to the Temple Mount in Jerusalem[257] one night, but the various collections are in disagreement as to whether this actually took place physically, or rather, in a dream. Many of these traditions relate that Muhammad was taken to Jerusalem (or Heaven) on a beast named "Buraq" by the angel Gabriel.[258] Later, Muhammad is said to have been raised into the "seven" heavens and saw (1) Adam - (2) John and Jesus - (3) Joseph - (4) Idris - (5) Aaron - (6) Moses - (7) Abraham, the last of whom took him to God. At first 50 daily prayers were made obligatory for Muhammad and his followers, but after talking to Moses, and returning to God to ask for a reduction, ten less daily prayers were made obligatory; and so on, until finally only five daily prayers remained. This tradition is obviously a later elaboration of the exegetes for Qur'an 17:1, since the strange name "Buraq"[259] never appears in the Qur'an, "Gabriel" is only known in Medinan passages (as well as the preference for Abraham), Muhammad never claims to have been in heaven or in God's presence in the Qur'an, the "reduction" in the number of daily prayers is also not referred to in the Qur'an (much less that there should be "five" daily prayers), etc. Moreover, the structure of the story seems to be based on other works: a spiritual journey to Jerusalem (cf. Ezek. 8:3),[260] seeing and speaking with other prophets in heaven (cf. The Revelation of Paul),[261] and "bargaining" from 50 to a lesser number (cf. Gen. 18:26-33).

Qur'an 17 begins with Muhammad's night journey from the holy mosque (Ka`ba) to the far-away mosque (Jerusalem or Heaven).[262] In v. 2 Moses is referred to again as having received the Book, which was a guide for the children of Israel, v. 3 mentions Noah and the vv. 4f seem to allude to the two destructions of the Temple in Jerusalem.[263] In v. 13 day and night are said to have been given for the calculation of years (and not for days; seasons would have been for years). The vv. 14f speak of the Judgment, and the vv. 23f seem to present some of the Ten Commandments, which have been interspersed with other Biblical and non-Biblical ordinances.[264] The instruction of v. 33, not to kill children, appears to refer to the pagan Arab practice of killing infant daughters. The v. 42 repeats the anti-pagan polemic of assigning daughters to God, but preferring sons for themselves, and the vv. 43f describe the Qur'an as a warner. The vv. 47f are a play on Ex. 34:34f (cf. II Cor. 3:13f) in which Muhammad has been exchanged for Moses, and v. 48 is similar to Is. 6:9-10. The vv. 52f give some of the Meccan arguments against the Resurrection, and the vv. 55f relate how Satan tried to instigate division among the servants of God. The v. 57 states that some prophets were made higher than others, and that David was given the Psalms. The vv. 58f relate the judgment of the polytheists, the vv. 62f summarize the narrative about Adam and Iblis, the vv. 68f describe God as both provider and punisher and the vv. 73f speak of the Judgment again. The vv. 75f appear to refer to the event of the Satanic inspiration,[265] v. 78 portrays the Meccans as trying to have Muhammad leave the land,[266] and v. 79 reports that such things occurred to the previous messengers. Two daily prayer times and a vigil are mentioned in the vv. 80f, and the vv. 84f tell of the witness of the Qur'an. The vv. 87f give the Qur'anic reply to someone who had asked about "spirit," which event is explained in some *Sira* traditions as follows: al-Nadr and `Uqba b. Abu Mu`ayt were sent to ask the Jews in Medina about Muhammad and his stories of the prophets, the Jews counseled them to ask him three things, one of which was "What is spirit?," they then asked Muhammad, who gave the belated answer that spirit was by the Lord's command (v. 87).[267] This tradition, however, is most probably the invention of later Muslim exegetes, since the other two questions the Jews supposedly recommended are rather things which Christians would have asked.[268] The question about "spirit" could have been asked by either the Meccans or the Jews, and was probably based on Muhammad saying that his mediator of revelation was a "spirit" (26:193)[269] The v. 90 describes the uniqueness of the Qur'an as not being imitable by humans or jinn, after which apparently Meccan requests for a miracle follow (vv. 91f). The v. 99 mentions the doctrine of Allah leading and leading astray, and the vv. 100f seem to refer to the Meccan rejection of the Resurrection. The vv. 103f give a very revealing narrative about Moses and Pharaoh, in which Moses is said to have been given nine signs (v. 103), as opposed to the ten plagues of the Bible (cf. Ex. 7:14f-12:33).[270] The vv. 105f not only contain the anomaly that Pharaoh tried to scare the Israelites out of the land, but it also seems clear now that the children of Israel were thought to have received Egypt as the Promised Land. Thus the notion of earlier suras, that Moses was thought to have aimed at driving the Egyptians from their own land (cf. 20:59, 66; 26:34), was fulfilled after the destruction of Pharaoh's armies. It is highly improbable that Muhammad could have misunderstood his informants to this extent, but rather likely that he modified the plots to fit his own situation with respect to the Meccans, who had evidently tried to scare him from the land (cf. v. 78). The v. 107 describes the Qur'an as being sent down piece by piece, v. 110 says that God can be called "Allah" or "al-Rahman" ("the Compassionate"), and v. 111 reiterates that God has no son or associate. In addition to the section of this sura, which seems to have the Jewish Law as its source (vv. 23f), several other verses in this sura are at least remotely similar to Bible passages, a work of Ephraem the Syrian, and the Talmud.[271]

Sura 27 gives mysterious letters, which are said to be the signs of the Qur'an and a clear Book; (v. 1) a guide and good news for the believers (v. 2). In v. 3 the believers are defined as those who pray, give alms and believe in the Resurrection. The vv. 4f speak of the destiny of unbelievers, and the vv. 7f give a brief narrative about Moses. The vv. 15f relate a narrative of David and Solomon, by which the latter is said to have learned the speech of birds (v. 16).[272] The vv. 17f continue the narrative of Solomon, in which he speaks with an ant,[273] communicates with the Queen of Sheba via a bird (vv. 20f),[274] and the "basmala" is mentioned as having been used by Solomon in a letter to the queen (v. 30). Some scholars think this was the first occurrence of the "basmala" in the Qur'an.[275] The vv. 46f give a narrative about Salih, following which a narrative of Lot appears (vv. 55f), where (in an obvious alteration by Muhammad) Lot's people (v. 57) are said to have wanted him and his family driven from the land (cf. 26:167).[276] The vv. 60f speak of God's provision and reproduce some of Muhammad's polemic against polytheists and their remarks. In v. 78 the Qur'an is said to instruct the children of Israel about things over which they are divided, and the verses following portray the (testimonies of the) Qur'an as signs from God. The vv. 85f tell of the Judgment, and Muhammad's mission is defined in the vv. 93f. The Queen of Sheba is mentioned for the first time in this sura, and Muhammad seems to have gotten his information about her by means of Jewish or Christian accounts of the legends about Solomon and the queen.[277] The v. 84 of this sura is reminiscent of Rev. 13:11. The vv. 42, 93 of this sura are thought to be missing some text.[278]

As mentioned above, some *Sira* traditions present al-Nadr and 'Uqba b. Abu Mu`ayt as having been sent to the Jewish rabbis in Medina to ask about Muhammad and his prophet stories. The Jews recommended that they ask Muhammad about three things, the answers to which only a prophet would know. They were to ask about the story of the men who disappeared in the past, the one who traveled to the bounds of the East and West, and about "spirit." Upon asking Muhammad, they were told he would give an answer to these questions the next day. After fifteen days, Gabriel is said to have come to Muhammad and revealed sura 18, which contains the stories of the Seven Sleepers and Dhu'l-Qarnayn ("the double-horned" - i.e. Alexander the Great).[279] In that both the legend of the Seven Sleepers[280] and the Qur'anic story about Alexander the Great[281] are known to have come from Christian sources, it is hardly probable to think that the Jews would have posed the questions concerning them. Moreover, Gabriel only seems to be known of in Medinan suras, and the *Sira* traditions place this event in Mecca, prior to al-Nadr's death. Nevertheless, although the occasions for these Qur'an passages may not be known for certain, it is evident that Muhammad was at least asked about "Dhu'l-Qarnayn" (cf. 18:82).

The first verses of **Qur'an 18** describe the purposes of the Book given to Muhammad, and among these is the notice that it is a warning to those who say God has a son (v. 3). The vv. 8f relate the Qur'anic version of the legend of the Seven Sleepers,[282] and al-Raqim (v. 8) is thought to have been a Syrian place name for a location in southern Palestine.[283] This Qur'anic account of the story also includes a Monotheistic message (vv. 13f) and a verse (v. 23) which is similar to the Bible verses Ja. 4:13, 15. The vv. 25f may have helped motivate some Muslims to reject the protection of polytheists, which some *Sira* traditions mention.[284] The vv. 28f contrast the destinies of sinners and those who believe, the vv. 31f give a parable of two men and gardens,[285] and v. 43 relates a water parable similar to Ps. 90:5f[286] in a passage (vv. 43f) which speaks of the temporal world and the Judgment. The vv. 48f give a summary of the Adam-Iblis narrative, and the vv. 50f describe the judgment of those who attribute associates to Allah. The vv. 52f present the Qur'an as a witness, and the vv. 59f give a long narrative about Moses, his servant and a prophet, which story seems to be based on various older legends.[287] As in the case of the Qur'anic story of the Seven Sleepers and the parable of the two men and gardens, the narrative about Dhu'l-Qarnayn (Alexander the Great) also seems to have come from Syrian sources.[288] Peculiar features of this story are the curious description of the sun setting in a "muddy spring" (v. 84),[289] and that Alexander appears as a Monotheist (vv. 94, 97f), who even speaks (v. 86) according to Qur'anic theology (cf. 18:29, 30). The vv. 99f relate of the Judgment, unbelievers, and those who believe and perform good works. Several verses of this sura are similar to Bible passages, and v. 44 is similar to Avot 6,9 (Talmud).[290]

Conclusions

The suras from this section indicate that Muslims practiced two daily prayers, and a some form of a vigil, (cf. 76:25f; 52:48f; 17:80f), which was gradually becoming another prayer time (cf. 50:38f; 20:130). The doctrine of Islamic Monotheism became more developed in this period, not only as opposed to polytheism (cf. 52:39; 37:149f; 43:15),[291] but also as opposed to Christianity (cf. 43:59, 81; 19:36, 91f; 23:93; etc.).[292] Muslim believers are described as praying, giving alms (23:1-4; 27:3); believing in the Resurrection (27:3) and performing good works (18:107). Some of the first moral requirements are prescribed for them (23:5f; 17:23f), and apostasy is referred to (43:35f, 72:16f, 24).

Characteristic for the suras of this period is the extensive use of prophet narratives in the form of punishment stories. Whereas the earlier suras of the Qur'an emphasized the theme of the Last Judgment, it is the doctrine of specific judgment which now becomes prominent with the implementation of these narratives.[293] Although Muhammad took many the of prophet's names and basic plots from the Bible, or from Jewish, Christian and Arabian lore, each prophet gradually takes on Muhammad's character, and each people assumes the traits of the pagan Meccans.[294] Frequently, the various peoples are destroyed as much for their rejection of the messenger's person, as for their disbelief in the message, whose content really only begins to be defined with Muhammad's realization of the importance of Monotheism. In turn, all of the messengers previous to Muhammad become apostles of Monotheism in the progressive narratives of the suras 37 - 71 - 44 - 20 - 26[295] and those which follow (cf. 21:25). Muhammad seems to have had little respect for chronology, and obviously altered many of the narratives to fit his own circumstances. Thus, with respect to Noah, the flood was sent because he was accused of lying (54:9f); Noah was a preacher of forgiveness (71:4, 9), who described rain as a blessing (71:10f), and is dismayed that his people have rebelled against him (71:21), scheming not to forsake the (Arabian) gods (71:22f). Moses is thought to have aimed at driving the Egyptians from the land (20:59, 66; 26:34), while Pharaoh is depicted as having wanted to drive the children of Israel from Egypt (17:105). The Egyptians are said to have been destroyed because they accused Moses and Aaron of lies (23:50), and even Lot was threatened with being driven away by his people (26:167; 27:57).[296] Again, in keeping with Muhammad's ministry, many of the prophets are presented as having preached obedience to Allah and themselves (cf. 71:3; 26:passim) and as not having asked for a wage for their services (26:passim).

Based on the amount of text and detail accorded the various narratives, Muhammad seems to have identified himself best with Noah[297] at first, and then later with Moses,[298] whereby the punishments of these narratives (a flood - drowning) and the natural hazards of living in Mecca may have initially played a significant role in his choice.[299]

Although some of the names for the Biblical characters of the Qur'anic narratives appear to have come from Jewish sources,[300] the vast majority of them seem to have been of Christian origin.[301] Conversely, the Biblical prophets who figure in the Qur'anic narratives are, for the most part, from the Old Testament.[302] The paradox of having narratives of Old Testament prophets where the prophets have "Christian" names, is not easily resolved. One Western scholar shows that the Ebionites are not only said to have accepted Abraham, Isaac, Jacob, Moses, Aaron and Joshua as prophets, but they are also said to have neglected "prophets of scripture" such as Isaiah and Jeremiah.[303] In addition to this possibility is Muhammad's apparent interest in "punishment narratives," which are much more abundant in the Old Testament than in the New.[304]

Most of the strange foreign vocabulary of this period also appears to have come from Christian sources,[305] and, in general, Muhammad seems to have understood Ethiopic better than Syriac.[306] As many scholars have pointed out, Muhammad must not have availed himself of written sources, but rather, he must have had informants who transmitted narratives to him verbally.[307] Thus, Mary the mother of Jesus is thought to have been the sister of Moses and Aaron; Isaac and Jacob (but not Ishmael) are claimed to be Abraham's sons; Satan is said to have led Adam to the Tree of Life ("eternity and kingdom"); a Samaritan is said to have countered Moses, etc. On the other hand, Muhammad appears to have corrected some earlier ambiguities as he became aware of them, e.g. the "old woman" of Qur'an 37:135 later becomes Lot's wife in 15:60.[308]

Many of the Biblical narratives of this period appear to have come from Jewish traditions and legends ultimately; some of them, however, were known to Christians and no doubt quite a few sects as well. Thus certain elements of the various Qur'anic narratives, e.g. Iblis' refusal to bow down to Adam,[309] or David's prostration in repentance,[310] are thought to have been Christian modifications of the Jewish stories. Whereas much of the material for the suras 38 and 27 seems to have come directly from Jewish sources, the suras 19, 36 and 18 reveal the heavy influence of sects which had separated from Christianity and (to a lesser degree) a dependence on Nestorian lore.[311] It is possible that the Qur'anic rejection of the Sonship and deity of Christ, played a major role in affecting the change from primarily Christian sources to Jewish ones.

The frequent allusion to "pairs" in Creation (cf. 51:49; 43:11; etc.) together with Muhammad's apparent affinity for pairs of rhyming names (which may have begun with Gog and Magog: "Yajuj wa Majuj"),[312] are somewhat reminiscent of the "doctrine of pairs" explained in the (Ebionite) Pseudo-Clementine literature.[313]

By comparison to the suras of the first period, the middle Meccan suras have
less in common with the works of Ephraem the Syrian, but more in common
with Bible passages, even though the similarity to these is often remote. As
one scholar has noted,[314] the Qur'an is more familiar with the book of Matthew
than any other book in the New Testament,[315] and it is known that of the
Gospel accounts the Ebionites used only the book of Matthew.[316] The Qur'anic
version of the Ten Commandments (17:23f) is also thought to have come from
Christians.[317]

With respect to the narratives of Arabian messengers, it is also obvious that
Muhammad modified their plots. Muhammad not only appears to have invented the names for Hud, Salih and Shu`ayb[318] to conform with the general
scheme of Qur'an 26, but in the same sura they are claimed to have been
preachers of Monotheism.

The internal evidence of the Qur'an indicates that Muhammad used a wide
variety of sources, and in the *Sira* traditions a twice-repeated remark of the
Medinan Nabtal b. Harith seems to imply the same.[319]

In the suras of the second Meccan period, the explanation of how Muhammad
received revelation changes from the pagan descriptions of the first period
(81:23f; 53:5f) to the more-developed mediation of a "spirit" (26:193; cf.
19:17, 19).[320] Moreover, the famous question concerning "spirit" (17:87) may
well have been asked Muhammad in this context.[321] Also during this period,
the first implications of Muhammad being a "prophet," as opposed to being
simply a "messenger" are made (43:5f; 25:31), and the Qur'anic doctrines
regarding "spirits" and "jinn" are not only expanded (37:10; 15: 18), but even
seem to have been applied in making the jinn responsible for the doctrine of
Christ's Sonship (72:1-15).[322]

The Meccans accused Muhammad of being possessed, a magician, a poet or a
liar (51:52; 52:29f; 37:35; 15:6; 38:3; 23:72; etc.). They charged him with
being a normal human who eats and drinks (21:3, 7f; 25:8f, 22), and blamed
him for receiving the assistance of others in composing the Qur'an (44:13;
25:5f). The Meccans rejected the doctrines of the Resurrection (44:33f; 50:2f;
38: 78f; etc.) and almsgiving (38:47); they asked for "signs" (20:130f;

17:92f), questioned why no angel had been sent to Muhammad (15:7; 25:8), and wanted to know when the Judgment should come (36:48).

Both the internal evidence of the Qur'an (25:6)[323] and the *Sira* traditions[324] show that the written composition of the Qur'an began no later than the second Meccan period. However, as will be shown later,[325] Muhammad was manifestly adverse to the idea that God's Word could be written down with human hands (cf. 2:73f), and thus the earliest copies of the Qur'an must have been simply used as memory aids.[326]

Notes:

[1] Blachère considered Qur'an 51 to be the first sura of this period; see Appendix B.

[2] Cf. Gen. 18:8.

[3] Geiger, *WMJA*, p. 127 references Bava Metzia 86,2.

[4] Although Jewish legends also present Pharaoh as thinking Moses was a "magician" (cf. Ginzberg, *Legends of the Bible*, p. 325), they say nothing of his claim that Moses was possessed. However, the accusation of possession was leveled at Muhammad by some of his countrymen; cf. Qur'an 68:2; 81:22; 51:52; 52:29; etc.

[5] Cf. *Sahih Bukhari*, vol. 6, pp. 365 f; *Sahih Muslim*, vol. 4, pp. 1467 f.

[6] Nöldeke and Schwally, *GQ*, vol. 1 , pp. 121 f; Rudolph, *Koran*, pp. 481 f, n. 2. Bell, in *Commentary*, vol. 2, p. 323, references the Ascension of Moses and also says that this Qur'an passage was meant eschatologically.

[7] *ECMD*, pp. 438 f, 556, 724.

[8] The Biblical account (Gen. 6:9f) shows that it was God who had determined to send the flood because of the wickedness of mankind, and not as a

result of Noah having been rejected by his people or having prayed for help against them. The legends of the Jews also follow the Biblical structure; cf. Ginzberg, *Legends of the Bible*, p. 71. Geiger (*WMJA*, p. 108) appears to have misinterpreted this Qur'an passage in noting a similarity between Noah being rejected by his people in 54:9-17 and Rabbinic writings which depict Noah as being mocked for building the ark.

[9] This is one of the earliest passages mentioning Lot by name, which name seems to have come from the Syriac and does not appear to have predated Muhammad in Arabic; Jeffery, *Vocabulary*, pp. 254 f. See n. 10, below.

[10] The Biblical narrations about both Lot and Pharaoh do not show that either the people of Sodom and Gomorrah, or Pharaoh's house were warned of their doom.

[11] Verse 43 also gives one of the first usages of the word "zabur," which although used here as "scripture," is thought to have come into Arabic prior to Muhammad's time as a corruption of Jewish or Christian terms for the Psalms; Jeffery, *Vocabulary*, pp. 148 f.

[12] The codex of Ibn Mas`ud; cf. Jeffery, *Materials*, p. 94.

[13] Cf. Rudolph, *Koran*, p. 477, n. 15.

[14] Blachére places Qur'an 68 directly after sura 54 in his list; cf. Appendix B.

[15] See pp. 49 f, above.

[16] Cf. Qur'an 26:223; 15:18; 72:9; etc. on the eavesdropping of spirits.

[17] Cf. Matt. 13:41f.

[18] Cf. I Pet. 1:17; Ps. 62:12; etc.

[19] Cf. Dt. 10:20.

[20] Cf. Rev. 2:11; 20:14.

[21] *SEI*, p. 490.

[22] See n. 8, above.

[23] Geiger, *WMJA*, pp. 121 f, gives Midrash Rabbah Genesis, parag. 17 as the source.

[24] See Appendix D, p. 365.

[25] See Appendix D, p. 365, and Tabari, *History*, vol. 2, pp. 82f. It is most probable that Isaac was meant in this passage, since Muhammad obviously did not know that Ishmael was also a son of Abraham until just prior to the break with the Jews in Medina (cf. Qur'an 19:50; 11:72f; 29:26; 6:84f).

[26] This word predates Muhammad in Arabic; Jeffery, *Vocabulary*, p. 276; Horovitz, *Untersuchungen*, p. 47. See Appendix D, p. 365, for a brief discussion of the sources for the name "Ishaq."

[27] The name for Aaron appears to have come from the Christian-Palestinian dialect of Syriac; Jeffery, *Vocabulary*, pp. 283 f.

[28] See Appendix D, p. 366.

[29] See Appendix D, p. 366.

[30] See Appendix D, p. 366.

[31] Bell and Watt, *Introduction*, p. 134, also show that Noah's description of rain as a blessing (71:10f), fits Muhammad's circumstances much better than Noah's.

[32] Nöldeke and Schwally, *GQ*, vol. 1, p. 124; Nöldeke, "Qur'an," p. 9. Muslim exegetes often give interesting explanations for this obvious error; see *Sahih Bukhari*, vol. 6, pp. 414 f, where Ibn ʿAbbas is reported to have said

that the Arabs later worshiped the same gods as the people did in Noah's time; cf. Ali, *Qur'an*, vol. 2, pp. 1619 f. For a description of these idols, see p. 9, n. 35.

[33] There appears to be no traditional source for such a prayer of Noah; however, Islamic hadith indicate that Muhammad prayed for his own relatives (even after their deaths) until Qur'an 9:114 was revealed; see Ibn Sa`d, *Classes*, vol. 1, 1, p. 136; Horovitz, *Untersuchungen*, p. 16.

[34] Nöldeke and Schwally, *GQ*, vol. 1, p. 124, n. 1.

[35] Guillaume, *Muhammad*, p. 136.

[36] Ibid; see also, n. 21, p. 57, above.

[37] Buhl, *Muhammad*, p. 161, (trans.): "The main contents of these prophet legends, which occupy such an important place in the Qur'an and come across as so extraordinarily tiresome by virtue of their repetition, is always the same: a prophet is sent to a people, who are unbelievers; and because they do not want to hear the divine admonition, they are struck with a destructive punishment. At the same time, generally everything these prophets say, and what the peoples reply, is a true reproduction of the discussions between him (Muhammad) and the Meccans. By contrast, the whole external apparatus (of these stories) is borrowed mainly from others: Jews and Christians." Rahman, *Islam*, p. 7: "The question of the 'historicity' of these details, i.e. of the extent of their conformity to earlier, pre-Islamic, stories and legends is in itself interesting but is beset with difficulties. Nor is the question of the 'material sources' of the Qur'anic prophetology very meaningful for assessing the real originality and import of the Prophet's message which must be located in the purpose to which these materials were turned and the service to which they were pressed. On the other hand, the Muslim need not fear and reject the historical approach to these materials." Cf. also Nöldeke, "Qur'an," pp. 8 f, and Horovitz, *Untersuchungen*, p. 9.

[38] Nöldeke, "Qur'an," p. 15.

[39] The problem of Muhammad being instructed by others, in light of his claim to have received his information as "revelations" from God is discussed below, see p. 145.

[40] Margoliouth in "Additions," *JRAS*, (1939), pp. 59 f, thinks that this term came from Ethiopic, and suggests that the phrase "Leave the sea tranquil..." could then be better rendered as: "leave the sea open..." (so that the Egyptians would enter and be drowned).

[41] Horovitz, *Untersuchungen*, pp. 102 f, shows that the name must have come from southern Arabia. Although Tubba` was referred to by early Arab poets, there seems to have been some confusion between Tubba` and Abraham among later Muslim writers. Horovitz thought that Muhammad probably did not know the original story of Tubba`, but that he simply took the name and made it conform to other punishment narratives.

[42] It is not known for certain who was meant here; Horovitz, *Untersuchungen*, pp. 94 f, cf. Qur'an 25:40; Tabari, *History*, vol. 4, p. 68. For various Islamic interpretations, see Suyuti, *El-Itkan*, vol. 2, p. 368.

[43] It is thought that Muhammad may have originally gotten this name from the works of earlier Arab poets, and then connected it with Shu`ayb (26:176f) and the Midianites (11:97f); Horovitz, *Untersuchungen*, pp. 93 f.

[44] See n. 41, above.

[45] Nöldeke and Schwally, *GQ*, vol. 1, p. 124.

[46] Cf. Qur'an 52:48f; 76:25f and the comments to these.

[47] Geiger, *WMJA*, p. 67 also references Othioth Derabbi Akiba 8,4; which comments on Is. 5:14.

[48] Guillaume, *Muhammad*, pp. 155 f. Nöldeke and Schwally, *GQ*, vol. 1, p. 125, also show that in some traditions different suras are said to have played a role in `Umar's conversion. Guillaume, *New Light*, p. 40, (Ibn Bukayr's Ibn Ishaq recension) gives Qur'an 81 in addition to sura 20.

[49] Cf. Nöldeke, "Qur'an," p. 17. This tradition is also important for research relating to the physical production of the Qur'an; see Nöldeke and Schwally, *GQ*, vol. 1, p. 46; Watt and Bell, *Introduction*, p. 37.

[50] See Appendix B, p. 351.

[51] Some Islamic sources claim that the letters "Ta Ha" here mean "O man" in Nabatean; cf. *Sahih Bukhari*, vol. 6. p. 231. This explanation is rejected by Western scholars; Nöldeke and Schwally, *GQ*, vol. 2, p. 71, n. 1.

[52] It is also possible, of course, that at least parts of this sura were composed during the boycott of the Hashimites.

[53] Cf. Qur'an 79:15.

[54] Tabari, *History*, vol. 3, shows that it was either winter (p. 48) or that it was night (pp. 50 f), whence the need for a fire.

[55] Cf. Qur'an 79:16. See Appendix D, p. 364.

[56] See n. 18, above.

[57] Cf. Ex. 3:4f.

[58] Command to perform the ritual prayer: Qur'an 17:80; etc. The coming "hour" of Judgment: Qur'an 79:42; 54:1, 46; etc. Reward according to deeds: Qur'an 37:38; etc.

[59] *Sahih Bukhari*, vol. 5, p. 47; *Sahih Muslim*, vol. 4, p. 1284; etc.

[60] This word appears to have come from the Ethiopic; Jeffery, *Vocabulary*, p. 88.

[61] Cf. Ex. 2:5 and Ginzberg, *Legends of the Bible*, p. 290.

[62] Cf. Ginzberg, *Legends of the Bible*, p. 326, where Pharaoh replies to Moses' allusion to God sending rain (cf. Qur'an 20:55) by saying that the Nile is sufficient for their agricultural needs. Muhammad for some reason overlooked this point, and even later has the crops in Egypt dependent on rain (Qur'an 12:49); see Nöldeke, "Qur'an," p. 9.

[63] Horovitz, *Untersuchungen*, p. 33.

[64] Geiger, *WMJA*, p. 157, references Midrash Yalkut 182, as a source.

[65] See Appendix D, p. 367.

[66] See Jeffery, *Vocabulary*, pp. 271, 177, respectively.

[67] See Appendix D, p. 367. The apparent aim of wishing to clear Aaron from the charge of having made the idol (cf. Ex. 32:2-4, 21-24), was realized by the addition of other characters and influences in Jewish lore; cf. also Ginzberg, *Legends of the Bible*, pp. 398 f. Muhammad probably heard of the Samaritans from another source and then placed them in this narrative.

[68] See Appendix D. p. 368.

[69] "Shaqiy(a)" appears in Qur'an 19:4, 33, 49 also.

[70] Eve is never mentioned by name in the Qur'an.

[71] Cf. Gen. 2:16f; 3:22. See also Geiger, *WMJA*, p. 100.

[72] See Jeffery, *Vocabulary*, pp. 50f (Adam), 47f (Iblis), 212f (Eden).

[73] Nöldeke and Schwally, *GQ*, vol. 1, p. 126, thought that these letters were to confirm the divine origin of this sura.

[74] Bell also considered Qur'an 26 to have been Meccan but revised in Medina (cf. *EI²*, s.v. "Kur'an," p. 418), and the mention of "book" in this predominantly Meccan sura poses a general problem for Bell's "Book" theory; cf. Watt, *Religionen*, pp. 206 f; Watt and Bell, *Introduction*, pp. 140 f.

[75] Cf. Ex. 1:8f, the slavery of the Israelites began before Moses' birth.

[76] Many of Muhammad's early followers were from the lower classes, or were slaves, as some of his informants reportedly were; Guillaume, *Muhammad*, p. 143f, 180, 193.

[77] See n. 4, above. Cf. Horovitz, *Untersuchungen*, p. 18.

[78] Geiger, *WMJA*, p. 157, gives Midrash Rabbah Exodus, parag. 5 as a reference.

[79] See n. 64, above.

[80] The vv. 81 f. describe the Resurrection, forgiveness of sins, the Judgment, Paradise and Hell in accord with earlier suras of the Qur'an. Intercession is also mentioned later (v. 100). Abraham also prays for his father, and Muhammad seems to have prayed some time for his (even dead) relatives; cf. n. 33, above; Horovitz, *Untersuchungen*, p. 18.

[81] See the comments to Qur'an 71, p. 80.

[82] See n. 76, above.

[83] Cf. Gen. 7:7.

[84] Cf. Qur'an 44:19; 11:93 and Buhl, *Muhammad*, p. 113.

[85] See Appendix D, p. 368.

[86] See Appendix D, p. 369.

[87] See Appendix D, p. 369.

[88] See Horovitz, *Untersuchungen*, p. 18, n. 1, who shows that Muhammad was apparently contrasting himself with soothsayers who expected gifts for their services, cf. Qur'an 26:40; 7:110.

[89] Cf. particularly v. 167, where Lot is threatened with being driven out of the land because of his preaching. Lot, however, was supposed to leave Sodom and Gomorrah and was driven out by angels; cf. Gen. 19:1f. On the hand, one of the apparent Meccan designs on Muhammad was to scare him from the land; cf. Qur'an 17:78.

[90] Moses was raised in Pharaoh's family (cf. v. 17), and Shu`ayb is later described as being the brother of the Midianites (Qur'an 11:85).

[91] See p. 47, above.

[92] Later "the faithful spirit" is identified as having been Gabriel; cf. Qur'an 2:91f and Rudolph, *Koran*, pp. 43f, n. 43.

[93] The learned of the Jews are said to have recognized Muhammad's mission in this passage. Cf. Nöldeke and Schwally, *GQ*, vol. 1, p. 126.

[94] Guillaume, *New Light*, p. 43. The usage of foreign vocabulary from Hebrew in all three phases of Meccan suras also indicates that Jews were present in Mecca; Speyer, in *SEI*, p. 638. See Wellhausen, *Medina*, p. 349.

[95] Guillaume, *Muhammad*, p. 117; Tabari, *History*, vol. 6, p. 88; Ibn Sa`d, *Classes*, vol. 1, 1, p. 231.

[96] Nöldeke and Schwally, *GQ*, vol. 1, p. 117.

[97] Cf. Nöldeke and Schwally, *GQ*, vol. 1, p. 127.

[98] Bell considered Qur'an 15 to have been a Meccan sura which had been revised or added to in Medina; Welch, in *EI²*, s.v. "Kur'an," p. 418. Cf. n. 74, above.

[99] See n. 4, above.

[100] Qur'an 17:61 is generally similar, in reference to which the Christian apologist al-Kindi comments; see *ECMD*, p. 439.

[101] Geiger, *WMJA*, p. 66, gives Sotah 10 and Sohar 2 as references.

[102] Cf. Qur'an 51:36 - "a house of Muslims."

[103] Cf. Qur'an 37:135 - "an old woman." See also Appendix D, p. 369, on Jewish and Syrian sources for Lot's wife having been evil.

[104] Geiger, *WMJA*, p. 58; Nöldeke and Schwally, *GQ*, vol. 1, pp. 114 f; Jeffery, *Vocabulary*, p. 257; Watt and Bell, *Introduction*, pp. 134 f. In his notes to his famous Qur'an translation, Bell (*Commentary*, vol. 1, pp. 428 f) wrote that Qur'an 15:87 would have to have been a Medinan passage if the word "mathani" really came from "mishnah" as Geiger maintained, and concerning the "mathani" he (Bell) wrote: "As Casanova points out, the phrase must refer to something other than the Qur'an; so that the Qur'an and the punishment stories must at this stage have been separate from each other." Bell thought the "Qur'an" may only have been revelations which were used for worship.

[105] E.g. *Sahih Bukhari*, vol. 6, pp. 189 f; Nöldeke, "Qur'an," p. 14.

[106] See Rudolph, *Koran*, p. 247, n. 24.

[107] For *Sira* traditions, see: Guillaume, *Muhammad*, p. 117; Tabari, *History*, vol. 6, p. 88. For Western opinions see: Nöldeke and Schwally, *GQ*, vol. 1, p. 129.

[108] Nöldeke and Schwally, *GQ*, vol. 2, p. 97.

[109] Ibid, vol. 1, p. 121; this word is most used in Qur'an 19. Watt and Bell, *Introduction*, pp. 152 f.

[110] Jeffery, *Vocabulary*, pp. 140 f.

[111] Nöldeke, "Qur'an," p. 19, 34 n. 36; *Sahih Bukhari*, vol. 8, pp. 13 f.

[112] Cf. Qur'an 25:61; Buhl, *Muhammad*, pp. 166 f. The traditions presenting Musaylima as "al-Rahman" may also have caused some misunderstanding; cf. Guillaume, *Muhammad*, pp. 134, 140.

[113] Nöldeke and Schwally, *GQ*, vol. 1, p. 121; Buhl, *Muhammad*, p. 167.

[114] Practically all of the Biblical narratives of these suras are out of chronological order.

[115] E.g. the reply to the accusation of Qur'an 44:13 is simply the threat of judgment; cf. 44:14. See also Qur'an 25:5f and 16:105f.

[116]   Jabr - Guillaume, *Muhammad*, p. 180.

> Sijill - *Sunan Abu Dawud*, vol. 2, p. 829. This was probably an exegetical assumption.

> Ibn Qammatha - Wellhausen, *Medina*, p. 55.

> Christian scribe - *Sahih Bukhari*, vol. 4, p. 523; *Sahih Muslim*, vol. 4, p. 1459.

[117] More than any others, the Noah narratives were radically altered (Qur'an 54:9f; 37:73f; 71; 26:105f) to fit Muhammad's own person; cf. *SEI*, pp. 450 f.

[118] *SEI*, p. 369; *EI²*, s.v. "Mecca,"p. 144. Meccan flood-control was one of the greater architectural concerns of the later Caliphs; ʿUmar and ʿUthman brought Christian engineers into the city to build structures to inhibit flooding; *EI²*, s.v. "Mecca," p. 147.

[119] Nöldeke and Schwally, *GQ*, vol. 1, p. 120, considered Muhammad to have identified himself the most with Moses for the entire middle Meccan period. Cf. *SEI*, pp. 414 f.

[120] Note the suspicious additions of Hud, Salih and Shu`ayb (nn. 84-86, above), none of whom are known to have predated Muhammad, and seem to be original with him; cf. Nöldeke, "Qur'an," p. 9; Horovitz, *Untersuchungen*, pp. 119, 123, 149 f; *SEI*, pp. 140, 499 f, 544.

[121] Cf. the Appendices D and E on the sources for the narratives and the origins of the Biblical names in Arabic.

[122] Idolatry appears to have been practically non-existent among the Jews in the first century AD.

[123] Tabari, *History*, vol. 6, p. 98.

[124] See references to Abraha's campaign against Mecca, p. 5. It is thought that Meccan persecution of the Muslims led Muhammad to change his earlier sympathies for the Persians to the Abyssinians; Andrae, *Ursprung*, pp. 22 f; *Mohammed*, p. 127; Buhl, *Muhammad*, p. 173, n. 116.

[125] See p. 4, above.

[126] Guillaume, *Muhammad*, p. 152. This tradition also seems to be in Yunus b. Bukayr's Ibn Ishaq recension; cf. *New Light*, p. 46.

[127] Nöldeke and Schwally, *GQ*, vol. 1, p. 130.

[128] Cf. Nöldeke, "Qur'an," pp. 21 f, for comments on Sprenger's interpretation of these letters.

[129] See n. 92, above.

[130] The sequence of these blessings is not to be overlooked. John was to have been blessed (have peace) on the days of his birth, death and resurrection, and in the same order, he was born, died and resurrected (in the afterlife). Jesus was also to be blessed (have peace) on the days of his birth, death and resurrection, which indicates that at the time this passage was composed, Muhammad may have believed Jesus had been crucified and died (cf. Qur'an 3:48).

[131] Cf. The Gospel of the Book of Mary; Appendix D, p. 370.

[132] Cf. Nöldeke and Schwally, *GQ*, vol. 1, pp. 8 f.

[133] Cf. The Protevangelion; Appendix D, p. 370.

[134] See n. 92, above.

[135] Cf. The Gospel of Pseudo-Matthew, where "Jesus" is in the place of "Mary's Lord"; Appendix D, p. 370.

[136] Cf. Pseudo-Matthew; Appendix D, p. 371.

[137] Later Christian polemicists had a field day with this discrepancy; *ECMD*, pp. x, 83, 139. See Appendix D, p. 371.

[138] Muslim commentators have been quite industrious in their search for possible explanations for these passages; *Sahih Muslim*, vol. 3, p. 1169; Tabari, *History*, vol. 4, p. 120; Abdelmajid Charfi, "Christianity in the Qur'an Commentary of Tabari," *Islamochristiana*, 6 (1980), pp. 111-113, Suyuti, *El-Itkan*, vol. 2, pp. 366, 503.

[139] Cf. The Arabic Infancy Gospel; Appendix D, p. 371.

[140] See n. 130, above.

[141] Horovitz, *Untersuchungen*, p. 129 f; Jeffery, *Vocabulary*, pp. 265 f; Andrae, *Mohammed*, p. 25.

[142] See Appendix D, p. 371.

[143] *SEI*, p. 640; see Appendix D, p. 372.

[144] See Bell, *Origins*, p. 129, who made this observation with respect to Qur'an 6:84f; cf. Horovitz, *Untersuchungen*, p. 91.

[145] *SEI*, pp. 178 f.

[146] For sources, see Appendix D, p. 372.

[147] Jeffery, *Vocabulary*, pp. 151 (Zacharias), 290 (John), 262 (Mary), 291 (Jacob), 63 (Ishmael), 51 (Idris).

[148] Although there is some evidence for pre-Islamic usage of the name in Arabic, it does not mean that this name was necessarily associated with John the Baptist; the Qur'an never mentions the apostle John.

[149] Welch, in *EI²*, s.v. "Muhammad," p. 365, cites Watt as thinking that some Muslims may have gone to Abyssinia to compete against Meccan merchants. Watt (*Muhammad*, pp. 65 f), in parting with Muslim tradition and the general opinion of Western scholars of Islam, maintains that the emigration to Abyssinia took place after and resultant to the event of the "Satanic verses."

[150] Ibn Sa`d, *Classes*, vol. 1, 1, pp. 235 f, 239 f.

[151] Buhl, *Muhammad*, p. 172, n. 115; *EI²*, s.v. "Muhammad," p. 365.

[152] Tabari, *History*, vol. 6, p. 101.

[153] Guillaume, *Muhammad*, pp. 146 f; *New Light*, pp. 38, 47 f; Ibn Sa`d, *Classes*, vol. 1, 1, pp. 235 f; Tabari, *History*, vol. 6, pp. 98 f.

[154] Cf. Tabari, *History*, vol. 6, pp. 100, 104. According to Ibn Sa`d's collection of traditions (*Classes*, vol. 1, 1, pp. 236, 238), Ibn Mas`ud is said to have gone to Abyssinia twice.

[155] Yunus b. Bukayr's Ibn Ishaq recension (*New Light*, pp. 34 f) also presents `Umar as having been sent with `Abdullah b. Abu Rabi`a and `Amr b. al-`As.

[156] Guillaume, *Muhammad*, pp. 150 f.

[157] Ibid. pp. 155 f; see n. 48, above.

[158] Ibid. p. 155.

[159] Ibid. pp. 157 f.

[160] Cf. *SEI*, p. 260.

[161] This boycott, whose regulations were allegedly written in a document, is said to have prevented intermarriage and trade with the Hashimites and the Muttalib; Guillaume, *Muhammad*, pp. 159 f; Ibn Sa`d, *Classes*,   vol. 1, 1, pp. 240 f; Tabari, *History*, vol. 6, pp. 105 f.

[162] Ibn Sa`d, *Classes*, vol. 1, 1, p. 241.

[163] Buhl, *Muhammad*, pp. 176 f.

[164] Ibid. p. 176.

[165] An alleged murder attempt on Muhammad: Ibn Sa`d, *Classes*, vol. 1, 1, p. 241; `Ali worked for a Jew in Mecca: Guillaume, *New Light*, p. 43 (cf. Andrae, *Mohammed*, pp. 139 f, where a version of this tradition is thought to have been set in Medina rather than Mecca); Attempts were made to smuggle food: Tabari, *History*, vol. 6, p. 106.

[166] Guillaume, *Muhammad*, pp. 161 f.

[167] Guillaume, *New Light*, pp. 38 f; Ibn Sa`d, *Classes*, vol. 1, 1, pp. 237 f; Tabari, *History*, vol. 6, pp. 107 f.

[168] "mosque" - (Tabari, *History*, vol. 6, p. 109); "large gathering"(Ibid. p. 111); "assembly near the Ka`ba" - (Ibn Sa`d, *Classes*, vol. 1, 1, p. 237; location not described in Guillaume, *New Light*, pp. 38 f. The objection to the use of the word "mosque" (مسجد = "place of prayer") in this tradition as being incompatible with the Meccan setting (cf. *EI²*, s.v. "Kur'an," p. 404) is not to be seen as serious, since the Ka`ba seems to have been a place of prayer for Meccan Muslims at the time, and this term (which is only found in one of

Tabari's traditions) was also used in other hadith about Mecca before the hijra; see Guillaume, *New Light*, p. 43 *Muhammad*, pp. 132, 161, etc.; cf. also Tabari, *History*, vol. 6, p. 109, n. 173.

[169] Although most *Sira* traditions present this sura as having been revealed to Muhammad on this occasion; other passages of the Qur'an, which appear to be related to this event (17:75; 28:87; cf. Ibn Sa`d, *Classes*, vol. 1, 1, pp. 237 f; Buhl, *Muhammad*, p. 178), would seem to indicate that this sura had already been composed and that Muhammad in effect was adding to its text.

[170] See Ibn Sa`d, *Classes*, vol. 1, 1, p. 237; one version of this tradition in Tabari, *History*, vol. 6, p. 111; and cf. Buhl, *Muhammad*, p. 178.

[171] Guillaume, *New Light*, pp. 38 f; Ibn Sa`d, *Classes*, vol. 1, 1, p. 238; Tabari, *History*, vol. 6, pp. 109, 112.

[172] Some Western scholars also see a discrepancy in that this verse is found in a Medinan sura and think the entire tradition of this event may have been invented as a "proof-text" for Qur'an 22:52; cf. *EI²*, s.v. "Kur'an,"   p. 404. However, *Sira* traditions frequently present later Qur'an passages as having been revealed much earlier. Qur'an 15:94 and 26:214 are often associated with Muhammad's public proclamation of Islam, whereas the much earlier passages 102:2f and 92:4 indicate that Muhammad had already begun to preach to others. Qur'an 36:78 (Guillaume, *Muhammad*, pp. 143, 165) is cited in reference to the early Meccan rejection of the doctrine of Resurrection, but the earlier passages 79:10-14 and 75:3f already substantiate this. In the case of the verses of Satanic inspiration, the earlier Qur'an 16:103f (cf. Buhl, *Muhammad*, p. 179) could also have been employed instead of 22:52.

[173] It is obvious that Ibn Hisham left these traditions out of his work, for, as Guillaume points out (*New Light*, p. 38), Ibn Hisham does not describe how the Meccans abruptly became Muslims; cf. Guillaume, *Muhammad*, p. 167. Other Muslim scholars have also noticed this deficiency and tried to improvise, see remarks on Ibn Kathir in *New Light*, p. 39. A modern Turkish translation of Ibn Hisham (*Islam Tarihi*, vol. 2, pp. 5 f, n. 1) is also at a loss to

explain the Meccans' conversion, and so gives Suhayli's description of the Satanic inspiration as a footnote.

[174] Cf. Nöldeke and Schwally, *GQ*, vol. 1, pp. 100 f; *EI²*, s.v. "Kur'an," p. 404.

[175] In *EI²*, s.v. "Muhammad," p. 365, Welch presumes that the tradition of the Satanic inspiration was not found in Ibn Ishaq, and appears to have based this presumption on that fact that the account is not given in Ibn Hisham. However, Ibn Hisham wrote that he had suppressed materials from Ibn Ishaq which were "disgraceful to discuss" and which "would distress certain people"; Guillaume, *Muhammad*, p. 691, n. 10. Moreover, it is certain that Ibn Hisham edited out traditions relating how the Meccans all of the sudden became Muslims; see n. 173, above. Traditions of the Satanic inspiration from Ibn Ishaq can not only be found in Tabari, (*History*, vol. 6, pp. 108 f), but also in Ibn Bukayr's Ibn Ishaq recension (Guillaume, *New Light*, pp. 38 f). Additionally, Suhayli states that these traditions were found in *both* Ibn Ishaq *and* the rival collection of Musa b. `Uqba (*New Light*, p. 39). Ibn Sa`d (*Classes*, vol. 1, 1, pp. 236 f) gives a version of the tradition independent from Ibn Ishaq, and Tabari also gives a second account (*History*, vol. 6, pp. 111 f), which comes from neither Ibn Ishaq nor Ibn Sa`d's sources.

[176] Some Western scholars hold that the sufferings of the Hashimites have been exaggerated in the tradition accounts; Watt, *Muhammad*, p. 77; in Tabari, *History*, vol. 6, p. xliv; *SEI*, p. 396; *EI²*, s.v. "Muhammad," p. 365.

[177] Some of the Quraysh pitied their countrymen and in effect ended the boycott; Guillaume, *Muhammad*, pp. 172 f; *New Light*, p. 35; Tabari, *History*, vol. 6, pp. 112 f.

[178] The document is said to have been eaten by: "worms" - Guillaume, *Muhammad*, p. 173; "white ants" - Ibn Sa`d, *Classes*, vol. 1, 1, p. 242; "termites" - Tabari, *History*, vol. 6, p. 114.

[179] Although failing to notice any relationship between the event of the Satanic inspiration and the end of the boycott, Buhl states that `Umar may have

contributed to Muhammad's recanting the verses, but sees no reason for Muhammad's followers to have compelled this retraction; *Muhammad,* p. 179, n. 129. *Sira* traditions depict the returning emigrants as having learned of Muhammad's recantation shortly before reaching Mecca, and that they then had to arrange for protectors prior to their entering the city; Guillaume, *Muhammad,* pp. 167 f; Ibn Sa`d, *Classes,* vol. 1, 1, p. 238.

[180] See Appendix D, p. 372.

[181] Tabari, *History,* vol. 3, p. 145.

[182] See Appendix D, p. 372.

[183] Speyer, *Erzählungen,* pp. 383 f; see Appendix D, p. 373.

[184] See Appendix D, p. 373.

[185] See Appendix D, p. 373.

[186] It is generally not known who was meant, and Muslim commentators have made a number of proposals; see p. 374, below, and *SEI,* pp. 76 f.

[187] Based on the text of Qur'an 6:84f, Bell (*Origins,* p. 129) and Horovitz (*Untersuchungen,* pp. 91 f) show that Muhammad only gradually came to realize who Ishmael was. However, this defect is already found in 38:45, 48, and 21:72, 85, both which probably predate the 6:84f passage.

[188] Nöldeke and Schwally, *GQ,* vol. 1, p. 131.

[189] See n. 88, above.

[190] Jeffery, *Vocabulary,* Job - pp. 73 f; David - pp. 127 f; Solomon - p. 178.

[191] Ibid. pp. 268 f. The term means "word" in Syriac, but Muhammad uses it more in the sense of "way." This expression is used figuratively for "religion" in both languages.

[192] See Appendix F, p. 410.

[193] Guillaume, *Muhammad*, p. 192.

[194] See Appendix D, p. 374.

[195] Nöldeke and Schwally, *GQ*, vol. 1, p. 131.

[196] Cf. *Sahih Bukhari*, vol. 6, pp. 309 f, where as an explanation of Qur'an 36:38, Muhammad is reported to have said that the sun sets under God's throne.

[197] Geiger, *WMJA*, p. 72, references Hagigah 16 and Taanit 11; cf. Qur'an 41:18f.

[198] Guillaume, *Muhammad*, p. 222; Ibn Sa`d, *Classes* vol. 1, 1, pp. 264 f.

[199] See p. 88, above, for a discussion of this polemical device.

[200] Cf. the modification of this in a *Sira* tradition, where this was revealed concerning "Jesus" being worshiped with God; Guillaume, *Muhammad*, pp. 163 f.

[201] Nöldeke and Schwally, *GQ*, vol. 1, p. 132.

[202] Horovitz, *Untersuchungen*, pp. 128 f; Jeffery, *Vocabulary*, pp. 218 f.

[203] Cf. Irenaeus, "Against Heresies," chs. 25 (parag. 6) and 26, *Ante-Nicene Fathers*, vol. 1, p. 351. The Gnostics, as practically all Christians also, denied that Jesus was physically the Son of God. In parting with Christianity, however, some Gnostics appear to have rejected the virgin birth; cf. Speyer, *Erzählungen*, p. 312, who references Irenaeus ("Against Heresies," ch. 25, parag. 1, *Ante-Nicene Fathers*, vol. 1, p. 350.)

[204] Cf. Augustine, "Reply to Faustus the Manichaean," book 23, *Nicene and Post-Nicene Fathers*, vol. 4, pp. 313 f.

[205] Andrae, *Ursprung*, p. 203, poses this question, without, however, really answering it. Ahrens, "Christliches," *ZDMG*, 84 (1930), pp. 188 f, did not think that Muhammad's Christology presented an unsolvable problem, but he also did not explain how this could have been worked out. Instead, Ahrens maintains that Muhammad's paying homage to the Ka`ba was the real reason for him not becoming a Christian. This nonetheless disagrees with the witness of pre-Islamic Christian poets, who also respected the Ka`ba; Andrae, *Mohammed*, p. 25. Some Arab Christians are even said to have participated in the pilgrimage to the Ka`ba; Buhl, *Muhammad*, p. 66; Andrae, *Ursprung*, p. 39; *Mohammed*, p. 25.

[206] Some jinn are said to have heard Muhammad praying, and as a result are said to have believed the Qur'an. Guillaume, *Muhammad*, pp. 192 f; Ibn Sa`d, *Classes*, vol. 1, 1, pp. 243 f; Tabari, *History*, vol. 6, pp. 117 f; *Sahih Bukhari*, vol. 6, pp. 415 f; *Sahih Muslim*, vol. 1, pp. 243 f; Nöldeke and Schwally, *GQ*, vol. 1, pp. 132 f.

[207] Guillaume, *Muhammad*, pp. 527 f; Ibn Sa`d, *Classes*, vol. 1, 1, p. 240; Tabari, *History*, vol. 9, p. 133.

[208] Umm Habiba, the former wife of `Ubaydullah, and Umm Salama are said to have seen pictures in an Abyssinian church named "Mariya": *Sahih Bukhari*, vol. 1, p. 251; vol. 2, p. 237; vol. 5, p. 136; *Sahih Muslim*, vol. 1, p. 268. There was a church of St. Mary at Axum; see *EI²*, s.v. "al- Nadjashi," p. 863 (which cites Muir's *Life of Mohammed*, p. 490).

[209] Cf. Andrae, *Mohammed*, p. 48.

[210] Irenaeus, "Against Heresies," book 5, ch. 1, *Ante-Nicene Fathers*, vol. 1, p. 527.

[211] Augustine, "Reply to Faustus the Manichaean," book 11, part 3, *Nicene and Post-Nicene Fathers*, vol. 4, p. 179.

[212] The Gospel of the Book of Mary as well as the Infancy Gospel are thought to have been used by Gnostics; cf. *Lost Books*, pp. 17, 38. See Appendix D, pp. 370 f.

[213] The book of The Acts of Andrew and Matthias was said to have been used by Gnostics, Manichaeans and others; cf. *Ante-Nicene Fathers*, vol. 8, pp. 356. See Appendix D, p. 374.

[214] See p. 51, above.

[215] Ibn Hisham in Guillaume, *Muhammad*, pp. 167 f.

[216] Ibn Sa`d, *Classes*, vol. 1, 1, p. 238.

[217] Ibn Sa`d, *Classes*, vol. 1, 1, pp. 136 f.

[218] Ibid., p. 139.

[219] Guillaume, *Muhammad*, p. 191; Ibn Sa`d, *Classes*, vol. 1, 1, p. 243; Tabari, *History*, vol. 6, p. 115.

[220] Buhl, *Muhammad*, p. 198; Watt, *Muhammad*, p. 79; Tabari, *History*, vol. 7, p. 8.

[221] Ibn Sa`d, *Classes*, vol. 1, 1, p. 244.

[222] Guillaume, *Muhammad*, p. 191 and Tabari, *History*, vol. 6, p. 115, report Muhammad to have said that the Quraysh never treated him poorly until after the death of Abu Talib. Watt and Bell, *Introduction*, p. 11, maintain that the composition of Qur'an 111 was probably a result of Abu Talib withdrawing his support and protection of Muhammad. An interesting comment of Zayd b. Haritha given in Ibn Sa`d, *Classes*, vol. 1, 1, p. 245, implies that Muhammad had been banished by the Quraysh; cf. Qur'an 17:78.

[223] Guillaume, *Muhammad*, pp. 192 f; Ibn Sa`d, *Classes*, vol. 1, 1, pp. 243 f; Tabari, *History*, vol. 6, p. 115.

[224] Guillaume, *Muhammad*, p. 193 and Tabari, *History*, vol. 6, p. 117, relate how Muhammad met a Christian slave from Nineveh named `Addas

during a visit to some of the leaders of al-Ta'if. Ibn Sa`d, *Classes*, vol. 1, 1, pp. 244 reports that some young men of al-Ta'if threw stones at Muhammad.

[225] Tabari, *History*, vol. 6, pp. 117 f, not only reports that they were seven in number, but also gives their names.

[226] Guillaume, *Muhammad*, pp. 193 f; Ibn Sa`d, *Classes*, vol. 1, 1, p. 245; Tabari, *History*, vol. 6, p. 118. Ibn Sa`d reports that the jinn heard Muhammad reciting sura 72!

[227] Ibn Sa`d, *Classes*, vol. 1, 1, p. 245; Tabari, *History*, vol. 6, p. 119.

[228] Geiger, *WMJA*, p. 63 references Hagiga 12,2.

[229] `Abdullah b. Abu Sarh was said to have been the scribe. Later Muslim Qur'an commentators, who obviously had problems with this tradition, often mention this event in conjunction with Qur'an 6:93, which rhetorically asks who would be more sinful than one who invented a lie against God. See Nöldeke and Schwally, *GQ*, vol. 1, p. 46, n. 4, for references to Islamic sources. Cf. Watt and Bell, *Introduction*, pp. 37 f.

[230] See p. 64, n. 82. It is also possible that Muhammad confused Mount Sinai with another mountain; e.g. the Mount of Olives; cf. Rudolph, *Koran*, p. 315, n. 5; p. 563, n. 2.

[231] Geiger, *WMJA*, p. 108, shows that the idea of a "hot water" flood is Jewish, and references Rosh Hashanah 16,2; Sanhedrin 108. Cf. Qur'an 11:42.

[232] See n. 229, above.

[233] The word seems to come from the Ethiopic word for "light" or "illumination"; Jeffery, *Vocabulary*, pp. 77 f.

[234] Nöldeke and Schwally, *GQ*, vol. 1, p. 133.

[235] The Meccans obviously rejected the doctrine of the Resurrection, and since the Bible shows that Jesus was worshiped as God and raised the dead, this question could hardly have been asked Christians. In noticing the problems incurred regarding Christians in this question, many modern Muslims contend that Jesus raised the dead only with God's permission; cf. Ali, *Qur'an*, vol. 2, p. 826, n. 2681.

[236] *ECMD*, p. 721, n. 10.

[237] See the comments on the suras 37, 71, 44, 20 and 26 on p. 106, above.

[238] The exact English equivalent for "furqan" is disputed, since Muhammad seems to have borrowed the word from Syriac and misunderstood its meaning; Nöldeke, "Qur'an," p. 14; Bell, *Origins*, p. 119; Jeffery, *Vocabulary*, pp. 225 f; Watt and Bell, Introduction, p. 139.

[239] See Appendix D, p. 372.

[240] See Appendix D, p. 374.

[241] See Appendix D, p. 372.

[242] See Appendix D, p. 375.

[243] See Appendix D, p. 373.

[244] See n. 187, above.

[245] See Appendix D, p. 375.

[246] Jeffery, *Vocabulary*, pp. 288 f.

[247] Ibid., p. 148. This word was known to Arabs prior to the advent of Islam. See n. 11, above.

[248] See n. 238, above.

[249] Jeffery, *Vocabulary*, pp. 163 f. A tradition in *Sunan Abu Dawud* (vol. 2, p. 829) claims that Muhammad had a secretary by this name, who was thought to be Abyssinian, however, this appears to be an innovation of later traditionists; see n. 116, above.

[250] Bell, parting with practically all other Western Qur'an scholars, considered these verses to have been Medinan; Watt and Bell, *Introduction*, p. 17, n. 1. Bell does not give the reason for this decision even in his notes (cf. *Commentary*, vol. 2, p. 2), but it seems it was based simply on the idea of his own theories: i.e. "writing" has to do with the production of the "Book," which period (according to Bell) began in Medina.

[251] See n. 116, above, for the names of some who are said to have been Muhammad's informants.

[252] This verb is also translated by some as causative; cf. Watt and Bell, *Introduction*, p. 36.

[253] In modern times, Muslims have invented many stories about the sea explorer Captain Cousteau accepting Islam after allegedly noting that salt and fresh water do not mix. The popular Islamic book by Bucaille (*The Bible, the Qur'an and Science*, pp. 179 f) also considers this to be a miracle in confirmation of this verse. Cousteau's denial of becoming a Muslim was published in the Turkish magazine *Gökyüzü* (March, 1985, p. 12), and Campbell (*The Qur'an and the Bible*, pp. 165 f) counters the Muslim claim, and notes, of course, that salt and fresh water do combine in the ocean.

[254] See n. 88, above.

[255] See Appendix F, p. 411, for sources.

[256] Guillaume, *Muhammad*, p. 179; the origin of these Christians is doubted, and Ibn Ishaq's personal reservations about this tradition are evident in the phrases "God knows"; cf. Ibid., p. xix.

[257] Or rather to Heaven; see *SEI*, p. 183.

[258] Guillaume, *Muhammad*, pp. 181 f; *New Light*, p. 58; Ibn Sa`d, *Classes*, vol. 1, 1, pp. 246 f; Tabari, *History*, vol. 6, pp. 78 f; *Sahih Bukhari*, vol. 1, p. 211; vol. 4, p. 287; vol. 5, p. 143; vol. 6, p. 196; vol. 7, p. 338; vol. 9, p. 449; cf. `Ali Tabari, in *ECMD*, pp. 591 f; Nöldeke and Schwally, *GQ*, vol. 1, pp. 134 f. The accounts in Ibn Sa`d differ considerably from the others. Originally, Muhammad's night journey to Jerusalem and his ascension into Heaven were related as having been two separate events. Later Islamic traditionists combined the two stories into one; cf. Welch in *EI²*, s.v. "Muhammad," p. 366; *Sahih Muslim*, vol. 1, pp. 100, 110.

[259] This name seems to come from the same root as the Arabic for "lightning"; *SEI*, p. 65.

[260] Nöldeke and Schwally, *GQ*, vol. 1, pp. 134 f, n. 7.

[261] *Ante-Nicene Fathers*, vol. 8, pp. 580 f; Nöldeke and Schwally, *GQ*, vol. 1, p. 136, n. 2.

[262] *SEI*, p. 183.

[263] Speyer, *Erzählungen*, pp. 322 f, sees a similarity between these verses and Homily 19 of Aphrahat or in *Opp.*, I, 440 A sqq. (Ephraem).

[264] Rudolph, *Koran*, pp. 262 f, n. 10; Ahrens, "Christliches," *ZDMG*, 84 (1930), pp. 177 f. Of the Ten Commandments I, II, V (all in 17:23), VI (17:35) and VII (17:34) or variations are given; cf. Ex. 20:1f and Dt. 5:6f. For other Biblical references, see Appendix F, p. 411.

[265] This passage is also mentioned in some of the *Sira* traditions on the Satanic inspiration; Ibn Sa`d, *Classes*, vol. 1, 1, p. 238; Tabari, *History*, vol. 6, p. 112; Cf. Nöldeke and Schwally, *GQ*, vol. 1, p. 139.

[266] It is improbable that this verse refers to the Jews of Medina, as some Muslims claim; Nöldeke and Schwally, *GQ*, vol. 1, p. 138.

[267] Guillaume, *Muhammad*, pp. 136 f. Some accounts given in canonical traditions place this event in Medina instead of Mecca, and have the Jews ask

Muhammad directly; *Sahih Bukhari*, vol. 1, p. 94; vol. 6, p. 207; vol. 9, pp. 295, 412; *Sahih Muslim*, vol. 4, p. 1464.

[268] See the comments on Qur'an 18:8f, 82f, below.

[269] See nn. 91 and 92, above. In the *Sira* tradition found in Guillaume, *Muhammad*, p. 255, Jewish rabbis ask Muhammad about "the spirit," and Muhammad answers that "the spirit" is Gabriel, who comes to him.

[270] See Appendix D, p. 375.

[271] See Appendix F, p. 411.

[272] See Appendix D, p. 375.

[273] See Appendix D, p. 376.

[274] See Appendix D, p. 376.

[275] Nöldeke and Schwally, *GQ*, vol. 1, pp. 116 f; cf. Watt and Bell, *Introduction*, p. 60.

[276] Cf. the comments on Qur'an 17:105f, above.

[277] Jeffery, *Vocabulary*, p. 160.

[278] Nöldeke and Schwally, *GQ*, vol. 1, p. 140.

[279] Guillaume, *Muhammad*, pp. 136 f.

[280] See Appendix D, p. 376.

[281] See Appendix D, p. 377.

[282] See Appendix D, p. 376.

[283] Jeffery, *Vocabulary*, pp. 143 f.

[284] Guillaume, *Muhammad*, pp. 169 f.

[285] See Appendix D, p. 377.

[286] See Appendix D, p. 377.

[287] See Appendix D, p. 377.

[288] See Appendix D, p. 377.

[289] Some pre-`Uthmanic Qur'an codices seem to have had "hot" instead of "muddy" (cf. Jeffery, *Materials*, p. 57; *Sunan Abu Dawud*, vol. 3, p. 1116).

[290] See Appendix F, pp. 411 f.

[291] See p. 88, above.

[292] See pp. 94 f, above.

[293] See p. 86, above.

[294] See pp. 86 f, above.

[295] See p. 86, above.

[296] See Appendix E, for other Qur'anic and Islamic descriptions of the prophets.

[297] See n. 117, above.

[298] Moses is at least mentioned in each of the last suras of this period, and is often described as having received the "Book" (37:117; 23:51; 25:37; 17:2); cf. Bell, *Origins*, p. 120. Of special interest is also the passage 17:47f, where Muhammad has been exchanged with the person of Moses; cf. Ex. 34:34; II Cor. 3:13f. Muhammad may have chosen to later identify himself more with Moses in order to be accepted as a prophet by the Jews.

[299] See p. 87, above.

[300] The Qur'anic names for the Samaritan, Adam and David seem to have come from Hebrew, and it is also possible that the names for Jacob and the Queen of Sheba came from Jewish sources; cf. Appendix E, below. Of these names, only the name for the Samaritan does not appear to have predated Muhammad.

[301] The Qur'anic names for Lot, Aaron, Elias, Baal, Isaac, Jonah, Iblis, Zacharias, John, Mary, Jesus (possibly), Ishmael, Idris, Israel, Solomon, Job, Gog and Magog appear to have come from Christian sources; cf. Appendix E. Qur'anic names which do not appear to have predated Muhammad are: Lot, Iblis, Zacharias, Mary, Jesus, Idris, Gog and Magog.

[302] Exceptions being, of course, the narratives of the suras 19, 36 and 18.

[303] Andrae, *Mohammed*, p. 102, cites Epiphanius, *Haer.* 30, 18. In the Pseudo-Clementine literature, (*Recognitions of Clement*, book 2, ch. 47, *Ante-Nicene Fathers*, vol. 8, p. 110) the prophets Adam, Enoch, Noah, Abraham, Isaac, Jacob, Moses and Jesus are mentioned by Simon.

[304] See p. 87, above.

[305] The word for "gourd" (n. 30) was possibly from Hebrew, the words for "manna" (n. 66), "quail" (n. 66), furqan (n. 238), milla (n. 191), al-Raqim (n. 282), seem to have come from Syriac, along with sijill (n. 249) which was at least influenced by the Greek; the words rahwun (n. 40), tabut (n. 60) and burhan (n. 233) appear to have come from Ethiopic.

[306] Generally speaking, Ethiopic terms found in the text of the Qur'an are used more in accordance with their original meanings than vocabulary borrowed from Syriac; cf. Appendix C, pp. 357 f. There is some evidence that Muhammad may have known at least some Ethiopic; Jeffery, *Vocabulary*, p. 11; *EI²*, s.v. "al-Nadjashi," p. 862.

[307] Nöldeke, "Qur'an," p. 9; Buhl, *Muhammad*, p. 161; Watt, *Muhammad*, p. 40; etc. Many Islamic traditions also give the names of informants (see n. 116, above) and only seldom mention any books as having been brought to Muhammad.

[308] Muhammad also later learned that Ishmael was Abraham's son; cf. the references in n. 144, above.

[309] See Appendix D, p. 368.

[310] See Appendix D, p. 372.

[311] Andrae, *Ursprung*, pp. 158 f, 197, shows that the Nestorian theologian Babai the Great (c. 580 AD) used the legend of the "Seven Sleepers" to explain the doctrine of "death-sleep," and that the Qur'anic Alexander legend probably came from Nestorian stories.

[312] Later Qur'anic "pairs" are: Harun - Qarun, Harut - Marut, Talut - Jalut; Horovitz, *Untersuchungen*, p. 81. Some scholars also think that "Musa - `Isa" may have also been one of these "pairs"; see Jeffery, *Vocabulary*, p. 218 for other references.

[313] Recognitions of Clement, book 3, chs. 59, 61 (*Ante-Nicene Fathers*, vol. 8, pp. 129, 130; *The Clementine Homilies*, hom. 2, chs. 15 sqq, 33 (*Ante-Nicene Fathers*, vol. 8, pp. 231 f, 235.

[314] Ahrens, "Christliches," *ZDMG*, 84 (1930), p. 172.

[315] Cf. Appendix F, pp. 410 f.

[316] Irenaeus (Against Heresies, book 1, ch. 26, 2): "They (the Ebionites) use the Gospel according to Matthew only, and repudiate the Apostle Paul, maintaining that he was an apostate from the law." (*Ante-Nicene Fathers*, vol. 1, p. 352. Ahrens, "Christliches," *ZDMG*, 84 (1930), p. 172, cites Eusebius (*Ecclesiastical History*, 5, 10, 3) as reporting that Pantaenus (c. 205 AD) found a people using a Hebrew Gospel of Matthew in "India," which location Ahrens interprets as having been in southern Arabia.

[317] Cf. n. 264, above. Ahrens, "Christliches," *ZDMG*, 84 (1930), pp. 177 f, thinks that Muhammad would have hardly neglected to mention the commandment of the Sabbath had he received his information from the Jews.

[318] See n. 120, above. Horovitz, *Untersuchungen*, p. 79.

[319] Guillaume, *Muhammad*, pp. 243, 622. These comments were reportedly made after the Hijra.

[320] See also n. 92, above.

[321] See n. 267, above.

[322] See pp. 95 f, above.

[323] Nöldeke and Schwally, *GQ*, vol. 1, p. 134; Watt and Bell, *Introduction*, pp. 36, 105 f.

[324] See n. 48, above; Watt and Bell, *Introduction*, p. 37.

[325] See p. 189, below.

[326] Watt and Bell, *Introduction*, pp. 105 f; 136.

Muhammad
The Hijra

In the aftermath of Abu Talib's death, Muhammad's position in Mecca became more precarious. Ever since his journey to al-Ta'if, Muhammad's desire to find new protection and support had become manifest, and *Sira* traditions also report that Muhammad had begun preaching to the various Arab tribes who came to Mecca for the annual pilgrimage.[1] Although Muhammad's message was rejected by almost all of the tribes, the first to show an interest in Islam was a young man from Medina,[2] who had come with a delegation to seek the aid of the Quraysh against another Medinan tribe known as the Khazraj.[3]

Generally, the suras of this last Meccan period are refinements of those of the previous period.[4] Not only are some new narratives added and some old ones expanded, but also a more dominant Jewish influence is noticeable, as Muhammad apparently began to identify himself more with them. Indeed, at first glance, Muhammad's understanding of Monotheism seemed to have much in common with Jewish theology, and because of this, he may have actively sought contact with them.

Qur'an 32 begins with mysterious letters, and v. 1 affirms that the "Book" has been sent by the Lord of the worlds. The v. 2 confronts the accusation that Muhammad composed the Qur'an without being divinely inspired, the vv. 3f present God as Creator, who made the heaven and earth in six days, and v. 4 is similar to Ps. 90:4. In the vv. 10f the Judgment of unbelievers and believers is described, v. 23 states that Moses was given the Book, and the disjointed imperative in this verse, in which Muhammad is commanded not to doubt, is thought to have been an interpolation.[5] The v. 25 speaks of the Judgment of those who are in disagreement regarding God's signs, v. 26 refers to the examples of past generations and v. 27 alludes to God's provision in Creation. The vv. 28f seem to present the Meccans question about when the Judgment should come, and Muhammad is commanded to reply that it will essentially be too late for them on the "Day of Decision"; Muhammad is then told to turn away from unbelievers.

Sura 41 also begins with mysterious letters, and states that the Qur'an has been sent by the Compassionate, in Arabic, as a bringer of good news and a warning (vv. 1f). The v. 4 is remotely reminiscent of II Cor. 3:13f. In the vv. 5f Muhammad is presented as being a man, to whom Monotheism was revealed, a woe is then expressed to pagans who do not give alms or believe in the Resurrection, and a good reward is promised those who believe and do good. Contrary to other Qur'anic passages, the vv. 8f describe the Creation of heaven and earth as having lasted 8 days, which inconsistency has also been noticed by Christian polemicists.[6] The vv. 12f speak of the thunder against the `Ad and the Thamud and then summarize these narratives. The vv. 18f relate that the various human body parts will testify at the Judgment, and this notion seems to be based on Jewish sources.[7] The vv. 25f give the remarks of unbelievers, and the vv. 30f tell about the future state of believers. In the vv. 34f Muhammad is counseled on how to deal with evil, the vv. 37f refer to the witness of Creation, and the vv. 41f describe the Qur'an as also being a sign. The v. 45 reiterates that Moses was given the Book, the vv. 47f speak of the Judgment and the vv. 52f relate the consequences of those who reject God's signs. 41:46 is remotely similar to Prov. 9:12. A *Sira* tradition depicts Muhammad as having recited 41:1-4 (approx.) to `Utba b. Rabi`a; however, this information does not seem to be very reliable.[8]

Qur'an 45 opens with mysterious letters, and describes the Qur'an as having been sent down by God. The vv. 2f speak of the witness of Creation, the vv. 5f portray the Judgment of unbelievers, and God is presented as provider in the vv. 11f. The v. 13 was thought by some to have been Medinan, and the address to "believers" no doubt influenced this view.[9] The vv. 15f state that the children of Israel received the Book, wisdom and prophethood, but that they soon fell into disagreement. In the vv. 17f Muhammad is said to have been placed on the Way,[10] the vv. 19f speak of unbelievers and those who believe, and v. 22 deals with the subject of predestination. The vv. 23f appear to reproduce pagan objections to the doctrine of the Resurrection, and the vv. 26f tell of the Judgment, in which, somewhat reminiscent of Is. 45:23 the peoples are shown to be on their knees. The verse 45:12 is also similar to Ps. 8:6f.

The *Sira* traditions relate that during one pilgrimage a number of the Khazraj listened to Muhammad's message and became Muslims.[11] The Khazraj are said to have become acquainted with Monotheism through the influence of their Jewish neighbors in Medina, whose apparent references to the coming Messiah seem to have at least partially induced the Khazraj to accept Muhammad as a prophet.[12] The new converts are then said to have propagated Islam in Medina,[13] and twelve men[14] are reported to have made the Qur'anic women's pledge (cf. 60:12) at al-'Aqaba (near Mecca) the following year.[15] After their return to Medina they requested that Muhammad send them a Qur'an teacher, and Mus'ayb b. 'Umayr was sent.[16] Mus'ayb later returned to Mecca, and the Medinan Muslims came to the pilgrimage to meet with Muhammad again.[17] Some 70 men and two women pledged to support and defend Muhammad as one of their own in this second meeting at al-'Aqaba, and twelve men were appointed to be the leaders of the people.[18]

During this time period, Muhammad is said to have dreamed he was to marry 'A'isha.[19] At first, Abu Bakr objected to giving his young daughter, on the grounds that Muhammad was his brother in Islam, but Muhammad replied that 'A'isha was permitted him.[20] 'A'isha is said to have been six years old when she was engaged to Muhammad, who was approximately 50 then.[21]

Not long after the second pledge of al-'Aqaba, some *Sira* traditions report that the command to fight against the pagans was given to Muhammad.[22] However, one version gives Qur'an 22:40-42 as the revealed command,[23] and another references Qur'an 8:40;[24] both of which appear to be Medinan passages dating from about the time of the battle of Badr.[25]

Although the *Sira* traditions are remarkably silent about how Muhammad came to assimilate Jewish ideas and rituals, the canonical hadith very strongly imply that there was such a period, which took place in Medina prior to Muhammad's break with the Jews in 2 AH. It is reported that the Jews (of Medina) used to read the Torah in Hebrew and then translate it for Muslims,[26] that in the absence of specific revelation Muhammad is said to have followed the practices of the People of the Book,[27] that he adopted the Jewish fast on the Day of Atonement[28] and the Jewish qibla (direction of prayer).[29] Furthermore, the Qur'an appears to show that the "middle" prayer (2:239)[30] and the abstention from carrion, blood, pork and things offered to other gods (6:146)[31] were the result of Jewish influences.

The mosque in Medina was also constructed according to the pattern of a Jewish synagogue,[32] and even the Islamic system of worship seems to have been adopted from Judaism.[33]

Western biographers of Muhammad have also noticed a brief period of assimilation during his first months in Medina, which they generally interpret as having been part of Muhammad's attempt to become accepted as a prophet by the Jews.[34] Despite this realization, however, Western scholarship on the Qur'an has frequently followed its Islamic counterpart in presuming a Medinan period which essentially began in 2 AH.[35] Nevertheless, relatively early on, Qur'an scholars recognized that some Meccan suras contained Medinan passages and vice versa.[36] Moreover, modern theories on the introductions of the "basmala"[37] and the mysterious letters[38] to the Qur'anic text also concede that Muhammad must have at least revised some typically Meccan passages in Medina. It is very unlikely that any Qur'anic "intermission" during Muham-mad's first months in Medina[39] would have escaped the notice of later Muslim traditionists, thus the question remains as to what sort of work was done on the Qur'an in Medina prior to 2 AH. One Western Qur'an scholar essentially linked this earliest Medinan period to the last Meccan one, without, however, really defining any of its distinctive characteristics.[40]

With respect to Muhammad's biography and Qur'anic studies, perhaps the most distinguishing feature of Medina was, again, the presence of a *practicing* Jewish community. Although Islamic traditions make virtually no mention of Jewish synagogues, there must have actually been quite a few in Medina, since some *Sira* accounts reveal the presence of no small number of rabbis and even a Jewish "school" there, which was led by a certain Finhas (Phinehas).[41] Additionally, the Jews of Medina are said to have possessed a copy of the Torah,[42] and some Qur'anic evidence suggests that they also had a collection of the Talmud.[43]

During this period of assimilation of Jewish doctrines and rituals, one would expect to find Qur'anic passages which not only spoke fairly favorably of the Jews, but also which would indicate more familiarity with traditional Judaism. Judging from the Islamic accounts about the Muslims' emigration to Medina, it appears that Muhammad only gradually came into "theological" contact with the Jews, and therefore it should not be surprising to notice a gradual, but ever-increasing knowledge of Judaism. Many Qur'anic passages, for example, refer to the exodus of the children of Israel, give instructions to "keep the covenant" and emphasize that Moses received "the Book,"[44] which also seem to reveal Jewish influence.[45]

Any allusion to "emigration" could also be suspect of being Medinan, and all passages regarding pagans should not automatically be thought to be Meccan, since Islamic traditions clearly testify to the presence of Medinan polytheists.

For the most part, the suras of what is often classified as the third Meccan period are actually mixed texts, which appear to contain Meccan as well as Medinan elements. Unfortunately, as with many other historically important events in early Islam, the Qur'an does not clearly state when the "emigration" (or Hijra) to Medina took place, thus only estimates can made as to when the Hijra occurred in the chronology of Qur'anic passages. For the sake of simplicity, the Hijra will be considered to have taken place about the time of the composition of sura 16 in this work. This does not mean that all of the passages of this and later suras are thought to be Medinan, but rather, that Qur'an 16 is one of the earliest suras definitely known to contain Medinan passages of substantial length.[46]

As opposed to Mecca, Medina (Yathrib) was located in a region with arable land. Not terribly much is known about the origins of the Jewish communities in Medina,[47] but they seemed to have dominated life there until Arab tribes from the south migrated into the area.[48] In general, nomadic Arabs were averse to agricultural activity,[49] and evidence seems to indicate that the Jews were largely responsible for the cultivation of Medina.[50] Eventually, the Arab tribes in Medina fought against the Jews and became more independent from them.[51] The later intermittent battles in Medina may have in part been caused by economic factors,[52] and the political situation there was very unstable. The battle of Bu`ath, which was between the Arab tribes of the Aws and the Khazraj, ended up involving most of the other Arab and Jewish tribes in Medina.[53] This conflict took place a few years before the Hijra, but was so inconclusive that no formal cessation of hostilities had been made prior to the arrival of Muslims in Medina.[54]

Sira traditions show that after the successful spread of Islam in Medina and the second pledge of al-'Aqaba, Muhammad's followers gradually began to emigrate to Medina.[55] The Meccans are said to have prohibited some Muslims from emigrating, and increased their persecution of them.[56] Muhammad himself reportedly waited for God's permission to emigrate,[57] which he is said to have received about the time some of the Quraysh had conspired to murder him.[58] Muhammad then left for Medina with Abu Bakr, both of whom are reported to have hidden themselves in a cave just south of Mecca for a few days to avoid capture.[59] After the Meccans had given up hope, Muhammad and Abu Bakr journeyed northward to Medina, and are said to have arrived in Quba' on the 24th of September 622 AD.[60] Later, 'Ali and the rest of Muhammad's and Abu Bakr's families reportedly emigrated from Mecca to Medina.[61]

Qur'an 16 begins by stating that God's commandment will come to pass and includes a phrase against "associators." The v. 2 presents God as sending the angels and spirit with His command, and v. 3 shows Him as Creator and higher than claimed associates. The vv. 4f speak of the Creation and God as the Provider, and the v. 9 presents a tenet of Qur'anic predestination. The vv. 23f deal with Monotheism, the Resurrection and Judgment, and the somewhat ambiguous v. 28 may refer to the Tower of Babel (Gen. 11:1f) or the destruction of Job's children (Job 1:19). The vv. 37f speak of former messengers and predestination, and the Ethiopic term for "idol" ("taghut") is used in v. 38.[62] The v. 40 presents some of Muhammad's opponents as swearing by Allah that there is no Resurrection, and one of the earliest allusions to an emigration is found in v. 43. Although some maintain that the emigration to Abyssinia is meant here,[63] it is more likely a reference to Medina (cf. 16:111)[64] In any event 16:43 is the only Qur'anic passage which mentions an emigration and predates the raids on the Meccan caravans. The v. 45 shows that previous messengers were also humans, and in case of doubt, that the "People of the Remembrance"[ذكر] (i.e. Jews or Christians) should be asked. The v. 47 seems to refer to Korah (cf. Num. 16:1f), and v. 53 claims that Allah said that "two gods" should not be accepted. The vv. 59f are directed against polytheists, v. 61 alludes to the then contemporary Arabian practice of burying new-born daughters, and v. 62 mentions the judgment of those who do not believe in the Resurrection. The vv. 65f relate that other messengers were sent before Muhammad, and in comparison to

Moses (cf. 32:23; 41:45)[65], Muhammad also is now said to have received "the Book" (v. 66). The vv. 67f speak of the wonder of Creation and God's provision, in which alcoholic beverages are spoken of favorably.[66] The vv. 79f depict the Judgment, the vv. 81f describe God's provision, and the vv. 86f speak of the Resurrection and Judgment. The v. 91 states that a witness from each people "umma"[67] will speak out against themselves and reiterates that Muhammad was given "the Book."[68] The v. 92 shows God as commanding good and forbidding "the shameful, unjust and wrong," and the vv. 93f speak of keeping God's covenant in a manner similar to Old Testament passages (e.g. Dt. 29:9, 12). The vv. 98f state that good works will be rewarded, and the vv. 100f instruct Muhammad in what to do when reciting the Qur'an. The v. 103 presents the Qur'anic doctrine of verse abrogation, and v. 104 maintains that the Holy Spirit brought the Qur'an to Muhammad.[69] The v. 105 reproduces the accusation that Muhammad was taught by others, and the Qur'anic rebuttal - i.e. that Muhammad's informant spoke another language[70] - does little more than confirm that Muhammad was indeed aided by other humans in the composition of the Qur'an.[71] *Sira* traditions, in attempting to explain this verse, claim that Muhammad's informant was either a Christian slave named Jabr[72] or a another slave known as Ibn Qammatha.[73] Other sources maintain that Salman al-Farisi was meant, but this is not very likely.[74] The vv. 108f speak of apostates from Islam, and the vv. 111-125 appear to be from a later period in Medina.[75] The vv. 126f are thought to be Meccan by some Western scholars,[76] although many *Sira* traditions associate this passage with the prohibition of extreme vengeance for Hamza's death at Uhud.[77] One peculiarity of sura 16 is that several of its verses approximate passages from Ps. 104,[78] and at least one Western scholar of Islam maintains that 16:2-36 is a good example of a Qur'an text which was probably structured on a Christian missionary sermon.[79] Other verses of this sura are also similar to Bible references.[80]

Sura 30 begins with mysterious letters. The vv. 1f describe a defeat of Byzantines, which specific event cannot be identified for certain, since they suffered many setbacks in their wars with the Persians.[81] The vv. 6f give a reply to the disbelief in the Resurrection, and the vv. 8f generally refer to the judgments against earlier peoples. The vv. 10f present the witness of Creation as evidence in favor of the Resurrection, and the vv. 16f are thought to have been Medinan, since the prayer times cited appear to be Medinan and not

Meccan.[82] The vv. 18f speak again of the Resurrection, and v. 29 gives one of the earliest usages of the word حنيف "hanif," which seems to have come from the Syriac "hanpa" (="heathen"), rather than the Aramaic "hanef" (="hypocrite").[83] The v. 30, which speaks of repentance, fearing God, performing the prayer and not associating any with God, is thought by some to have been Medinan.[84] The vv. 32f illustrate the hypocritical character of pagans, and the vv. 37f, which were thought to be Medinan,[85] instruct to give alms instead of lending money out to usurers. The vv. 39f are concerned with the Resurrection and the Judgment, v. 44 states that Allah does not love unbelievers, and the vv. 45f depict God as the sender of signs and the Provider. The vv. 49f return to the subject of Judgment, and the vv. 58f speak of the witness of the Qur'an and Muhammad.

Qur'an 11 opens with mysterious letters and speaks of a "Book." The vv. 2f describe Muhammad as a warner and proclaimer of repentance and forgiveness. The vv. 5f show that God is the all-knowing, and v. 9 mentions the six-day Creation and the Jewish notion that God's throne was on the waters.[86] The vv. 10f display some pagans' reactions to the doctrine of Resurrection, v. 15 reproduces question as to why no treasure nor angel was sent to Muhammad,[87] and v. 16 presents the reply to the accusation that Muhammad authored the Qur'an. The vv. 18f speak of the reward of those who love life on earth, and v. 20 describes the Qur'an as having been preceded by the Book of Moses.[88] The vv. 21f relate about the Judgment, and the vv. 27f give a narrative about Noah. The comment of an alleged leader of Noah's people (v. 29) may well have been the words of a Meccan leader, since the accusations of Muhammad being only a human, whom only the vilest follow, etc. seem to have been Meccan charges (cf. 21:3f, 7; 25:8f, 22; 26:111). The statement that Noah did not seek a wage from his people (v. 31), is typical of previous narratives (cf. Qur'an 26:109) and is also a disclaimer which Muhammad himself made (cf. Qur'an 52:40; 68:46; 38:86). The replies of Noah to the apparent question of why no treasure nor angel was sent to him (v. 33), parallels the accusations made against Muhammad (cf. 11:15). The v. 34 suggests that Muhammad had disputed with the Meccans many times, and produces an unmistakable echo of the Meccan's dare to see the threatened punishment on their city. The v. 37 inadvertently departs from the Noah narrative to present Muhammad's reply to the charge of authoring the Qur'an, after which the Noah narrative continues in vv. 38f. The alleged revelation given to Noah (v. 38), was more probably a reason for Muhammad to leave Mecca, but the idea of Noah being ridiculed as he built the ark seems to have been Jewish,[89] as well as the notion that the waters of the flood were warm (v. 42).[90] The origin of the anomaly that one of Noah's sons drowned in the flood is uncertain (vv. 44f),[91] and it appears that Muhammad meant to localize the final resting place of the ark to Arabia in v. 46.[92] The narrative about Hud (vv. 52f) presents him as not only not asking for a wage (v. 53), similar to Noah (cf. v. 31), but also has Hud call his people to be Monotheists, repent and to ask for forgiveness (vv. 52, 54), as the character Salih does (v. 64) in the narrative about him (vv. 64f).[93] The vv. 72f give a narrative about Abraham, in which Isaac and Jacob were said to have been proclaimed to his wife, and no mention is made of Ishmael.[94] The vv. 79f tell of Lot as the angels came to him, and in general, this version of the narrative, although not flawless,[95] appears to follow the Biblical accounts better than previous ones (cf. 54:33f; 37:133f; 26:160f; 15:61f). A narrative about Shu`ayb, who is now said to have been from Madyan,[96] is told in the vv. 85f, and he also calls his people to be Monotheists (v. 85), request forgiveness and repent (v. 92). Shu`ayb's preaching style is based on Muhammad's own (cf. vv. 86, 89f), and the replies of the people were no doubt the same as the Meccans' to Muhammad (v. 93). The vv. 99f briefly mention Moses and Pharaoh. In general, the narratives of this sura represent an improvement over those of Qur'an 26, as even their chronology has been "corrected."[97] In the vv. 112f the themes of the example punishments of previous peoples and the Judgment are interrupted by the statement that the Book given to Moses is disputed over (v. 112), and a listing of three prayer times (v. 116), in which the night vigil has become another time for prayer.[98]

Sura 14 begins with mysterious letters and mentions that (the) "Book" has been sent down. The vv. 2f speak of God's judgments, and v. 4 describes the Qur'an doctrine of predestination. The vv. 5f speak of Moses, and Muhammad (cf. v. 1) is compared with Moses (v. 5) as bringing the people "from the darkness(es) into the light," which phrase is actually based on something which was told the apostle Paul (cf. Acts 26:18). The v. 9 alludes to Noah, the `Ad and the Thamud, the vv. 10f generally concern the messengers and the peoples to whom they were sent, and v. 16 reiterates the notion that the various peoples tried to drive their messengers from the land,[99] but that the latter will dispossess the former (of their land).[100] The vv. 18f tell about the Judgment, and the vv. 29f give both the gist of Ps. 1:3 and its converse.[101] The vv. 33f speak of apostates from Islam, v. 36 states that believers should pray and give alms, and v. 37 describes God's provision. The vv. 38f are from a later period,[102] and the vv. 43f explain the Judgment again. Other verses of this sura similar to Bible passages are 14:19 - cf. Rev. 21:1; Is. 65:7, and 14:21 - cf. Ps. 1:4.

Qur'an 12 is one of the most remarkable narrative suras, which deals almost solely with "the most beautiful story" (v. 3) of Joseph. Hardly any other Qur'anic narration of comparable length is so dependent on the Jewish Mid-rashim and Talmud,[103] and certainly no other attains the plot complexity of this story. *Sira* traditions generally place the composition of this sura in Mecca,[104] and Islamic and Western Qur'an scholars usually agree.[105] Although it is possible that this sura was indeed composed in Mecca, based on its strong exploitation of customary Jewish sources, one would rather expect an early Medinan setting, not far from the synagogues and school of the Jews there.[106] According to the theories of one Western Qur'an scholar, at least parts of this sura were thought to have been revised in Medina.[107] Sura 12 begins with mysterious letters and implies that these are the signs of a "clear Book" (v. 1), which was "sent down" as an Arabic Qur'an, so that it could be understood (v. 2). In vv. 4f the narrative about Joseph[108] opens with him telling his father about his dream of the eleven stars, the sun and the moon bowing down to him,[109] and Jacob warns Joseph not to relate this dream to his brothers (v. 5). Later, while making their plans, one of Joseph's brothers says that a caravan will pull Joseph out of the well (v. 10), and the brothers then ask Jacob why he does not entrust Joseph to them (v. 11), as they would also protect him (v. 12). Jacob fears "the wolf" will eat Joseph (v. 13), and later the brothers claim that "the wolf" ate him (v. 17). A water-drawer finds Joseph in the well (v. 19), and "they" sell Joseph (v. 20) to an Egyptian (v. 21). Joseph would have sinned with the Egyptian's wife, but he was warned (v. 24),[110] and Joseph's shirt is examined to see if it was torn from the front or the back.[111] Instead of being condemned, Joseph is justified (vv. 28f),[112] and Egyptian women shame the . Egyptian's wife (v. 30).[113] Upon seeing how handsome Joseph was, the Egyptian women then cut their hands (vv. 31f),[114] and Joseph chooses to go to prison rather than to obey the wishes of the Egyptian's wife (v. 33). Joseph says that he has left the religion of those who do not believe in God (v. 37), and preaches Monotheism to the two servants in prison (vv. 39f), one of whom is to be crucified (v. 41). When the king has his dream, the other servant goes to Joseph to get its interpretation (vv. 45f), which inplies a fifteenth year of rain (v. 49).[115] The Egyptian's wife admits her guilt when the king investigates Joseph's case (vv. 50f).[116] After Joseph's brothers come to Egypt, for which no reason is given (v. 58), the money is put back in their sacks in hopes that they will return (v. 62). The brothers complain to Jacob that they would have been able to bring one more load if their brother [Benjamin] had gone with them (vv. 63f). The return of all the brothers to Egypt seems to have been immediate (vv. 65f), and their father advises them to enter the city through doors separate from one another (v. 67).[117] Joseph secretly tells his brother [Benjamin] his identity (v. 69).[118] It is said that it would have been illegal for Joseph to arrest his brother, and when the brother [Benjamin] is brought before Joseph for the theft of his chalice, the other brothers accuse both him and his brother [Joseph] of theft (v. 77).[119] The confused text of vv. 81f clearly shows that the brothers then returned to Jacob without their brother [Benjamin] and also without knowing Joseph's identity. Jacob, however, knows that Joseph is alive (vv. 86, 97).[120] The brothers return to Egypt again, and when they ask for alms (v. 88), they are confronted by Joseph (v. 89) and realize who he is (v. 90). The brothers then take Joseph's shirt, to place it on Jacob's face and heal his blindness (v. 93).[121] Jacob smells Joseph's scent when the caravan set off from Egypt (v. 94), and he receives his sight when Joseph's shirt is placed on his face (v. 96). Joseph then welcomes his parents to Egypt (v. 100),[122] and later prays to die a Muslim (v. 102). The story of Joseph is said to have been revealed to Muhammad (v. 103), who requests no wage for it (v. 104).[123] The vv. 105f speak of the disbelief in God's signs and punishment, and the vv. 109f allude to the previous messengers to other peoples. Oddly enough, the Qur-'anic narrative of Joseph mentions neither the names of his brothers, nor does it refer to the king of Egypt as "Pharaoh."[124] The Qur'anic version of this story is at times so ambiguous that the reader has to have read the Biblical accounts to understand the plot.[125] The Arabic name for Joseph [Yusuf] is thought to have come from the Jews,[126] the foreign word for "cattle" (v. 65) probably came from Aramaic (or Syriac),[127] and the word for "cup" (v. 72) is from the Ethiopic.[28]

Sura 40 begins with mysterious letters, and mentions "the Book" as having been sent down by God. The vv. 2f describe God as forgiving, and the vv. 4f refer to earlier unbelievers and their messengers. The vv. 7f deal with the subject of intercession, the vv. 15f speak of the Judgment, and the vv. 22f return to the subject of previous peoples and messengers. The vv. 24f present a new version of a narrative about Moses, in which Moses is said to have been sent to Pharaoh, Haman and Korah,[129] who call Moses a magician and liar (v. 25). The command to kill the sons of Moses' people is said to have come about after Moses was sent to these three (v. 26), and Pharaoh then wants to kill Moses, in part because he is afraid the latter will cause others to change their religion (v. 27). It can hardly be overlooked that Muhammad has placed himself in the role of Moses, and this is also substantiated in the allusion to a "believer from Pharaoh's people," whose rhetorical question (about killing a man for saying his Lord is Allah; v. 29) appears in the *Sira* and canonical traditions as having been said by Abu Bakr when the Quraysh once tried to kill Muhammad.[130] This alleged believer in Moses' time also makes an allusion to Noah's people, the `Ad, the Thamud (v. 32) and Joseph (v. 36).[131] Pharaoh then commands Haman to build a tower to Heaven for him (vv. 38f),[132] and the unnamed believer later gives a sermon (vv. 41f), which is very much in the style of Muhammad's. The vv. 48f relate that this believer was protected and then describe the judgment of Pharaoh and his people. The vv. 54f refer to previous messengers, and v. 56 presents Moses as having received guidance, and the children of Israel "the Book." In v. 57 Muhammad is commanded to request forgiveness for his own sins,[133] and only two daily prayer times are mentioned. The vv. 59f speak of the witness of Creation, and the vv. 61f refer to the Judgment. The vv. 63f describe God as Provider, Creator and being one, the vv. 69f show God as Creator again, and the vv. 71f return to the theme of the Judgment. For the most part, the vv. 78f compare Muhammad with previous messengers. Some of the verses of this sura are similar to the Jewish Tefillah, the apocrypha or the Bible,[134] the Arabic name for Haman appears to have come from the Jews,[135] and the form "Qarun" (for Korah) may have been created by Muhammad to rhyme with "Harun" (for Aaron).[136]

Qur'an 28 begins with mysterious letters, which are said to be "the signs of the clear Book" (v. 1). The vv. 2f give a narrative about Moses. The v. 3 implies that the Israelites were part of the people of Pharaoh, and v. 4

that they were to inherit the land of Egypt.[137] The v. 5 mentions Haman as being a contemporary of Pharaoh, v. 8 depicts Moses as being adopted by Pharaoh's wife (rather than his daughter),[138] and the Qur'anic account assumes that the same Pharaoh reigned from the time of Moses' birth until his return to Egypt. In the vv. 14f Moses is shown as killing and then repenting,[139] and v. 27 maintains that Moses served eight or ten years in order to marry his wife.[140] In the vv. 33f Moses is depicted as being afraid to return to Egypt, because of the previous murder, and he requests that Aaron be sent with him. In v. 38 Haman is commanded to build a tower (cf. 40:38f), v. 43 shows Moses as having received "the Book," and in the vv. 44f Muhammad is compared with Moses. The vv. 48f reproduce the possibly Jewish questions as to why Muhammad was not given the same as Moses, and such questions may have induced Muhammad to begin editing "the Book" portions of the Qur'an.[141] The v. 49 may have referred to the Torah, and v. 52 must allude to either Jews or Christians.[142] The vv. 57f give some of Muhammad's discussions with pagans, the vv. 62f speak of the Judgment, and the vv. 67f describe those who believe and God's power. The vv. 76f, which seem to have been a later addition,[143] contain a narrative about Korah, who is described as having been wealthy.[144] In the vv. 85f the Qur'an and "the Book" are said to have been given to Muhammad, and the vv. 86-87 may refer to the event of the Satanic inspiration.[145] The message of 28:60 is similar to that of I Jn. 2:17.[146]

Sura 39 opens with "the sending down of the Book from God..." which is shown to have been given Muhammad (v. 2). The vv. 4f speak of polytheism, state that God does not lead liars or unbelievers (v. 5), and give an unclear denial of God having a son (v. 6). In the vv. 7f God is shown to be the Creator, who created the "eight pairs" (v. 8).[147] The vv. 11f speak of unbelievers and those who believe, and v. 14 presents Muhammad as the "first of the Muslims."[148] The vv. 17f refer to the Judgment, and v. 19 mentions "Taghut" (cf. 16:38). The vv. 22f speak of God's provision, and the sending down of "the most beautiful stories" (v. 24). The vv. 25f return to the subject of the Judgment, and v. 29 mentions "the Arabic Qur'an, in which nothing is crooked." The vv. 37f speak of predestination, and the vv. 39f reproduce some discussions with polytheists. In v. 42 "the Book" is said to have been sent down to Muhammad, and the content of v. 43 may be related to the Nestorian doctrine of death-sleep.[149] The vv. 44f deal with intercession, and the vv. 46f speak of the Resurrection and Judgment. The vv. 50f are very similar to the passage in vv. 11f, v. 54 concerns forgiveness, and the vv. 55f describe the Judgment, which is preceded by "two" trumpet blasts.[150] The vv. 54-56 or 61 are considered to have been Medinan by some,[151] and v. 67, which already reveals Biblical influence (cf. Is. 34: 4; 40:12), is said to have been recited to a Jewish rabbi.[152] Many of the verses in this sura are similar to Bible passages or Talmudic references.[153]

Qur'an 29 begins with mysterious letters, and the vv. 1-10 are thought to have been Medinan,[154] because they obviously allude to the "hypocrites." The vv. 11f relate how unbelievers tried to mislead believers, and the vv. 13f briefly mention Noah, who is said to have been 950 years old at the time of the flood.[155] The vv. 15f give a narrative about Abraham, whose preaching style is quite similar to that of Muhammad's. The v. 23 contains a mistake of person,[156] and in v. 26 Isaac and Jacob are spoken of as having been given to Abraham (cf. 19:50); again, Ishmael is missing.[157] The vv. 35f speak of Shu`ayb, v. 37 mentions the `Ad and the Thamud, and v. 38 refers to Korah, Pharaoh and Haman. The v. 40 compares polytheists with a spider, and v. 43 mentions God as Creator. The vv. 44f deal with Qur'an recitations and prayer, and v. 45 seems to refer to the Jews.[158] The v. 47 indicates that Muhammad had neither read (recited) nor written a book previously, but many Western scholars presume that only the Bible was meant here.[159] Taken in context with v. 48, however, this passage shows that up until this time Muhammad only wanted the Qur'an to be recited from memory, since his writing it down would have only incurred doubt (cf. 25:6).[160] The vv. 49f essentially present the Qur'an as Muhammad's miracle, and the vv. 53f give the apparently Meccan challenge for Muhammad to hurry the alleged punishment, which is then described as being Hell. The v. 56 alludes to an emigration, but not necessarily the one to Medina.[161] The vv. 59f give some of the discussions with pagans, and v. 69 is thought by some to have been Medinan, provided it refers to armed conflict.[162] The word for "hypocrite" in 29:10 appears to have come from the Ethiopic,[163] and a few verses of this sura are similar to Bible passages.[164]

According to *Sira* traditions, the "hypocrites" were those pagan Arabs in Medina who "pretended to accept Islam" but secretly sided with the Jews against Muhammad.[165]

Sura 31 opens with mysterious letters, which are said to be the signs of the wise Book. The vv. 2f describe the Book as a guidance for those who practice good (works), pray, give alms and believe in the Resurrection. The identity of the person referred to in the vv. 5f, who is said to buy vain stories, was a matter of speculation for later Qur'an commentators.[166] The vv. 7f describe the reward of those who believe and practice good (works), and the vv. 9f speak of God's Creation and provision. The vv. 11f tell about Luqman,[167] which narrative is abruptly interrupted by the subject of honoring one's parents in the vv. 13-14.[168] The story of Luqman continues in the vv. 15f, and v. 15 is thought to be missing some text.[169] The vv. 19f reproduce some of Muhammad's discussions with pagans, and v. 26 is similar to Qur'an 18:109.[170] The vv. 27f speak of God's signs, and v. 34 of His knowledge. The v. 31 of this sura is similar to a Talmud passage.[171]

Qur'an 42 begins with mysterious letters, and there was apparently a discrepancy about these in the codices of Ibn Mas`ud,[172] and Ibn `Abbas.[173] The vv. 1f describe God in praise, and v. 3 deals with the ministry of angels. The v. 5 indicates that the Qur'an was given to warn "the mother of cities," (Mecca) and those surrounding it, v. 6 speaks of predestination, and v. 7 presents God as protector. In the vv. 9f God is shown to be the Creator and Provider, and the vv. 11f depict God as having given (Muslims) the same faith as He gave Noah, Abraham, Moses and Jesus. Not only is this latter list in chronological order, but the names of the "Arabian" prophets are missing. This in turn seems to show that Muhammad was in closer contact with Christians, and possibly Jews also, at the time this verse was composed.[174] The v. 13 speaks of division among the (religious) groups, v. 14 gives a sermon of Muhammad, v. 15 concerns those who argue about God, and v. 16 declares that God sent "the Book." The vv. 18f describe God's provision, and v. 20 speaks of polytheism and Judgment. In v. 22 Muhammad is to say that he does not seek a wage,[175] but rather the love of relatives. The v. 23 gives an accusation of the pagans, the vv. 24f speak of believers and unbelievers, and the vv. 27f tell of God's provision and signs. The vv. 34f return to the subject of believers and unbelievers, and v. 38 presents Allah as not loving the unrighteous. The vv. 42 and 45 are concerned with predestination, and the vv. 48f show God as Creator and Predestinator. Several verses in this sura are similar to Bible passages.[176]

Sura 10 begins with mysterious letters, which are said to be the signs of the Book. The v. 2 speaks of Muhammad's ministry as a warner, and the vv. 3f describe God's witness in Creation and the Judgment. The vv. 12f show God's application of punishment, and v. 13 is similar to other Qur'an passages (cf. 16:55f; 39:11f, 50f; etc.). The vv. 16f deal with someone's request for a different Qur'an, v. 19 mentions a pagan belief about intercession, and v. 21 gives the question as to why no miracle was sent down for Muhammad. The vv. 22f speak of human reactions to God's judgment (punishment) and compassion, and v. 25 relates a brief parable, in which the earthly life is compared with the water cycle (cf. 18:43).[177] The vv. 26f tell about predestination and Judgment, and the vv. 32f present God's provision as a witness against humanity. The v. 38 maintains that the Qur'an could not have been composed without Allah and that the Qur'an confirms previous scripture. The vv. 39f repeat the accusation of Muhammad's authorship of the Qur'an, and as a reply, the challenge is made to produce a similar sura. The vv. 41f give some of the reactions to Qur'an recitations, and v. 47 expresses the possibility that Muhammad will not see the coming judgment (punishment) in his own lifetime. The v. 48 states that each people has its own messenger, and the question as to when the judgment (punishment) will take place is answered with an allusion to the end Judgment (vv. 49f). The vv. 60f give an adverse Qur'anic reaction to the Jewish dietary laws, and this indicates that Muhammad was becoming acquainted with practical Judaism at the time. The v. 62 shows again that everything is being recorded for the Judgment, the vv. 64f speak of those who believe, and v. 69 claims that God did not have a Son. The account about Noah (vv. 72f) resembles previous Noah narratives, but the narration concerning Moses (vv. 76f) differs somewhat from the earlier Moses stories. In v. 84 Moses is reported to have said that those who believe and trust in God are Muslims,[178] and v. 87, which gives perhaps the earliest Qur'anic usage of the term "qibla" (the direction faced during prayer), appears to be based on a Jewish anachronism crediting Moses with the institution of synagogues in Egypt.[179] The ultimately Jewish notion that Pharaoh repented appears in v. 90,[180] but the Qur'an adds that in so doing Pharaoh became a Muslim.[181] In v. 94, Muhammad is commanded to consult those who read the scriptures before him, should he have any doubts, and this verse was also used by later Christian polemicists.[182] The v. 98 makes a brief reference to Jonah, in which "his people" are said to have believed to avert punishment.[183] The vv. 99f, which contradict the doctrine of "jihad," must have predated 2 AH,[184] and the vv. 104f counter polytheism. 10:19 is similar to Is. 44:10, and 10:62 is similar to Is. 40:15.[185]

According to Islamic traditions, the "mosque" (place of prayer) in Medina was initially only Muhammad's residence, which had two huts (for Safiya and `A'isha) and a wall enclosing a court of earth.[186] The huts are reported to have been constructed like those of Moses,[187] and the "qibla" side of the mosque is said to have faced Jerusalem (similar to synagogues),[188] to which Qur'an 10:87 seems to refer. *Sira* traditions present the location of the mosque in Medina as having been determined by Muhammad's camel, which property is then reported to have been bought from two young orphans.[189]

Qur'an 34 begins with praises to God, and the vv. 3f contain some of the remarks of unbelievers. Apparently, the Jewish approval of the Qur'anic message is referred to in v. 6.[190] The narratives about David and Solomon (vv. 10f) generally follow previous Qur'anic accounts, with the exception of the incident regarding Solomon's death (v. 13),[191] where the strange word for "scepter" is used, which probably came from Hebrew.[192] The vv. 14f tell about two gardens and a flood in Saba',[193] and the vv. 21f reproduce some discussions with polytheists, in which v. 43 implies that Muhammad had contact with "studying" Jews (cf. 68:37).[194] The v. 46 reiterates Muhammad's claim not to be seeking a wage for his services.[195] The ambiguous passage in vv. 50f probably refers to the Judgment, and may have been at least partially based on the Biblical Lk. 16:19f. Qur'an 34:30 is remotely similar to I Cor. 8:10-13, and 34:46, whose content is repeated in many other Qur'anic passages, is similar to Mt. 10:8 and the Talmudic Avot 1,3.[196]

Sura 35 also opens with praises to God and a description of angel wings, which is reminiscent of Is. 6:2.[197] The vv. 3f are a call to repentance, the vv. 7f describe the situation of unbelievers at the Judgment, and v. 9 speaks of predestination. The vv. 10f present the witness of God in Creation, and the vv. 16f tell of His power. In the vv. 21f Muhammad is said to be sent as a warner, and that all peoples had a warner. The vv. 25f show God to be the Provider, and the vv. 26f states that those who read (recite) God's Book, pray and give alms will be rewarded. The vv. 28f maintain that the revelation given to Muhammad confirms the previous (Books), the vv. 30f describe Paradise, and the vv. 33f speak about Hell and unbelievers. The vv. 37f are thought to be a later addition, because of a change in the rhyme,[198] and the vv. 38f present an interesting polemic against pagans, in which they are asked what their gods have created, and where their book is. The v. 40 refers to those who swore by Allah that they would follow a future warner, but that they rejected Muhammad; it could be that the Messianic hopes of the Jews of Medina were alluded to in this verse.[199] The vv. 41f maintain that those meant in v. 40 will be punished. Qur'an 35:19 is similar to Gal. 6:5, and 35:44 is vaguely reminiscent of Ps. 130:3.[200]

Qur'an 7 begins with mysterious letters, following which a book is said to be sent down to Muhammad, in order to warn and as an admonition to believers. The vv. 3f refer to previous peoples and their punishments, and the vv. 7f speak of the scales at the Judgment.[201] The vv. 9-11 contain a grammatical mistake in persons,[202] the v. 9 shows God's provision, and the vv. 10f give a narrative about Adam, which is generally based on earlier Qur'anic accounts. The vv. 25f present admonitions addressed to the "children of Adam," in which the pagans are said to have Satan as their protector, since God clothed Adam, and yet the polytheists practice the custom of nudity at their shrines (vv. 29f).[203] The v. 32 maintains that the judgment (punishment) can neither be delayed nor expedited, the vv. 33f speak of unbelievers and their judgment, and the vv. 40f relate about believers in Paradise and their discussions with those in Hell. The vv. 52f present God as Creator and Provider, and a narrative about Noah is given (vv. 57f), which is based on previous Qur'anic Noah stories. The vv. 63f present a narration about the `Ad and Hud, and the vv. 71f relate about the Thamud and Salih. Both of these accounts generally agree with earlier Qur'anic stories, with the exception that v. 76 shows that the punishment of the Thamud was an earthquake (cf. 11:70 - "shout"). The vv. 78f give a narrative about Lot, which is based on previous Qur'anic stories, but in the account of Shu`ayb (vv. 83f) he is threatened with being driven out (of the land) with the believers (v. 86), and the punishment of his peoples (v. 89) is also now said to have been an earthquake (cf. 11:97 - "shout"). The vv. 92f speak about previous peoples and their messengers. The vv. 101f give a narrative about Moses, in which he is said to have performed the miracle of the leprous hand (v. 105),[204] and all of the works and buildings of Pharaoh are said to have been destroyed (v. 133). In v. 142 God is shown as having written on the tables of stone, and the mysterious "Samaritan" of earlier Qur'anic accounts is missing in the passage about the golden calf (vv. 146f). More in conformity to the Biblical narrative (cf. Ex. 32:1f), Moses is said to have been angry with Aaron (v. 149), v. 154 shows that Moses chose 70 men (cf. Num. 11:16f), and without giving a reason for their selection, appears to have them be punished with an earthquake.[205] The v. 155 depicts God describing Muhammad's followers as those who fear God, give alms and believe in God's signs, and the passage vv. 156-158 appears to have been a later addition.[206] The v. 159 may refer to either the Muslims in general, or Jewish converts, and the vv. 160f give the continuation of the Moses narrative, in which the events of water from the rock, and the provision of manna and quail are related. The vv. 161f show the entrance of the Israelites into "the city, " whereby they were to eat of all they wanted, and say "forgiveness."[207] Then the unrighteous among them exchanged the word with another, and the Israelites were punished (v. 162).[208] By comparison to the narratives of Qur'an 11, the stories of this suras follow the same chronological sequence, but a narrative about Abraham is missing. The vv. 163f tell a story about fish who only came to a city on the Sabbath,[209] and the v. 166 depicts Sabbath-violators as having been turned into apes.[210] The v. 170 speaks of a mountain having been shaken over the children of Israel,[211] and the vv. 174f relate about an unbeliever whose identity is not known.[212] The v. 175 gives a peculiar parable about those who regard God's signs to be lies, v. 177 deals with the subject of predestination, v. 178 speaks of unbelievers, and v. 179 states that God's names are the most beautiful. The vv. 180f return to the theme of believers and unbelievers, the vv. 183f describe the rejection of Muhammad and his message, and the vv. 186f reproduce some of Muhammad's discussions with others. The vv. 189f are against polytheism, where v. 194 is based upon Ps. 115:4-6 (cf. Qur'an 7:178 also). The vv. 198f give instructions to Muhammad, and v. 204 refers to prayer as only being performed in the evening and morning.[213] The strange term al-A`raf in v. 44 seems to have come from Ethiopic, and the Arabic for "Sabbath" probably came from Aramaic[214] Many verses of this sura are reminiscent of Bible passages.[215]

Sura 46 opens with mysterious letters, and mentions the sending down of the Book. The vv. 2f seem to repeat some of Muhammad's discussions with pagans, whereby he asks for their "book" (v. 3). Muhammad is accused of authoring the Qur'an (v. 7), and he maintains that he is not something new among the messengers (v. 8). The vv. 9f give some of Muhammad's discussions with the Jews, in which he claims that at least one Jew confirms the Qur'anic message.[216] The vv. 12f give what appears to be one of the earliest Islamic creeds, and the vv. 14f seem to describe the exemplary life of an ideal Muslim.[217] The vv. 18f tell of the Judgment, and the vv. 20-35, which were doubtless added to this sura,[218] give a narrative about "the brother of the `Ad" (i.e. Salih), in which this people is destroyed (v. 23) by a wind (cf. 7:76 - earthquake; 11:70 - a shout). The vv. 25f seem to compare the Meccans with the `Ad. The vv. 28f relate Muhammad's reciting the Qur'an to the jinn (cf. 72:1f),[219] who are now quoted as saying the Qur'an was sent after and in confirmation of Moses' Book. These call their "people" to hear and believe God's summoner for the forgiveness of sins (v. 30). The v. 32 gives argument in favor of the Resurrection, and the vv. 33f speak of the Judgment. 46:14 is similar to the Talmudic Avot 5,21; and 46:19 is similar to Luke 16:25.[220]

In the former passage where jinn are said to have overheard Muhammad as he recited the Qur'an (72:1f), the jinn were essentially accused of having forged the doctrine of Christ's Sonship. In this additional story about the jinn, however, these beings are said to have testified (among other things) that the Qur'an confirmed the Book of Moses (46:28f). It is highly unlikely that such stories would have carried much weight with either Christians or Jews, but they probably were intended for Arab pagans or Muslims who had converted from polytheism.

Sura 6 begins with praise to God (vv. 1f), and then speaks of unbelievers and Muhammad's discussion with them (vv. 4f). The v. 7 seems to answer the implied question of why the Qur'an was not sent down on parchment,[221] and v. 8 repeats the question as to why no angel was sent down to Muhammad. In v. 14 Muhammad claims to be the first to profess Islam,[222] and the v. 34 states that no one changes God's Words (cf. v. 115). The vv. 50f are instructions to Muhammad, and the vv. 56f return to discussions with unbelievers, in which v. 60 seems to show that God was believed to have taken souls to Himself as they slept.[223] The vv. 74f give a narrative about Abraham, in which his father is said to have been Azar (v. 74),[224] and Abraham rejects the presumption that the stars, moon and sun are gods (vv. 76f).[225] In v. 84 Isaac and Jacob are said to have been given Abraham, and Muhammad still does not seem to have known how Ishmael was related, since his name appears among other prophets in v. 86.[226] This listing of the prophets (vv. 84f) is not only out of chronological order, but the names of the Arab messengers (Hud, Salih, Shu`ayb) are missing.[227] The v. 88 speaks of predestination, and v. 90 shows that Muhammad requested no wage for his services.[228] The v. 91 relate some of Muhammad's discussions with the Jews, in which they are said to write Moses' Book on parchment, and v. 92 states that "this Book" (i.e. the Qur'an) was sent down to warn the "mother of cities" (Mecca) and those surrounding it as well. The vv. 92f speak of the Resurrection, and the vv. 96f describe the witness of creation. The vv. 100f seem to counter both polytheism and Christianity, whereby v. 111 states that if signs had been given, no one would have believed them (cf. 17:61).[229] The v. 115 reiterates that none can change God's Words (cf. v. 34; Qur'an 18:26). The vv. 118f, which are thought to have been an addition to the text,[230] deal with the Jewish dietary laws, and the vv. 122f speak of unbelievers. The v. 125 is concerned with predestination, and the vv. 137f are against pagan sacrifice and the killing of new-born daughters (cf. 16: 61). The v. 144 speaks of the "eight pairs" again (cf. 39:8),[231] v. 146 shows compliance with some points of the Jewish dietary laws,[232] but the vv. 147f counter these laws generally. The vv. 149f reproduce a discussion with pagans, and the vv. 152f give some moral regulations, in which keeping the covenant of God is referred to in v. 153. Some text is thought to be missing before v. 155,[233] and this passage (vv. 155f) speaks of "the Book" having been given Moses. The vv. 157f admonish others not to claim that "the Book" was sent down on only two groups previously (the Jews and the Christians), and v. 159 appears to depict Muhammad as telling others to wait for God's signs, whereby a punishment (or the Judgment) was probably being referred to. The vv. 160f may have been a later addition.[234] The Qur'anic term for "swine" (6:146) comes from Aramaic,[235] and this sura has many verses which are similar to Bible passages.[236]

Although one collection of *Sira* traditions relates how Muhammad came to part with the Jews,[237] Qur'anic evidence from this time period seems to provide more information about the theological developments which led up to this separation. Muhammad not only said that he was a messenger like Moses, but it appears that he also claimed to have been the awaited prophet of the Jews (cf. 35:40). Moreover, the Qur'an was said to have confirmed the previous Books (10:38; 35:28f; 46:9f). Even though some Jews (rabbis) are reported to have converted to Islam,[238] the vast majority were no doubt disinclined to accept either Muhammad as God's messenger, or the Qur'an as God's Word. Nevertheless, Muhammad's first open disagreement with the Jews appears to have been over their dietary laws. In Qur'an 10:60 Muhammad rhetorically asks the Jews if God had not allowed them to eat everything He had provided, and implies that the Jews imposed the dietary restrictions on themselves (the implied accusation of their inventing a lie against God is mentioned in 10:61). For their part, the Jews could show that the dietary laws were found in the "Book" of Moses, and even some Qur'an passages indicate that Muhammad had seen copies of the Torah on parchment (cf. 6:7, 91). Although Muhammad seems to have adopted some of the Jewish dietary regulations (cf. 6:146), he definitely must have rejected others.[239] Nevertheless, after the Qur'an was said to have confirmed previous scriptures, which were also sent down by God, Muhammad's options for justifying this rejection were limited. By way of a story unknown of from other sources, Qur'an 7:160-162 (cf. 2:55f) accuses the unrighteous among the Jews for having substituted God's word for another, and seems to imply that the dietary laws were a punishment on the Jews.[240] In Qur'an 6:147 a generalization of the Judaic dietary regulations is said to have been a punishment, and the Jewish reaction to all of this can be surmised from Qur'an 6:148, which anticipates that Muhammad will be accused of lying.

Qur'an 13 begins with mysterious letters, which are said to be the signs of "the Book." The vv. 2f describe God as the Provider in creation, and the vv. 5f mention the rejection of the doctrine of Resurrection and speak of unbelievers. The v. 8 reiterates the request for miracles, the vv. 9f describe God's knowledge of the hidden, and the vv. 13f repeat discussions with unbelievers. The vv. 20-26 are thought by some to have been later revisions,[241] since they speak of those who keep God's covenant (vv. 20f), and those who break God's covenant (vv. 25f). The vv. 27f repeat the requests for miracles, and the vv. 29f show the apparently Meccan rejection of the term "al-Rahman" (the Compassionate) for Allah. The vv. 31f state that the Judgment will come, and the vv. 33f speak of unbelievers and the God-fearing. The v. 36 shows the partial rejection of the Qur'an by some

Jews (or Christians), and v. 37 maintains that the Qur'an was sent down in
Arabic and warns Muhammad not to give in to the demands of others. The v.
38 shows that no miracles are given without God's permission, and the v. 40
tells Muhammad he may die before the punishment comes (cf. 10:47). The v.
41 may refer to an immigration, and the v. 43 reproduces the accusation of
"unbelievers" that Muhammad was not sent by God.

Conclusions

During this Qur'anic period, it appears that the night vigil had basically
become a third prayer time (11:116),[242] and also that a simple form of the
Islamic creed was slowly evolving (cf. 16:23; 46:28). Jerusalem may have
been instituted as the Islamic qibla at this time (cf. 10:87), and the mosque
(Muhammad's residence) may have been constructed in this period (cf. 10:87).
Muslim believers are described as fearing God (30:30; 7:155), as giving alms
(41:5f; 30:37f; 14:36; 31:2f; 35:26f; 7:155), as praying (30:30; 14:36; 31:2;
35:26f), as believing in the Resurrection (41:5f; 31:2f), as not associating
(equating) others with God (30:30), as practicing good works (31:2f), as
reciting God's Book (35:26f) and as believing God's signs (7:155). A brief
moral code is given (6:152f), and apostates from Islam are referred to (16:
108f; 14:33f). The Qur'anic doctrine of predestination became more developed
in this period (16:9, 37f; 14:4; 39:37f; 42:6, 42, 45, 48f; 10:26f; 35:9; 7: 177;
6:88, 125).

Many of the developments in the Qur'anic narratives of this period are noteworthy. Although the themes and major characters of the punishment stories
are generally retained, modifications have been made. The narratives of Qur'an
11, for instance, reveal that a chronological "correction" had been made since
the composition of those in Qur'an 26.[243] The alleged messenger Shu`ayb is
now connected with Midian (11:85; 29:35; 7:83),[244] the people of Midian are
at first said to have been destroyed by a "shout" (11:97), but this is later said to
have been an "earthquake" (7:89). Similarly, the `Ad are at first shown to have
been destroyed by a "shout" (11:70), later this is said to have been an "earthquake" (7:76), and in another passage it is said to have been a "wind" (46:23).
The character Luqman appears in 31:11f, but the role of "the Samaritan" has
been dropped from the Moses narrative (7:146f). In the apparently later
passages of this period, all of the legendary Arab figures disappear completely

from the lists of messengers (42:11; 6:84f). Nevertheless, Jesus (42:11; 6:85), Zacharias and John (6:85) are mentioned in these same verses, even though no narratives about them appear in this period. With respect to the Qur'anic narratives which are based on Biblical characters, these modifications seem to indicate that Muhammad attempted to accommodate the Jews at first, but later either Christians or the members of sects which had broken off from them.

The narratives of this period also show that Muhammad had begun to identify himself with Moses, and this seems to have been part of Muhammad's attempt to win over the Jews. The character of Moses is accorded more text (and generally more detail) than any other of the Qur'anic messengers in this period, and he is the only messenger mentioned as having received the "Book" (32:23; 41:45; 11:20, 112; 28:43).[245] The apparently Jewish question as to why Muhammad was not given the same as Moses (28:48f), seems to have been at least partially answered by verses which now show Muhammad to have received the "Book" (16:66; 6:92). Muhammad is openly compared with Moses (cf. 14:1, 5; 28:44f), and in 17:47f (see the previous period) he even appears to have been substituted for Moses (cf. Ex. 34:34; II Cor. 3:13f).

As opposed to the last Qur'anic period, the names of the Biblical characters which were introduced in these suras all seem to have come from Jewish sources, rather than Christian ones.[246] The amount of foreign vocabulary from the Jews has also increased,[247] although a number of terms seem to have come from Ethiopic,[248] but practically none from Syriac.[249]

Quite a few of the narratives in the suras of this period are generally repetitions of the previous Qur'anic accounts. However, new narratives have been introduced (e.g. those about Joseph and the Sabbath) and older ones have been expanded (e.g. those about Moses, Haman and Korah). Many of these new narratives are heavily dependent on the Talmud and Jewish legends, but the influence of Christian sources on these new narratives appears to have been minimal. Nevertheless, many errors were made in the Qur'anic versions of these stories, which again indicates that Muhammad relied on oral sources.[250] Accordingly, one of Noah's sons drowns (11:44f); Joseph, among many other inconsistencies,[251] welcomes his parents to Egypt (12:100);

Moses was sent to Pharaoh, Haman and Korah (40:25); Haman is to build a
tower for Pharaoh (40:38f); Moses is adopted by Pharaoh's wife (28:8); Moses
asks for forgiveness for killing the Egyptian (28:14f); Moses served 8 or 10
years for his wife (28:27f); Noah was 950 years old at the time of the flood
(29:13); Moses performs the miracle of the leprous hand before Pharaoh
(7:105); Moses requests to see God, but a mountain is destroyed instead
(7:139f); fish which would only come on the Sabbath (7:163f); Sabbath
violators were transformed into apes (7:166); Abraham's father was Azar
(6:74).

Although the heavy influence of Judaism is obvious in the suras of this period
(see also the references to "keeping covenant": 16:93f; 6:153; 13:20f), there is
some evidence which reveals that Muhammad was still in contact with Christians. The instruction to give alms instead of lending to usurers (30:37f),[252] the
references to Jesus (42:11; 6:85) Zacharias and John (6:85), and the denial
that "the Book" was not previously sent down to just "two" groups (6:157f), all
seem to reveal a Christian presence in Medina. Moreover, the Qur'an verses
from this period which are similar to New Testament passages[253] (particularly
Qur'an 14:5f - Acts 26:18), and the notion that the Jewish dietary laws were
meant to be a punishment on the Jews (7:160f; 6:147)[254] also indicate the
influence of Christians or pseudo-Christian sects. Muslim scholars have
generally thought that Medinan passages concerning Christianity were due to
the Christians of distant Najran,[255] and though this idea cannot be categorically
rejected,[256] it is more probable that Muhammad had frequent contact with the
Christians of the nearby Wadi al-Qura.[257]

As was shown in the last chapter, it may have been pagan Arab understandings
of Monotheism which led Muhammad to reject the doctrine of the Sonship of
Christ and turn away from Christianity.[258] Muhammad then seems to have
favored Judaism, and no doubt learned about the previous scriptures from
them (16:45; 10:94), until he became cognizant of the Jewish dietary laws.
Perhaps after a period of partial conformance to these regulations, Muhammad
rejected them as a whole,[259] and retained a dietary code, which as it turns out,
would have been most acceptable for Arabs or Ethiopian Christians.[260] The
later Qur'anic references to Jesus (42:11, 6:85), Zacharias

and John (6:85) also suggest that Muhammad again turned to Christians after his disagreement with the Jews concerning their dietary laws.

During this period, requests were still made for a miracle or sign on Muhammad's behalf (10:21; 29:49; 13:8, 27f). Muhammad replied that miracles were of God (10:21; 29:49; cf. 13:38), and once even rhetorically asked if the sending down of the Book was not enough (29:50). Some of Muhammad's hearers also seem to have asked him to expedite the threatened punishment (29:53f; 7:32), and once he answered by alluding to the Judgment (29:54f). In other passages, Muhammad states that the awaited punishment may not come during his own lifetime (10:47; 13:40). Muhammad still asks for no wage for his services (12:104; 42:22; 34:46; 6:90), and he has not yet directly claimed the title of a prophet for himself (cf. 7:92; 6:112). Muhammad's statement about not being anything new among the messengers (46:8) is contradicted by his assertion that he is the first Muslim (39:14) or the first to profess Islam (6:14).[261] Muhammad was commanded to request forgiveness for his own sins in 40:57.

The Qur'an is presented as a revelation in Arabic (41:2; 12:2; 39:29; 13:27),[262] which confirms the previous Books (10:38; 35:28; 46:28f). Muhammad was accused of authoring the Qur'an himself (11:16; 10:39f; 46:7) and of having received "foreign" help (16:105). The Qur'an was "preserved" by memory (29:47f), and Muhammad seems to have had reservations about having it committed to writing (6:7), even though he was earlier accused of such (perhaps as a memory aid - cf. 25:6) and knew that the Jews copied out the Book of Moses on parchment (6:91).

Notes:

[1] Guillaume, *Muhammad*, pp. 194 f; Ibn Sa`d, *Classes*, vol. 1, 1, pp. 249 f; Tabari, *History*, vol. 6, pp. 120 f.

[2] Iyas b. Mu`adh - Guillaume, *Muhammad*, pp. 196 f; Tabari, *History*, vol. 6, pp. 123 f. The name "Medina," actually means "town" and was adopted much later, Medina was known as "Yathrib," before the Hijra; cf. *EI²*, s.v. "al-Madina."

[3] The battle of Bu'ath, between the Aws and the Khazraj, is said to have taken place shortly after this delegation returned to Medina.

[4] Nöldeke and Schwally, *GQ*, vol. 1, p. 143.

[5] Ibid., p. 144.

[6] Cf. e.g. Campbell, *The Qur'an and the Bible*, pp. 177f.

[7] Geiger, *WMJA*, p. 72, references Hagigah 16 and Taanit 11; cf. Qur'an 36:65.

[8] Nöldeke and Schwally, *GQ*, vol. 1, pp. 144 f; Guillaume, *Muhammad*, pp. 132 f.

[9] Nöldeke and Schwally, *GQ*, vol. 1, p. 145.

[10] شريعة.

[11] Guillaume, *Muhammad*, pp. 197 f; Ibn Sa'd, *Classes*, vol. 1, 1, pp. 250 f; Tabari, *History*, vol. 6, pp. 124 f. The number of those who converted is given as one, two, six or eight in traditions known to Ibn Sa'd.

[12] Guillaume, *Muhammad*, pp. 197 f; Tabari, *History*, vol. 6, pp. 124 f.

[13] Guillaume, *Muhammad*, p. 198; Ibn Sa'd, *Classes*, vol. 1, 1, p. 253; Tabari, *History*, vol. 6, pp. 125 f. Ibn Sa'd reports that the first mosque (place of prayer) in Medina was that of the Banu Zurayq.

[14] Ten of these are said to have from the Khazraj and two from the Aws; Ibn Sa'd, *Classes*, vol. 1, 1, p. 254.

[15] Guillaume, *Muhammad*, pp. 198 f; Ibn Sa'd, *Classes*, vol. 1, 1, pp. 254 f; Tabari, *History*, vol. 6, pp. 126 f.

[16] Guillaume, *Muhammad*, p. 199; Ibn Sa'd, *Classes*, vol. 1, 1, p. 255;

Tabari, *History*, vol. 6, p. 127. Ibn Hisham's report contains the anachronisms of placing the institution of the Friday prayers (as a heading) and the call to prayer in this time period.

[17] Guillaume, *Muhammad*, pp. 201 f; Ibn Sa`d, *Classes*, vol. 1, 1, pp. 255 f; Tabari, *History*, vol. 6, pp. 130 f.

[18] Guillaume, *Muhammad*, pp. 203 f; Ibn Sa`d, *Classes*, vol. 1, 1, pp. 256 f; Tabari, *History*, vol. 6, p. 136. The twelve are likened to the twelve leaders Moses chose from the Israelites and the twelve disciples of Jesus in Ibn Sa`d, which also anachronistically mentions Gabriel. Ibn Sa`d shows that there were some 500 Muslims among the Khazraj and the `Aws at this time. The accounts of Ibn Hisham and Tabari speak of the Muslims as having a qibla, however, the introduction of the qibla probably occurred later in Medina.

[19] *Sahih Bukhari*, vol. 5, p. 152; vol. 7, p. 42; vol. 9, p. 155; *Sahih Muslim*, vol. 4, p. 1298.

[20] *Sahih Bukhari*, vol. 7, p. 12.

[21] *Sahih Bukhari*, vol. 5, p. 152; vol. 7, pp. 50, 65; *Sahih Muslim*, vol. 2, pp. 715 f (one of these hadith show `A'isha to have been seven years old); *Sunan Abu Dawud*, vol. 2, p. 569. `A'isha is reported to have been 18 years old when the 63 year-old Muhammad died; *Sahih Muslim*, vol. 2, p. 716; vol. 4, p. 1253.

[22] Guillaume, *Muhammad*, pp. 212 f; Tabari, *History*, vol. 6, p. 139.

[23] Guillaume, *Muhammad*, p. 213.

[24] Tabari, *History*, vol. 6, pp. 137, 139.

[25] Nöldeke and Schwally, *GQ*, vol. 1, pp. 187, 214; Buhl, *Muhammad*, pp. 232 f. See also Watt in Tabari, *History*, vol. 6, p. xxiv. Muslim scholars also place the revelation of the suras 8 and 22 in Medina; cf. *EI²*, "Kur'an," p. 416; Suyuti, *El-Itkan*, vol. 1, pp. 4 f. Although 22:40 is thought to have dated from the Hijra in one canonical hadith (cf. Suyuti, *El-Itkan*, vol. 1, pp. 32 f), later

Muslims recognize the passage as having been Medinan; cf. Ali, *Quran*, vol. 2, p. 861, n. 2816. The debate over the translation of يقتلون as an active or passive (22:40), is not terribly important, since both active and passive readings of this verse: "Permission is given those who fight (or are fought against)..." indicate that the armed struggle between the Meccans and emigrants had already begun. The attempt to place these verses in a Meccan setting may well have been a reaction of Islamic traditionists to the Christian accusation that, in contrast to the Old Testament prophets, Muhammad had received no divine authority for opening the armed conflict against the Meccans; cf. *ECMD*, pp. 358, 447 f.

[26] *Sahih Bukhari*, vol. 6, p. 13; vol. 9, pp. 338 f.

[27] *Sahih Bukhari*, vol. 5, p. 193; vol. 7, p. 525; *Sahih Muslim*, vol. 4, p. 1248.

[28] The claims that the pagan Arabs fasted on the 10th of Muharram (*Sahih Bukhari*, vol. 3, p. 65; vol. 6, p. 24; *Sahih Muslim*, vol. 2, pp. 548 f) are not very reliable, since the Arabic `Ashura comes from the Hebrew through the Aramaic (`asor = "the tenth day"), which corresponds to the 10th of Tishrey, or the Jewish Day of Atonement; Lev. 23:27f; Nöldeke and Schwally, *GQ*, vol. 1, p. 179, n. 1; Buhl, *Muhammad*, p. 216. The idea that this fast was held by the Jews to commemorate their deliverance from Pharaoh (*Sahih Bukhari*, vol. 6, pp. 165, 233; *Sahih Muslim*, vol. 2, pp. 548 f) also appears to have been an Islamic corruption. Some hadith show how this fast was held by the Muslims in Medina; *Sahih Muslim*, vol. 2, pp. 552 f.

[29] Ever since the days of Solomon, Jews faced the Temple Mount in Jerusalem when praying; I Kgs. 8:29f; Dan. 6:10; Talmud Berakhot 31a. The first Islamic qibla was also Jerusalem (*Sahih Bukhari*, vol. 6, pp. 16 f; *Sahih Muslim*, vol. 1, pp. 267 f), after this was learned from the Jews; Tabari, *History*, vol. 7, p. 25; cf. also Nöldeke and Schwally, GQ, vol. 1, p. 179, n. 1; Buhl, *Muhammad*, p. 216. The Medinan Qur'anic passage 2:136f also indicates that the Muslims prayed in the same direction as the Jews, before the qibla was changed in 2 AH. Welch, in *EI²*, s.v. "Muhammad," p. 368, also

points out that the Ebionites and Elkesaites also prayed facing Jerusalem, and thus that this borrowing may have been from them.

[30] Buhl, *Muhammad*, p. 215; *SEI*, p. 492.

[31] Although some discount the influence of the Jews in these matters (e.g. *SEI*, p. 316) it can hardly be a coincidence that the Jews are mentioned in this passage (16:119), which is generally recognized as being one of the earliest regarding dietary regulations. Cf. also Speyer, *Erzählungen*, p. 320. The New Testament restrictions (Acts 15:20f), which are similar to those given in Qur'an 16:115f, were essentially given out of respect for Jewish practice. Although Acts 15:20f does not forbid pork, Ethiopian Christians usually do not eat it. It also does not appear that the pagan Arabs ate pork either; Crone, *Trade*, p. 190, n. 104.

[32] Buhl, *Muhammad*, p. 204, *SEI*, p. 398.

[33] Guillaume, "The Influence of Judaism on Islam," *The Legacy of Israel*, pp. 155 f.

[34] Nöldeke and Schwally, *GQ*, vol. 1, p. 179, n. 1; Buhl, *Muhammad*, pp. 212 f; Bell, *Origins*, p. 127; Andrae, *Mohammed*, pp. 136 f; Watt, *Muhammad*, pp. 98 f.

[35] Qur'an 2, which for the most part is thought to have been composed in 2 AH, is generally considered to have been the first Medinan sura; Suyuti, *El-Itkan*, vol. 1, pp. 1 f; Nöldeke and Schwally, *GQ*, vol. 1, p. 173; *EI²*, s.v. "Kur'an," pp. 416 f. Nöldeke and Schwally suggest that earlier Medinan suras may have been lost.

[36] Suyuti, *El-Itkan*, vol. 1, pp. 1 f.

[37] Nöldeke and Schwally, *GQ*, vol. 2, pp. 79 f; cf. also *Sunan Abu Dawud*, vol. 1, p. 202.

[38] Nöldeke and Schwally, *GQ*, vol. 2, pp. 68 f; *EI²*, s.v. "Kur'an," p. 414.

[39] The first 16-18 months after Muhammad's arrival in Medina.

[40] Bell, *Qur'an*, vol. 1, pp. vi f, simply described his "Qur'an period" as "covering the later part of Muhammad's activity in Mecca and the first year or two of his residence in Medina, during which he is producing a Qur'an, giving in Arabic the gist of previous revelation"; cf. Bell, *Origin*, p. 125; Watt and Bell, *Introduction*, pp. 137 f; *EI²*, s.v. "Kur'an," pp. 417 f. Bell also attributed the composition of various Qur'an passages to this period; e.g. concerning Qur'an 29:46-48 he writes: "a little earlier than 2 AH"; *Qur'an*, vol. 1, p. 388.

[41] Guillaume, *Muhammad*, pp. 239f, 260, 263. "Finhas" appears to have been one of the few typically Jewish names of those living in Medina and the surrounding area; cf. Horovitz, *Untersuchungen*, p. 163.

[42] See the references in n. 26, above, together with *Sahih Bukhari*, vol. 8, pp. 529 f; *Sahih Muslim*, vol. 3, pp. 918 f. Cf. Qur'an 3:87.

[43] Note the many references to the Talmud in the "Medinan" suras in Appendix F, pp. 414 f; cf. also Buhl, *Muhammad*, p. 20.

[44] See p. 162, above.

[45] Bell, *Origin*, p. 120; most of these earlier passages only mention Moses as having received "the Book," but no other prophet from a later age.

[46] Cf. Nöldeke and Schwally, *GQ*, vol. 1, pp. 145 f.

[47] The deficiency of Jewish names among the Jews of Medina, has led some to suspect that they were either Arab converts to Judaism, or "Arabized" Jews; Guillaume, *Muhammad*, pp. 239 f; Buhl, *Muhammad*, pp. 18 f; *SEI*, pp. 292 f; *EI²*, s.v. "al-Madina," p. 994.

[48] *EI²*, s.v. "al-Madina," p. 995.

[49] Buhl, *Muhammad*, p. 202; cf. *Sahih Bukhari*, vol. 3, p. 296.

[50] Guillaume, *Islam*, p. 12; *SEI*, p. 293; *EI²*, s.v. "al-Madina," p. 994.

[51] Watt, *Muhammad*, p. 85; *SEI*, p. 292; *EI²*, s.v. "al-Madina," p. 995.

[52] Watt, *Muhammad*, p. 87.

[53] Among others, the Arab leader ʿAbdullah b. Ubayy did not participate in this battle; Buhl, *Muhammad*, p. 202, n. 5; *EI²*, s.v. "al-Madina," p. 995

[54] Buhl, *Muhammad*, pp. 202 f; *EI²*, s.v. "al-Madina," p. 995.

[55] Guillaume, *Muhammad*, pp. 213 f; Ibn Saʿd, *Classes*, vol. 1, 1, pp. 261 f; Tabari, *History*, vol. 6, pp. 139 f.

[56] See the references in n. 55, above.

[57] Guillaume, *Muhammad*, p. 221.

[58] Guillaume, *Muhammad*, pp. 221 f; Ibn Saʿd, *Classes*, vol. 1, 1, pp. 263 f (presents Muhammad as having recited Qur'an 36:1-10 on this occasion); Tabari, *History*, vol. 6, pp. 140 f.

[59] Guillaume, *Muhammad*, pp. 223 f; Ibn Saʿd, *Classes*, vol. 1, 1, pp. 266 f; Tabari, *History*, vol. 6, pp. 147 f.

[60] Actually 12 Rabiʿ I, 1 AH; Guillaume, *Muhammad*, p. 227; Ibn Saʿd, *Classes*, vol. 1, 1, p. 271; Tabari, *History*, vol. 6, p. 150.

[61] Guillaume, *Muhammad*, pp. 223 (n. 3), 227; Tabari, *History*, vol. 7, p. 8.

[62] Jeffery, *Vocabulary*, p. 202.

[63] Blachère, *Coran*, p. 295, n. to v. 43.

[64] Suyuti, *El-Itkan*, vol. 1, p. 27; Nöldeke and Schwally, *GQ*, vol. 1, pp. 145 f.

[65] See p. 162, above.

[66] This verse was obviously composed before the drinking of wine (or other alcoholic beverages) was forbidden (cf. Qur'an 5:92).

[67] This word appears to have been a pre-Islamic borrowing from the Jews; Horovitz, *Untersuchungen*, pp. 51 f; Jeffery, *Vocabulary*, p. 69. However, the theological idea of this verse— that a people would have their own witness against themselves— appears to come from the Talmud; Andrae, *Ursprung*, p. 69, references Avodah Zarah 2a-3b.

[68] See n. 65, above.

[69] See p. 108, above. This appears to be one of the earliest Qur'anic usages of term "the Holy Spirit."

[70] عجمى = "a barbaric language," i.e. non-Arabic.

[71] cf. Buhl, *Muhammad*, p. 169.

[72] Guillaume, *Muhammad*, p. 180, also n. 2. This name appears to be of Ethiopic origin; see also the references given in Nöldeke and Schwally, *GQ*, vol. 1, p. 148.

[73] Wellhausen, *Medina*, p. 55. Waqidi also maintains that the Qur'an passage 16:105-111 was revealed about the time of the battle of Badr; Ibid.

[74] Cf. Nöldeke and Schwally, *GQ*, vol. 1, p. 148, where it is pointed out that Islamic commentators seem to have been misled by the word عجمى in Qur'an 16:105.

[75] Nöldeke and Schwally, *GQ*, vol. 1, pp. 147 f; see p. 199, below.

[76] Ibid., p. 149.

[77] Guillaume, *Muhammad*, p. 387, Tabari, *History*, vol. 7, pp. 133 f; Wellhausen, *Medina*, p. 135.

[78] See Appendix F, p. 412..

[79] Andrae, *Ursprung*, pp. 168 f, outlines this style and compares Qur'an 16:2-36 with the sermons found in Acts 17:24f; 14:15-17; Ps. 146:6; I Clem. XIX:3-XXIII; Clem. Hom. 1:7.

[80] See Appendix F, p. 412.

[81] Nöldeke and Schwally, *GQ*, vol. 1, pp. 149 f.

[82] Ibid., pp. 150 f; see p. 41, above.

[83] Somehow the terms "hanpa" or "hanef," which Syrian Christians or Jews may have called pagan Arabs, came to assume a positive religious meaning among Arabs predating Muhammad. Eventually, however, "hanif" came to mean "Muslim," especially during Muhammad's ministry in Medina (cf. Qur'an 3:60). See Buhl, *Muhammad*, pp. 70 f; Horovitz, *Untersuchungen*, pp. 56 f; Andrae, *Mohammed*, pp. 108 f; *SEI*, pp. 132 f; EI², s.v. "Hanif"; Watt and Bell, *Introduction*, p. 16. In their discussions with Muslims, Syrian Christian polemicists argued that "hanif" actually meant "pagan"; see *ECMD*, pp. 290, 343 n. 27, 412 f.

[84] Rudolph, *Koran*, p. 368, n. 10.

[85] Cf. Qur'an 2:263f, 276, Rudolph, *Koran*, p. 369, nn. 14-15.

[86] Geiger, *WMJA*, p. 64, references the Midrash (Rashi) for Gen. 1:1f.

[87] The Jews of Medina are thought to have been implied in vv. 15 and 20; Nöldeke and Schwally, *GQ*, vol. 1, p. 151.

[88] See n. 87, above.

[89] Geiger, *WMJA*, p. 108, cites Midrash Tanhuma.

[90] Ibid., p. 108, where Rosh ha-Shanah 16,2 and Sanhedrin 108 are referenced.

[91] See Appendix D, p. 378.

[92] See Appendix D, p. 378.

[93] These stories are also similar to those found in sura 26.

[94] See p. 89, above.

[95] Cf. Gen. 19f.

[96] It is thought that Muhammad may have tried to identify Shuʿayb with Jethro from the Bible, as he is shown among the people of Madyan (Midian) in the suras of this period; cf. Horovitz, *Untersuchung*, pp. 119 f; *SEI*, p. 544.

[97]	Sura 26	Sura 11
	Moses	Noah
	Abraham	Hud
	Noah	Salih
	Hud	Abraham
	Salih	Lot
	Lot	Shuʿayb
	(Shuʿayb)	Moses

[98] See p. 105, above.

[99] See p. 106, above.

[100] See pp. 103, 106, above.

[101] Speyer, *Erzählungen*, p. 458, also references the Talmud, Avot 3,22.

[102] See p. 199, below.

[103] See Appendix D, pp. 378 f.

[104] In Wellhausen, *Medina*, p. 349, Waqidi gives a tradition reporting that a certain Ethiopian Jewish slave named Jabr became a Muslim as a result of hearing sura 12 prior to the emigration to Medina. See also Nöldeke and Schwally, *GQ*, vol. 1, pp. 152, for references to later Islamic sources.

[105] See Appendix B, pp. 351 f..

[106] Another possibility, of course, is that an early Jewish convert to Islam may have provided the materials for this sura.

[107] Cf. *EI²*, s.v. "Kur'an," p. 418.

[108] See Appendix D, pp. 378 f.

[109] According to a tradition in Suyuti, *El-Itkan*, vol. 2, p. 498, a Jew is said to have asked Muhammad which stars Joseph saw in his dream. Gabriel is reported to have told Muhammad, who then told the Jew that they were: Harsan, Tarik, Dhu'l-Qatafayn, Dhu'l-Fark, Wassab, Amudan, Qabis, Dharuh, Musabbih, Faylak, Ziya and Nur, the last two of whom are said to have represented Joseph's mother and father.

[110] See Appendix D, p. 379.

[111] See Appendix D, p. 379.

[112] See Appendix D, p. 379.

[113] See Appendix D, p. 379.

[114] See Appendix D, p. 379.

[115] Nöldeke, "Qur'an," p. 9, shows that Muhammad thought Egypt's agriculture was dependent on rain; cf. p. 114, n. 62, above.

[116] See Appendix D, p. 379.

[117] See Appendix D, p. 379.

[118] See Appendix D, p. 379.

[119] See Appendix D, p. 380.

[120] See Appendix D, p. 380.

[121] See `Abdullah b. Ubayy, p. 271, below.

[122] See Appendix D, p. 380.

[123] See p. 116, n. 88, above.

[124] Cf. Jeffery, *Vocabulary*, p. 225.

[125] Nöldeke, "Qur'an," p. 12. Contemporary Islamic films on the life of Joseph often reveal that Muslim writers have availed themselves of Biblical sources to fill in the Qur'anic narrative.

[126] Ibid., p. 295.

[127] Ibid., p. 82.

[128] Ibid., p. 177.

[129] See Appendix D, p. 380.

[130] Guillaume, *Muhammad*, p. 130; Tabari, *History*, vol. 6, p. 102; *Sahih Bukhari*, vol. 5, pp. 123 f; vol. 6, pp. 320 f.

[131] Some early Muslim Qur'an commentators thought this Joseph to be someone other than Joseph the son of Jacob; see Appendix E, p. 405.

[132] See Appendix D, p. 380.

[133] Cf. *ECMD*, p. 723.

[134] See Appendix F, p. 412.

[135] Jeffery, *Vocabulary*, p. 284.

[136] Horovitz, *Untersuchungen*, pp. 81, 131; Jeffery, *Vocabulary*, pp. 231 f.

[137] Cf. Qur'an 17:105f, and p. 103, above.

[138] See Appendix D, p. 381.

[139] See Appendix D, p. 381..

[140] See Appendix D, p. 381. The ambiguity of this statement is reported to have caused one Jew to ask a Muslim which of these two time periods Moses served. The Muslim then asked Ibn `Abbas, who supposed that Moses served ten years; cf. *Sahih Bukhari*, vol. 3, p. 525.

[141] Cf. Bell, *Qur'an*, vol. 1, pp. vi-vii; Watt and Bell, *Introduction*, pp. 141 f; *EI²*, s.v. "Kur'an," p. 418.

[142] The comments of Nöldeke and Schwally (*GQ*, vol. 1, p. 153) on 28:52 only show that this verse must have been composed before Muhammad's break with the Jews in 2 AH. This verse could have very well dated from Muhammad's first months in Medina.

[143] Nöldeke and Schwally, *GQ*, vol. 1, pp. 153 f.

[144] See Appendix D, p. 381.

[145] See p. 91, above.

[146] See Appendix F, p. 412.

[147] See p. 107, above.

[148] The Christian apologist al-Kindi comments on the discrepancy between the Qur'an depicting Abraham (and other prophets) as having been Muslims, and Muhammad's claim of being the first Muslim; *ECMD*, p. 415.

[149] Cf. Andrae, *Ursprung*, pp. 160 f; *Mohammed*, pp. 89 f.

[150] Cf. Andrae, *Ursprung*, p. 142; Ahrens, "Christliches," *ZDMG*, 84 (1930), pp. 54 f. This notion of "two" trumpet blasts is thought to have come from the works of Ephraem the Syrian.

[151] Nöldeke and Schwally, *GQ*, vol. 1, p. 154.

[152] Several versions of canonical traditions show that a rabbi came to Muhammad and said that on the Day of Judgment God would essentially hold the earth and all creation in His hand and would say that He is Lord (or King), upon which Muhammad is reported to have recited Qur'an 39:67; *Sahih Bukhari*, vol. 9, p. 409; *Sahih Muslim*, vol. 4, p. 1461. Apparently later, however, Muhammad is depicted as having repeated what the rabbi had told him as true; *Sahih Bukhari*, vol. 8, pp. 345 f; *Sahih Muslim*, vol. 4, p. 1462. It is rather possible that Muhammad actually got the idea for Qur'an 39:67 from a rabbi in the first place.

[153] See Appendix F, pp. 412 f.

[154] These verses are thought to have date from after the battle of Badr, or probably even Uhud; Nöldeke and Schwally, *GQ*, vol. 1, pp. 154 f.

[155] See Appendix D, p. 382.

[156] Allah, who is generally referred to in first person plural (vv. 14, 26, 30, 34), is spoken of in third person singular in v. 23; Horovitz, *Untersuchungen*, p. 23.

[157] See p. 89, above.

[158] Nöldeke and Schwally, *GQ*, vol. 1, p. 155, consider the phrase "with better means" (v. 45) to refer to Muhammad's armed conflict with the Jews.

However, this verse was used in a much less belligerent sense by both early Muslim and Christian polemicists; cf. *ECMD*, pp. 384, 479.

[159] E.g. cf. Bell (*Qur'an*, vol. 1, p. 388; *Commentary*, vol. 1, p. 65), considering this verse to be Medinan and predating 2 AH, thinks that Muhammad only meant to say that he was neither a Christian scribe nor Jewish rabbi, who could read (recite) or write scripture.

[160] See Appendix F, p. 356.

[161] Nöldeke and Schwally, *GQ*, vol. 1, pp. 156 f, this verse may have also caused early Muslim scholars to think that this one was of the last suras to be revealed before the Hijra; cf. Appendix B, pp. 352 f.

[162] Nöldeke and Schwally, *GQ*, vol. 1, p. 156.

[163] Jeffery, *Vocabulary*, p. 272.

[164] See Appendix F, p. 413..

[165] Guillaume, *Muhammad*, p. 239.

[166] This person is often held to have been Nadr b. Harith, but this is by no means certain; cf. Rudolph, *Koran*, p. 373, n. 3; Ali, *Qur'an*, vol. 2,   p. 1080, n. 3584.

[167] See Appendix D, p. 382.

[168] It is conjectured that these verses were intended to have been placed after v. 18; Nöldeke and Schwally, *GQ*, vol. 1, p. 157.

[169] Nöldeke and Schwally, *GQ*, vol. 1, p. 157.

[170] Rudolph, *Koran*, p. 374, n. 10.

[171] Geiger, *WMJA*, p. 88, references Yevamot 4,10.

[172] Ibn al-Nadim, *Fihrist*, trans. Dodge, vol. 1, p. 57; Jeffery, *Materials*, p. 85.

[173] Jeffery, *Materials*, p. 205.

[174] The reference to Jesus in this passage indicates Christian influence. In speaking of Qur'an 6:83f, Horovitz, *Untersuchungen*, p. 37, felt that Muhammad intentionally left out the names of the "Arabian" messengers. A tradition in Ibn Sa`d, *Classes*, vol. 1, 2, p. 286, claims that Qur'an 42:11 was recited at the time the qibla was changed from Jerusalem to Mecca.

[175] See p. 116, n. 88.

[176] See Appendix F, p. 413.

[177] See Appendix D, p. 377..

[178] See n. 148, above.

[179] See Appendix D, p. 382.

[180] See Appendix D, p. 382.

[181] See n. 148, above.

[182] See *ECMD*, p. 308, where this Qur'an 10:94 was used to counter the later Muslim charge that the Bible had been altered.

[183] See Appendix D, p. 383.

[184] The Christian apologist al-Kindi also noticed that these verses stood in contradiction to the doctrine of Jihad; *ECMD*, p. 478.

[185] See Appendix F, p. 413.

[186] Ibn Sa`d, *Classes*, vol. 1, 2, pp. 281 f; Buhl, *Muhammad*, p. 204; *SEI*, pp. 330 f. A canonical hadith reports that `A'isha lived in the house of

Harith b. al-Nuʿman in Medina until her marriage with Muhammad was consummated; Ibn Saʿd, *Classes*, vol. 1, 1, p. 160, cf. *Sahih Bukhari*, vol. 5, p. 152.

[187] Ibn Saʿd, *Classes*, vol. 1, 2, p. 282.

[188] Ibid., p. 281.

[189] Guillaume, *Muhammad*, pp. 228 f; Ibn Saʿd, *Classes*, vol. 1, 2, pp. 280 f; Tabari, *History*, vol. 7, p. 5.

[190] Cf. Nöldeke and Schwally, *GQ*, vol. 1, p. 158.

[191] Cf. Tabari, *History*, vol. 3, p. 174.

[192] Margoliouth, "Additions," *JRAS*, (1939), pp. 53 f.

[193] See Appendix D, p. 383.

[194] See p. 64, n. 79.

[195] See p. 116, n. 88.

[196] See Appendix F, p. 413.

[197] See Appendix F, p. 413.

[198] Nöldeke and Schwally, *GQ*, vol. 1, p. 158.

[199] See pp. 141, 160. The v. 41 of this passage could also refer to the Jews of Medina.

[200] See Appendix F, p. 413.

[201] See p. 46, n. 105.

[202] Horovitz, *Untersuchungen*, p. 37, points out that Allah is referred to in the first person plural in the vv. 9-10, but as third person singular in the vv. 11f.

[203] A canonical tradition connects this passage with Muhammad's later prohibition of nudity at the Ka`ba (*Sahih Muslim*, vol. 4, p. 1555), however, Nöldeke and Schwally (*GQ*, vol. 1, p. 159) suggest that these verses were composed during a pre-Hijra pilgrimage.

[204] See Appendix, D, p. 383.

[205] Muhammad probably confused this with Korah's destruction; cf. Num. 16:23f.

[206] Nöldeke and Schwally, *GQ*, vol. 1, pp. 159f. See p. 209, below.

[207] The city the Jews are said to have entered was thought by some Muslim scholars to be Jerusalem (!); Tabari, *Tafsir*, vol. 2, p. 704. The word "hittatun" (="forgiveness") came from either Hebrew or Aramaic; Jeffery, *Vocabulary*, p. 110.

[208] Cf. 2:55f, this passage seems to imply that the Jewish dietary laws were self-imposed. According to Islamic sources, a group of the Jews is said to have exchanged either the word "habbatun" (="grain"); *Sahih Bukhari*, vol. 6, pp. 7 f, 131; or the word "hintatun" (="barley"); Tabari, *Tafsir*, vol. 2, p. 705, (cf. also Guillaume, *Muhammad*, p. 250); for the word "hittatun" (="forgiveness"). Geiger, *WMJA*, pp. 18 f, maintained that the word "khati'yatun" (="sin") may have been meant as the exchanged word, a form of which is found in both Qur'anic passages mentioning this supposed event (cf. 7:161; 2:55). In itself, this story of the Jews entering a city and being commanded to ask for forgiveness does not appear in any Jewish sources, and was probably due to Muhammad himself (a very similar story is also told in 4:153f about the Jews disobeying Sabbath commandment).

[209] See Appendix D, p. 383.

[210] See Appendix D, p. 384.

[211] See Appendix D, p. 384.

[212] Some later Islamic sources claim that Balaam was meant, while others mention Umayya b. Abu'l-Salt; see Nöldeke and Schwally, *GQ*, vol. 1, p. 160.

[213] See p. 41.

[214] Jeffery, *Vocabulary*, al-A`raf - p. 65, Sabbath - pp. 160 f.

[215] See Appendix F, p. 413.

[216] Some Islamic sources think that `Abdullah b. Salam was meant; cf. Nöldeke and Schwally, *GQ*, vol. 1, p. 160, but it may be that Moses was being alluded to; cf. Rudolph, *Koran*, p. 454, n. 5.

[217] It is thought that the described conversion at 40 years old may have been a reference to either Muhammad or Abu Bakr; cf. Rudolph, *Koran*, p. 454, n. 11.

[218] Nöldeke and Schwally, *GQ*, vol. 1, p. 160.

[219] See also: Guillaume, *Muhammad*, p. 194; Tabari, *History*, vol. 6, p. 118.

[220] See Appendix F, p. 413.

[221] Cf. v. 91; 52:3; Rudolph, *Koran*, p. 136, n. 3.

[222] See n. 148, above.

[223] Cf. 39:43; Rudolph, *Koran*, p. 140, n. 19; see also n. 149, above.

[224] See Appendix D, p. 384.

[225] See Appendix D, p. 384.

[226] See Bell, *Origin*, p. 129; see Appendix D, p. 365.

[227] Horovitz, *Untersuchungen*, p. 37, felt that Muhammad left off these names intentionally.

[228] See p. 89.

[229] Cf. Al-Kindi in *ECMD*, p. 439.

[230] Nöldeke and Schwally, *GQ*, vol. 1, p. 162.

[231] See n. 147, above.

[232] It has been suggested that the Qur'an probably only maintained the eating habits of the pagan Arabs; *SEI*, p. 316.

[233] Nöldeke and Schwally, *GQ*, vol. 1, p. 162.

[234] See p. 198, below.

[235] Jeffery, *Vocabulary*, p. 126.

[236] See Appendix, F, pp. 413 f.

[237] Guillaume, *Muhammad*, pp. 239 f.

[238] Some are shown to have been sincere in their conversions; Guillaume, *Muhammad*, pp. 239 f, while others are said to have been hypocritical; Ibid., pp. 246 f. In the canonical traditions, Muhammad is reported to have said that if ten Jewish scholars had followed him, that all Jews would have done the same; *Sahih Muslim*, vol. 4, p. 1463; cf. *Sahih Bukhari*, vol. 5, p. 192.

[239] Although the Qur'an and Islamic traditions do not illuminate Muhammad's reasons for partially rejecting the Jewish dietary laws, one would very strongly suspect that it had to do with the fact that camel meat, which was one of the staples of the Quraysh (cf. e.g. Tabari, *History*, vol. 7, p. 31), is forbidden as unclean in the Torah (Lev. 11:4). See also p. 253, n. 64.

[240] See nn. 206-207, above; cf. Speyer, *Erzählungen*, pp. 318 f.

[241] Rudolph, *Koran*, p. 233, n. 1.

[242] Even though Qur'an 40:57 still mentions only two prayer times.

[243] See n. 97, above.

[244] See n. 96, above.

[245] See p. 135, n. 298, above. In *Sahih Bukhari*, vol. 8, pp. 344 f, (and related traditions) an argument between a Muslim and a Jew is said to have occurred, in which Muhammad was claimed to have been greater than Moses. When Muhammad was informed of this, he is reported to have said that he was not to be considered as being greater than Moses.

[246] Joseph - n. 126, Haman - n. 135, Korah - n. 136.

[247] `Ashura - n. 28, cattle - n. 127, scepter - n. 192, forgiveness - n. 207, Sabbath - n. 214, swine - n. 235.

[248] Idol - n. 62, cup - n. 128, watchtower - n. 132, hypocrite - n. 163, al-A`raf - n. 214.

[249] "hanif" (which seems to have predated Islam) - n. 83, cattle (which could have come from Aramaic) - n. 127.

[250] See p. 53.

[251] See the commentary on the Joseph narrative (Qur'an 12) for anomalies which cannot be attributed to Jewish or Christian sources.

[252] Andrae, *Ursprung*, pp. 185 f.

[253] See Appendix F, pp. 412 f.

[254] See Andrae, *Ursprung*, p. 198; Speyer, *Erzählungen*, pp. 318 f.

[255] Cf. e.g. Guillaume, *Muhammad*, pp. 270 f; Nöldeke and Schwally, *GQ*, vol. 1, p. 177, n. 2.

[256] Christians from Yemen on pilgrimage to Jerusalem would probably have passed through Medina.

[257] See p. 1, above. Other sources of Christian influence in Medina are also possible; the Medinan Abu Qays b. Abu Anas is said to have rejected idols and lived as a monk before he accepted Islam. He is reported to have considered becoming a Christian before he accepted Islam; Guillaume, *Muhammad*, pp. 236 f.

[258] See p. 95, above.

[259] See p. 160, above.

[260] See n. 31, above.

[261] See n. 148, above.

[262] The matter of the Qur'an having been "revealed" in Arabic and not containing foreign vocabulary has long been disputed by Muslim and Christian authorities; Kindi, *ECMD*, pp. 460 f; Nöldeke, "Qur'an," pp. 14 f; Jeffery, *Vocabulary*, pp. 5 f; Margoliouth, "Additions," *JRAS*, (1939),   pp. 53 f.

Muhammad
Break with the Jews

Sira traditions report that shortly after Muhammad arrived in Medina, the Friday prayers were held,[1] Muhammad gave his first message,[2] and a constitution was drawn up to define the relationship between the Muslims, Medinans and the Jews.[3] However, evidence shows that the institution of the Friday prayers was a result of Muhammad's later contact with the Jews,[4], the traditional texts of Muhammad's first sermon differ widely from one another,[5] and the present form of the constitution describes situations which could hardly have predated the battle of Badr.[6]

From an Islamic standpoint, the inhabitants of Medina and its surrounding areas were: the emigrants from Mecca, the Ansar (="helpers"; the Muslims of Medina), the hypocrites (those who feigned to accept Islam), the Jews, their Arab allies and the Arab pagans. In *Sira* traditions, Muhammad is said to have paired the emigrants and the Ansar with each other in order to bond them into a sort of clan.[7] Nevertheless, the two Muslim groups appear to have been somewhat independent, since, for example, none of the Ansar are said to have participated on the raids predating Badr.[8]

The bonding of emigrants to the Ansar also had an economic side to it. Ever since their arrival in Medina, the emigrants had been staying in the homes of the Ansar.[9] These no doubt supported them financially, as the alleged terms of their bonding to the emigrants stipulated that they would support and be able to inherit from one another.[10] In that the emigrants had left their own homes in Mecca, their economic situation was probably not the best, and even the Qur'an describes them as having been "poor" (59:8).[11]

Economically, Muhammad himself probably did not fare much better than his followers. There are quite a few Islamic traditions about the poverty of Muhammad and his family,[12] which though generally discredited by Western scholars,[13] may have originally been based on Muhammad's first months at Medina. Some *Sira* traditions attempt to show that Muhammad began the raids on the Meccan caravans as a result of revelation, but the Qur'an verses cited in these traditions indicate that the armed conflict had already begun before these verses were composed.[14] The poverty of the emigrants along with the possible fear that the Ansar were getting tired of supporting them are thought to have moved Muhammad to begin the raids on the Meccans,[15] and it is probably no coincidence that Muhammad's disclaimer about not asking for a wage[16] does not appear in any suras of this period. Later passages in the Qur'an attempt to justify the Muslim attacks by accusing the Meccans of having driven the emigrants from their homes (2:79; 3:194; 22:41). But, to the contrary, the *Sira* traditions depict the Meccans as generally having wanted to prevent the emigration to Medina. Moreover, only much later passages sanction the Muslims' attacks on the other polytheist (Arab) tribes (9:5), the Jews, Byzantines and other Christian Arabs (9:29). Despite these obvious inconsistencies, one thing is relatively clear: the armed conflict with the Meccans was started by Muhammad.[17]

The first attempted raid on Meccan caravans was led by Muhammad's uncle Hamza some seven months after Muhammad's arrival in Medina. The 30 Muslims intercepted the caravan, which was being escorted by 300 men under Abu Jahl, near al-'Is on the Arabian coast. After arraying themselves for battle, the neutral Majdi b. 'Amr al-Juhani negotiated with both sides until they left the field without engaging in combat.[18]

About a month after this event Muhammad is reported to have married the nine year-old 'A'isha.[19]

A second raid was sent out to Rabigh, where 60 Muslims under 'Ubayda al-Harith met 200 Meccans under Abu Sufyan. Although some arrows were shot (allegedly the first in the name of Islam), there was no further fighting.[20]

In the ninth month after the Hijra, 20 Muslims were sent out with Sa'd b. Abu Waqqas to al-Kharrar, but they arrived there one day after the caravan had already passed.[21]

Qur'an 2 begins with mysterious letters, which are inferred to be the title of the Book without doubt and which is a guidance for those who fear God (v. 1). The vv. 2f describe those who believe as believing in the "hidden," performing prayer, giving alms, as believing that which was sent down to

Muhammad and that which was sent down previous to him and as trusting in the Resurrection. The vv. 5f refer to "unbelievers" and hypocrites, who only profess to believe in Allah and the end Judgment, and the vv. 19f seem to contain a sermon of Muhammad, which is addressed "O you people." The vv. 119a are thought to have been composed in about the beginning of 2 AH by some Western Qur'an scholars.[22] The vv. 28f give a narrative about Adam, which is pretty much in keeping with the earlier Qur'anic stories about him, and the vv. 38f open with the phrase "O you children of Israel." In v. 38 the notion about "keeping covenant" is referred to, and afterwards admonitions are given to accept the Qur'an, not to hide the truth (v. 39), to pray, give alms and bow down (v. 40). The narratives about Pharaoh, Moses and the calf (vv. 46f), which are actually directed to the "children of Israel" (as part of the preceding sermon) reveal some modifications and improvements on earlier Qur'anic versions of these accounts. The short story in the vv. 55f, about the Jewish dietary laws (cf. Qur'an 7:161f),[23] has now been added to the Moses narrative. The v. 59 states that "those who believe" and the Jews, Christians and Sabians,[24] who believe in God and the Resurrection and practice good, will be rewarded and will have nothing to fear. The v. 61 again relates how the Sabbath-violators of the children of Israel were allegedly turned into apes (cf. 7:166), and the vv. 63f indicate that Muhammad confused the law about the red heifer (Num. 19:2f) with the heifer whose neck was to be broken for someone killed by an unknown (Dt. 21:1f).[25] The v. 70 seems to refer to a group of the Jews who are accused of intentionally altering God's word after having understood it, and v. 71 must also apply to the Jews, who appear to have decided not to tell Muhammad or the Muslims about the Bible, because the information the Jews give is simply being used against them. The vv. 73f indicate that there were unlearned (or possibly proselytes)[26] among the Jews who did not know "the Book." In this same passage those are condemned, who write out "the Book" with their hands and claim that their work is from God, with the object of selling it.[27] Thus Muhammad still seems to have been averse to the notion of God's word being copied out by hand,[28] although he must have later changed his mind. The v. 74 appears to be about the Jews and God keeping covenant, but a description of the covenant with the children of Israel (vv. 77f) contains some pretty novel ideas, such as speaking only good things about people and performing (the ritual) prayer. The covenant referred to in the vv. 78f may also have been the constitution which Muhammad made in

Medina, which the Jews are said to have broken later. The v. 81 mentions
Moses as having been given the Book, and states that Jesus was given clear
signs and strengthened with the Holy Spirit. The Jews are charged in the same
verse with having accused some messengers of lies and of having killed others.
The vv. 82f tell of the Jews' rejection of the Qur'an, which book is said to have
confirmed what the Jews (already) had. The v. 86 mentions the Israel's rebellion both in the matter of the golden calf and when the mountain was said to
have been raised over them (cf. 7:170).[29] The vv. 88-90 and 91-97 are thought
to have been directed at specific individuals,[30] and in Islamic traditions the
Jews are said to have been Gabriel's enemy (v. 91).[31] The names of Gabriel
and Michael are mentioned together in v. 92,[32] and the vv. 93f indicate that at
least some of the Jews rejected the Qur'an. In v. 96 Solomon is declared not to
have been an unbeliever,[33] and the figures Harut and Marut are named.[34] The
v. 98 seems to show how a derogatory greeting of the Jews was to be
avoided,[35] and many traditions also give other alleged Jewish greetings which
were used against the Muslims.[36] The v. 99 mentions "unbelievers" among the
"People of the Book," v. 100 explains the Qur'anic doctrine of abrogation, and
v. 103 presents many of the People of the Book as looking for converts among
the Muslims, whereby the word "unbelief" seems to be used in the sense of
disbelief in the Qur'an or Muhammad's messengership (cf. v. 99). The v. 104
gives an exhortation to prayer and paying alms, v. 105 reproduces the claim
that only Jews or Christians will go to Paradise, and v. 107 gives the alleged
remarks of Jews against Christians and Christians against the Jews. The v. 108
seems to refer to a Meccan prohibition of Muslims praying at the Ka`ba,[37] and
the denial of God having a son was probably directed against Christians.[38] The
v. 114 contains the complaint that the Jews and Christian are not satisfied until
one follows their religion(s), and v. 115 states that those who recite the
scriptures correctly, also believe them. The vv. 118f represent perhaps one of
the earliest Qur'anic passages to mention the Abraham legend, in which
Abraham and Ishmael are credited with the building of the Ka`ba,[39] and
Ishmael is recognized as being one of Abraham's sons.[40] The v. 118 describes
Abraham as having been an "imam" (leader of a people or religion),[41] and the
vv. 119f mention the "maqam (station) of Abraham" (here probably the Ka`ba
complex) as a place of prayer, giving an alleged command of God for Abraham and Ishmael to purify the house (Ka`ba).[42] Islamic traditions usually show
that `Umar influenced the revelation, declaring the "maqam of

Abraham" to be a place for prayer,[43] and it may well be that he suggested this new identification altogether, since this association does not predate the Medinan period.[44] The vv. 121f have Abraham and Ishmael anachronistically pray to be Muslims,[45] and makes them also pray for a future messenger, in which Muhammad is implied (v. 123). In v. 124 the "way" (religion) of Abraham is alluded to, and in v. 126 Jacob is said to have told his children to become Muslims.[46] In v. 127 Muhammad has become aware that Abraham was the father of Ishmael and Isaac, and v. 129 modifies the earlier discussions about divine guidance (v. 114) by implying that guidance could be found in the religion of Abraham. The v. 130 gives a primitive creed, in which the prophets named are all Biblical characters and in chronological order (Abraham, Ishmael, Isaac, Jacob, Moses and Jesus). The v. 132 contains an obscure reference to baptism, and v. 136 gives the famous rhetorical question about whether Abraham, Ishmael, Isaac and Jacob were Jews or Christians. The vv. 136f relate about the change of the Islamic qibla (direction of prayer), and many Islamic traditions report that the qibla was changed from Jerusalem to the Ka`ba.[47] The v. 138 implies that Muhammad had had the Ka`ba as a qibla earlier, and some Islamic traditions show that Muhammad at least prayed at the pagan Ka`ba prior to the Hijra.[48] The v. 139 reveals that Muhammad himself wanted to change the qibla, and v. 140 indicates that those to whom the Book was given would not accept Muhammad's new (idol-filled) qibla. The v. 141 implies that the Jews in Medina knew the Book as well as their own sons, and some canonical traditions attempt to connect the charge about the Jews "hiding the truth" (also v. 141) with the subject of the punishment of stoning for adultery.[49] The Islamic doctrine about martyrs (v. 149) may have been remotely related to a Christian teaching,[50] and v. 151 gives a standard Islamic saying for those in ominous situations. In v. 153 the two Meccan hills Safa and Marwa are declared holy, and a canonical tradition shows that some early Muslims had thought these were pagan sites.[51] Since v. 153 abruptly deals with the Hajj, some Western scholars think this verse was a later addition (ca. 7 AH) which has more in common with the vv. 185f.[52] The vv. 154f show that those who hide God's signs and guidance will be cursed, and the vv. 156f present unbelievers as also being accursed. The v. 158 is similar to the Monotheistic creed of Dt. 6:4, and the vv. 158f speak of God's provision in creation. The vv. 160f are directed against polytheists, and v. 163 states a general dietary precept. The vv. 165f speak about unbelievers, and the vv.

167f return to the subject of dietary regulations. Some Western scholars consider the vv. 163-166 to have been Meccan,[53] but it is also quite possible that they were Medinan, since the vv. 163-169 deal generally with dietary regulations and the rejection of what was "sent down." In the vv. 169f those who hide the scriptures and sell them are condemned to Hell, and v. 172 gives a definition of those who fear God. The vv. 173f sanction revenge for murder, and some Western scholars consider this passage to have been composed shortly before Ramadan of 2 AH.[54] The vv. 176f speak of inheritance, the vv. 179f make the fast of Ramadan obligatory, the v. 185 mentions the Hajj, and the vv. 186f allow Muslims to fight those who fight against them. The vv. 192f make the Hajj or a sacrifice obligatory, and v. 194 allows business during the Hajj and mentions "rushing down from" the hill of "Arafat" in Mecca. Western scholars think that most of the passage vv. 185-199 was composed not earlier than 6 AH.[55] The vv. 200f give the examples of two types of people, v. 206 shows that some may have expected a miracle such as God coming in the shadow of a cloud with angels, and v. 207 encourages one to ask the children of Israel about the signs which were given them. The vv. 209f speak of divisions among mankind, and v. 211 gives a question regarding alms. The vv. 212f show that some of Muhammad's followers were apprehensive about participating in the fighting, v. 214 must refer to the raid on Nakhla[56] as described in Islamic traditions,[57] and v. 215 states that those who (among other things) participate in Allah's way (Jihad) will be able to hope for Allah's compassion. The v. 216 is against wine and games, but they are not yet forbidden, and the vv. 218f speak of being benevolent to orphans. The vv. 220f forbid marriage to "associators," which has been expanded to include Christians in canonical traditions,[58] and v. 222 (contrary to Muslim opinion) is actually similar to the Jewish regulations on menstruating women.[59] The Qur'anic description of women as being tillable fields for men (v. 223),[60] was later used by early Christian polemicists.[61] The v. 224 contains an instruction about oaths, and v. 225 declares that Allah will not punish for unintentional oaths.[62] The vv. 226f describe the Islamic regulations concerning divorce, in which remarriage to the same former husband is only allowed after an interim marriage to someone else (v. 230).[63] The vv. 234f give regulations for widows, and the vv. 237f speak of divorce before the consummation of marriage. The v. 239 mentions the "middle prayer," which is thought to have been adopted from Judaism,[64] and v. 240 provides for praying while walking or riding when in danger.[65] The vv. 241f return to the subject of widows, and the v. 244f refers to the Jihad, in which v. 244 seems to be based somewhat on Ezek. 37:1f.[66] The vv. 247f relate a narrative about Saul, Goliath and David, in which the Israelites' request for a king has been combined with the Muslims' will to fight (since they have been driven from their homes, etc.; v. 247). The Jewish ark of the covenant is mentioned anachronistically (v. 249),[67] and the story about Saul has been confused with that of Gideon (vv. 250f).[68] In v. 254 Jesus is mentioned as having been given "clear signs" and as having been strengthened by the Holy Spirit. The v. 255 is an exhortation to almsgiving, and v. 256 describes God generally. The vv. 257f state that there is no compulsion in religion, and the word "taghut" (for "idol") appears twice.[69] The narratives about someone [Nimrod] arguing with Abraham (v. 260),[70] the man who slept 100 years (v. 261)[71] and the four birds (v. 262)[72] are all used as examples in favor of the Resurrection. The vv. 263f appear to deal with the subject of alms, and the vv. 266f give related parables about two types of ground. The vv. 276f forbid usury and encourage one to give alms, and the vv. 282f give a law about the recording of debts, whereby provision is made for the illiterate.[73] The v. 285 gives a short creed, in which (among other things) no difference is said to have been made between God's messengers (cf. Qur'an 17:57), and the v. 286b is a prayer text. The Qur'anic names for Gabriel and Michael (v. 92) and Marut (v. 96) appear to have come from the Syriac,[74] whereas the Qur'anic names for Saul and Goliath seem to have been corruptions of their Hebrew names.[75] The Arabic term for baptism (v. 132) probably came from a Palestinian-Christian dialect of Syriac,[76] and the terms for the "(twelve) tribes" (v. 130)[77] and the shekinah (v. 249)[78] may have come from the Hebrew through Syriac. The Qur'anic for the "ark" of the covenant most probably came from the Ethiopic.[79] This sura contains many verses which are at least remotely similar to passages in the Bible or Talmud.[80]

Just as it is obvious that Muhammad learned much from the Jews (Qur'an 16:45; 10:94),[81] it is equally evident that many of his discussions with the Jews cannot have occurred as Islamic traditions relate.[82] Muhammad's information about Judaism probably came from Jewish converts to Islam,[83] (indirectly) from the Torah,[84] from questioning the Jews[85] and through his passive contact with them.[86] Muhammad is even said to have allowed the relating of Jewish traditions.[87] Qur'anic evidence seems to indicate that Muhammad's first disagreement with the Jews was with respect to their dietary laws.[88] It may well have been the restrictions on camel meat[89] which led Muhammad to reject the Judaic dietary regulations and opt for pagan Arab or Ethiopian Christian practices.[90] The Jews could certainly prove that their dietary laws were found in the Torah (Lev. 11:1f), but Muhammad's refusal was so staunch, that he then accused them of having corrupted the scriptures (cf. Qur'an 7:161f; 2:55f).[91] This no doubt only served to further the Jewish rejection of Muhammad and the Qur'an.

Muhammad then appears to have begun to find fault with the Jews wherever he could, and his sermon to the "children of Israel" which follows a narrative about Adam in sura 2 provides a good example of his anti-Jewish polemic. By way of admonition, the Jews are charged with selling God's "signs" (v. 38b), with cloaking the truth in lies and hiding the truth contrary to their knowledge (v. 39). In an allusion to the narrative about Satan not bowing down to Adam (vv. 28f), the Jews are commanded to bow down (v. 40). They are accused of having sinned in the matter of the (golden) calf (v. 48), of not believing Moses (v. 52) and of exchanging a word of God for another (v. 56). In v. 58 the Jews are said to have brought God's wrath upon themselves in that they denied God's "signs," killed the prophets, rebelled and became transgressors. The Jews are blamed for violating the Sabbath (v. 61), hardening their hearts (v. 69) and altering God's Word (vv. 70f, cf. vv. 55f). The Jews are accused of breach of covenant (vv. 79f), and are said to have been cursed by Allah (v. 82). They are said to have rejected the Qur'an (v. 83) and brought God's anger upon themselves (v. 84). The Jews are shown as only believing what was "sent down" to themselves (v. 85). They are again accused of having killed the prophets (v. 85b) and of having said "we hear and rebel" (v. 87b - cf. Ex. 24:3, 7) in a play on words.[92] They are said (no doubt mistakenly) to have regarded Gabriel as an enemy (vv. 91f)[93] and seem to have addressed Muhammad as being an evil person (v. 98).[94]

In the canonical traditions the Jews are further accused of robbing graves for cloth,[95] of exercising inequality in their punishments,[96] of being the cause for the spoiling of meats[97] and of being destroyed when their women wore wigs.[98] Muhammad is even said to have cursed the Jews later, because they sold fat which was forbidden them.[99]

The Jews of Medina are reported to have cast spells on Muhammad effectively[100] and they are moreover thought to have been responsible for the initial barrenness of the Muslim women after the Hijra.[101]

The Qur'an accuses the Jews of having hidden the truth (2:39, 141, 154f, 169f), and the reason for this can be pretty well ascertained from Islamic sources. Both the Qur'an and hadith show that Muhammad received a substantial amount of theological information from the Jews.[102] However, Qur'an 2:71 reveals that (apparently) the Jews had decided not to teach the Muslims anything about their Books, after noticing that the information they had given was only being used against them. A *Sira* tradition also shows that some Jewish rabbis once refused to answer Muslims' questions about the Torah,[103] and a well-known canonical hadith depicts the Jews as complaining that Muhammad opposed them in everything.[104] The Jews may have even furnished Muhammad with false information,[105] and a classic example of this is related in the many Islamic traditions about the punishment of stoning for adultery.[106]

The Jews are said to have ridiculed the Qur'an and Muhammad,[107] and at least two of their derisive sayings seem to be preserved in the Qur'an 2:87b, 98).[108]

Muhammad must have soon realized that his attempts to become accepted by the Jews as a prophet were doomed to failure, but in order to break away from the Jews, and yet retain his former claim of being a messenger in the line of the Biblical prophets, Muhammad needed a theological argument. As a result of his contact with the educated Jews of Medina, Muhammad must at least have learned to what major extent his previous Qur'anic narratives were flawed.[109] It can hardly be presumed, however, that Muhammad was formerly oblivious to his own intentional alterations of Biblical narratives, by which, for example, the earlier prophets' ministries were made to conform to Muhammad's own circumstances.[110] Indeed, even in the Meccan period, Muhammad seems to have had no reservations about changing Biblical materials to suit his own interests and aims, and the solution for his situation with respect to the Jews in Medina would be no different.

In Medina Muhammad appears to have learned not only that Ishmael was Abraham's (older) son (cf. 2:127, 130),[111] but probably also that Ishmael was considered to have been a father of the Arabs by the Jews.[112] Muhammad could not have helped but to notice that Abraham predated the Mosaic Law (cf. 2:136) and had doubtless become acquainted with the pilgrimages of the Jews and Christians to Jerusalem, which for the Jews were ultimately based on the Abraham - Moriah - Temple doctrine.[113] Muhammad then claimed that Abraham and Ishmael purified "God's house" (the Ka`ba - 2:119) and built its foundations (2:121). Islam was then defined to be the "way" (religion) of Abraham (2:124), which predated Judaism and Christianity (2:132). Islamic tradition generally credits `Umar with the idea of choosing the "maqam of Abraham" (most probably the whole Ka`ba complex) as a place of prayer,[114] and Muhammad is later reported to have said that if any among his followers were inspired, `Umar would have been one of them.[115]

For the Jews at least, the Temple area in Jerusalem (cf. I Kgs. 8:30; Dan. 6:10; etc.) was also their "qibla" (direction of prayer). Muhammad is said to have wanted to change the qibla previously (2:139), and in 2:136f the Islamic qibla was apparently changed from Jerusalem to pagan Mecca. This open break with the Jews is said to have occurred some 16-18 months after the Hijra.[116]

Whereas Muhammad had earlier sought to adopt practices from Jews and Christians, he now seems to have turned against them. Canonical traditions report Muhammad as having said that one should neither pray as a Jew,[117] nor dress as they do for prayer.[118] Muhammad is quoted as having said that the Muslims were not to follow the Jews and Christians,[119] and he even seems to have encouraged others to do the opposite of the People of the Book.[120] Muhammad appears to have rejected the Sabbath as a day of worship (cf. Qur'an 16:125), and chose Friday as a day of assembly.[121] Not to be outdone by Jews and Christians, prayer is said to have been instituted and an Islamic call to prayer (adhan) was introduced, which was intentionally distinct from those of the Judaism and Christianity.[122]

Interestingly enough, most of the rites which Muhammad then developed for Islam are essentially based on Jewish practices.

The Jewish "qibla" (Jerusalem) also served as their place of pilgrimage, and the change of the Islamic qibla now "sanctified" the heathen pilgrimage to the Ka`ba. Although some Muslims seem to have had their reservations about this adaptation,[123] Safa and Marwa were declared holy (Qur'an 2:153). The Hajj is also spoken of in Qur'an 2:185, 192f, and one need not necessarily date all of these passages much later, since at least some aspects of the institution of the Islamic Hajj must have been concurrent with the change of the qibla.

Both *Sira* and canonical traditions attempt to connect the Jewish fast on the Day of Atonement (`Ashura) with the introduction of the fast of Ramadan.[124] However, although some Western scholars have noticed similarities to this Jewish fast,[125] which is held in autumn, there is a substantial disagreement in months, since this Islamic rite is reported to have been begun 19 months after the Hijra (in March 624 AD). A canonical tradition describing `Ashura as being a day highly esteemed by Jews and Christians[126] together with the consistent (although incorrect) testimony of Islamic hadith that `Ashura commemorated Israel's deliverance from Pharaoh,[127] indicate that instead of the Day of Atonement, the Jewish Passover and Christian Easter were meant, which are celebrated in the spring. Other Islamic traditions show that Muhammad collected the "zakat al-fitr"[128] at the end of Ramadan,[129] and this is similar to the Jewish payment of redemption which was also collected at the Passover.[130] Some Western scholars of Islam have viewed the fast of Ramadan as coming from the Christian observance of Lent, but this is not very probable, since the Christian "fasting" during Lent is not very similar to the Islamic practice.[131] The Manichaeans apparently had a fast which lasted 30 days and which was broken at each sunset, and the Harranians are said to have had a similar fast.[132] Another Western scholar thinks that since Ramadan was the first month of the year and the night of Qadr may have been New Years day, the Islamic practice may have been related to the pagan practice of "i`tikaf."[133] It is generally thought that Muhammad combined quite a number of sources in introducing the fast of Ramadan.[134]

According to Islamic traditions, the battle of Badr would have occurred during the first fast of Ramadan.[135] Some accounts depict Muhammad as only keeping the fast for the first one or two days,[136] whereas others present him and his followers as not having kept the fast at all.[137] One tradition maintains that Muhammad kept the fast on returning from Badr,[138] but another indicates that the Muslims ate during the daytime immediately after returning from Badr.[139] Thus, in the opinion of some Western scholars, the fast of Ramadan was probably not instituted at all before the battle of Badr.[140]

Another plausible theory concerning Ramadan and the battle of Badr is that the Islamic fast was to commemorate the Muslims' victory over the pagans, similar to the Passover (or according to Islamic sources: `Ashura) celebration in remembrance of how God delivered the Israelites from Pharaoh.[141] Moreover, the narratives about Saul, Goliath and David actually seem to have been composed after the battle of Badr, where even the confusion of Saul for Gideon together with the example of Goliath's defeat at the hands of the youthful David appear to have been used in commemoration of the Muslims' victory over a superior force at Badr.[142]

After his open break with the Jews, Muhammad also appears to have introduced a number of regulations for his "communitized" followers. In Qur'an 2 some of the basic Islamic laws governing revenge for murder (vv. 173f), inheritance (vv. 176f), marriage (vv. 220f), divorce (vv. 226f, 237f), widowhood (vv. 234f, 241f) and debts (vv. 282f) are given, for example. These new regulations seem to have had Judaism as their reference, although in at least one case (concerning divorce and remarriage; 2:230) the Islamic law is contrary to both the Old and New Testament.[143]

The passage **Qur'an 6:160f** may also have been composed about this time. Jews and Christians could have possibly been meant in v. 160, and the comment about Muhammad having nothing to do with such may mean that he was slowly giving up the hope of being accepted by them as a messenger of God. The v. 161 speaks of a ten-fold reward for good and a simple "reward" for evil, and the v. 162 refers to the "way" (religion) of Abraham. In v. 163 Muhammad claims to be the first Muslim,[144] v. 164 is similar to Qur'an 39:9 and v. 165 is reminiscent of Qur'an 2:28.

The verse **Qur'an 73:20** could have been composed in this period. This verse seems to refer to a congregational night vigil, the continuation of the raids and that Muhammad was to pray for forgiveness.

Qur'an 16:111-125 is probably also early-Medinan. The v. 111 mentions the emigration and shows that the armed conflict with the Meccans had already begun, and the v. 112 speaks of the rewards in the Judgment. The parable in the vv. 113f no doubt refers to Muhammad and the Meccans,[145] in which the success of the Muslim raids is alluded to (v. 113b). The vv. 115f are in essence a reaction to the Judaic dietary laws, and v. 120 says that forgiveness will be granted those who in ignorance performed evil. The v. 121 describes Abraham as having been an "imam" (cf. 2:118), and v. 124 speaks of the "way" (religion) of Abraham (cf. 2:124; 6:162). In v. 125 the Sabbath is said to have been appointed only for those who were in disagreement, and it appears that Muhammad had rejected the importance of the Sabbath for his own followers. The v. 126 encourages Muhammad to invite others to the way of the Lord and to argue with them in a better manner (cf. 29:45), v. 127 gives an ambiguous statement about vengence,[146] and v. 128 shows that Muhammad was to have patience with respect to those who opposed him. Two of the verses of this passage (vv. 115, 127) are similar to Bible or Talmud references.[147]

Qur'an 14:38-42 was probably also composed in this period. The v. 38 contains an alleged prayer of Abraham, whereby he prays to be turned away from idolatry with his sons, and this obviously contradicts Qur'an 16:121, which claims that Abraham was not among the idolaters. The v. 40 depicts Abraham as having left a part of his family near the Ka`ba, v. 41 mentions Ishmael and Isaac, and v. 42 has Abraham pray for forgiveness for himself and his parents.[148]

Along with parts of two other suras, **Qur'an 98** is thought to partially date from before the battle of Badr, but in the year 2 AH.[149] The vv. 1f speak of the unbelievers among the People of the Book, who were so named because they rejected the Qur'an. In v. 4 prayers and alms are described as being rituals of the faith related in the Qur'an, v. 5 states that the unbelievers of the People of the Book and pagans will be sent to Hell, and the vv. 6f claim that believers and those who practice good (works) will go to Paradise. Some Islamic sources claim that this sura was originally much longer than it is today.[150]

Sura 64 opens in praise of God (vv. 1f), and v. 5 speaks about the punishments of previous unbelievers. The v. 6 reproduces the rhetorical question used against Muhammad about being led by a human, and the vv. 7f seem to repeat a discussion with pagans regarding the Resurrection. As a parallel to the earlier Qur'anic doctrine of obedience to God and Muhammad[151] v. 8 seems to initiate the notion of belief in God and His messengers. The v. 9 maintains that those who believe in God and practice good (works) will have their sins covered and will be admitted into Paradise, and v. 10 describes those who deny God's signs (accounting them to be lies) as being the inhabitants of Hell. The v. 11 declares that no mishaps occur without God's permission, and the v. 12 commands obedience to God and Muhammad, who is described as "his messenger." The vv. 14f deal with the subject of almsgiving, and appear to show that some were reluctant to give alms because of their families.

Qur'an 62 also begins in praise of God (vv. 1f), in which Muhammad is described as having been a messenger to the "unlearned" (or "heathen")[152] The v. 5 uses a Jewish byword against the Jews themselves,[153] and the vv. 6f address Jewish claims of being the "friends of God." The vv. 9f provide the only allusion to the Islamic Friday assemblies,[154] and v. 11 depicts the "worldliness" of the first Muslims.[155]

After the first three attempted raids on Meccans were unsuccessful, Muhammad himself led a raid to Waddan 12 months after the Hijra, but he was also unable to find a caravan. A treaty with the Banu Damra was said to have been made on this expedition, which lasted 15 days.[156]

In some Islamic traditions the practice of "mut`a" (temporary marriage)[157] is said to have been allowed by in Muhammad on a raid in which he participated.[158] Some hadith say that this practice was allowed in 8 AH,[159] whereas others report that it was forbidden at Khaybar in 7 AH.[160] A few traditions show that Mut`a was first forbidden in the caliphate of `Umar,[161] nevertheless, some Shiite and Sunni groups still practice it.[162]

One *Sira* tradition relates that Muhammad's cousin `Ali married Muhammad's daughter Fatima at the end of the twelfth month after the Hijra, and another states that this marriage took place in the 22nd month after the Hijra.[163]

In about the 13th month after the Hijra, Muhammad is said to have led a raiding party of about 200 men to Buwat, without, however, engaging the 100 Meccans who were escorting a caravan of 2500 camels.[164]

During the same month, Muhammad is reported to have gone as far as Safawan in pursuit of Kurz b. Jabir, who had stolen herds grazing near Medina. Muhammad did not find him.[165]

In the 16th month after the Hijra, Muhammad tried to intercept a Meccan caravan on its way to Syria, but it eluded him. He had assembled 150-200 men,[166] who rode 30 camels in alternation. This expedition reached al-'Ushayra, and Muhammad is said to have made treaties with the Banu Mudlij and Banu Damra there. The battle of Badr took place when Muhammad tried to raid this caravan on its return from Syria. 'Ali is also reported to have been called Abu Turab at al-'Ushayra.[167]

In the 17th month after the Hijra, during the pagan holy month of Rajab, Muhammad sent out a raiding party of 8 (12 or 13) Muslims under the command of 'Abdullah b. Jahsh with a sealed message (evidently to prevent possible spies from knowing their destination).[168] After two days' journey, the Muslims opened the letter, those who did not wish to continue were to return to Medina, and the others were to go to the valley of Nakhla (not far from Mecca) to wait for a caravan. Two of the Muslims claimed to have lost their camel and went looking for it. At Nakhla the remaining Muslims saw a Meccan caravan, which was escorted by four men. Because of the heathen 'umra, fighting was generally forbidden in the month of Rajab, but faced with either breaking this tradition or letting the caravan reach Mecca, the Muslims, some of whom were posing as pilgrims, decided to attack. One Meccan was killed, two were captured and one got away. The Meccans seem to have captured the two Muslims who had lost their camel.[169] When the Muslims returned to Medina with the booty of camels, wine, raisins and leather, Muhammad was accused of having violated the peace of the "holy" month, but he denied responsibility for the armed conflict. Qur'an 2:214 was then revealed, in which the sacredness of the pagan month of Rajab was maintained, and the Meccans were accused (among other things) of the greater sin of seducing some from "Allah's way."[170] After the Muslims were returned,[171] Muhammad let the Meccans ransom his captives, one of whom became a Muslim. Islamic traditions contradict one another in both the matter as to whether or not Muhammad paid the blood-money for the Meccan who was killed,[172] and in the question as to when the booty was divided.[173] Western scholars generally feel that Muhammad was well aware of the risk of breaking the peace of Rajab when he sent out the raiding party.[174]

Most collections of the *Sira* traditions show that the change of the qibla and Muhammad's break with the Jews occurred in this time period.[175]

In the 19th month after the Hijra (Ramadan), Muhammad assembled a group of just over 300 men[176] and 70 camels to raid the returning Meccan caravan, which they had failed to intercept about three months earlier. The caravan was led by Abu Sufyan, who on hearing of Muhammad's plans, alerted Mecca. The Meccans, who had not forgotten the raid at Nakhla, quickly raised an army of 950 men, 700 camels and 100 horses led by Abu Jahl to confront the Muslims. Unknown to Muhammad, the caravan had given them the slip again, and when they arrived at Badr expecting to find it, they discovered that the numerically superior Meccan forces were there instead (cf. Qur'an 8:45).[177] After realizing their situation, Muhammad nevertheless encouraged his followers to advance against the Meccans. In planning for the fight, Muhammad is said to have made a mistake, and an alternative suggestion of al-Hubab b. al-Mundhir is reported to have been so clever[178] that even Gabriel agreed with it.[179] The battle of Badr is said to have taken place on either the 17th or 19th of Ramadan and began with a series of duels, which were won by the Muslims. In the general combat which ensued, the polytheists were routed. About 70 Meccans are reported to have been killed and approximately an equal number were captured.[180] Abu Jahl and other Meccan leaders were among the dead. Muslim casualties totaled only 14. The booty is said to have been 150 camels, 10 horses, equipment, weapons and much leather.[181] Initially, Muhammad wanted to have all the prisoners executed, but 'Umar persuaded him to let many be ransomed.[182] Among those executed was Muhammad's verbal antagonist al-Nadr b. al-Harith.[183]

Although some Muslim sources imply that Muhammad received one-fifth of the spoils (cf. Qur'an 8:42) after the raid to Nakhla or the battle of Badr, it seems more likely that this practice was actually first instituted after the raid on the Banu Qaynuqa.[184] The booty from the battle of Badr was divided equally[185] among the Muslims on the way back to Medina,[186] and each man was said to have received either a camel with riding equipment, two camels or a couple of leather blankets.[187] Islamic reports show that there were serious disagreements about the division of the spoils, until Qur'an 8 was revealed.[188]

Muhammad returned to Medina shortly after his daughter Ruqayya, the wife of 'Uthman b. 'Affan, was buried.[189] Some of the prisoners had been killed, some died,[190] some taught the boys of the Ansar to write (in return for their freedom),[191] and others were ransomed. Among those who were to be ransomed was Abu'l-'As, the husband of Muhammad's daughter Zaynab. When Zaynab sent a ransom for her husband, Muhammad noticed a necklace of Khadija which was sent. Muhammad then decided to return the ransom and set Abu'l-'As free, on the condition that Zaynab be allowed to come to Medina. Abu'l-'As later became a Muslim and was reunited with his wife in Medina.[192]

Qur'an 8 opens with the reply to a question about the spoils, in which the booty is declared to belong to God and Muhammad (v. 1). Further, the believers are instructed to fear God and obey God and Muhammad (v. 1).[193] In the vv. 2f, believers are described as having hearts which fear when Allah's name is mentioned, being those whose faith grows when they hear God's signs, who trust God, observe prayer and give alms. The vv. 5f are about Muhammad's ministry leading up to the battle of Badr, in which the Meccans are shown to have argued with Muhammad about the truth (v. 6). In v. 7 the Muslims are described as having actually wanted to raid a relatively unprotected caravan, but that God wanted to confirm the truth in having them confront the larger relief force (cf. v. 45). The v. 9 states that 1000 angels helped the Muslims at Badr, and this disagrees with Qur'an 3:119f, where they are said to have been 3000.[194] The rain before the battle of Badr is spiritualized in v. 11. The vv. 15f speak of Hell for those who turned from the fight, and the vv. 17f say that it was God who fought. The v. 20 commands obedience to God and Muhammad, and the vv. 21f encourage the believers not to be as those who say they hear, but actually do not. The vv. 24f essentially reiterate the command for obedience, and the vv. 27f admonish those who believe not to deceive God and

Muhammad. The vv. 30f speak of the plans of the unbelievers to capture, murder or exile Muhammad, and the vv. 32f explain that the proclaimed "punishment" (judgment) did not take place earlier, since Muhammad was living among the pagans then. In the vv. 35f the prayers of the unbelievers at the Ka`ba are described as being worthless, and the unbelievers are said to have attempted to seduce some from "God's way." The vv. 37f condemns the unbelievers to Hell, and v. 40 gives a call to fight against them. The v. 42 declares that one-fifth of the spoils belong to God, Muhammad, his relatives, orphans, the poor and traveler. The vv. 43f are again concerned with the battle of Badr, and v. 45 describes Allah as having given Muhammad a false vision about the size of the enemy forces,[195] so that the Muslims would not have lost their courage. The v. 48 again commands obedience to God and Muhammad, and the vv. 49f return to the subject of Badr, describing the influence of Satan and the hypocrites. In the vv. 54f the unbelievers are compared with Pharaoh's people, and in the vv. 57f unbelievers are described and prisoners are mentioned. The v. 60 instructs Muhammad on how to deal with traitors, and the vv. 61f give another call to war against the unbelievers. The vv. 68f reveal Muhammad's initial intention of killing all of the prisoners from Badr, and the vv. 71f show that the prisoners were to be called on to become Muslims. The v. 73 seems to refer to the bonding of the emigrants to the Ansar,[196] and v. 74 describes unbelievers as being relatives of one another. In v. 75 the Muslims who emigrated, fought in "Allah's way," those who provided lodging and gave help are said to deserve forgiveness and generous provision. The v. 76 states that those who believed later, emigrated and fought were also of the other Muslims. The v. 24 of this sura is remotely similar to I Jn 3:20 and v. 67 is reminiscent of Lev. 26:8.[197] Some Islamic sources claim that Qur'an 9 was originally part of this sura, but based on the obviously vastly different times of composition for these suras, Western Qur'an scholars generally do not accept this theory.[198]

Qur'an 74:31-34 could have been composed in this period, possibly after Muhammad had once recited the preceding verses (74:1-30) and the unbelievers and hypocrites had made remarks about them (cf. v. 32). The v. 31 says that (the number of) the angels guarding Hell was a sign (cf. 8:52) and mentions the increase of the believers' faith (cf. 8:2). The v. 34 states that only God knows about His host, or forces (cf. 8:9; 3:120f).

Sura 47 begins in condemnation of unbelievers who seduce others from Allah's way (v. 1), and v. 2 states that those who practice good and believe what was sent down to Muhammad will have their transgressions covered. The v.4 says that unbelievers are to be killed, and the vv. 5f speak of Paradise for martyrs. The v. 8 declares that God helps those who help Him, the vv. 9f tell about unbelievers, and v. 11 refers to the punishments of previous peoples. The v. 13 speaks about believers and Paradise, and v. 14 again alludes to the punishments of previous peoples. The vv. 16f contrast the alleged rivers of water, milk, wine and honey[199] to the boiling water which is said to be drunk in Hell. The v. 18 appears to show that Jews attempted to dissuade others from following Muhammad, and v. 19 speaks of those who are said to be guided. The v. 21 shows that Muhammad was commanded to pray for forgiveness for his own sins, along with the sins of others (cf. 40:57; 110:1f). The vv. 22f speak of those who did not want to fight (the hypocrites),[200] and v. 34 mentions those who seduce others from Allah's way. The v. 35 commands obedience to God and Muhammad, and v. 36 states that there will be no forgiveness of sins for those who die as unbelievers. The v. 37 instructs Muhammad not to seek peace with the Meccans, v. 38 speaks of earthly life and v. 40 solicits contributions for the armed conflict and appears to refer to a reply of the Jews in this matter.[201]

During the last five days of Ramadan in 2 AH, the blind `Umayr b. `Adi murdered the poetess `Asthma bt. Marwan at home in her sleep, because she had allegedly reviled Islam in verse.[202]

In the 20th month after the Hijra, Salim b. `Umayr murdered the 120 year-old Abu `Afak in his sleep. He was a Jew who had composed poetry against Muhammad.[203]

In the same month, on a Sabbath day, the expedition against the Medinan Jewish Banu Qaynuqa began. Although many traditions depict the Jews as having broken the covenant with Muhammad, it is fairly clear from the references to Qur'an 8:60 in these accounts, along with the testimony of another hadith,[204] that Muhammad broke his covenant with them.[205] The Jews, who were in their fortresses, were besieged for 15 days and surrendered without offering any resistance. At first, Muhammad wanted to have them excuted, but after `Abdullah b. Ubayy interceded, Muhammad decided to have them exiled from Medina. Under the terms of the agreement, the Banu Qaynuqa abandoned their property and goods, which were taken as booty by the Muslims. Muhammad received one-fifth of the spoils (cf. Qur'an 8:42).[206]

The first feast of the sacrifice (`Id al-Adha) is said to have been held in the 22nd month after the Hijra.[207]

Also in the 22nd month after the Hijra, Muhammad and 200 Muslims are said to have left Medina in pursuit of Abu Sufyan, who with 200 Meccans[208] had killed two men and burned two houses and a field near Medina. In order to expedite their escape, Abu Sufyans riders threw off sacks of barley (sawiq), which were collected by the Muslims as booty. There was no confrontation on this expedition.[209]

Qur'an 3 begins with mysterious letters and a Monotheistic statement (v. 1). In v. 2 the Qur'an is alleged to be a book of truth, which confirms what was previous to it, i.e. the Torah and the Gospel, which were also "sent down" by God. The v. 3 states that there will be a punishment for those who deny God's signs. The v. 5 shows that some of Muhammad's contemporaries tried to cause division by looking for the meanings of ambiguous Qur'an passages, and in reply, it is said that only God knows the meanings of such verses, and that those established in knowledge believe all (of the Qur'an). The vv. 6f give a prayer against being led astray, and the vv. 8f speak of unbelievers, who are compared with Pharaoh's people (v. 9). The v. 11 may refer to the battle of Badr, and the vv. 12f contrast the temporal pleasures of life to the eternal pleasures of Paradise. The vv. 14f speak of believers, v. 16 makes a monotheistic statement, and v. 17 claims that religion before God is Islam. The v. 18 refers to discussions with those who were given the Book, and v. 19 gives the call to them and the unlearned[210] to be Muslims. The vv. 20f seem to allude to the Jews in the statement about killing the prophets, and the vv. 22f appear to give the response of "those who were given the Book" to Muhammad's invitation to Islam. The prayer of the vv. 25f probably came from Jewish sources.[211] The vv. 27f show that believers are not to accept unbelievers as their protectors, and v. 29 stipulates that those who love Allah should follow Muhammad, and that Allah would then love them and forgive their sins; a command of obedience to Allah and Muhammad follows. The v. 30 states that God chose

Adam, Noah, the family of Abraham and the family of `Imran (Amram),[212] and the vv. 31f begin a long narrative about Mary (and Jesus), in which Zacharias plays a role.[213] The vv. 37f give a Qur'anic form of the Annunciation,[214] v. 40 depicts Jesus as being a Word from God (cf. John 1:1, 14) and the "Messiah," which is one of the earliest Qur'anic usages of this title. The alleged prophecy about Jesus speaking from the cradle (v. 41) is similar to Qur'an 19:31. The v. 43 states that God was to teach Jesus the Book, the Wisdom, the Torah and the Gospel, and says further that Jesus was to make clay birds live,[215] to heal those who were born blind, to heal lepers and to raise the dead. Jesus was also to proclaim what should be eaten and stored (?), and this, together with the statement about Jesus confirming the Torah but allowing some things which were forbidden (v. 44), seems to have been part of Muhammad's (Christian-based) polemic against the Jewish dietary laws. In v. 45 Jesus' disciples ("hawariyun") are described as being God's helpers and Muslims.[216] The v. 48 shows that God was to let Jesus die before His ascension, and Muslim exegetes have been largely unsuccessful in reconciling this verse with the traditional interpretation of Qur'an 4:156.[217] In v. 52 Jesus is said to have been created as Adam was, and v. 54 seems to refer to a cursing challenge Muhammad made to Christians.[218] Although v. 57 appears to search for common ground between Muslims and the People of the Book, the vv. 58f, which mention the Torah and Gospel again, state that Abraham was neither a Jew, nor a Christian. In v. 61 the claim is made that Muhammad and the Muslims were the closest to Abraham. The v. 62 shows that some of the People of the Book were actively trying to influence Muhammad followers, the vv. 63f depict the People of the Book as having rejected the Qur'an and accuses them of cloaking the truth in lies. The v. 68 maintains that some of the People of the Book are trustworthy in financial matters, and v. 69, which allegedly quotes People of the Book as saying that they were not obligated concerning the "unlearned,"[219] appears to refer to the Jewish practice of exacting interest from gentiles.[220] In v. 72 some of the People of the Book are accused of corrupting the Book verbally (not in written form), v. 73 may be an implied rejection of Christ's deity (in which encouragement is given to be "rabbani" who learn and study the Book), and v. 74 forbids accepting angels or prophets as lords. The vv. 75f speak of God's covenant with the prophets and allude to Muhammad, who was to confirm the Book. The v. 78 expresses the belief in what was given to Muhammad, Abraham, Ishmael, Isaac, Jacob, the tribes, Moses and

Jesus without discriminating between them. The v. 79 says that those who accept other religions instead of Islam are bound for Hell, and this idea seems to contradict Qur'an 2:59 and 5:73. The vv. 80f say that a people who become unbelievers after having believed will be punished eternally (cf. v. 74b). The v. 86 is an encouragement to financial contributions (as opposed to alms), and v. 87 relates that all foods were allowed Israel, but that they had forbidden themselves some things *before* the Torah was "sent down"; the Jews are then requested to bring the Torah and read from it. In v. 88 those who compose lies against God are considered evil. The v. 89 is an instruction to follow the "way" (religion) of Abraham, v. 90 claims that the first house established for humans was the Ka'ba, and v. 91 mentions the maqam of Abraham (in which the Ka`ba may have been meant)[221] and makes the pilgrimage a duty to Allah. The v. 93 implies that the People of the Book rejected the Qur'an, and v. 94 accuses them of seducing others from Allah's way. In v. 95 those who obey a group of the People of the Book are said to make their belief unbelief (cf. vv. 74b, 80f), the vv. 96f give instruction for Muslims to remain Muslim. The vv. 101f forbid sectarianism and this is linked to the sin of unbelief after belief (cf. v. 95). In v. 106 the Muslims are described as having been the best community formed for humans, but that the People of the Book did not believe, although some are believers. The vv. 107f allow fighting those People of the Book who fight against the Muslims, v. 108 probably implies Jews in the accusation of having murdered the prophets, and the vv. 109f describes believers among the People of the Book. The vv. 112f were probably composed after the battle of Uhud.[222] The apparently pre-Islamic name of `Imran and title "Masih" (Messiah), as well as the term "rabbani" (v. 73) appear to have come from the Syriac.[223] The Arabic word for Torah seems to have come from Hebrew,[224] and terms for the Gospel and Jesus' disciples appear to have Ethiopic as their source.[225] Many of the verses of this sura are at least remotely similar to the Bible and other non-canonical works.[226] One collection of *Sira* traditions relates that some of the passages of this sura were composed in connection with a meeting of Jews and Christians (from Najran) before Muhammad.[227] It is, however, more likely that these passages came about as a result of Muhammad's conversations with individual Christians nearer Medina.

Qur'an 7:156-158 may have been composed during this period. In v. 156 Muhammad claims to have been an "unlearned" (or gentile)[228] prophet, who was foretold of in the Torah and Gospel as (among other things) allowing the good and forbidding the bad, and taking off burdens and bonds. This description seems to describe Muhammad's position with respect to the Jewish dietary regulations and the Law in general. The alleged prophecy of Muhammad in v. 156 says further that they would prosper who would believe Muhammad, strengthen him, help him and follow the light sent down to him. In v. 157 Muhammad claims to be a messenger of Allah for all mankind, and v. 158 instructs to believe God and His words. The word for "help" (`azzara) in v. 156 appears to have come from Hebrew.[229]

In the 23rd month after the Hijra, Muhammad and 200 men went out to engage the Banu Sulaym and Ghatafan, who were said to have assembled themselves together at al-Kudr. After not being able to find them there, Muhammad captured a shepherd and later a herd of 500 camels.[230] Muhammad then took one-fifth of the booty and the rest was divided among the Muslims who participated. The captured shepherd was later freed after he became a Muslim.[231]

During the 25th month after the Hijra, Muhammad had the Jewish poet Ka`b b. al-Ashraf murdered for composing verses against Muhammad and inciting others against him.[232]

Also in the 25th month after the Hijra, Muhammad and 450 Muslims undertook an expedition to Dhu Amarr, where he had heard that the Banu Tha`laba and Muharib had assembled, intending to attack them. The Muslims took a man prisoner, who served as an informant and later became a Muslim. During a stop for a rest, a man is said to have become a Muslim after attempting to murder Muhammad. There was no fighting on this expedition.[233]

In the 27th month after the Hijra, Muhammad and 300 Muslims went to al-Furu`, where they had heard that some of the Banu Sulaym were preparing for an attack against them. It is said that by the time the Muslims had arrived, the Banu Sulaym had already dispersed. There was no fighting on this expedition.[234]

During the 28th month after the Hijra, Muhammad sent Zayd b. Haritha and 100 Muslims mounted on horses to intercept a caravan of the Quraysh at al-Qarada. A man was captured, who upon the threat of death became a Muslim and was freed. Muhammad is reported to have received 20,000 dirhams as one-fifth of the booty.[235]

It is said that Muhayyisa b. Mas'ud murdered a Jew after hearing Muhammad command the killing of all Jews within the power of the Muslims.[236]

In about the 30th month after the Hijra, Muhammad is reported to have married 'Umar's daughter Hafsa, who was the widow of a Muslim killed at Badr.[237]

During the 32nd month after the Hijra, the Meccans under Abu Sufyan assembled an army of some 3000 men and marched toward Medina. Although 'Abdullah b. Ubayy counselled against leaving their fortresses in Medina, Muhammad, on the advice of other Muslims, decided to confront the Meccans. Muhammad is said to have rejected the aid of Medinan polytheists,[238] and his force of 1000 became a force of 700 on the way to Uhud, after 'Abdullah b. Ubayy decided to leave them. According to reports, the Meccans had two cavalry units right and left of their center, and Muhammad had placed a rear-guard of archers on a piece of higher ground. At first, the battle went so well for the Muslims in the center that they began to plunder the Meccan camp. Apparently afraid they would miss out on the spoils, most of the archers in the Muslim rear-guard left their position. After noticing this mistake, Khalid b. Walid led the Meccan cavalry in storming the reduced rear-guard, and Muslim began to kill Muslim in the ensuing chaos. The polytheists seem to have thought at one point that they had killed Muhammad, but in actuality he had only been wounded in the face and had had a tooth broken. In the end, some 65 Muslims were killed,[239] among them Muhammad's uncle Hamza. Meccan losses are said to have been 22, and Muhammad executed the Muslims' only Meccan prisoner.[240]

The day after the battle of Uhud, Muhammad, his Muslim soldiers and others went as far as Hamra al-Asad, where the Meccans returning from Uhud had killed two Muslim scouts. Muhammad and his forces defiantly camped so near the Meccans that both sides could see each others fires at night. No further fighting took place during this expedition.[241]

The remainder of **Qur'an 3 (vv. 112f)** is thought by some to have been revealed after the battle of Uhud.[242] The vv. 112f speak of unbelievers, v. 114 dictates that believers are only to make friends with believers, and vv. 115f shows that some believers liked unbelievers. The vv. 117f refer to the battle of Uhud, v. 119 alludes to the battle of Badr, v. 120 states that 3000 angels helped the Muslims at Badr (cf. 8:9 - "1000" instead of "3000"), v. 121 says that God would help them with 5000 angels if the Muslims would remain steadfast and godfearing. The vv. 125f are against usury and in favor of making contributions, v. 133 tells of victory for those who remain believers, and the vv. 134f essentially describe war as being (necessary) for the selection of martyrs and destruction of the enemy. The v. 138 implies Muhammad's mortality,[243] and v. 139 says that death is only by God's permission. The v. 140 speaks of many prophets having been helped by myriads (of angels) in battle, and v. 141 gives the alleged prayer of the prophets in which, among other things, forgiveness of sins is requested. The v. 142 commands believers not to obey unbelievers, v. 143 presents God as Lord and Helper, and v. 144 states that unbelievers will go to Hell. The vv. 145f refer to the battle of Uhud in saying that God had kept His promise and all went well until some Muslims disagreed with a command and rebelled. The v. 148 shows the regrets of some Muslims that they had fought (at Uhud), and replies that death is predestined. In v. 149 Satan is said to have made some (Muslims) retreat (at Uhud), and the vv. 150f return to the theme of Muslim regrets and predestination. The v. 153 shows Muhammad's compassion on his soldiers, and v. 154 encourages trust in God. The v. 155 seems to indicate that Muhammad was accused of fraud with respect to booty.[244] The vv. 158f give a brief recapitulation of Muhammad's ministry, make an allusion to the Muslim victory at Badr and then speak of the loss at Uhud. The v. 162 speaks again of the regrets of some of the Muslim soldiers (cf. vv. 148, 150), and v. 166 makes allusion to the defeat at Uhud. The v. 169 says that the believers were to fear Muhammad, and v. 174 gives the commandment to believe God and Muhammad. The vv. 175f encourage contributions, and v. 177 seems to have been levelled at the Jews (the accusation of killing the prophets). The *Sira* traditions describe an event with respect to this verse.[245] The statement in v. 179, which seems to have come from the Jews, that they would accept no prophet until fire was sent down from heaven to consume a sacrifice, appears to refer to Elijah (cf. I Kg. 18:21f), and v. 180 says that (even) prophets sent with signs were murdered (by the Jews). The vv. 182f speak of Judgment. The vv. 184f deal with the Jews, who were commmanded to proclaim God's Word and not to hide it, but they refused and resorted to selling it (cf. Qur'an 2:73). The vv. 187f relate of God's witness in Creation, the prayer, which begins in v. 188b includes the request for forgiveness (v. 191). The v. 194 speaks of Paradise for those who emigrated, were driven out of their houses and suffered and died in Allah's way. The vv. 196f show that Muhammad was not to be troubled by unbelievers, for they are bound for Hell, and v. 197 says that those who fear God will go to Paradise. The vv. 198f show that the believers among the People of the Book (who do not sell God's Word) will go to Paradise, and v. 200 exhorts believers to be patient. The Arabic word for "myriads" (v. 143) seems to have come from Syriac.[246] Many of the verses of this sura are at least remotely similar to Bible passages,[247] and *Sira* traditions relate that more than a few verses of this section (vv. 112f) were composed with respect to and after the battle of Uhud.[248] A Christian scribe of Muhammad (from the Banu Najjar), who is said to have recited Qur'an 2 and 3, is reported to have reverted (to Christianity).[249]

Qur'an 61 begins in praise of God (v. 1). The vv. 2f make an allusion to hypocrites, whom Allah hates, and speaks of believers who fight (in ranks) in "Allah's way" as being loved by Allah.[250] In v. 5 it appears that Muhammad is compared to Moses, and v. 6 makes the claim that Jesus, who confirmed the Torah, had told the children of Israel about the advent of a prophet named Ahmad (Muhammad).[251] The v. 6 goes on to say that although this prophet (most probably Muhammad) had come to them with "clear signs," they (the Jews) had rejected him. The vv. 7f maintain that God provides for victory over other religions, and the vv. 10f claim Paradise for those who fight in Allah's way. The v. 13 may refer to the victory over the Banu Nadir,[252] and v. 14 calls for those who believe to be Allah's helpers as Jesus' disciples were (cf. Qur'an 3:45).

Sura 57 also opens in praise of God (vv. 1f), and the vv. 7f give a command to believe Allah and Muhammad. The vv. 12f show that believers will go to Paradise and the unbelievers to Hell, and the vv. 15f instruct believers not to be as those who were given the Book previously. The v. 17 gives an encouragement to give alms, and v. 18 tells of rewards for believers and punishment for unbelievers. The vv. 19f contrast temporal earthly life to eternal life in Paradise. The v. 22 relates that no catastrophe occurs without God's permission, and v. 24 says that if others are greedy, God is rich. The vv. 25f tell of God's sending the former messengers and the Book, where Noah, Abraham and Jesus are mentioned, and monasticism is said to have been an innovation of man. The vv. 28f essentially command believers to fear God and believe Muhammad, and then describe the benefits of those who live accordingly. Some of the verses of this sura are at least remotely similar to Bible passages.[253]

Qur'an 4 opens with a command to fear God (v. 1), the v. 2 speaks about being benevolent and just to orphans, and v. 3 allows a Muslim to have two, three or four wives.[254] The vv. 4f return to the subject of orphans, the vv. 8f give some regulations regarding inheritance, and v. 9 is directed against injustice to orphans. The vv. 10f speak of inheritance again, v. 17 presents these as the regulations of Allah saying that those who obey Allah and Muhammad will be led into Paradise, and v. 18 says that those who rebel will be sent to Hell. The vv. 19f speak of adultery and witnesses (no punishment is mentioned), and v. 22 rules out death-bed repentance. The v. 23 forbids that one's wives be inheritable. The vv. 24f give some of the Qur'anic laws for marriage,[255] in which the practice of "mut`a" is referred to[256] and married slaves who commit adultery are to receive half of the punishment of free-women (again no punishment is described). The vv. 33f appear to forbid blood-feuds among Muslims, v. 36 gives commandment against covetousness, and v. 37 speaks of inheritance. The v. 38 explains why men are more dominating than women, and prescribes the warning, restriction and beating of rebellious women. The v. 39 instructs that an arbitrator should be used to settle disputes between man and wife. The v. 40 commands to serve God, be a Monotheist and (essentially) be good to all. The v. 41 admonishes against greed, and the vv. 42f speak of alms. The vv. 45f describe the Judgment, and v. 46 gives regulations for prayer, in which the restriction about drunkeness in prayer and the provision for ritual washings with sand (where no water is available) seem to have come from Jewish sources.[257] Islamic traditions generally report that the latter of these laws was instituted once as `A'isha lost her necklace on an expedition.[258] The vv. 47f describe Jewish activities against

Muhammad,[259] v. 48 contains the statement about hearing and rebelling (cf. Qur'an 2:87),[260] and v. 49 refers to their use of the term "ra'ina."[261] The v. 51 seems to have been directed against polytheists, v. 54 seems to be against the Quraysh allies of the Jews, who are said to worship "jibt" and "taghut,"[262] and v. 55 concludes that they are cursed by Allah. The v. 56 appears to refer to the Jews as not having contributed to the Muslim cause, and the vv. 57f describe the people of Abraham as having been given the Book, wisdom and a kingdom, but that some turned away and were sent to Hell. The v. 60 says that believers will go to Paradise, v. 61 commands to be just in judgment, and v. 62 commands to obey Allah and Muhammad and bring judicial cases before them. The vv. 63f are directed against the hypocrites, who are said to consult "taghut," and v. 71 says that those who obey Allah and Muhammad will be with the prophets, etc. (in Paradise). The v. 73 instructs to attack in groups, and v. 74 gives the expression of some that they were glad not to have been with the others (at Uhud). The vv. 76f encourage to fight in Allah's way, the v. 80 speaks of death as being predestined, and v. 83 describes the behavior of the hypocrites. The v. 84 states that if the Qur'an had not been God's Word, they would have found many contradictions, and v. 86 commands fighting in Allah's way. The v. 87 speaks of intercession for good and evil, and v. 88, which probably referred at first to the Jews, instructs to answer the greetings of others in like manner.[263] The v. 89 makes a monotheistic statement, and the vv. 90f show that there was a division of opinion (among Muslims) concerning the hypocrites. The vv. 92f give regulations about allies and those seeking peace, v. 94 forbids believers to kill other believers, and v. 95 show that those who kill other believers intentionally will be sent to Hell. The v. 96 dictates that (an arranged) peace is to be maintained, even if it was made with unbelievers, and v. 97 stipulates that those who remain at home, without a disablement, are not to be considered equal to those who fight in Allah's way. Islamic traditions present the excuse of disablement in v. 97 as being added during Muhammad's dictation of this verse, when a blind Muslim interrupted to ask about his own situation.[264] The vv. 99f appear to show that those who did not emigrate with the Muslims, excepting those who could not, would be punished in Hell, and the vv. 102f are similar to Jewish guidelines making provision for prayers in the presence of a enemy.[265] The v. 105 commands not to be weary in seeking out pagans (in raids), and v. 106 presents Muhammad as being a judge, who was not to intercede for traitors. The vv. 107f show that Muhammad was not to help those who deceived one another, the vv. 110f speak of sin and forgiveness, and the vv. 113f say that Allah protected Muhammad from being led astray by others and then tells of rewards and punishments. The vv. 116f are generally against polytheism, in which v. 116 states that God does not forgive the sin of polytheism, but He does forgive everything else.[266] The vv. 121f claim that those who believe and practice good (deeds) will go to Paradise, and v. 124 describes Abraham as having been God's friend (cf. II Chr. 20:7; Ja. 2:23). The vv. 126f deal with regulations for women, where the vv. 127f are about reconciliation and v. 129 concerns the subject of divorce. The vv. 130f describes Allah, v. 134 speaks of believers, and v. 135 implies that these believe in God, the angels, the Books, His messengers, and the Resurrection. The vv. 136f speak about the hypocrites, and the vv. 138f warn about not making friends with unbelievers. The vv. 149f seem to describe the partial rejection of some of the messengers on the part of the Jews, and those who believe Allah and Muhammad are said not to discriminate between God or His messengers. In the vv. 152f the People of the Book are depicted as having asked Muhammad to send them a Book from Heaven, and Muhammad answers that they (the Israelites) rebelled anyway when they asked Moses to show them God. The v. 153 gives a variation on the Qur'anic parable about the Jewish dietary laws, in which the commandment not to violate the Sabbath takes the place of the alleged commandment to say "forgiveness" (cf. 7:161; 2:55). The accusation of having murdered the prophets (v. 154) and the statement about having uncircumcised hearts imply the Jews, and they also seem to be charged with defaming Mary (v. 155).[267] In v. 156 the Jews claim to have killed the Messiah Jesus,[268] but, similar to certain Gnostic doctrines,[269] this only appeared to be so to the Jews, they actually killed and crucified someone else. The v. 158 presents the Jewish dietary laws as having been a punishment,[270] and 159 declares that the Jews will be punished for the sin usury.[271] In v. 160 some Jews are said to have believed that which was sent down to Muhammad and previous to him, and are said to perform the prayer, give alms, believe in God and the Resurrection. The v. 161 alleges that Muhammad was given revelation as other prophets, and then lists Noah, "prophets after him," Abraham, Ishmael, Isaac, Jacob, the tribes, Jesus, Job, Jonah, Aaron, Solomon, and David, in which the last five of these are out of chronological order, and may have been added later. The v. 162 states that

God spoke (directly) to Moses,[272] and the vv. 165f show that unbelievers will be sent to Hell. The v. 168 gives a command to believe that Muhammad was a messenger from God. The v. 169 declares that Jesus was a messenger, Word and Spirit of God,[273] and this verse goes on to deny a false understanding of the Trinity and makes an ambiguously phrased rejection of His Sonship. The vv. 170f show that the proud are to be punished, the v. 174 claims that the proof and light has come, and v. 175 answers a question regarding inheritance. The Arabic word for "crime" in v. 2 appears to have come from Syriac, and the term "jibt" in v. 54 came from Ethiopic.[274] Some of the verses of this sura are at least remotely similar to passages in the Bible or Talmud.[275]

Sura 65 begins by giving regulations with respect to divorce (vv. 1f), and the vv. 8f refer to the punishments of previous peoples. The vv. 11f show that those who believe and practice good (works) will go to Paradise, and v. 12 mentions the "seven heavens."[276] The v. 11 contains a phrase which is similar to an expression in Acts 26:18.[277]

Conclusions

The Qur'anic evidence from this period shows that the "middle prayer" was added (2:39), and some form of ablution was performed (4:46). Islamic worship appears to have become congregationalized in this period, and in opposition to Jewish and Christian practices, Friday was chosen as a day of assembly (62:9f). As a result of Muhammad's turning away from Judaism, the Islamic Abraham legend was forged (2:118f) in order to theologically justify the change of the qibla (apparently)[278] from Jerusalem to the Ka`ba (2:136f), the Hajj was adopted and modified from Arabic polytheism (2:185, 192f; 3:91), and the fast of the month of Ramadan was instituted (2:179f). Additionally, traditions show that the feast of the sacrifice and the "zakat al-fitr" were introduced, and these seem to have been based on the Jewish celebrations of Passover.[279] Although some general creeds can be found in this section of suras (2:285; 4:135), the traditional Islamic "shahada" cannot be found in the Qur'an at all.[280] According to the suras of this period, believers are described as having believed the "hidden" (2:2f), as peforming the prayer and giving alms (2:2f; 8:2f), of believing what was revealed to Muhammad and the previous Books (2:2f); of believing in angels, the Books, the messengers (4:135), and the Resurrection (2:59, 4:135). They were to practice good works

(2:58; 98: 6f; 64:9; 47:2; 4:121f; 65: 11f), to fear God (8:1), to fear Muhammad (3:169), to obey God and Muhammad (64:12; 8:1, 20, 24f, 48; etc.), to believe God and Muhammad (64:8; 3:174; 57:7f, 28f; 4:135), not to deceive God and Muhammad (8:27f), not to have unbelievers as protectors (3:27f), not to have unbelieving friends (3:114; 4:138f), not to obey unbelievers (3:142), not to be as those who were given the Book (57:15). They were encouraged to participate in armed conflict (61:2f; etc.), commanded not to kill each other (4:94); they were to be Allah's helpers (61:14). They were not to make any discrimination between the messengers (4:151), and they are now clearly called "Muslims" (3:57).

Distinctive of these suras is their regulatory nature. With the formation of a Muslim "community," laws and guidelines became necessary, and in this period regulations were made governing inheritance (2:176f; 4:8f, 23, 37, 175), marriage (2:220f; 4:3, 24f, 126f), divorce (2:226f, 237f; 4:129; 65: 1f), widows (2:234f, 241f), usury (2:276f; 3:125f), debt instruments (2:282f), revenge for murder (2:173f), and the division of booty (8:1, 42). Some of these laws were derived from Jewish sources, and in the absence of a civil authority in the Hijaz, the theocratic legal system of the Jews in Medina generally served as a pattern for the Muslim community.

Certain passages of this period indicate that the general prohibition of wine had not yet been given (2:216; 47:16f; 4:46).

After Muhammad realized that Ishmael was a son of Abraham, the Qur'anic narratives became preoccupied with the development and exploitation of the Abraham legend (2:118f), which was to justify Muhammad's break with the Jews.[281] Whereas Muhammad appears to have identified himself most with the characters of Noah and Moses earlier, he does not seem to have portrayed himself as Abraham (as one might have expected) in the suras of this section. Rather, by way of anachronism Muhammad has Abraham and Ishmael pray for his advent (2:123), he has himself be foretold of in the Torah and Gospel (7:156f), and even makes Jesus prophesy of him as "Ahmad" (61:6).

Relatively few new characters appear in the narratives of these suras, and the sources for their Arabic names seem to have been diverse.[282] The amount of vocabulary borrowed from Syriac has increased,[283] whereas the number of terms borrowed from Hebrew[284] and Ethiopic[285] appears to have been minimal.

Among the new narratives of this period are the Abraham legend (2:118f), the story about Saul, Goliath and David (2:247f), and the materials concerning the family of `Imran (3:30f). As in earlier Qur'anic accounts, a number of inconsistencies can also be found in the narratives of this period. Aside from the association of Abraham and Ishmael with the Ka`ba (2:118f) and other problems, the laws of the red heifer were confused with the law of the heifer which was to have its neck broken for someone murdered by an unknown (2:63f), the return of the ark of the covenant was to confirm Saul's kingship (2:249), Saul was obviously confused with Gideon (2:250), and `Imran (Amram) was evidently thought to have been the father of Moses and Mary, the mother of Jesus (3:30f).

Doctrinally, quite a few contradictions can also be found in the suras of this section. Qur'an 2:285 claims in essence that God made all prophets equal, but 17:57 shows that some were made higher than others; 14:38 depicts Abraham as praying for himself and his sons to be turned away from idols, whereas 16:121 claims that Abraham was not an idolater; in 3:48 God is reported to have said He would let Jesus die, but 4:156 implies that He did not; 3:79 shows that those who desire another religion other than Islam will be lost, but 2:59 (and 5:73) show that some Jews and Christians also will have nothing to fear or be sad about; 8:9 maintains that 1000 angels helped the Muslims at Badr, whereas 3:119f claim that 3000 assisted them there. Another inconsistency can be found in the anti-Jewish story about the children of Israel entering a city in which they were commanded to say the word "forgiveness" (2:55; cf. 7:161). Another version of this account, however, claims that the children of Israel were instead commanded not to violate the Sabbath on this occasion (4:153).

The suras of this period indicate that Muhammad had come to realize that Ishmael was Abraham's son (2:119f), and the terms for "the Messiah" (3:40; etc.), Torah and Gospel (3:43; etc.), and the names for Gabriel and Michael (2:91f) appear to have been used for the first time.

Also somewhat characteristic of the suras in this section (and to some extent the suras of the former period) is that the subject of forgiveness is mentioned quite frequently (14:42; 47:2, 21, 34; 3:29; 3: 141, 188b; 4:110f, 116), and Muhammad was also commanded to pray for forgiveness for his own sins in one verse (47:21).[286]

Sira traditions indicate that the economic situation of Muhammad and the emigrants[287] seems to have motivated them to begin to plunder both Meccan caravans and the herds belonging to other Arab tribes. Some passages in these suras reveal that some Muslims were reluctant about joining the raiding parties (2:212f) and this disinclination only seems to have increased under the influence of the hypocrites (8:51; 47:22) especially after the Muslim defeat at Uhud (3:148, 150f, 162). At least two approaches were used to motivate the Muslims to the armed conflict: Paradise was promised to those who would be killed (47:5f; 3:194; 61:10f) and Hell was promised for those who turned from the fight (8:15f). Moreover, regulations were made to deal with traitors (8:60; 4:106). The hypocrites were alluded to as being unbelievers (4:90f), who were hated by God (61:2f), and for whom there would be a punishment (4:136f).

Other Qur'an passages show that some Muslims either hesitated or refused to pay their alms (64:14f), and it appears that even at this early stage some of them were inclined to dispute the meanings of ambiguous Qur'an verses. (3:5). At one point Muhammad even seems to have been accused of fraud (3:155) in his division of the spoils.[288]

After his theological break with the Jews,[289] Muhammad began to use the force of arms against them. Thus the 120 year-old Abu `Afak was murdered in his sleep,[290] the Banu Qaynuqa was driven into exile[291] the poet Ka`b b. al-Ashraf was murdered,[292] and Muhammad is reported to have commanded that all Jews within the power of Muslims should be killed.[293]

Muhammad also still seems to have had contact with Christians or later sects since references to Jesus (2:81, 130, 254; 3:37f) now present him as the Messiah (3:40; 61:6; 57:27; 4:156, 161, 169), Word and Spirit of God (4:169), who confirmed the Torah (3:44; 61:6) and was taught the Gospel (3:43). Additionally, polemic against the deity of Jesus (3:52), the Trinity and

His Sonship (4:169) are given, and Mary (3:31f; 4:155), Zacharias (3:32f) and John [the Baptist] (3:34) are mentioned at least.

The polemic connected with the Abraham legend (2:136; 3:58f) was apparently directed against both Jews and Christians, whereas the accusations about selling God's Word (2:38, 73, 169f; 3:184, 198), hiding the truth (2:39, 141, 154f, 169f; 3:184) and killing the prophets (2:58, 81, 85; 3:20f, 177; cf. 4:156) were probably levelled at the Jews. For their part, the Jews seem to have continued asking Muhammad for miracles to prove his prophethood (3:179f; 4:152f).

Muhammad's revelations also seem to have been quite susceptible to the direct influence of others. Canonical traditions state that God agreed with `Umar in the matter of the "maqam of Abraham" (2:119),[294] another speaks of inspiration and `Umar.[295] Still other Islamic traditions claim that the verses of the Qur'an were more similar to `Umar's words than Muhammad's, and that the Qur'an was often revealed in accordance with `Umar's opinion.[296] Muhammad is said to have originally wanted to kill the prisoners from Badr (8:68f), but it was `Umar who moved him to let them be ransomed.[297] Similarly, Muhammad is reported to have wanted to kill the Banu Qaynuqa, who had surrendered (also cf. 8:68f), but it was `Abdullah b. Ubayy who influenced him to let them be exiled instead.[298] The question of a blind Muslim reportedly contributed to the final form of Qur'an 4:97,[299] and al-Hubab persuaded Muhammad to use another battle plan at Badr.[300] Other problems with respect to Muhammad's revelations were that he apparently wanted to have the qibla changed in the first place (2:139), he was unable to intercept either the Meccan caravans or an alleged enemy on some raids he led personally,[301] and he is even said to have received a false vision from Allah (8:45).

The "punishment" of Allah for the Meccans, which was often referred to in earlier suras, is now said to have been delayed because Muhammad was in Mecca at the time (8:32),[302] and one verse even seems to indicate that Muhammad's raids on the Meccans were in effect Allah's punishment of that town (16:121). Some (perhaps Meccans) are said to have had plans to capture, murder or exile Muhammad (8:30f).

Many of the suras of this section seem to be composed of fragmentary passages (from diverse time periods), which give the general impression of having been more or less haphazardly thrown together. At least one Western scholar has proposed a theory to account for the "disjointedness" of the Qur'an, in which some of the suras of this group provide classic examples.[303]

Notes:

[1] Guillaume, *Muhammad*, pp. 228 f; Tabari, *History*, vol. 7, pp. 1 f.

[2] Guillaume, *Muhammad*, pp. 230 f; Tabari, *History*, vol. 7, pp. 2 f.

[3] Guillaume, *Muhammad*, pp. 231 f.

[4] For example, the "middle prayer" (Qur'an 2:239), which is the time of the congregational prayer on Fridays, is based on the Jewish prayer times. The introduction of the Friday service is also thought to have somehow been related to the day of preparation for the Sabbath; Buhl, *Muhammad*, pp. 214, 228; Watt, *Muhammad*, p. 99; *EI²*, s.v. "Muhammad," p. 368. The institution of the call to prayer must have been contemporary with the introduction of the congregational Friday prayer.

[5] The text given by Tabari is longer than that found in Ibn Hisham. The account given by Ibn Hisham also contains a Biblical phrase (about one being killed and leaving his flock without a shepherd; cf. I Kgs. 22:17; II Chr. 18:16; Zech. 13:7; etc.), which does not appear in the Qur'an.

[6] The mention of "war" in the constitution betrays a time period after the start of Muhammad's raids, and the description of the Jews as having "their own religion" presumes that Muhammad's break with the Jews had already occurred. Most Western scholars of Islam consider this document to have been drawn up in 2 AH; cf. Buhl, *Muhammad*, pp. 211 f; Andrae, *Mohammed*, pp. 135 f; Guillaume, *Islam*, p. 41; Watt, *Muhammad*, pp. 95 f; *EI²*, s.v. "Muhammad," p. 367.

[7] Guillaume, *Muhammad*, pp. 234 f; Ibn Sa`d, *Classes*, vol. 1, 2, pp. 278 f. Buhl shows, for example, that the pairing of Muhammad with `Ali in these traditions must be fallacious, since both were not only emigrants, but also close relatives; Buhl, *Muhammad*, p. 208.

[8] Wellhausen, *Medina*, p. 33, where Muhammad is said to have thought that he had only obligated the Ansar to defend Medina; cf. Ibn Sa`d, *Classes*, vol. 2, 1, pp. 2 f. See, however, n. 165, below.

[9] Guillaume, *Muhammad*, p. 218; Ibn Sa`d, *Classes*, vol. 1, 1, p. 160.

[10] Ibn Sa`d, *Classes*, vol. 1, 2, p. 279.

[11] Buhl, *Muhammad*, p. 231.

[12] *Sahih Bukhari*, vol. 7, pp. 241 f; *Sahih Muslim*, vol. 4, pp. 1534 f; etc.

[13] Cf. e.g. Andrae, *Mohammed*, p. 140.

[14] See p. 166, n. 25.

[15] Buhl, *Muhammad*, p. 231; Andrae, *Mohammed*, p. 139.

[16] See pp. 84, 164, above.

[17] Cf. Buhl, *Muhammad*, p. 234.

[18] Guillaume, *Muhammad*, pp. 283 f; Ibn Sa`d, *Classes*, vol. 2, 1, pp. 2 f; Tabari, *History*, vol. 7, pp. 10, 13; Wellhausen, *Medina*, p. 33.

[19] Tabari, *History*, vol. 7, pp. 6 f.

[20] Sa`d b. Abu Waqqas was said to have shot the first arrows for the Muslims, and it was he who was selected to lead the next raid; Guillaume, *Muhammad*, p. 281; Ibn Sa`d, *Classes*, vol. 2, 1, pp. 3 f; Tabari, *History*, vol. 7, pp. 10 f, 12 f; Wellhausen, *Medina*, p. 33.

[21] Guillaume, *Muhammad*, p. 286; Ibn Sa`d, *Classes*, vol. 2, 1, p. 4; Tabari, *History*, vol. 7, p. 11.

[22] Nöldeke and Schwally, *GQ*, vol. 1, p. 173.

[23] See p. 157, above for a discussion of this story. Cf. Wellhausen, *Medina*, pp. 247 f.

[24] Owing largely to the fact that the Qur'an only mentions the Sabians without describing their beliefs or practices (5:73; 22:17), much speculation has been made about their identification. Western scholars usually maintain that the name of the Sabians comes from the Hebrew root meaning "to immerse," and that a similar term in Mandaean "s^{e}ba" means "to baptize." According to various views, the Sabians could have been followers of John the Baptist, Mandaeans, Elkasaites, Gnostics, or even Hanifs; Buhl, *Muhammad*, p. 67; Andrae, *Mohammed*, pp. 105, 108; Horovitz, *Untersuchungen*, pp. 121 f; Jeffery, *Vocabulary*, pp. 191 f; *SEI*, pp 477 f. Islamic traditions also show that Muhammad was called a "Sabian" by some contemporaries (*Sahih Bukhari*, vol. 1, pp. 204 f; vol. 4, p. 477; *Sahih Muslim*, vol. 4, pp. 1316 f). The tradition stating that the Sabians used to read the Psalms (*Sahih Bukhari*, vol. 1, p. 240) is more probably a later innovation of Muslim exegetes, based on the correspondence of the Torah to the Jews and the Gospel to the Christians.

[25] See Appendix D, p. 384.

[26] Muhammad and early Islamic scholars seem to have understood the word "ummi" to mean "unlearned" (cf. Qur'an 7:156f; 3:19, 69; 62: 2). Western scholars, however, generally consider this word to have come from a Jewish term for "gentile," thus they often translate "heathen" instead; cf. Nöldeke and Schwally, *GQ*, vol. 1, pp. 14 f; Watt and Bell, *Introduction*, pp. 33 f; see also p. 34, n. 47. In any event, the word "ummi" implies someone who had not read the Bible.

[27] Canonical hadith relate that copies of the Qur'an were also sold later; *Sunan Abu Dawud*, vol. 2, p. 755, and they are still sold today. From a theological standpoint this verse has also become self-condemning for Islam.

[28] See pp. 100, 151, 311, above.

[29] See Appendix D, p. 384.

[30] Nöldeke and Schwally, *GQ*, vol. 1, p. 176.

[31] *Sahih Bukhari*, vol. 6, pp. 8 f; Guillaume, *Muhammad*, p. 255.

[32] See Appendix D, p. 384.

[33] See Appendix D, p. 385.

[34] See Appendix D, p. 385.

[35] The word "ra'ina" (approximately "look to us") seems to have been used by the Jews as a play on words from the Hebrew where the same phrase has the approximate meaning of "our evil one" ; Geiger, *WMJA*, p. 17; Rudolph, *Koran*, p. 45, n. 48.

[36] Instead of giving the greeting "peace be upon you" the Jews are reported to have said "death be upon you"; *Sahih Bukhari*, vol. 8, pp. 32 f, 181; *Sahih Muslim*, vol. 3, pp. 1183 f. Cf. Geiger, *WMJA*, p. 18.

[37] Nöldeke and Schwally, *GQ*, vol. 1, pp. 176 f.

[38] It is improbable that the Christians of Najran were meant here; Nöldeke and Schwally, *GQ*, vol. 1, p. 177 (see also n. 2).

[39] See Appendix D, p. 385.

[40] See pp. 89, 196.

[41] See Appendix D, p. 385.

[42] See Appendix D, p. 385.

[43] E.g. *Sahih Bukhari*, vol. 6, p. 11; *Sahih Muslim*, vol. 4, pp. 1280 f, where some traditions contain the problematical phrase about God concurring with 'Umar (!) in at least three Qur'anic verses. See p. 220, below.

[44] Wellhausen, *Reste*, p. 76.

[45] See p. 177, n. 148, above.

[46] See p. 177, n. 148, above.

[47] Guillaume, *Muhammad*, p. 289; Ibn Sa'd, *Classes*, vol. 1, 2, p. 283; Tabari, *History*, vol. 7, pp. 24 f; *Sahih Bukhari*, vol. 1, pp. 35, 237; vol. 6, pp. 14, 18; *Sahih Muslim*, vol. 1, p. 236; *Sunan Abu Dawud*, vol. 1, p. 132.

[48] See pp. 46, 90, above.

[49] Cf. e.g. *Sahih Bukhari*, vol. 4, pp. 532 f.

[50] Andrae, *Ursprung*, pp. 162 f.

[51] *Sahih Bukhari*, vol. 6, p. 21.

[52] Nöldeke and Schwally, *GQ*, vol. 1, pp. 177 f.

[53] Ibid., p. 178.

[54] Ibid.

[55] Ibid., pp. 180 f. The vv. 196b-198 are thought to have been possibly Meccan, the vv. 190, 192a from 6 AH, and v. 192 b from 10 AH.

[56] Ibid., p. 182.

[57] Guillaume, *Muhammad*, pp. 286 f; Ibn Sa'd, *Classes*, vol.2, 1, pp. 7 f; Tabari, *History*, vol. 7, pp. 18 f.

[58] *Sahih Bukhari*, vol. 7, p. 155.

[59] Nöldeke and Schwally, *GQ*, vol. 1, p. 183.

[60] Cf. *Sahih Bukhari*, vol. 6, pp. 38 f; *Sahih Muslim*, vol. 2, p. 731.

[61] *ECMD*, pp. 93, 142.

[62] This doctrine is contrary to the Bible; cf. Eccl. 5:4-6.

[63] This Islamic doctrine, which is sufficiently illustrated in canonical traditions (*Sahih Bukhari*, vol. 3, p. 489; vol. 7, pp. 136 f; *Sahih Muslim*, vol. 2, pp. 729 f), is also contrary to the Bible (cf. Dt. 24:1f; Mt. 5:32; etc.) and was a popular topic with early Christian polemicists (*ECMD*, pp. 129, 142, 399, 475, 540).

[64] See p. 41. In *Sahih Muslim*, vol. 1, pp. 272 f, conversation is said to have been allowed during prayer prior to the "revelation" of this verse (cf. p. 59, n. 37, above).

[65] Geiger, *WMJA*, pp. 84 f, references Mishnah Berakhot 4,5 shows this as generally conforming with Jewish practice.

[66] Rudolph, *Koran*, p. 65, n. 130.

[67] Cf. I Sam. 6. The Qur'an presents the return of the ark as a confirmation of Saul's kingship.

[68] See Appendix D, p. 386.

[69] See p. 144, above.

[70] See Appendix D, p. 387.

[71] See Appendix D, p. 387.

[72] See Appendix D, p. 387.

[73] See. p. 33, n. 39, above.

[74] Jeffery, *Vocabulary*, pp. 100 (Gabriel), 275 (Michael).

[75] Ibid., pp. 97f (Goliath), 204 (Saul).

[76] Ibid., p. 192.

[77] Ibid., p. 57.

[78] Ibid., p. 174.

[79] Ibid., p. 88.

[80] See Appendix F, pp. 414 f.

[81] Cf. Tabari, *History*, vol. 7, p. 25, where the Jews are reported to have said that they had in effect taught Muhammad where the qibla was in the first place.

[82] Buhl, *Muhammad*, p. 218, n. 50, remarks that the traditions unreliably always depict Muhammad as the winner of these discussions.

[83] Guillaume, *Muhammad*, p. 240 f; *Sahih Bukhari*, vol. 5, p. 189.

[84] The Jews are reported to have read the Torah in Hebrew, and explained it in Arabic; *Sahih Bukhari*, vol. 6, p. 13.

[85] *Sahih Bukhari*, vol. 9, p. 338.

[86] Some traditions relate how a Jewess told ʿAʾisha about the "torment in the grave." ʿAʾisha then asked Muhammad, who at first denied there would be such a thing, only later to confess that there would be a "torment in the grave"; *Sahih Bukhari*, vol. 2, p. 256; vol. 8, p. 251; *Sahih Muslim*, vol. 2, p. 428.

[87] *Sunan Abu Dawud*, vol. 3, p. 1039.

[88] See p. 160, above.

[89] See p. 184, n. 239, above, and p. 253, n. 64.

[90] See p. 164, above.

[91] See p. 157, above.

[92] *SEI*, p. 639.

[93] See n. 31, above. Since Gabriel (Dan. 9:21) and Michael (Dan. 10:13) are both mentioned as being angels of God in the Hebrew scriptures, it is more than probable that the remarks of the Jews were either taken out of context or misquoted.

[94] See n. 35, above.

[95] *Sahih Bukhari*, vol. 4, p. 437.

[96] *Sahih Bukhari*, vol. 5, pp. 58f.

[97] *Sahih Bukhari*, vol. 4, p. 345.

[98] *Sahih Muslim*, vol. 3, p. 1166.

[99] *Sahih Bukhari*, vol. 4, p. 442; *Sahih Muslim*, vol. 3, p. 380.

[100] *Sahih Muslim*, vol. 3, pp. 1192 f; Guillaume, *Muhammad*, p. 240; Ibn Sa'd, *Classes*, vol. 2, 2, pp. 244 f.

[101] The first child of the Muslims is said to have been born some 20 months after the Hijra; *Sahih Bukhari*, vol. 7, p. 273; Tabari, *History*, vol. 7, pp. 9 f. Interestingly enough, one canonical tradition credibly relates how childless Arab women of Medina would promise to have a prospective child raised as a Jew; *Sunan Abu Dawud*, vol. 2, p. 743; cf. I Sam. 1:1f.

[102] See p. 193, above.

[103] Guillaume, *Muhammad*, p. 259.

[104] *Sahih Muslim*, vol. 1, pp. 175 f. See also Nöldeke and Schwally, *GQ*, vol. 1, p. 183, n. 1, for references to other Islamic sources.

[105] *Sahih Bukhari*, vol. 6, pp. 73 f. See also Bell, *Origin*, p. 101.

[106] The Jews are said to have brought two adulterers to Muhammad, who was then asked what their punishment should be. Some traditions present the Jews as having innovated a non-capital punishment for adulterers, but Muhammad is said to have asked that a Torah be brought and read. The Jews are then reported to have read from the Torah, and covered the "verse about stoning" with a hand. When they were requested to show what they were hiding, the verse of stoning became manifest, and the adulterers were then stoned to death; *Sahih Bukhari*, vol. 8, p. 529; *Sahih Muslim*, vol. 3, pp. 918 f; Guillaume, *Muhammad*, pp. 266 f.

[107] Guillaume, *Muhammad*, pp. 246 f, 264; Buhl, *Muhammad*, p. 218; Andrae, *Mohammed*, p. 137.

[108] See nn. 35 and 92, above; cf. n. 36, above, for other Jewish greetings.

[109] Buhl, *Muhammad*, p. 219, in speaking of the threat of the Jews undermining Muhammad's prophetic authority, states (trans.) : "He (Muhammad) could not possibly concede that his earlier prophet stories were incorrect, since they had appeared with the stamp of revelation, and on the other hand he could not all of the sudden disavow the earlier revelations, to which he had appealed up until then." (cf. Buhl, in *SEI*, p. 398). Although this same idea is followed by Welch, in *EI²*, s.v. "Muhammad," p. 368, Muhammad was certainly aware of such blatant corruptions of Biblcal narratives as are found, for example, in Qur'an 71:20-24.

[110] See pp. 86 and 112, n. 37, above.

[111] See Appendix D, pp. 385 f.

[112] Josephus, *Ant.*, 1, 12, 4.

[113] See Appendix D, pp. 385 f.

[114] See n. 43, above.

[115] *Sahih Muslim*, vol. 4, p. 1280.

[116] Islamic datings for the change of the qibla range from 9-19 months after the Hijra; see Nöldeke and Schwally, *GQ*, p. 174, n. 1, for a listing of Islamic sources.

[117] *Sahih Bukhari*, vol. 4, p. 427; *Sahih Muslim*, vol. 1, p. 275.

[118] *Sunan Abu Dawud*, vol. 1, p. 167.

[119] *Sahih Bukhari*, vol. 4, p. 440; *Sahih Muslim*, vol. 4, p. 1403. Cf. Qur'an 57:15.

[120] *Sahih Bukhari*, vol. 4, p. 442; vol. 7, p. 519; *Sahih Muslim*, vol. 3, p. 1156.

[121] *Sahih Bukhari*, vol. 2, p. 1; vol. 4, p. 457.

[122] Islamic sources usually describe this event as having taken place soon after the construction of the "mosque" in Medina; *Sahih Muslim*, vol. 1, p. 207; Guillaume, *Muhammad*, pp. 235 f; Ibn Sa'd, *Classes*, vol. 1, 2, pp. 290 f. Contrary to Islamic claims, the present text of the "adhan" (cf. *SEI*, p. 16) does not seem to predate 690 AD in archaeological finds; cf. Nevo, "Prehistory," *JSAI*, vol. 17 (1994), p. 110.

[123] *Sahih Bukhari*, vol. 6, p. 21.

[124] Tabari, *History*, vol. 7, pp. 25 f; *Sahih Bukhari*, vol. 3, p. 124; *Sahih Muslim*, vol. 2, pp. 548 f.

[125] Goitein is cited in *SEI*, pp. 468 f, as showing that Jewish traditions maintain that Moses received the second stone tablets on the Day of Atonement. According to Qur'an 2:181, the fast of Ramadan was instituted because

the Qur'an was "sent down" in that month. Based on Qur'an 2:180a ("numbered days") and the practices of the Jews 10 days prior to the Day of Atonement, Goitein proposes that the fast of Ramadan was only held for 10 days initially.

[126] *Sahih Muslim*, vol. 2, p. 552.

[127] See p. 167, n. 28, above.

[128] This was said to have predated the institution of the Zakat (Ibn Sa`d, *Classes*, vol. 1, 2, p. 293) and is continued today (*SEI*, p. 156).

[129] Ibn Sa`d, *Classes*, vol. 1, 2, p. 293; Tabari, *History*, vol. 7, p. 26; *Sahih Bukhari*, vol. 2, pp. 341 f.

[130] Ex. 34:18f (Ex. 13:13f; Num. 18:15f).

[131] Buhl, *Muhammad*, pp. 226 f, cites Sprenger and Grimme as being of the opinion that the fasting of Ramadan came from Lent, but disagrees with them using this and other arguments.

[132] Buhl, *Muhammad*, p. 227, (nn. 71-72) references the *Fihrist*. Cf. Buhl, in *SEI*, p. 398.

[133] Buhl, *Muhammad*, pp. 227 f, cites Wensinck. Cf. *SEI*, p. 189.

[134] Buhl, *Muhammad*, p. 228.

[135] Guillaume, *Muhammad*, pp. 289 f; Ibn Sa`d, *Classes*, vol. 2, 1, pp. 9 f; Tabari, *History*, vol. 7, pp. 26 f; Wellhausen, *Medina*, pp. 37 f.

[136] Wellhausen, *Medina*, p. 46.

[137] Ibn Sa`d, *Classes*, vol. 2, 1, pp. 21 f.

[138] Ibn Sa`d, *Classes*, vol. 2, 1, p. 22.

[139] Guillaume, *Muhammad*, p. 309; Tabari, *History*, vol. 7, p. 67.

[140] Watt, *Muhammad*, p. 114; Tabari, *History*, vol. 7, p. 26, n. 52.

[141] Watt makes a similar suggestion in *Muhammad*, p. 114.

[142] See Appendix D, p. 386.

[143] See n. 63, above.

[144] See p. 177, n. 148.

[145] See Appendix D, p. 387.

[146] Cf. Al-Kindi in *ECMD*, p. 451.

[147] See Appendix F, p. 415.

[148] In Qur'an 6:74, Abraham's father "Azar" (!) is shown to have been an idolater. It seems that Muhammad also prayed for his own parents, who had most certainly been idolaters; see. p. 112, n. 33.

[149] Nöldeke and Schwally, *GQ*, vol. 1, p. 185.

[150] Ibid., vol. 1, pp. 240, 242; vol. 2, p. 97.

[151] See pp. 80, 106.

[152] See p. 34, n. 47.

[153] Speyer, *Erzählungen*, p. 461. The first part of this verse is also remotely similar to Mt. 23:4.

[154] See the references for n. 121, above.

[155] Some canonical hadith report that this verse was revealed as once, upon the arrival of a caravan on Friday, all but 12 Muslims left Muhammad (in

the mosque) and went to meet the caravan; *Sahih Muslim*, vol. 2, p. 409.

[156] Guillaume, *Muhammad*, p. 281; Ibn Sa`d, *Classes*, vol. 2, 1, pp. 4 f;
Tabari, *History*, vol. 7, pp. 11 f, 15; Wellhausen, *Medina*, p. 34.

[157] Cf. *SEI*, pp. 418 f.

[158] *Sahih Bukhari*, vol. 6, p. 110; *Sahih Muslim*, vol. 2, pp. 705 f.

[159] *Sahih Muslim*, vol. 2, pp. 707 f.

[160] *Sahih Bukhari*, vol. 5, p. 372; vol. 7, pp. 36, 311; vol. 9, p. 76; *Sahih
Muslim*, vol. 2, p. 708; vol. 3, p. 1071.

[161] *Sahih Muslim*, vol. 2, pp. 610, 706.

[162] *SEI*, p. 420.

[163] Tabari, *History*, vol. 7, pp. 18, 92.

[164] Guillaume, *Muhammad*, p. 285; Ibn Sa`d, *Classes*, vol. 2, 1, pp. 5 f;
Tabari, *History*, vol. 7, pp. 13, 15; Wellhausen, *Medina*, p. 34. See n. 166.

[165] Guillaume, *Muhammad*, p. 286; Ibn Sa`d, *Classes*, vol. 2, 1, p. 6;
Tabari, *History*, vol. 7, pp. 14, 16; Wellhausen, *Medina*, p. 34.

[166] Since the number of emigrants could hardly have been more than 90
men, it is obvious that either some of the Ansar must have participated in this
action, or that these traditions have been corrupted. Cf. n. 176, below.

[167] Guillaume, *Muhammad*, pp. 285 f; Ibn Sa`d, *Classes*, vol. 2, 1, pp. 6 f;
Tabari, *History*, vol. 7, pp. 13 f, 16; Wellhausen, *Medina*, p. 34.

[168] This letter was said to have been written by Ubayy b. Ka`b; Well-
hausen, *Medina*, p. 35; cf. Watt and Bell, *Introduction*, pp. 35 f.

[169] Guillaume, *Muhammad*, pp. 286 f; Ibn Sa`d, *Classes*, vol. 2, 1, pp. 7 f; Tabari, *History*, vol. 7, pp. 18 f, 21 f; Wellhausen, *Medina*, pp. 34 f.

[170] Guillaume, *Muhammad*, pp. 287 f; Tabari, *History*, vol. 7, p. 20; Wellhausen, *Medina*, p. 37.

[171] Some accounts show that the two simply returned to Medina after they had found their camel (Ibn Sa`d, *Classes*, vol. 2, 1, p. 8; Wellhausen, *Medina*, p. 36). If they had indeed been captured by the Meccans, one would have to ask why the Meccans had not demanded a ransom for them, particularly in light of what the Muslims had done with the Meccan prisoners.

[172] Wellhausen, *Medina*, p. 37.

[173] Some accounts report that one fifth of the booty was given to Muhammad (before Qur'an 8:42 was composed), others claim that the booty was divided after the battle of Badr; Guillaume, *Muhammad*, pp. 288 f; Ibn Sa`d, *Classes*, vol. 2, 1, pp. 8 f; Wellhausen, *Medina*, p. 37.

[174] Buhl, *Muhammad*, pp. 236, shows that granting the option of return (at the start of the expedition) was actually in anticipation of fighting in the month of Rajab; cf. Andrae, *Mohammed*, pp. 141 f; Watt, *Muhammad*, pp. 109 f.

[175] See pp. 195 f, above.

[176] Islamic accounts generally give 305-319 Muslims, 74-83 of whom were said to have been emigrants. Guillaume in *Muhammad*, p. xv, mentions that the early Islam historian Shurahbil b. Sa`d used to delete the names of Badr warriors from traditions if their posterity did not bring him "presents" upon visiting him.

[177] In comparing Qur'an 8:5-9, 43-46, with the traditional accounts of the battle of Badr, Buhl (*Muhammad*, p. 240, n. 95) shows that the Muslims had no knowledge of the Meccan relief force. The events surrounding the interrogation of the Meccan water-bearers clearly indicates that the Muslims thought

they would be facing a weak caravan escort at the most; cf. Guillaume, *Muhammad*, p. 295; Tabari, *History*, vol. 7, pp. 43 f; Wellhausen, *Medina*, p. 48.

[178] The Meccans had unwisely not bothered to occupy a water source, and al-Hubab counseled to take possession of a well nearest the Meccans, make a cistern and then stop up all other available water sources. al-Hubab's suggestion was then carried out; Guillaume, *Muhammad*, pp. 296 f; Tabari, *History*, vol. 7, p. 47.

[179] Wellhausen, *Medina*, p. 35.

[180] Islamic traditions give totals varying from 50 killed and 43 captured, to 74 killed and 74 captured.

[181] Wellhausen, *Medina*, p. 67.

[182] Ibid., p. 69.

[183] For Islamic accounts of the battle of Badr see: Guillaume, *Muhammad*, pp. 289 f; Ibn Sa`d, *Classes*, vol. 2, 1, pp. 9 f; Tabari, *History*, vol. 7, pp. 26 f; Wellhausen, *Medina*, pp. 37 f; *Sahih Bukhari*, vol. 5, pp. 196 f.

[184] Cf. Ibn Sa`d, *Classes*, vol. 2, 1, p. 33; Wellhausen, *Medina*, p. 93; Nöldeke and Schwally, *GQ*, vol. 1, p. 187, n. 4.

[185] Wellhausen, *Medina*, p. 66.

[186] Ibid., p. 71.

[187] Ibid., p. 66.

[188] Guillaume, *Muhammad*, pp. 321 f; Tabari, *History*, vol. 7, p. 64.

[189] Owing to the illness of his wife, `Uthman was not present at Badr. Waqidi presents Muhammad as having arrived in Medina as Ruqayya was being buried; Wellhausen, *Medina*, p. 71.

[190] Wellhausen, *Medina*, p. 78 f.

[191] Zayd b. Thabit is said to have learned to write from some of the Meccan prisoners; Ibn Sa`d, *Classes*, vol. 2, 1, p. 23.

[192] Guillaume, *Muhammad*, pp. 314 f; Tabari, *History*, vol. 7, pp. 73 f.

[193] See p. 106, above.

[194] Rudolph, *Koran*, p. 176, n. 6.

[195] See n. 177, above.

[196] See p. 187, above.

[197] See Appendix F, p. 415.

[198] Nöldeke and Schwally, *GQ*, vol. 2, pp. 80 f. Cf. Watt and Bell, *Introduction*, p. 60; *ECMD*, p. 457.

[199] The idea for such rivers in Paradise seems to have come from the apocryphal Secrets of Enoch or Apocalypse of Paul; see Appendix F, p. 415.

[200] See p. 187, above.

[201] Cf. Guillaume, *Muhammad*, p. 263, where Finhas the Jew voiced his dissatisfaction at being asked to contribute for the Muslims' war against the Meccans.

[202] Guillaume, *Muhammad*, pp. 675 f; Ibn Sa`d, *Classes*, vol. 2, 1, pp. 30 f; Wellhausen, *Medina*, pp. 90 f. Ibn Hisham shows that Muhammad instigated her murder. Ibn Sa`d and Waqidi present `Umayr as having vowed to kill her.

[203] Guillaume, *Muhammad*, p. 675; Ibn Sa`d, *Classes*, vol. 2, 1, p. 31; Wellhausen, *Medina*, pp. 91 f. Cf. *ECMD*, p. 430.

[204] Wellhausen, *Medina*, p. 94.

[205] Cf. Buhl, *Muhammad*, p. 248; *SEI*, p. 399; *EI²*, s.v. "Muhammad," p. 370. Islamic sources generally present this conflict as beginning from a Jewish prank in which a Jew and an Arab were killed.

[206] Guillaume, *Muhammad*, pp. 363 f; Ibn Sa`d, *Classes*, vol. 2, 1, pp. 32 f; Tabari, *History*, vol. 7, pp. 85 f; Wellhausen, *Medina*, pp. 92 f.

[207] Tabari, *History*, vol. 7, pp. 87 f.

[208] Ibn Sa`d gives 200 or 40 men; Waqidi gives 200 or 400 men.

[209] Guillaume, *Muhammad*, pp. 361 f; Ibn Sa`d, *Classes*, vol. 2, 1, pp. 33 f; Tabari, *History*, vol. 7, p. 89; Wellhausen, *Medina*, p. 94.

[210] Or "heathens"; see p. 34, n. 47.

[211] Nöldeke and Schwally, *GQ*, vol. 1, p. 191.

[212] See Appendix D, p. 388.

[213] See Appendix D, p. 388.

[214] See Appendix D, p. 388.

[215] See Appendix D, p. 388.

[216] See p. 177, n. 148.

[217] See Appendix D, p. 388.

[218] In Guillaume, *Muhammad*, p. 277, Ibn Hisham gives an unreliable tradition which presents these Christians as having been a deputation from Najran, who decided not to accept Muhammad's challenge.

[219] See p. 34, n. 47.

[220] Cf. Dt. 23:19-20. Thus in this case, the term "`ummiyun" would perhaps best be translated "heathen."

[221] See p. 196.

[222] Rudolph, *Koran*, p. 73, n. 1; cf. Nöldeke and Schwally, *GQ*, vol. 1, pp. 192 f.

[223] Jeffery, *Vocabulary*, pp. 217 (`Imran), 265 (Masih), 137 f (rabbani).

[224] Ibid., p. 95 (Tawra).

[225] Ibid., pp. 71 (Gospel - "Injil"), 115 (hawariyun).

[226] See Appendix F, p. 415.

[227] Guillaume, *Muhammad*, pp. 260 f.

[228] See p. 34, n. 47, above.

[229] Jeffery, *Vocabulary*, pp. 213 f.

[230] Waqidi also reports that at least 1400 camels were in this herd; Wellhausen, *Medina*, p. 95.

[231] Guillaume, *Muhammad*, p. 360; Ibn Sa`d, *Classes*, vol. 2, 1, pp. 34 f; Tabari, *History*, vol 7, pp. 88 f; Wellhausen, *Medina*, pp. 94 f.

[232] Muhammad also hired Hasan b. Thabit to write poetry against those aiding Ka`b; Guillaume, *Muhammad*, pp. 364 f; Ibn Sa`d, *Classes*, vol. 2, 1, pp. 35 f; Tabari, *History*, vol. 7, pp. 94 f; Wellhausen, *Medina*, pp. 95 f.

[233] Guillaume, *Muhammad*, p. 362; Ibn Sa`d, *Classes*, vol. 2, 1, pp. 39 f; Tabari, *History*, vol. 7, p. 93; Wellhausen, *Medina*, pp. 99 f.

[234] Guillaume, *Muhammad*, p. 362; Ibn Sa`d, *Classes*, vol. 2, 1, p. 41; Tabari, *History*, vol. 7, pp. 88, 93; Wellhausen, *Medina*, p. 100.

[235] Guillaume, *Muhammad*, p. 364; Ibn Sa`d, *Classes*, vol. 2, 1, pp. 41 f; Tabari, *History*, vol. 7, pp. 98 f; Wellhausen, *Medina*, pp. 100 f.

[236] Guillaume, *Muhammad*, p. 369.

[237] Tabari, *History*, vol. 7, p. 105; *Sahih Bukhari*, vol. 5, pp. 228 f.

[238] The account in Waqidi says that these were Jewish allies of `Abdullah b. Ubayy; Wellhausen, *Medina*, p. 106.

[239] Waqidi gives the Muslim killed as 74; Wellhausen, *Medina*, p. 138.

[240] Guillaume, *Muhammad*, pp. 370 f; Ibn Sa`d, *Classes*, vol. 2, 1, pp. 42 f; Tabari, *History*, vol. 7, pp. 105 f; Wellhausen, *Medina*, pp. 101 f.

[241] Guillaume, *Muhammad*, p. 390; Ibn Sa`d, *Classes*, vol. 2, 1, pp. 57 f; Tabari, *History*, vol. 7, pp. 138 f.

[242] Rudolph, *Koran*, p. 73, n. 1.

[243] Owing to `Umar's belief that Muhammad was not dead after his last illness in 11 AH, some Western scholars thought that this and other Qur'anic passages regarding Muhammad's mortality where later additions to the text of the Qur'an; Nöldeke and Schwally, *GQ*, vol. 2, pp. 81 f.

[244] This accusation was made with respect to the spoils from Badr; Nöldeke and Schwally, *GQ*, vol. 1, p. 193, reference (among others) Waqidi - see Wellhausen, *Medina*, p. 67.

[245] Guillaume, *Muhammad*, p. 263; Wellhausen, *Medina*, p. 146. Cf. Qur'an 47:40.

[246] Jeffery, *Vocabulary*, p. 138.

[247] See Appendix F, p. 415.

[248] See e.g. Wellhausen, *Medina*, pp. 145 f.

[249] *Sahih Bukhari*, vol. 4, p. 523; *Sahih Muslim*, vol. 4, p. 1459.

[250] This passage is thought to refer to the battle of Uhud; Nöldeke and Schwally, *GQ*, vol. 1, p. 194.

[251] Appendix D, p. 389.

[252] Nöldeke and Schwally, *GQ*, vol. 1, p. 194.

[253] See Appendix F, p. 415.

[254] This idea may have been influenced by Jewish practice; Rudolph, *Koran*, p. 96, n. 4, cites Yevamot 44a; Ketubbot 90a-96b; Keritot 15a.

[255] For v. 27 cf. Lev. 18:6-18.

[256] See p. 200, above; cf. Nöldeke and Schwally, *GQ*, vol. 1, p. 198.

[257] Geiger, *WMJA*, p. 86, references Berakot 31,2 and Berakot 46 respectively. Nöldeke and Schwally, *GQ*, vol. 1, p. 199, n. 5 cite Berakot 15a, (for the use of sand in ablutions) and think that the Qur'anic regulation may have also come from a Christian source which followed the Talmudic practice. For a discussion of the problems in trying to date this verse, see *GQ*, vol. 1, pp. 199 f.

[258] *Sahih Bukhari*, vol. 6, pp. 88, 103; vol. 7, p. 69; etc.

[259] The Banu Nadir are thought to have been meant here; Nöldeke and Schwally, *GQ*, vol. 1, pp. 200 f.

[260] *SEI*, p. 639; p. 195, above.

[261] Geiger, *WMJA*, p. 17; p. 195, above.

[262] Nöldeke and Schwally, *GQ*, vol. 1, p. 200.

[263] See n. 36, above; *Sahih Bukhari*, vol. 8, pp. 32 f, 181.

[264] Zayd b. Thabit was said to have been the scribe at the time; *Sahih Bukhari*, vol. 6, pp. 94 f.

[265] Geiger, *WMJA*, p. 86, cites Berakhot 4, 4; cf. Nöldeke and Schwally, *GQ*, vol. 1, p. 202, n. 1.

[266] Such a verse may have played a role in the attempts of later Islamic theologians to absolve Muhammad from the sin of ever having been an idolater. See pp. 26 and 28, above.

[267] This could refer to Qur'an 19:28f (cf. *SEI*, p. 329) or perhaps to references to Mary in the Talmud (Rudolph, *Koran*, p. 115, n. 71).

[268] Cf. Sanhedrin 43a.

[269] See Appendix D, p. 389.

[270] See p. 160, n. 240.

[271] See n. 220, above.

[272] See Appendix D, p. 389.

[273] See Appendix D, p. 389.

[274] Jeffery, *Vocabulary*, pp. 116 f (hub = "defeated, guilty"), 99 f (jibt = "new god").

[275] See Appendix F, pp. 415 f.

[276] Cf. Qur'an 67:3; Geiger, *WMJA*, pp. 63 f.

[277] See p. 147.

[278] One work of Crone and Cook, which has not been very well accepted by many other Western scholars of Islam, refer to archaeological finds in early mosques indicating that the qibla was not officially changed prior to 705 AD; Crone and Cook, *Hagarism*, pp. 23 f, 173 (as cited by J.H. Smith in an unpublished paper). Cf. Watt in Tabari, *History*, vol. 6, pp. xvii f.

[279] See p. 197, above, and the nn. 129 and 207.

[280] At present, there seems to be no archaelogical evidence that Muhammad's name was used in either official or non-official religious writings before 690 AD; cf. Nevo, "Prehistory," *JSAI*, vol. 17 (1994), p. 109 f.

[281] See pp. 195 f, above.

[282] Gabriel and Michael are thought to have come from Syriac (n. 74), Saul and Goliath from Hebrew (n. 75), and the "disciples" of Jesus from Ethiopic (n. 225).

[283] See nn. 76-78, 223, 246, 274, above.

[284] See nn. 224, 229, above.

[285] See nn. 79, 225, 274, above.

[286] Cf. *ECMD*, p. 723.

[287] See pp. 187 f, above.

[288] See n. 244, above.

[289] See pp. 193 f, above.

[290] See p. 205, above.

[291] See pp. 205 f, above.

[292] See p. 209, above.

[293] See p. 210, above.

[294] See the references in n. 43, above.

[295] See the reference in n. 115, above.

[296] Suyuti, *El-Itkan*, vol. 1, p. 75; cf. Nöldeke, "Qur'an," p. 8.

[297] See n. 182, above.

[298] Ibn Sa`d, *Classes*, vol. 2, 1, pp. 32 f; Tabari, *History*, vol. 7, p. 86.

[299] See n. 264, above.

[300] See nn. 178-179, above.

[301] See nn. 156, 167, 183, 209, 233, 234.

[302] Andrae, *Ursprung*, p. 62.

[303] See the work of Bell, as referred to in Watt and Bell, *Introduction*, pp. 101 f; *EI²*, s.v. "Kur'an," p. 418.

Muhammad
Victory and Death

During the 35th month after the Hijra, 150 Muslims under Abu Salama were sent to Qatan to confront the Banu Asad, who were allegedly planning to attack them. When the Muslims arrived, they only found three shepherds and some camels and sheep, which they captured and brought back to Medina. Abu Salama died on the return journey, from wounds which he had sustained at Uhud.[1]

Also in the 35th month after the Hijra, `Abdullah b. `Unays was sent out to kill Sufyan b. Khalid, who was said to have been planning to attack the Muslims. `Abdullah later brought Sufyan's head to Muhammad.[2]

In the 36th month after the Hijra, Muhammad sent 70[3] Ansar Qur'an reciters with Abu Bara to present Islam to his people. A messenger was sent out in advance with a letter, and when he reached `Amir b. al-Tufayl, the latter had him killed. Together with allies from among the `Usayya and Ri`l,[4] `Amir and his forces backtracked the Muslim messenger's trail and attacked the Muslims at Bi'r Ma`una. Only one Muslim escaped death to return and tell Muhammad of the attack.[5]

Muhammad is reported to have been very grieved by the deaths of his reciters, and an allegedly abrogated Qur'an verse is said to have been revealed concerning this defeat.[6]

Also during the 36th month after the Hijra, some of the `Adal and al-Qara requested that Muhammad send some Muslims[7] to teach them the Qur'an and the laws of Islam. They were betrayed at al-Raji`, where all but three Muslims were killed by the Hudhayl. Of the remaining Muslims (all of whom were taken prisoner), one was killed while trying to escape, and the other two were sold to the Meccans, who had them executed.[8]

In the 37th month after the Hijra, the Jewish Banu Nadir are said to have made plans to kill Muhammad.[9] When this became known, however, Muhammad is said to have given them an ultimatum to leave Medina. Hoping for assistance from `Abdullah b. Ubayy and the Banu Qurayza, the Banu Nadir are said to have withstood the Muslims. After a 15 day-long siege, however, the Banu Nadir surrendered, and they were exiled from Medina. Since this action was a siege, and not an expedition, Muhammad then took all of the booty and divided it primarily among the emigrants, to the exclusion of the Ansar (cf. Qur'an 59:5, 8-9). The palm trees of the Banu Nadir were felled, and some of the children of the Ansar, who had been covenanted (I Sam. 1:1f) to be raised up as Jews among the Banu Nadir were returned to their original families.[10]

The drinking of wine is thought to have been forbidden in this time period.[11]

Qur'an 59, which appears to have been composed after the Banu Nadir were driven from Medina,[12] begins with the statement that everything in Heaven and on earth praises God (v. 1). The vv. 2f maintain that God drove out the unbelievers among the People of the Book (the Banu Nadir), and claim that neither Muslims, nor the others believed this would happen (to the Banu Nadir). The v. 4 accuses them (the Banu Nadir) of having opposed Allah and Muhammad, and asserts that even the palm trees were felled with Allah's permission.[13] The v. 6 shows that Muhammad changed the regulation about booty in this case, since the Muslims did not even have to be mounted (it was a siege).[14] The v. 7 declares that the spoils from all city dwellers belong to Allah and Muhammad (alone) for distribution among his relatives, the orphans and poor, etc. In v. 8 the (economically) poor emigrants are described as having been the true ones, and v. 9 admonishes the Medinans not to be jealous. The v. 10 gives an alleged (or example) prayer of later converts to Islam, and v. 11 depicts the hypocrites as having said that they would also go into exile and help the People of the Book (Jews), whereby the hypocrites are accused of lying. The v. 12 says that the hypocrites would not go into exile, nor help, etc., they are said to have been without understanding (v. 13), and would remain in their fortresses (v. 14). In the vv. 15f the hypocrites are compared with previous unbelievers and Satan himself, both of whom are destined for Hell. The v. 18 admonishes believers to fear God, and v. 21 seems to make an ambiguous reference to

Mount Sinai with respect to a hypothetical "sending down" of the Qur'an. The vv. 22f are in praise of God. The vv. 23f are similar to the Jewish Tefillah.[15]

During the 43th month after the Hijra, Muhammad is said to have married Zaynab b. Khuzayma, who had been divorced.[16]

In the 44th month after the Hijra, Muhammad is reported to have married Umm Salama, whose husband had died on the return journey from Qatan.[17]

During the 45th month after the Hijra, Muhammad and 1500 Muslims reportedly went to Badr in order to accept the challenge of Abu Sufyan.[18] The polytheists are said to have left Mecca with 2000 men, only to return later (supposedly because it was a year of drought) without engaging the Muslims. The only reported spoils from this action were the profits from the sale of the goods the Muslims had taken with them to the market at Badr.[19]

Allegedly during the 46th month after the Hijra,[20] Muhammad had the Jew Abu Rafi`murdered in his home at Khaybar. It is said that he had been planning to attack the Muslims.[21]

In the 47th month after the Hijra, Muhammad is said to have heard that the Anmar and Tha`laba were planning to attack him, so he and 400 Muslims[22] went to Dhat al-Riqa to engage them. When the Muslims arrived, they only found some women, whom they captured. The main forces are said to have been up on the mountains not far away, and in that Muhammad was afraid they might attack them, he prayed the prayer of fear (Qur'an 4:102f). On the return journey, one Muslim was wounded, and a murder attempt on Muhammad is reported to have taken place.[23]

During the 49th month after the Hijra, Muhammad and 1000 Muslims are reported to have set out for Dumat al-Jandal, where some were said to have been preparing to attack them.[24] Just outside of the town, the Muslims found camels and sheep, which they seized after fighting the shepherds. Upon hearing about this, the townspeople fled, and there was no further fighting. One man was taken prisoner, and he became a Muslim. Muhammad later made a treaty with `Uyayna b. Hisn concerning grazing rights.[25]

In the 54th month after the Hijra, Muhammad is said to have received information that the Banu Mustaliq and other nomad Arabs were planning to attack him. Muhammad left Medina with 30 Muslims, `A'isha, Umm Salama and a number of the hypocrites. During the journey, one man is said to have met them and become a Muslim, and another was captured as a spy and executed by `Umar. When the Muslims arrived at al-Muraysi`, the Arab nomad allies of the Banu Mustaliq had already fled. Muhammad set his forces in battle array, and after an alleged exchange of arrows, the Muslims began a general attack. The Muslims won quickly, having killed 10 of their enemies, while losing one of their own, who was accidently killed by another Muslim.[26] Some 2000 camels and 5000 sheep were taken, and the rest of the men, women and children were taken prisoner, of whom the women alone are said to have numbered 200. Among the captured was the beautiful Juwayriya,[27] who accepted Islam and was married by Muhammad. A substantial number of her people were then freed,[28] including the women whom the Muslims had already slept with. With Muhammad's approval, some of the Muslims had had relations (`Azl)[29] with the captured women before they allowed them to be ransomed, and it is reported that none of the women wanted to remain with the Muslims. A contention over the water at al-Muraysi` pitted the emigrants against the Medinans, after which `Abdullah b. Ubayy is said to have made a threatening remark (cf. Qur'an 63: 8). Some Muslims called on Muhammad to murder him, but in the end, Muhammad refused to do so.[30] Qur'an 63 is said to have been revealed in reference to `Abdullah b. Ubayy.[31]

Sura 63 begins by speaking of the hypocrites (vv. 1f). They are described as turning others from Allah's way (v. 2), and they are to be killed by Allah (v. 4). In the vv. 5f Muhammad offers to pray for their forgiveness, v. 7 shows that the hypocrites were against contributing to the Muslim cause, and v. 8 is said to reproduce the threat of `Abdullah b. Ubayy. The v. 9 commands the believers not to let their wealth or children inhibit them from meditating on God, and the v. 10a gives a command for almsgiving. The v. 10b-11 maintain that Allah will not hear last minute prayers to buy more time to give alms.

On the return journey from al-Muraysi`, `A'isha (who had not been happy with the prospect of Muhammad's marriage to Juwayriya)[32] is said to have lost her necklace. While everyone was searching for it, a prayer time occurred, and as the Muslims were not near a water source, the verse about "tayammum" was said to have been revealed (Qur'an 4:46 or 5:9).[33] At another point on the journey, `A'isha lost her necklace again, and by the time she had found it, Muhammad and the other Muslims had already moved on. Safwan b. al-Mu`attal, who had lagged behind the other Muslims, found `A'isha and mounted her on his camel. They did not reach Muhammad and the others until the next morning, and rumors, whose sources were said to have been `Abdullah b. Ubayy, Mistah bt. Uthatha, Hamna bt. Jahsh, and the poet Hassan b. Thabit, began to abound. After arriving in Medina, a conflict between the Aws and the Khazraj arose as to who would support Muhammad in this matter. Muhammad then asked for the counsel of `Ali and Usama; the former suggested that Muhammad find another wife (which fostered `A'isha's dislike of `Ali) , and the latter supported `A'isha's plea of innocence. About about a month later, Qur'an 24:1-11 is said to have been revealed to Muhammad, which absolved `A'isha of any guilt. Since those who had defamed her (i.e. Mistah, Hamna and Hassan)[34] could not have been witnesses (cf. Qur'an 24:4, 12-13), they were said to have been given 80 lashes each.[35]

Qur'an 24 claims to be a legal sura (v. 1), in which the punishment for adulterers and adulteresses is set at 100 lashes, the number of witnesses for condemnation was set at four, and the punishment for a false witness is fixed at 80 lashes (vv. 2f). According to the vv. 6f a husband accusing his wife of unfaithfulness is to swear four times, but the accused wife is to be spared the punishment if she swears four times that she did not commit adultery; on the fifth time, both parties are to wish that Allah curse themselves should the other party have said the truth. The vv. 11f refer to the matter of `A'isha on the return from al-Muraysi`,[36] and the appeal to forgive (v. 22) is said to have been directed at Abu Bakr.[37] The v. 24 states that the various parts of one's body will testify at the Judgment.[38] The vv. 28f dictate that all are to ask for permission before entering someone else's dwelling, and the vv. 30f give a command against the lust of the eyes along with the regulation regarding to whom women can expose themselves. It would appear that these measures were also possibly connected to Zayd b. Haritha's divorce of Zaynab b. Jahsh.[39] The v. 32 basically commands Muslims to marry, and v. 33 speaks of those who cannot find a wife, encourages manumission of slaves, and prohibits forcing women slaves to be prostitutes. The v. 34 is thought by some to refer to the two examples of Joseph (Qur'an 12:23f) and Mary (Qur'an 19:16f) both of whom were accused of adultery,[40] the v. 35 describes God as being the light of Heaven and earth, and v. 36 may have referred to churches.[41] The vv. 37f claim that believers who are not inhibited by business or wealth from meditating on God, and those who also perform the prayer and give alms, will be rewarded. The vv. 38f compare the works of unbelievers with a mirage in the desert and darkness at sea. The vv. 41f speak of the witness of God in Creation, and the vv. 46f concern themselves with the hypocrites (cf. 63:5f). The vv. 50f describe believers as being those who say that they "hear and obey,"[42] after which instruction is given not to swear obedience, but to show it. Those who believe and perform good (works) are promised that they will be made successors (v. 54), and those who perform the prayer, give alms and obey Muhammad, are told that they will possibly find mercy. The v. 56 says that unbelievers are bound for Hell, and the vv. 57f return to the subject of asking permission before entering the dwellings of others, because of the possible nakedness of the host. The v. 60 shows that it was no sin to dine in the houses of relatives or with those who were handicapped, and v. 61 command believers to give the greetings of God upon entering a house. In v. 62 believers are defined as those who believe Allah and Muhammad, these are to ask leave of Muhammad at meetings, and Muhammad is to pray for those who do not. The v. 63 states that Muhammad was to be addressed differently than others, and a warning is given not to disobey Allah's commands. The v. 64 says that God knows everything. A number of verses in this sura are similar to passages in the Bible, Talmud or text of the Jewish Tefillah.[43] This sura is said to have had more than 100 verses,[44] or to have been as long as Qur'an 2 originally.[45]

In canonical traditions, 'Umar is quoted as saying that there was a verse regarding the stoning of married adulterers in the Qur'an originally.[46] Evidently, however, this verse was not found in the Qur'an codices of his day, for 'Umar states that he would have added the verse himself, were it not for those who would have accused 'Umar of adding to the Qur'an.[47] The notable Ubayy b. Ka'b claimed that the verse of stoning was originally found in Qur'an 33,[48] although the rhyme of the given text, as well as the subject matter, actually fits Qur'an 24 better.[49] The stoning of adulterers and adulteresses appears to have been practiced by Muhammad and his followers.[50] In earlier times, the former Gnostic Bardesan (d. ca. 224-230 AD) wrote that even those suspected of adultery were stoned to death by the Arabs of his day,[51] and it is at least probable that this punishment was still being practiced by pagan Arabs contemporary with Muhammad. In any event, early Islam theologians were faced with the difficulty of deciding whether or not the alleged verse of stoning was abrogated by Qur'an 24:2f.[52] A solution to this problem was found in the judgment that the punishment of stoning was for married adulterers and adulteresses, while flogging was the punishment for the unmarried transgressors.[53]

Sura 58 begins with a certain divorce case (vv. 1f),[54] in which the heathen statement of divorce is essentially declared to be ineffectual. The vv. 4f describe the punishment for those who continue to use such statements, and the vv. 6f give a warning not to disobey Allah and Muhammad. The v. 8 shows that God knows everything (even what is spoken in secret discussions), and v. 9 mentions some who held secret discussions although they were forbidden to do so; these also greet Muhammad with other than Allah's greeting. The vv. 10f are against gossip, and declare that secret conversations are of Satan, The v. 12 commands to make room for others in the mosque (place pf prayer), and to stand up when told to do so. The v. 13 dictates that those wishing to speak with Muhammad should pay alms first; those who do not are to perform the prayer, give alms and obey Allah and Muhammad (v. 14). The vv. 15f seem to deal with the hypocrites who had Jewish protectors,[55] who (the hypocrites) will be heavily punished, because they turn others from Allah's way; Satan is in them and they are Satan's allies. The v. 21b declares that Allah and Muhammad will be victorious, and v. 22 claims that those who believe in God and the Judgment would not love those who oppose Allah and Muhammad; the believers will be sent to Paradise, they are said to be Allah's allies. The v. 8 of this sura is at least remotely similar to Mt. 18:20 and Avot 3,7.[56]

Some of the exiled of the Banu Nadir are said to have gone and encouraged the Meccans, Ghatafan and Sulaym to attack the Muslims in Medina.

In the 57th month after the Hijra, a Meccan force under Abu Sufyan with its allies is said to have advanced on Medina. The Meccans and their allies are reported to have numbered 10,000 men, and the Muslims are said to have had

3000 men. As part of the defences of Medina, Muhammad is said to have commanded the digging of a ditch (as a hindrance to attackers), whose construction was reportedly suggested by the Persian Salman al-Farisi. The Meccans are said to have convinced the Jewish Banu Qurayza to break their covenant with Muhammad. During the 15 day-long siege,[57] only a small contingent of Meccans is reported to have crossed the ditch once. Muhammad is said to have employed a spy, who was at least somewhat successful in sowing discord among the Meccans and their allies. Abu Sufyan allegedly wanted to plan a large-scale attack on the Muslim positions, but when the Banu Qurayza were approached, they refused to participate on the grounds that it was the Sabbath. That evening a severe wind storm is said to have induced the Meccans and their other allies to lift the siege and retire. In the end, the Meccans are reported to have lost three men to the Muslims' six dead, one of whom died later.[58] Many verses of Qur'an 33 are said to have been revealed concerning this siege.[59]

Also during the 57th month after the Hijra, Muhammad is said to have married Zaynab b. Jahsh; the divorced wife of Zayd b. Haritha, who was Muhammad's adopted son. It is reported that Muhammad once went to visit Zayd, who was not home. While there, Muhammad saw Zaynab, who was only partially clothed. Upon seeing her, Muhammad reportedly said: "Praise to Allah, the changer of hearts." When Zaynab told Zayd about the incident later, Zayd offered to divorce his wife, so that Muhammad could then marry her. Initially, Muhammad refused, but then later accepted after verses were revealed regarding Zayd's status and his offer (cf. Qur'an 33:4f, 37f).[60]

Also in the 57th month after the Hijra, Muhammad is said to have been commanded to move against the Banu Qurayza by Gabriel. Some 3000 Muslims besieged them for 15 days, but the Jews offered no resistance.[61] The Jews sent to Muhammad for terms of surrender, but he refused them. Eventually, the Banu Qurayza surrendered, no doubt in hopes of being exiled as the Banu Qaynuqa and Banu Nadir had been. The Aws also asked for leniency for their former allies, and Muhammad then had Sa`d b. Mu`adh (one of the Aws who was dying from wounds he sustained at the ditch) decide their fate. Sa`d said that all of the men of the Banu Qurayza were to be executed, their women and children were to become slaves, and their goods were to be divided among the Muslims (cf. Qur'an 33:26f). When Muhammad heard of Sa`d's decision, he is reported to have said: "That is the decision of Allah in the seventh Heaven!"[62] The execution of the 600-700 Jewish men[63] by `Ali and al-Zubayr is said to have lasted into the evening, and only one man is reported to have become a Muslim and eaten camel meat.[64] One Jewish woman was also executed for allegedly having killed a Muslim with a millstone. Her expression of joy in the face of death left `A'isha with an unforgettable impression. The spoils are reported to have totalled 1500 swords, 300 coats of mail, 1000 spears, 1500 shields, wine (which was spilled out), camels and livestock. Muhammad took the Jewish Rayhana bt. `Amr as a slave (concubine).[65] Sa`d is reported to have died the same night, and the gates of Heaven are said to have been open, and the throne is said to have shaken because of him.[66]

Qur'an 33 opens with a command addressed to Muhammad as a prophet, which says that he was to fear God and not obey unbelievers and hypocrites, but to follow what was revealed to him. The v. 3 gives that command to trust God as Protector, and v. 4 rejects the pre-Islamic declaration of divorce (cf. 59:2), and the pagan Arab customs concerning the status of adopted sons. The v. 5 is about naming adopted sons, and v. 6 claims that Muhammad is nearer the believers than they are to themselves. This verse also declares that Muhammad's wives are "the mothers of the believers," and says that (Muhammad's) blood relatives are nearer than the emigrants or the Medinans. The v. 7 makes an allusion to a covenant of God, which was made with Noah, Abraham, Moses and Jesus. The vv. 9-26 seem to refer to the battle of the ditch.[67] The vv. 12f repeat the words of the hypocrites, v. 13 shows that some heeded them and left the field, although they had covenanted not to desert (v. 15). The vv. 17f say that God will punish those who desert and hinder others (from fighting),[68] and v. 20 voices the thoughts of the hypocrites. The v. 21 says that Muhammad is a good example of a believer, and in v. 22 the believers are said to have seen a confirmation of Muhammad's words when they saw the allies (the Meccans and others). The v. 23 states that some kept their word (to fight), while others did not. Much later, when Zayd b. Thabit was collecting verses for the Qur'an he is reported to have found this verse only by Khuzayma al-Ansari.[69] In v. 25 God is said to have turned backed the unbelievers, v. 26 seems to mention the alleged treachery of the Banu Qurayza, and v. 27 seems to refer to their defeat. The vv. 28f confront Muhammad's wives about loving wealth or Allah and Muhammad, and although some canonical traditions mention these verses, without giving a possible context,[70] this passage may refer to disputes about the abundant spoils from the Banu Qurayza and how Muhammad's share was divided among his wives. In v. 30, Muhammad's wives are told that their punishment will be more severe than for others, if they would commit something shameful, but v. 31 states that they would receive a double reward for obedience to Allah and Muhammad. The v. 32 warns Muhammad's women about speaking properly to others, and v. 33 commands his women not to adorn themselves as they did in pre-Islam, but to pray, give alms and obey God and Muhammad. The v. 34 says that Muhammad's women are to consider the signs and wisdom (Qur'an) which were read (recited) in their houses, and v. 35 states that Muslims are to be obedient, true, steadfast, humble, to give alms, to fast, to shun sexual immorality, and meditate on God often. The v. 36 declares that God's and Muhammad's decisions are final, and that they are to be obeyed. The vv. 37f refer to the incident with Zaynab and Zayd,[71] and v. 40 depicts Muhammad as not having a son,[72] but as being Allah's messenger and the "seal of the prophets." The v. 41 gives the commandment to meditate on God and praise Him mornings and evenings, and v. 42 states that God and His angels pray for believers to be led from the darkness into the light. The v. 43 says that believers will greet God with the word "peace," and in v. 44 Muhammad is addressed as a prophet and is said to have been sent as a witness, bearer of good news and a warner. In v. 47 Muhammad is commanded not to obey unbelievers and hypocrites, and v. 48 speaks of divorce prior to the consummation of marriage. In the vv. 49f Muhammad is basically allowed to marry any woman who presents herself to him as a special privilege, and ʾAʾisha's alleged reaction to v. 51 in the canonical traditions is well known.[73] The v. 52 must have been composed later,[74] since Muhammad is not allowed to have more wives now. The v. 53 dictates that those wishing to visit Muhammad were to ask for permission,[75] and that no one was to marry his wives after him. The v. 55 allows Muslim women to speak with their relatives without the veil, and v. 56 maintains that God and His angels pray for Muhammad.[76] The v. 59 commands Muhammad's wives and daughters and those of the believers to cover (or veil) themselves. The vv. 60f give a severe warning to the hypocrites, and v. 63 reproduces a question about the advent of "the hour," which is answered by the statement that only God knows. The vv. 64f are about unbelievers and their destiny Hell, and the vv. 66f give their alleged regrets about not having obeyed Allah and Muhammad, but rather their lords and powerful men. The vv. 69f instruct believers not to be as those who hurt Moses (verbally), but rather to fear God and speak words of sincerity. The message of v. 72 is ambiguous, and v. 73 is a request for God to punish the hypocrites and unbelievers, and turn Himself to the believers. `A'isha is said to have reported that this sura contained 200 verses in Muhammad's time.[77]

In the 59th month after the Hijra,[78] Muhammad sent Muhammad b. Maslama and 30 Muslims to raid the Banu Bakr (al-Qurata). Along the way they plundered some of the Muharib and took their livestock. When they raided the al-Qurata, they are said to have killed about 10 men and seized their livestock as well. The spoils reportedly totalled 150 camels and 3000 sheep, from which Muhammad took his one-fifth.[79]

During the 61st month after the Hijra,[80] Muhammad and 200 Muslims left Medina on short notice in an attempted surprise attack on the Banu Lihyan at al-Raji`, where these had killed some of Muhammad's followers in the 36th month after the Hijra. When the Muslims arrived, however, the Banu Lihyan had already left the area, and they could not find anyone. Muhammad is said to have sent Abu Bakr with 10 horsemen to al-Ghamim in order to frighten the Meccans, who had allegedly not yet executed their two prisoners from al-Raji`.[81]

Also in the 61st month after the Hijra, the polytheist `Uyayna b. Hisn raided al-Ghaba with 40 horsemen. They killed a Muslim, captured his wife and seized 20 of Muhammad's milch-camels. Some of the Muslims immediately pursued them and were able to engage them. Three[82] of `Uyayna's men were said to have been killed; the Muslims lost one man and were able to retrieve 10 of the camels. Muhammad eventually assembled 500 Muslims,[83] but then decided it was too late to continue the pursuit. The woman who had been captured allegedly escaped and returned to Muhammad.[84]

In the same month, Muhammad sent `Ukkasha b. Mihsan with 40 Muslims to raid al-Ghamr. When they arrived, the Banu Asad had already fled, but the Muslims were able to capture a man who showed them where a herd of camels was. The Muslims took 200 camels and set the man free.[85]

During the 62nd month after the Hijra, Muhammad sent Muhammad b. Maslama with 10 men to attack the Banu Tha'laba at Dhu al-Qassa. Arriving at night, the Muslims were said to have been surrounded by 100 men, who were then allegedly joined by nomads. Three Muslims are said to have been killed, and Muhammad b. Maslama was wounded and brought back to Medina.[86]

Muhammad then sent out Abu 'Ubayda with 40 men to the same location, but they were only able to find camels and sheep, which they took.[87]

Also in the 62nd month after the Hijra, Muhammad sent Zayd b. Haritha to raid the Banu Sulaym at al-Jamum. The Muslims captured a woman who showed them where the camels and sheep were, which they subsequently seized.[88]

During the 63rd month after the Hijra, Muhammad sent Zayd b. Haritha with 170 horsemen to intercept a caravan of the Quraysh at al-'Is. The Muslims are said to have captured the entire caravan (allegedly with much silver), along with Zaynab bt. Muhammad's husband Abu al-'As. After arriving in Medina, Zaynab gave her husband protection.[89]

In the 64th month after the Hijra, Muhammad sent out Zayd b. Haritha with 30 men to raid the Banu Tha'laba at al-Taraf. When the Muslims arrived, they could find no one, but were able to take 20 camels and some sheep.[90]

Also during the 64th month after the Hijra, Muhammad sent out Zayd b. Haritha with 500 men to raid the Hisma. The Muslims killed some of the Hisma, captured 100 women (and children), and seized 1000 camels and 5000 sheep. Not long afterwards, however, the Hisma accepted Islam, and all of their women and children and livestock were returned to them.[91]

In the 65th month after the Hijra, Muhammad sent Zayd b. Haritha to raid Wadi al-Qura.[92]

During the 66th month after the Hijra, Muhammad sent 'Abdulrahman b. 'Awf with 700 men to Dumat al-Jandal to invite the people there to Islam, and to fight them if they did not become Muslims or pay the "jizya."[93] The leader al-Asbagh b. `Amr[94] is said to have converted with many others, and those who were not willing to accept Islam are said to have agreed to pay the "jizya." `Abdulrahman married a daughter of al-Asbagh and returned to Medina.[95]

Also in the 66th month after the Hijra, Muhammad sent out `Ali b. Abu Talib with 100 men to raid the Banu Sa`d b. Bakr at Fadak. The Banu Sa`d is said to have conspired with the Jews of Khaybar and was reportedly planning to attack the Muslims. Along the way, the Muslims captured a man, who on the promise of freedom, showed them where the herds of camels and sheep were. The Muslims attacked and seized 500 camels and 2000 sheep.[96]

In the 67th month after the Hijra, Muhammad sent Zayd b. Haritha at the head of a Muslim caravan to Syria. Not far from Wadi al-Qura, some of the Banu Badr seized the caravan and beat Zayd. Zayd returned to Muhammad, who then sent him out to attack the Banu Badr. The Muslims captured the elderly Umm Qirfa with her daughter and killed the former by binding her legs to two camels, which were then driven in opposite directions. The daughter was later married off to a Muslim.[97]

During the 68th month after the Hijra, Muhammad sent `Abdullah b. Ruwaha and 30 Muslims to murder Usayr b. Rizam, the newly-selected leader of the Jews at Khaybar. It is said that he had been planning to attack Muhammad. After Usayr was told that Muhammad wanted to appoint him as the ruler of Khaybar, he left for Medina with 30 Jewish escorts who also rode double on the camels of the Muslims. Along the way, the Muslims killed all of the Jews except for one who escaped. The Muslims are said not to have had any losses.[98]

Also in the 68th month after the Hijra, eight men of the `Urayna who had accepted Islam were given permission to drink from some of Muhammad's milch camels until they recovered from their illnesses. Once in good health, however, they killed one of Muhammad's shepherds[99] and took the 15 milch camels. Muhammad sent Kura b. Jabir and 20 horsemen to pursue them. All eight were captured and brought back to Medina, where Muhammad had their hands and feet cut off, gouged out their eyes[100] and crucified them. Qur'an 5:37 is said to have been revealed on this occasion.[101]

After a Meccan attempt to murder Muhammad failed,[102] Muhammad sent out two Muslims to murder Abu Sufyan b. Harb. This attempt also failed, but three other polytheists were killed, and one was captured.[103]

Qur'an 22 is composed of many passages which are thought to have been Meccan.[104] The vv. 1f speak of the Judgment, and the vv. 5f are about the Resurrection. The 11f describe "weak" believers, who call on pagan gods, and v. 14 says that those who believe and perform good (works) will be sent to Paradise. The v. 17, which states that God will judge between the Jews, Sabians, Christians, Magians and polytheists, is thought to have been a later addition, and v. 18 says that all nature bows down to God. The vv. 20f show that unbelievers will be sent to Hell, but that believers will go to Paradise. The vv. 25-38 are thought to date from 6 or 7 AH.[105] The vv. 25f say that those who lead astray from Allah's way and the Ka`ba will be punished, v. 27 speaks about Abraham and the Ka`ba, in which an alleged command of God was given to him, and the v. 28 speaks of the Hajj. The vv. 31f are about honoring God's commandments and rituals, but shunning polytheism, and the vv. 34f deal with sacrifice. In v. 37 camels are claimed to have been given as sacrificial animals by God (which is contrary to the Jewish Law), and v. 39 maintains that God protects the believers but does not love unblievers. The v. 40 allows the fighting of those who were fought against, and v. 41 compares those who were driven from their homes with those whose places of worship were destroyed; this verse says that God used a people to defend them, and that God helps those who help Him. The v. 42 describes some as performing the prayer, giving alms, commanding the right and forbidding the wrong, and the vv. 43f speak of the punishments of previous peoples, in which the peoples of Noah, the`Ad, the Thamud, Abraham, Lot, Midian and Moses are referred to. The v. 48 claims that Muhammad was just a warner, and v. 51, which is often alluded to in the traditions about the Satanic inspiration,[106] differentiates between messengers and prophets.[107] The v. 52 refers to the hypocrites, v. 53 deals with the Jews and v. 54 speaks of unbelievers and "the hour." The v. 55 says that those who believe and perform good (works) will go to Paradise, and v. 56 shows that those who do not believe God's signs will go to Hell. The vv. 57f speak of martyrs and Paradise, v. 60 says that God regulates day and night, and v. 61 states that God is truth and that pagan deities are lies. The vv. 62f speak about the witness of God in Creation and the Resurrection, and v. 66 says that each religion was given its (own) rituals. The vv. 67f states that at the Judgment God will decide between those who argue with Muhammad, and the vv. 70f show that the polytheists who reject God's signs will be sent to Hell. The v. 73 says that God is not honored by polytheists, and v. 74 maintains that God chooses messengers from among angels and men. In the vv. 76f the believers are commanded to bow down, serve God, perform good (works), and strive in Allah's way. This passage claims that God chose the believers, obligated them to the religion (way) of Abraham and named them "Muslims." In v. 78 commandment is given to perform the prayer, give alms and hold fast to Allah. The word for "animal" in v. 29 appears to have come from Hebrew,[108] and the term for monasteries in v. 41 may have come from Ethiopic.[109] The v. 38 is similar to Is. 1:11 (etc.), and the v. 46 is reminiscent of II Pet. 3:8.[110]

In the 69th month after the Hijra, Muhammad and 1400 Muslims[111] approached Mecca dressed as pilgrims (with 70 animals for sacrifice) in order to perform the `Umra.[112] The Meccans sent out reconnaisance to shadow the Muslims, who eventually stopped at al-Hudaybiya, not far from Mecca. In the long negotiations with the Meccans, the Muslims thought at one point they would have to resort to armed force, when it was falsely rumored that Muhammad's negotiator `Uthman had been killed. An agreement was finally made with the Quraysh, by which 10 years of peace were to prevail, and the Meccans would be allowed to stay in Mecca for three days[113] the following year. Other conditions were that those of the Quraysh dependents who fled to Muhammad without permission were to be returned, but those who fled from Muhammad to the Meccans were not to be given back. Owing to the objections of the Meccans, the treaty document began with the words: "In your name Allahumma" instead of the basmala, and Muhammad was referred to as Muhammad b. `Abdullah rather than "the messenger of God." `Ali is said to have written the original, and a copy was given to the Meccans. Many of Muhammad's followers were highly dissatisfied about the apparent concessions Muhammad had made with the Meccans. The Muslims later sacrificed their 70 sacrificial animals. Some of the Muslims cut their hair and others shaved their heads. On the return from Hudaybiya, Qur'an 48:1-2 is said to have been revealed.[114]

Sura 48 opens with the statement that Muhammad has been given victory (v. 1), and says that his former and later sins have been forgiven (v. 2). The v. 4 claims that the Shechinah is in the hearts of the believers, v. 5 says that the believers will be sent to Paradise, and v. 6 concludes that the hypocrites and polytheists will be sent to Hell. The v. 8 describes Muhammad as having been sent as a witness, bringer of good tidings and a warner, so that others may believe God and Muhammad, etc. and praise God mornings and evenings. The vv. 10f encourage to keep covenant, show that some did not go up with the Muslims (to Hudaybiya), and give a reproof of them.[115] The v. 13 states that whoever does not believe God and Muhammad will be sent to Hell, and v. 14 says that God forgives and punishes whom He will. The vv. 15f return to the subject of the Arab allies who did not go up (to Hudaybiya) with the Muslims,[116] and the v. 17 dictates that those who obey Allah and Muhammad will be sent to Paradise, but those who turn their backs on them will be punished in Hell. The fragment v. 18a seems to refer to Hudaybiya, as the Muslims took an oath before they thought they would have to fight the Meccans, and the vv. 18f are thought to have been composed after the battle at Khaybar.[117]

After the treaty of Hudaybiya, Muhammad is reported to have begun sending out messengers to the various Arab tribes and the kings of nearby countries in order to invite them to accept Islam.[118]

In the 75th month after the Hijra,[119] Muhammad assembled a force of 1400 and marched on Khaybar. After deploying between Khaybar and the Ghatafan, the Muslims began attacking the Jews, taking fortress by fortress (some captured Jews are said to have told the Muslims how the fortresses could be entered). In the end, some 93 Jews and 15 Muslims[120] are said to have been killed. After the battle, a Jewish woman prepared a meal for Muhammad and some of his followers, and put poison in the lamb which was to be eaten. Bishr b. al-Bara ate some of the meat and died, and Muhammad, who had a piece of the lamb in his mouth, quickly spit it out.[121] Muhammad had the woman executed.[122] The remaining Jews asked Muhammad to spare their lives, and then surrendered. Muhammad took their property and is said to have enslaved their women.[123] The Jews were allowed to work their land and the palm trees, and were allowed to keep one half of the harvest. The consumption of donkey meat is said to have been forbidden at Khaybar.[124] Of the women captives, Muhammad married Safiya bt. Huyayy.[125] Among the spoils from Khaybar were the books of the Torah, which were returned to the Jews at their own request.[126]

After the battle of Khaybar, the Jews of Fadak came to Muhammad, and asked for and received the same terms as the Jews of Khaybar.[127] Since no fighting was involved, Muhammad took the properties of Fadak for himself (cf. the raid on the Banu Nadir).[128] These properties later became a source of dispute among Fatima and Abu Bakr after Muhammad's death.[129]

Also after the battle of Khaybar, Ja`far b. Abu Talib returned from Abyssinia with other Muslims, among whom was Umm Habiba, who had been promised to Muhammad.[130]

Muhammad married Umm Habiba, whose former husband had become a Christian in Abyssinia and had died there.[131]

The remainder of **Qur'an 48 (vv. 18-29)** may have been composed in this time period. The vv. 18f say that Allah was pleased with those who gave their oaths (at Hudaybiya), that the Shechinah was sent down, and they were rewarded with a victory and abundant booty (Khaybar). The v. 22 (and possibly v. 20)[132] seems to refer to the inability of the Meccans to aid those at Khaybar, because of the newly-signed treaty of Hudaybiya. The vv. 24f also seem to refer to Hudaybiya, and v. 26 depicts the discontent of some of Muhammad's followers there, and claims that the Shechinah was sent down. The v. 27 refers to a vision which Muhammad is said to have had with respect to performing the `umra, and in v. 29 Muhmammad's followers are said to have marks on their heads from (frequent) prostrations, which is similar to descriptions of Christian monks.[133] This verse also makes the claim that a parable about a plant (cf. Mk. 4:26f)[134] is found in the Torah and Gospel, and promises forgiveness and a reward to those who believe and perform good (works).

Reportedly in response to Muhammad's letter inviting him to Islam, the Muqawqis of Alexandria (who did not become a Muslim) sent Muhammad

Mariya (the Copt), her sister Sirin (or Shirin) and other presents. Muhammad kept Mariya for himself (as a concubine), and gave Sirin to Hassan b. Thabit.[135]

One day Muhammad is said to have visited with Mariya in Hafsa's dwelling, without the latter's knowledge. When Hafsa found out about it, Muhammad allegedly swore not to visit Mariya again, and Hafsa was not to tell anyone else. After Muhammad discovered that Hafsa had not kept her word, Muhammad is said to have divorced his wives for a month.[136]

Qur'an 66 apparently begins with the incident about Mariya and one of Muhammad's wives telling others about something which he spoke to her about in secret. The v. 4 is said to have referred to `A'isha and Hafsa,[137] and v. 5 mentions the threat of divorce.[138] The v. 6 is a commandment for believers to save themselves and their families from Hell, and v. 7 says that unbelievers will not have an excuse. In v. 8 believers are to repent sincerely, so they will possibly have their sins forgiven and go to Paradise. In v. 9 Muhammad is addressed as a prophet and is told to strive against the unbelievers. The v. 10 claims that the wives of Noah and Lot went to Hell,[139] v. 11 gives an alleged prayer of Pharoah's wife, and v. 12 states that God's Spirit was breathed into Mary, and she believed.[140] These pairs of believing and unbelieving women were no doubt intended to serve as examples for Hafsa and `A'isha originally.

Later, Muhammad defeated the Jews of Wadi al-Qura and made a pact with them concerning their lands. The Jews of Tayma' ageed to pay the "jizya." Years later the Caliph `Umar expelled the Jews of Khaybar and Fadak, but allowed those of Wadi al-Qura and Tayma' remain, because they were not considered to be in the Hijaz.[141]

In the 78th month after the Hijra, Muhammad sent `Umar b. Khattab with 30 Muslims to raid the Hawazin at Turaba. When they arrived, they could not find anyone there.[142]

Also in the 78th month after the Hijra, Muhammad sent Abu Bakr to raid the Banu Kilab in Najd. At least seven families were killed, and prisoners were taken. In Medina, Muhammad asked for one of the beautiful female captives, and traded her for Muslim prisoners in the hands of polytheists.[143]

Also during the 78th month after the Hijra, Muhammad sent Bashir b. Sa`d with 30 men to raid the Banu Murra in Fadak. They seized camels and sheep, but were then attacked and lost them soon afterwards. Bashir b. Sa`d was reportedly killed, but then returned to Medina later to lead of force of 200 men to the same location. They are then said to have seized about 2000 camels.[144]

In the 79th month after the Hijra, Muhammad sent Ghalib b. `Abdullah with 130 men to raid the Banu `Uwal and the Banu Tha`laba. They killed everyone they fought with and seized camels and sheep.[145]

In the 80th month after the Hijra, Muhammad sent Bashir b. Sa`d and 300 men to engage `Uyayna b. Hisn and part of the Ghatafan at Yaman and Jamar. They took some camels, and on their return journey, they captured two men who later accepted Islam and were set free.[146]

During the 81st month after the Hijra, Muhammad and 2000 Muslims with 60 animals for sacrifice left for Mecca to perform the "`umra" which was agreed upon the year before at Hudaybiya. The polytheists left Mecca, and the Muslims entered. Muhammad circumambulated the pagan Ka'ba as he was mounted on his camel, and then rode to Safa and Marwa. The sacrifices were slaughtered near Marwa. Muhammad wanted to marry Maymuna bt. al-Harith[147] in Mecca, but on the fourth day, the Meccans asked Muhammad to leave the city as he had agreed to the year before. The Muslims left Mecca, and Muhammad had to consummate his marriage to Maymuna outside of the town.[148]

In the 82nd month after the Hijra, Muhammad sent Ibn Abu al-`Awja with 50 men to raid the Banu Sulaym. The Muslims were surrounded and many were killed. Ibn Abu al-`Awja was wounded, but was able to return to Medina.[149]

During the 84th month after the Hijra, `Amr al-`As, Khalid b. Walid and `Uthman b. Talha are reported to have come to Medina and accepted Islam.[150]

Also in the 84th month after the Hijra, Muhammad sent Ghalib b. `Abdullah with 13 to 19 men to raid the Banu Mulawwih in al-Kadid. Along the way they captured a prisoner. They attacked the Banu Mulawwih, killing some, and capturing women and children as they seized their livestock. A sudden rainstorm sent by Allah is said to have enabled them to escape those of the Banu Mulawwih who were pursuing them.[151]

Also during the same month, Muhammad sent Ghalib b. `Abdullah with 200 men to Fadak, to avenge the attack made on Bashir b. Sa`d by the Banu Murra.[152] When the Muslims arrived, they are said to have killed some of the Banu Murra and reportedly took their camels.[153]

In the 85th month after the Hijra, Muhammad sent Shuja` b. Wahb and 24 men to raid the Hawazin in al-Siyyi. When they arrived there, the Muslims killed some people, took female captives and much livestock.[154] After the clans sent representatives to Muhammad and accepted Islam, the women were returned, except for one girl, who remained the wife of Shuja`.[155]

Also in the 85th month after the Hijra, Muhammad sent Ka'b b. `Umayr and 15 men to raid Dhat Atla. The Muslims invited the people there to Islam, but after they refused to become Muslims, the fighting began. Only one wounded Muslim survived to return to Muhammad.[156]

During the 87th month after the Hijra, Muhammad and 3000 men set out for Mu'ta to avenge the death of one of his envoys. They were reportedly met by a force of 100,000 men,[157] including some of the Byzantines. The Muslims lost three commanders (among them Zayd b. Haritha and Ja`far b. Abu Talib) before giving the flag to Khalid b. Walid, who essentially organized the retreat. The Muslims are said to have had heavy losses.[158]

In the 88th month after the Hijra, Muhammad sent `Amr al-`As and 300 men to attack some of the Baliyy and Qusa`a, who were allegedly planning to attack the Muslims. Muhammad later sent 200 men as reinforcements. When the unified force arrived at Dhat al-Salasil, most of their foe had already fled, so the Muslims only drove away the few who remained.[159]

During the 89th month after the Hijra, Abu ʿUbayda b. al-Jarra and 300 men went out to raid a group of the Juhayna near the sea. The Muslims could not find them, however, and were so weakened by hunger that they ate tree leaves (al-Khabt). A giant fish is said to have washed up on the shore, from which they reportedly ate for 12 days.[160]

In the 90th month after the Hijra, Muhammad sent Abu Qatada and 15 men to raid some of the Ghatafan at al-Ghaba. The Muslims are said to have surrounded and defeated them. Four women and some children were captured, and some 200 camels and 1000 sheep[161] were seized.[162]

Qur'an 60 begins with a command for believers not to make friends with the enemy, and in v. 4 Abraham is referred to as being an example of one who did not make friends with polytheists, but still prayed for his father. The vv. 5f give the text of a prayer, and in v. 9 believers are forbidden to have unbelieving friends. The v. 11 appears to encourage the Medinans to give those fleeing from Mecca the same gifts which the Meccans give those who flee to them, and v. 12 gives the women's oath of allegiance.[163] The command for believers not to make friends with those with whom Allah is angry is most probably an allusion to the Jews (v. 13). The vv. 1-9 of this sura are thought to have been composed in 8 AH, but prior to the conquest of Mecca (al-Fath),[164] and the vv. 10f are thought to have date from directly after Hudaybiya.[165]

Also during the 90th month after the Hijra, the Quraysh are said to have broken the treaty of Hudaybiya by attacking a tribe allied with the Muslims. The Meccans are reported to have attempted to have their treaty renewed, but the damage had already been done.[166]

In the 91st month after the Hijra, Muhammad and his allies set out for Mecca with a force of 10,000 men. Since Muhammad had intentionally chosen an approach which did not reveal his destination, the Meccans are said to have been caught by surprise. Abu Sufyan met them before the town, and on the threat of death, accepted Islam. The Muslims entered Mecca without resorting to the use of force. Muhammad commanded that six men and four women be executed, but of these, only three of the men and at least one of the women were actually put to death.[167] One of Muhammad's former scribes, Ibn Abu Sarh[168] (who had fled from Muhammad to Medina), was only spared death because of the intercession of `Uthman b. `Affan. Only Khalid b. Walid is reported to have encountered resistance, whereby 24 Quraysh, 4 of the Hud-hayl and 2 Muslims were killed. Later, Muhammad circumambulated the Ka`ba as he was mounted on his camel, and he is said to have destroyed the 360 idols around the Ka`ba as he recited Qur'an 17:83. Muhammad then went (or sent others) into the Ka`ba in order to wash away the pictures within. Allegedly, only the pictures of Abraham,[169] Mary and Jesus[170] were allowed to remain. Muhammad gave a sermon, commanded the destruction of all house-hold idols and declared the sanctity of Mecca. No spoils were taken from Mecca. Fasting in this month (Ramadan) was voluntary,[171] and Muhammad did not fast for the entire month.[172] It is said that Muhammad borrowed a large sum of money from others, in order to distribute it to the poor. Muhammad forbade the trade in wine, pork and idols, and prohibited payments to pagan religious officials for their services. Muhammad expressed his anger at the Jews for selling fat, and is said to have forbidden the practice of temporary marriage (Mut`a).[173]

In **sura 110** (vv. 1-3) Muhammad is commanded to praise God and pray for forgiveness when the victory comes and many accept Islam. This sura is considered by some to have been the last sura of the Qur'an composed.[174]

Also during the 91st month after the Hijra, Muhammad sent Khalid b. Walid with 30 horsemen to destroy the idol al-`Uzza[175] at Nakhla. In addition to the idol, Khalid is also said to have killed a naked black woman there, whom Muhammad later identified as having been al-`Uzza herself.[176]

In the same month, Muhammad sent `Amr b. al-`As to destroy the idol of Suwa,[177] the god of the Hudhayl. The priest of Suwa became a Muslim after the idol was destroyed.[178]

During the same month, Muhammad sent Sa`d b. Zayd with 20 horsemen to al-Mushallal to destroy the idol Manat.[179] Zayd rpeortedly also killed a naked woman on this expedition.[180]

In the 92nd month after the Hijra, Muhammad sent Khalid b. Walid with 350 men to invite the Banu Jadhima to Islam, but not to fight them. Although the Banu Jadhima claimed to be Muslims, Khalid had them taken as prisoners and had some of them executed. Khalid is also said to have killed someone. On his return, Khalid claimed that Muhammad had commanded him to attack the Banu Jadhima, but Muhammad denied the responsibility for Khalid's actions and had the blood-money paid for those who had been killed.[181]

Also in the 92nd month after the Hijra, Muhammad and his allies left Mecca for the valley of Hunayn with a force of 12,000 men to attack the Hawazin and the Thaqif, who were allegedly planning an attack on the Muslims. Along the way, Muhammad is said to have hung his weapons on a tree, fell asleep and was protected from a would-be assassin by Allah.[182] In another tradition, some of the newly converted Muslims are said to have asked Muhammad to give them a tree to hang their weapons on[183] (and sacrifice to the gods), but Muhammad refused and made an allusion to Moses.[184] When the Muslims began their assault in the valley of Hunayn, they were ambushed, and many of the Muslims began to flee. A small group around Muhammad is said to have held its ground, and Muhammad reportedly prayed as Moses had at the Red Sea.[185] Muhammad was able to rally those who had fled, and the Muslims' counter-attack was so severe that some began killing children. When Muhammad inquired about this, one replied that they were only pagan children (who were being killed). Muhammad forbade this and asked rhetorically if not even the best of the Muslims had not been pagan children.[186] The spoils from the battle are said to have been 6000 slaves, 24,000 camels, 40,000 sheep and much silver. In the division of the booty, which took place at al-Ji`rana after the siege of al-Ta'if,[187] the new Meccan converts to Islam (who were to be reconciled)[188] were favored, and the Ansar received nothing.[189] The Hawazin accepted Islam not long afterwards, and their women and children were returned to them, but not their possessions.[190] Islamic sources only give the names of four Muslims who fell at Hunayn.[191]

In the 93rd month after the Hijra, Muhammad sent al-Tufayl b. `Amr to destroy the idol Dhu al-Khaffayn[192] with his tribe. He burned the idol and brought 400 of his people to al-Ta'if to assist with the seige there.[193]

Also in the 93rd month after the Hijra, Muhammad and his forces advanced to al-Ta'if, where the Banu Thaqif had fled into their fortress after the battle of Hunayn. The Muslims beseiged them for three weeks.[194] The Muslims tried to assault the walls, but the casualties caused by the defenders' archers were too high. The Muslims then tried to undermine the walls of the fortress, but the defenders threw red-hot plowshares down on the Muslims' testudo, which caught fire. Muhammad then began destroying the vineyards of the Banu Thaqif.[195] The Muslims then asked the women of their tribes in the fortress (who had intermarried), to come out to them, but the women refused. The Muslims then offered to free all the slaves who would come out to them, and more than 13 are said to have escaped.[196] Still the Muslims were unable to enter the fortress, and so they abandoned their seige of al-Ta'if. The Muslims are reported to have lost 12 men.[197]

The booty from the battle of Hunayn was then divided at al-Ji`rana after the seige of al-Ta'if.[198]

In the 94th month after the Hijra, Mariya the Copt gave birth to Ibrahim b. Muhammad, which made Muhammad's other women very jealous of her.[199]

Also during the 94th month after the Hijra, the pilgrimage was held according to the pagan Arab rituals.[200]

In the 95th month after the Hijra, Muhammad sent `Uyayna b. Hisn[201] and 50 horsemen to raid the Banu Tamim. Muhammad's forces are said to have captured 11 men, 11 women and 30 children. Some of the Banu Tamim came to Muhammad later and are said to have called for him incessantly. After an alleged poetry contest between the Banu Tamim and the Muslims (which the latter are said to have won), the Banu Tamim accepted Islam, and their captive relatives were returned to them. Qur'an 49:1f is said to have been revealed at this time.[202]

Muhammad had sent a tax-collector (cf. Qur'an 9:60) to the (now) Muslim Banu Mustaliq. Through a misunderstanding, blood was almost shed, but the situation was corrected finally. Qur'an 49:6 is said to have been revealed on this occasion.[203]

Qur'an 49 begins with the command for believers to let Muhammad go ahead of them and speak louder than themselves, and it is said that those who speak more quietly in his presence are those who will be forgiven and rewarded (vv. 1f). The vv. 4f are against calling to Muhammad from outside of his house, and the vv. 6f seem to refer to the tax collection incident with the Banu Mustaliq.[204] The v. 9 gives regulations for two parties of believers who are at odds with each other, and v. 10 says that believers are brothers (of one another). The vv. 11f forbid mockery and defamation, etc. among the community, and v. 14 speaks of Arab nomads who profess to believe, but in reality do not. In v. 15 believers are described as believing Allah and Muhammad without doubting later, and they are those who contribute and fight in "Allah's way." The v. 16 is a reply to someone about not trying to teach God about their religion, and v. 17 maintains that God leads believers and that they did not accept Islam themselves. The v. 18 says that God knows all.

During the 96th month after the Hijra, Muhammad sent Qutba b. `Amir and 20 men to raid the al-Kath`am. They captured a man whom they later killed as he tried to warn his tribe. The Muslims captured women, camels and sheep, and were only able to elude those pursuing them because of a sudden rainstorm which flooded a valley.[205] The spoils, after Muhammad's one-fifth was deducted, were said to have been 4 camels or 40 sheep per man.[206]

In the 97th month after the Hijra, Muhammad sent al-Dahhak b. Sufyan to raid the Banu al-Kilab at al-Zujj. The Muslims invited the al-Kilab to accept Islam, but after they refused, the Muslims attacked them. One Muslim fought with his pagan father, who was then killed by another Muslim (in order that it not be said that the one had killed his own father).[207]

During the 98th month after the Hijra, Muhammad sent `Alqama b. Mujazziz with 300 men to attack Abyssinians, who had been seen from the coast. The Muslims returned without having engaged anyone.[208]

Also in the 98th month after the Hijra, Muhammad sent `Ali b. Abu Talib with 150 men to destroy the idol al-Fuls. The Muslims are said to have destroyed the idol, taken prisoners and seized livestock. The male captives who refused to accept Islam were executed.[209]

In the same month, Muhammad sent 'Ukkasha b. Mihsan to raid al-Jinab.[210]

During the 101st month after the Hijra, Muhammad is said to have received news that the Byzantine Emperor Heraclius had assembled the Lakhm, Judham, Ghassan and 'Amila, and that their advance guard had reached al-Balqa. As Muhammad mobilized his forces, some of the hypocrites[211] and the Ghifar[212] asked for permission to remain behind. Muhammad and 30,000 men advanced to Tabuk. Muhammad sent Khalid b. Walid with 420 horsemen from Tabuk to raid the Christian king Ukaydir b. 'Abdulmalik in Dumat al-Jandal. The Muslims captured Ukaydir, who was hunting wild cows outside of his fortress. Using Ukaydir as a hostage, Khalid had him demand entrance to the fortress for the Muslims. After they were refused, the king promised Khalid 2000 camels, 800 cattle,[213] 400 coats of mail and 400 spears, if he let him be released. Ukaydir was freed, entered the fortress, kept his word, and later agreed to pay the "jizya" (tribute) in Muhammad's presence.[214] Upon hearing of Ukaydir's fate, the king (governor) of Ayla, a Christian named Yuhanna b. Ruba is said to have come to Tabuk with the inhabitants of Jarba and Adhruh. They also agreed to pay the "jizya." The Muslims are also reported to have subjected the Jews of Maqna to pay the "jizya." Without engaging any of the Byzantine forces, the Muslims, who had been suffering from the heat and lack of water,[215] began their return to Medina. Many verses of Qur'an 9 are said to have been revealed with repect to the expedition to Tabuk.[216]

While Muhammad was preparing for the expedition to Tabuk, some of the Banu Sulaym came to him and said that they had built a mosque for the ill and poor and as a shelter in bad weather. They requested that Muhammad come to their mosque and lead the prayers for them, and Muhammad said he would come when he had more time. On his return from Tabuk, however, Qur'an 9:108 is said to have been revealed to Muhammad, and he then came to learn that this "mosque of opposition" had been built for (a mysterious) Abu 'Amir. Muhammad sent some of his men, who destroyed the mosque and had it burned.[217]

During the 103rd month after the Hijra, the Banu Thaqif[218] is reported to have accepted Islam.[219]

In the 105th month after the Hijra, one of the alleged leaders of the hypocrites, `Abdullah b. Ubayy, died. According to canonical traditions, Muhammad had Ibn Ubayy's corpse removed from the grave,[220] placed it on his knees, breathed on it,[221] placed his saliva on it and dressed it in his own shirt.[222] Canonical hadith also report that Muhammad's family would breathe on their hands and wave them over an ill person while reciting parts of the Qur'an,[223] and the use of saliva as a treatment for illness is also documented.[224] The Qur'an itself (12:93) shows that the shirt of Joseph was believed to have instrumentally brought healing to Jacob. Nothing of this sort, however, is reported to have taken place in Ibn Ubayy's case, and many traditions give varying accounts, which generally depict either Ibn Ubayy (on his deathbed), or Ibn Ubayy's son as requesting that Muhammad clothe the corpse with his shirt and perform the funeral prayers.[225] `Umar appears to have been against praying for Ibn Ubayy from the outset, and Qur'an 9:81, 85 are said to have been revealed on this occasion.[226]

Qur'an 9 is the only sura missing the basmala.[227] The first 30-40 verses of this sura are said to have been read by `Ali at the Hajj in 9 AH.[228] The vv. 1f declare that there is no compulsion on polytheists who had made a treaty with Muhammad previously, but a four month period of grace would be given for the other polytheists, after which those persisting in polytheism were to be killed. The vv. 18f state that only those who believe in Allah and the Resurrection, who perform the prayer, give alms and fear Allah alone, are permitted to visit the mosque (in Mecca). The vv. 20f say that those who emigrated and participated in the fight have a high position with Allah and will go to Paradise. The v. 23 commands not to have unbelievers as friends, and v. 24 maintains that pagans are not to fear for a lack of business. The v. 25 refers to the battle of Hunayn, and in v. 26 it is claimed that the Shechinah was sent down upon Muhammad and the Muslims, and angels are also said to have been sent to fight alongside them. The v. 27 states that God turns whom He will to repentance, and v. 28 declares that the pagans are unclean, but that they were allowed to hold the pilgrimage in that year only. The v. 29 commands to fight the Jews and Christians until they pay the "jizya," v. 30 makes the claim that the Jews accept Ezra as God's son[229] and the Christians accept Jesus as

God's Son; both Jews and Christians are then cursed. The v. 31 maintains that rabbis and monks were accepted as lords with Allah and the Messiah, and v. 32 charges that the People of the Book wanted to extinguish God's Light, but that God will perfect it. The v. 33 says that Muhammad was sent with guidance and true religion, in order to make it appear over every other religion. In the vv. 34f rabbis and monks are accused of having misappropriated contributions and of turning others from "Allah's way," and those who do not contribute to "Allah's way" will reportedly be sent to Hell. In the vv. 36f the intercalary month is abolished,[230] and a command is given to fight idolaters. The vv. 38f encourage to go forth in "Allah's way," where fighting is meant, and it is said that Allah will punish those who do not participate. The v. 40 reportedly refers to Muhammad and Abu Bakr's escape during the Hijra, and v. 41 encourages to fight in "Allah's way." The v. 42 appears to be a complaint against those who did not want to go to Tabuk because it was too far away. The v. 43 requests that God forgive Muhammad for permitting some not to go out (to Tabuk), and the vv. 44f claim that those who requested permission (not to go out) were unbelievers, and that it was better they did not go out anyway. The v. 50 says that the unbelievers are sad if all goes well (for the Muslims), but they are happy not to have been with them when a defeat occurs. The v. 51 says that God allows what happens to Muslims and that He is their defender, and v. 52 shows that the Muslims awaited God's punishment of the unbelievers. In v. 58 Muhammad is accused of unjust distribution of the alms, and v. 60 explains that the alms are for the poor and needy, the collectors, those whose hearts were to be won,[231] and others. The v. 61 shows that Muhammad felt hurt by the accusation of being called an "ear,"[232] and v. 62 claims there will be a punishment for those who hurt Muhammad. The v. 63 speaks of the hypocrites, and v. 64 states that those who are against Allah and Muhammad will be sent to Hell. The v. 65 says that the hypocrites were afraid that a sura would be revealed about themselves, and the canonical traditions indicate that such fears were also shared by Muslims.[233] The v. 66 refers to some uncertain question asked the hypocrites, who replied that they were just conversing and joking, and Muhammad asks if they were not rather mocking Allah, the Qur'an (signs) and himself. The v. 67 says that they (the hypocrites) became unbelievers after belief, and v. 68 presents them as having commanded the wrong, forbidden the right, and of having closed their hands (to making contributions); the hypocrites are said to have forgotten God, and God is said to have forgotten them. The v. 69 promises Hell for the hypocrites and unbelievers. In v. 71 Muhammad is said to have received the stories about the peoples of Noah, the `Ad, the Thamud, Abraham, Midian and the unrepentant (Sodom and Gomorrah?)[234] as having been punished. In v. 72 believers are described as commanding the right, forbidding the wrong, performing the prayer, paying the alms tax, and obeying Allah and Muhammad; v. 73 says that Allah has promised them (believers) Paradise. In v. 74 Muhammad is commanded to fight against the unbelievers and hypocrites, whose home is Hell, and v. 75 says that they give oaths and then lie; they are given a chance to repent. The vv. 76f maintain that some had said they would give alms if God gave them of His bounty, but that after they received thereof, they did not. The v. 81, about Muhammad vainly asking for the forgiveness of hypocrites, was allegedly revealed with respect to `Abdullah b. Ubayy. The v. 82 reproduces some of the complaints of Muhammad's followers that the weather was too hot (to go to Tabuk), and the reply is given that Hell is even hotter; the participation of such in future raids was to be denied (v. 84). The v. 85 forbids the praying for dead hypocrites, and this verse is also said to have been revealed concerning `Abdullah b. Ubayy.[235] The v. 87 maintains that some wished to remain at home when a sura was revealed about fighting with Allah and Muhammad, and the vv. 89f claim that all will go well (Paradise) for those who participate in the fighting. In v. 91 some nomad Arabs are said to have lied about their excuses (for not going to Tabuk), and it is said that there will be a punishment for them. The v. 92 shows that the weak and ill were excused, and v. 93 seems to refer to those for whom Muhammad had no mounts (to go to Tabuk), and whom he had to send away weeping.[236] In v. 94 some are condemned for asking permission to remain home because they already possessed wealth, and in the vv 95f the believers are instructed not to believe them, even if they swear. The v. 98 refers to the unbelief of the nomad Arabs, and v. 99 says that some of them viewed the "zakat" as a tribute tax. This verse depicts the nomad Arabs as waiting for fortunes to change, and they are answered that things will change for them - for the worse. In v. 100 some of the nomads are said to believe in God and the Judgment, and they are said to consider their alms as a means of coming nearer to God and the prayers of Muhammad; it is said that these will find compassion. The v. 101 speaks of Paradise for the first emigrants and helpers, and v. 102 says that the nomad Arab hypocrites and those of Medina will be sent to Hell. The v. 103 states that some of these hypocrites

confessed their sins, and v. 104 describes Muhammad as purifying and
sanctifying those from whom he accepts alms.[237] The vv. 108f seem to refer to
the "mosque of opposition,"[238] and v. 109b appears to allude to the Ka'ba. In v.
112 the claim is made that the Torah, Gospel and Qur'an contain a promise for
believers whom Allah has purchased for Paradise, who are to kill and be killed
in "Allah's way." The v. 113 is grammatically incomplete, in v. 114 Muhammad and the believers are commanded not to pray for forgiveness for
pagans,[239] and v. 115 claims that Abraham only prayed for his (pagan) father,
because of a former promise. The v. 117 gives a short description of God's
power, and v. 118 says that God helped Muhammad, the emigrants and the
helpers in their time of trouble. The v. 119 appears to refer to three who were
left behind (Tabuk).[240] The vv. 120f give a commandment to fear God and an
encouragement to participate in raids, but in an apparent reversal, v. 123
dictates that not all should go out; some should remain and learn about religion. In v. 124 the believers are commanded to fight the unbelievers, v. 125
gives a question as to who was strengthened in faith by a sura. The vv. 126f
present the hypocrites as dying as unbelievers, and that (as a group) they are
(so) tried once or twice a year. In v. 128 the hypocrites are said to have asked
who sees them, when a sura (probably concerning them) is revealed. The v.
129 presents Muhammad as a messenger sent from among them (the Arabs),
who is burdened by their troubles. The v. 130 makes a statement of Monotheism. Zayd b. Thabit said that, as he was collecting the verses of the Qur'an, he
was only able to find the vv. 129-130 with (Abu) Khuzayma.[241] The Arabic
name for Ezra (v. 30) is thought to have come from Hebrew.[242] Some of the
verses of this sura are at least remotely similar to passages in the Bible and
Talmud.[243]

In the 106th month after the Hijra, Muhammad sent Abu Bakr and (later)`Ali
with 300 pilgrims and 20 camels for sacrifice to perform the Hajj in Mecca.
Abu Bakr led the Hajj and declared that no polytheists would be allowed to
participate in the Hajj the following year and that no one would be permitted to
circumambulate the Ka`ba naked then. `Ali is reported to have read the first 30
or 40 verses of Qur'an 9 on the day of sacrifice.[244]

The alms tax ("zakat") is said to have been made obligatory (cf. Qur'an 9:11), and Muhammad reportedly sent out his representatives to collect it from the various tribes (cf. Qur'an 9:60).[245]

The intercalary month of the pagan Arabs, which adjusted the lunar calendar to compensate for the seasons (and thus postponed the "holy months"), was abolished (cf. Qur'an 9:36f). With respect to the Gregorian calendar, the months of the Islamic calendar begin about 10-12 days earlier in each successive year.

During the 109th month after the Hijra, Muhammad sent Khalid b. Walid to raid the Banu `Abdulmadan at Najran.[246]

In the 110th month after the Hijra,[247] Khalid b. was said to have been sent to the Banu al-Harith b. Ka`b at Najran. After inviting them to Islam, they are reported to have accepted. Khalid is said to have taught them Islam and the book of Allah, and later accompanied their deputation to Muhammad.[248]

According to one tradition, Khalid was in Yemen for six months, and then `Ali arrived to relieve him.[249]

During the 115th month after the Hijra, Muhammad sent `Ali b. Abu Talib and 300 men to Yemen with orders to be mild on them, in order to win them over to Islam. The Muslims raided the Banu Madhhij and captured women and children and seized livestock. After a force of the Banu Madhhij had mobilized, `Ali invited them to Islam, but they refused. The Muslims attacked, killing 20 men, and their enemy fled. Instead of pursuing them, however, `Ali invited them to Islam again. This time the Banu Madhhij accepted and agreed to pay the alms tax.[250]

Especially after the Hajj of 9 AH and the sending out of the tax collectors, many of the Arab tribes are said to have sent deputations to Muhammad.[251]

During this time period, the three "false" prophets, Musaylima in al-Yamama,[252] al-Aswad in Yemen[253] and Tulayha in the country of the Asad[254] are said to have risen up against Muhammad.[255] Of these, Musaylima

275

is said to have sent Muhammad a letter with the proposal of dividing the land between themselves, but Muhammad refused.[256]

Qur'an 5 appears to be composed of very many fragments from various time periods.[257] The vv. 1f essentially forbid hunting during the pilgrimage, and v. 3b shows that the former hate against the Meccans was to be laid aside. The v. 4 speaks of dietary laws and forbids arrow casting as divination. The v. 5 states that faith has been perfected[258] and that the dietary laws can be broken if one is suffering from hunger. The vv. 6f continue with the subject of dietary regulations, and v. 7b abruptly begins to speak of marriage laws, whereby the marriage to a Jew or Christian seems to be allowed. The vv. 8f deal with ablutions before prayer, and v. 10 seems to refer to Ex. 24;3, 7. The v. 15 speaks about an alleged covenant made with the children of Israel, in which those who perform the prayer, give alms, and believe the messengers are said to have their sins forgiven and will be sent to Paradise. The v. 16 says that the Jews broke the covenant, exchanged some of the words and forgot parts of what was told them. The v. 17 states that a covenant was also made with the Christians, but they forgot part of it and (as a punishment) hate and enmity was sown among them. The v. 18 says that Muhammad has come to proclaim what the People of the Book had hidden— a light from Allah by which people are led from the darkness to the light (cf. Acts 26:18). The v. 19 states that the unbelievers say that God is the Messiah, and asks who would have had more power than God in order to have killed Him. The v. 20 says that God has power over everything, and in v. 21 the Jews and Christians, who claim to be the sons of God are asked why God punishes them for their sins. The v. 22 maintains that Muhammad has come after an intermission in the prophetic ministry. The vv. 23f give a narrative in which Moses anachronistically alludes to God as having already appointed kings from among the Israelites (v. 23); the people's (spies) answer to the commandment to enter the land is referred to (v. 25), an ambiguous story about two men who disobeyed and did not enter a city is given (vv. 26f), and the forty years of wandering is mentioned as having been a punishment (v. 29). The vv. 30f give a short narrative about the two sons of Adam [Cain and Abel],[259] The v. 37 says that those who oppose Allah and Muhammad by making destruction in the earth, are to be punished by being killed and crucified with their (alternate) hands and feet being cut off, or by banishment.[260] The v. 38 excludes the punishment of those who come and repent before they come into the hands of the Muslims. The v. 39 encourages to fight in "Allah's way," and the vv. 40f show that the unbelievers would never be able to ransom themselves from Hell. The v. 42 declares that thieves (male or female) are to have their hands cut off, and v. 43 describes repentance after the punishment. The v. 44 says that God punishes and forgives whom He will, and the vv. 45f are against the hypocrites and the Jews (who are said to have exchanged words from their places). In v. 47 the Jews are described as having not accepted Muhammad because they have the Torah, and v. 48 presents the Torah as containing guidance and light, and maintains that the prophets were Muslims who judged the Jews. This verse also forbids the selling of God's signs (cf. 2:73), and v. 49 gives the laws of vengeance or forgiveness.[261] The v. 50 states that Jesus was sent to confirm the Torah and was given the Gospel, in which is guidance and light confirming the Torah; the Gospel is, moreover, said to be a guide and warning to those who fear (God). The v. 51 says that the People of the Gospel are to judge according to what God sent down in the Gospel (cf. 5:72),[262] and in the vv. 52f the Qur'an is said to have been sent down to Muhammad to confirm the previous Books, and Muhammad is to judge according to what was sent down. The v. 56 commands those who believe not to have Jewish or Christian friends, (since) they are the friends of one another. The v. 57 depicts the hypocrites as waiting for a change in fate, and in v. 58 the believers accuse the hypocrites of having broken their oaths. In v. 59 the Muslims are told that if they turn away, God will choose another people, and in vv. 60f the protectors are described as being Allah, Muhammad and the believers who perform the prayer, pay the "zakat" and bow down. The vv. 62f command believers not to have the Jews or Christians as friends (those who mock Islam), and not to have unbelieving friends either. The v. 64 rhetorically asks the People of the Book if they reject Muslims because they believe in God, the Qur'an and what was sent down previously. The v. 65 says that some of them (the Jews) were turned into apes (cf. 2:61; 7:166) and swine, and concludes that those who serve "taghut" are in a bad situation. The v. 68 asks why the rabbis do not forbid the sinful speech of the Jews and their ingestion of the forbidden. In v. 69 the statement of the Jews, that God's hands are bound, is reproduced, and it is said that God will punish them. The v. 70 states that if the People of the Book would believe and fear God, they would be sent to Paradise, and says further that they would have been essentially better off if they had fulfilled the Torah and the Gospel. In v. 71 Muhammad is commanded to proclaim everything that was sent down to him, and v. 72 says that the People of the Book have nothing to stand on until they fulfill the Torah and the Gospel.[263] The v. 73 says that those who believe and Jews, Sabians and Christians who believe in God, the Resurrection and practice good (works) will have nothing to fear (cf. 2:59). In v. 74 the children of Israel are said not to have liked the message of the messengers; they accused them of lies and killed them. The v. 75 says that the Jews were made (spiritually) blind and deaf as a punishment (cf. Acts 28:26f). In v. 76 those who say that God is the Messiah are described as being unbelievers, and Jesus is quoted as telling the children of Israel to serve His and their Lord. This verse says further that those who ascribe partners to God will go to Hell. The v. 77 is against those who say that God is the third of three; there is only one God. The v. 79 says that the Messiah was only a messenger, his mother was a just person, and they both ate food, etc.[264] The vv. 80f speak of the People of the Book as worshipping others beside God, and command them not to transgress the truth in their faith(s). In the vv. 82f the unbelievers of the children of Israel are said to have been cursed by David and Jesus, because they (the children of Israel) rebelled. The vv. 83f claim that the Jews made friends with unbelievers (the allied polytheist Arabs), and the v. 85 depicts the Jews and polytheists as being for the most part enemies of the Muslims, whereas the Christians are said to be the nearest the Muslims. In the vv. 86f some (of the Christians) are reported to have accepted the Qur'an, and have been rewarded with Paradise, but the unbelievers will be sent to Hell. The vv. 89f speak generally of the Islamic dietary laws, and v. 91 claims that God does not punish for unintentional oaths, nevertheless, an expiation for the same is given. In the vv. 92f wine, games, stones for sacrifice,[265] and arrows for divination are forbidden. The v. 94 maintains that believers who practice good (works) are not accused of sin for what they ate previously, and the vv. 95f state that wild game (excepting fish) is forbidden on the pilgrimage and gives the expiation for transgression. In v. 98 the Ka`ba is declared to be a refuge for mankind, etc., and the vv. 98b-99 say that Allah punishes, and Muhammad is only responsible for the proclamation. In v. 101 believers are told not to ask about things, which if made manifest would trouble them, and a canonical tradition (in reference to this verse) implies that some things were forbidden, simply because someone had asked Muhammad about them.[266] The v. 102 forbids some heathen practices with respect to sacrifice, and v. 103 shows that some (pagans) wanted to remain in the traditions of their forefathers. The vv. 105f make provision for verbal testaments and how they could be contested. The vv. 109f give a narrative about Jesus and His disciples, in which Jesus is said to have been strengthened by the Holy Spirit cf. 2:81, 254), and that He spoke in the cradle (cf. 19:30f). Moreover, it is said (v. 110) that God taught Him the Torah and the Gospel (cf. 3:43), and with God's permission He is said to have made clay birds live, He healed the blind and lepers and raised the dead (cf. 3:43). Some are said to have thought his miracles were magic (also v. 110), and Jesus' disciples are said to have been inspired and also Muslims.[267] In the vv. 112f the sending down of a table is claimed to have been a sign,[268] which was to have been a feast day for His disciples and those who followed.[269] In v. 116 it is said that Allah will ask Jesus if He commanded others to accept Himself and His mother as two gods beside Allah, and it is said that Jesus will then deny this.[270] In v. 117, Jesus will reportedly say that He only commanded to serve God, His Lord and their Lord (cf. v. 76). The vv. 118f speak of punishment and Paradise, and v. 120 states that God has the power over all things. The word for "making clean" in v. 4 probably came from the Jews,[271] the term for "unlawful" in the vv. 46, 67f may have come from the Syriac,[272] and the word for "table" came from Ethiopic.[273] Many of the verses of this sura are similar to passages in the Bible or Talmud.[274]

Islamic traditions report that Ibrahim b. Muhammad died as an infant on the same day a solar eclipse occurred.[275]

In the 117th month after the Hijra, Muhammad and his followers left Medina to perform the Hajj. `Ali and his forces returned from Yemen and met Muhammad in Mecca. Muhammad showed the pilgrims how the Hajj was to be performed, and gave what was later to be known as his farewell sermon.[276]

During the 121st month after the Hijra, Muhammad sent out Usama b. Zayd[277] to raid Mu'ta. On the day they were to set out, however, they received news that Muhammad's illness had become severe. The Muslim forces returned to Medina.[278]

At the end of the 120th month after the Hijra, Muhammad became ill (with a headache, and later a fever) after praying at a Muslim cemetery at night. During the almost two weeks of his illness, many remedies were tried, including pouring cold water over him,[279] giving him medicine[280] and breathing on his hands and then waving them over his body.[281] Muhammad also prayed for healing and later for forgiveness for himself.[282] When his illness became more severe, Muhammad appointed Abu Bakr to lead the congregational prayers. Muhammad is said to have been moved to ʿA'isha's apartment, after his condition had worsened at Maymuna's apartment. In Muhammad's presence, Umm Salama and Umm Habiba are said to have spoken of the church "Mary," which they had seen in Abyssinia,[283] and Muhammad said that such places of worship were near graves. Muhammad later cursed Jews and Christians for making graves a place of worship.[284] Muhammad asked for materials to write something by which none would go astray, but the materials were refused him, because he was said to have been delirious.[285] Muhammad is reported to have spoken with his daughter Fatima[286] and Usama b. Zayd,[287] who was to lead the second raid to Mu'ta. Muhammad is also said to have told Umm Bishr that he was feeling the effects of the poisoning attempt at Khaybar (from which her son had died).[288] Muhammad is said to have died in ʿA'isha's lap,[289] and they covered his corpse.[290] ʿUmar did not believe that Muhammad was dead, threatened those who said he was, and claimed that Muhammad would return as Moses did.[291] According to another tradition, the people maintained that Muhammad would be raised (from the dead) as Jesus was.[292] Abu Bakr said that as for those who worshipped Muhammad, he was dead; but as for those who worship God, He is alive and does not die. ʿUmar is then said to have been reminded of a Qur'an verse (3:138) by Abu Bakr, which described Muhammad's mortality, and ʿUmar is only then said to have believed that Muhammad was dead.[293] Nevertheless, Muhammad is reported to have died on a Monday, and his followers are said to have waited to bury him, until his corpse began to decay.[294] Muhammad's corpse was washed (with shirt on) by some of his companions, and not his wives.[295] Muhammad is said to have been buried at night on Wednesday the same week,[296] and even ʿA'isha is reported not to have known about it, until she heard them digging the grave,[297] (which was in her own apartment).[298] Muhammad was said to have been 63 years old at his death,[299] in the 121st month after the Hijra.[300]

Conclusions

The suras of this period do not introduce any new prayer times, although ablutions are mentioned (5:8f). *Sira* traditions relate that the five daily prayers were performed by Abu Bakr at the Hajj in 9 AH,[301] and then later by Muhammad in 10 AH,[302] but the silence of the Qur'an on the number of daily prayers casts serious doubts on the reliability of such traditions. The "zakat" seems to have been instituted in this period, essentially as an addition to almsgiving. The tribute tax for Jews and Christians was introduced (9:29), and they were not given the ultimatum to become Muslims as the pagans were (9:5). In the passages of this period, Muslim believers are described as praying (24:37, 55; 22:78; 9:8, 72; 5:15, 60), giving alms (24: 37, 55; 33:35; 22:78; 9:18, 72; 5:15), fasting (33:25) and contributing and fighting in "Allah's way" (49:15). The believers were to be true (33:35) and obedient (24:55; 33:35; 9:72); they were not to let wealth (24:37; 63:9), children (63:9) or business (24:37) hinder them from meditating on God (24: 37; 63:9; cf. 33:35), praying or paying the "zakat" (24:37). Muhammad claimed to have been nearer to the believers than they were to themselves (33:9), and Muhammad's wives were called "mother(s) of the believers" (33:9). The Muslim believers were to shun sexual immorality (33:35), and God and His angels are said to have prayed for them (33:42). Believers were not to love those who oppose Allah and Muhammad (58:22), they were not to make friends with the enemy (60:1f), and they were not to have unbelieving (60:9; 9:23; 5:62f), Jewish or Christian (5:56, 62f) friends. The believers were declared to be brothers of each other (49:10), who were not to pray for the forgiveness of pagans (9:114). Believers, who were said to be Allah's allies (58:22), were commanded to fight unbelievers (9:5, 124), Jews and Christians (9:29), and those who killed and were killed in "Allah's way" were promised Paradise (9:112). Weak believers are said to have called on pagan gods (22:11f). It is maintained that God chose the believers, obligated them to Araham's religion and named them "Muslims" (22:77). Believers were to let Muhammad go before them and speak louder than themselves (49:2f), and they were not to ask (Muhammad) about things whose answer would trouble them (5:101). The Shechinah was said to have been sent down on the Muslims (49:26; 9:26) and is even said to have been in the believers' hearts (49:4).

Aside from the typical description of the hypocrites as having an illness in their hearts, these suras of the Qur'an also show that some of the hypocrites had Jewish protectors (58:15), they broke their oaths (9:75; 5:57) and were against contributing to the Muslim cause (62:7; 9:68). The hypocrites are said to have turned others from "Allah's way" (63:2; 58:17) and to have become unbelievers after belief (9:67; cf. 3:101). The hypocrites were reportedly waiting for a change in fate (5:57; cf. 9:99), the deaths of their fellows were to be taken as a warning (9:126f) and the funeral prayers were not to be offered for them (9:81, 85). The hypocrites are said to have commanded the wrong and forbidden the right; they forgot God, and God forgot them (9:68). The hypocrites were afraid that a sura would be revealed about themselves (9:65), and God is requested to punish them (33:73). The hypocrites are compared with unbelievers and Satan (59:15f), they are said to have been Satan's allies (58:15f) and Satan is said to have been in them (58:15f). The hypocrites are said to have been destined for Hell (48:6; 9:69, 74; cf. 9:102).

The Qur'an passages of this period also contain regulations and laws for the Muslim community with respect to divorce (58:1f; 33:4), adultery (24:1f), marriage (5:76), theft (5:42) and dietary matters (5:1f, 94f). The drinking of wine and some pagan practices were also forbidden (5:92, 102).

In addition to these, some verses of this period are concerned with Muhammad's wives (33:28f, 37f, 53, 55, 59; 66:1f), a few instructions are given for the assemblies at the mosque (58:12), and camels are declared to be acceptable for animal sacrifices (22:37). One of the only passages in the Qur'an dealing with the subject of religious learning for Muslims can be found in this section (9:123).

In comparison to earlier suras of the Qur'an, there are relatively few narratives in this period. An explanation is given for Abraham's prayer for his pagan father (9:115), a distorted narrative about Moses and the spies is given (5:23f), a story about Adam's sons [Cain and Abel] is presented (5:30f), Jesus is spoken of (5:50, 76, 82f) with David (5:82f), an altered version of the Eucharist is given (5:109f), together with an innovated story about Jesus before Allah (5:116f). The odd statement about the Jews believing that

`Uzayr is God's son (9:30), seems to be the only fairly direct Qur'anic reference to Ezra.

Interestingly, the peoples of the pre-Islamic Arab legends seem to return to the text (9:71), and one wonders if this might not have had something to do with the confirmation of previous Qur'an passages for the massive influx of pagan (or particularly Meccan) Arabs to Islam.

The Arabic name for Ezra seems to have come from the Hebrew, and the other foreign vocabulary of these suras appears to have come from Hebrew (or Aramaic),[303] Syriac,[304] or Ethiopic (from Christians or members of sects).[305]

The evidence of foreign vocabulary (as given) in this and the previous sections indicate that the earliest passages of the Qur'an were generally influenced by Syriac, the "middle" suras reveal more borrowings from Hebrew or Aramaic, and the last suras imply an increasing dependence on Ethiopic (Christian) terms. This later influence of Ethiopic may have come about through the return of Muslims from Abyssinia. Furthermore, although the Qur'anic cognates from Ethiopic generally always approximate their counterparts in meaning,[306] the derivatives from Hebrew, Aramaic or Syriac are frequently nearest their original meanings in the later suras of the Qur'an.

There are numerous inconsistencies in the last years of Muhammad's ministry. It does not appear that the entire fast of Ramadan was held very often by the early Muslims, since the battle of Badr (2 AH),[307] the raid to murder Umm Qirfa (6 AH),[308] the raid on the Banu `Uwal and Banu Tha`laba (7 AH),[309] the conquest of Mecca (8 AH),[310] and `Ali's mission to Yemen (10 AH),[311] all occurred in Ramadan. The Qur'an confirms that the Torah is God's Word (cf. 3:2f; 5:48, 50; etc.), but when the Muslims had a copy in their possession (from the spoils of Khaybar), they gave it back to the Jews, keeping only their women and material goods as booty.[312] The Jews are accused of having exchanged some of God's words (cf. 5:16), but they are encouraged to practice the Torah (5:72). Although Mecca was already in Muslim hands, the pilgrimage of 8 AH was performed according to pagan customs. Moreover, in 9 AH the participation and accompanying rituals of the pagan Arabs were still allowed, even though pagans were considered to have been "unclean" (9:28).

Although Muhammad's forces had already attacked pagan Arabs, Jews and Christians (who had not attacked them first),[313] general commands to fight the polytheists (9:5) and Jews and Christians (9:29) appear only in this section of suras. The Banu Nadir was expelled,[314] the men of the Banu Qurayza were executed and their women and children became slaves.[315] The Jews of Khaybar, Wadi al-Qura, Tayma'[316] and Maqna[317] were subjected to various treaties or tribute. The Christians of Dumat al-Jandal and Ayla were also forced to pay tribute.

Theologically, Muhammad came to realize that the Jews did not accept him as a prophet because they possessed the Torah. (5:48) The Jews are accused of having broken the covenant given them, of having exchanged words (in God's Word) and of having forgotten parts of what had been told them (5:16). Christians, however, are not charged with having tampered with God's Word, but are only said to have forgotten parts of the covenant made with them (5:17). Jews are claimed to have accepted Ezra as God's son, whereas Christians accept Jesus as God's Son (9:30). Both Jews and Christians are even said to have called themselves the sons of God. (5:20). The People of the Book are accused of taking rabbis and monks as lords beside Allah and the Messiah (9:31) and of trying to extinguish God's Light. (9:32) The rabbis and monks are charged with having misappropriated contributions and with having turned others from Allah's way (9:34f). The Jews are said to have had unbelievers for friends (5:83f), and Jews and Christians were alleged to be friends of each other (5:56). Whereas the Jews (and polytheists) are described as being mostly enemies of the Muslims (or Muhammad), Christians are said to be the nearest to them (5:85). Some Christians are depicted as having accepted the Qur'an, (5:86f). Both the Torah (5:48) and the Gospel (5:50) are described as being a guidance and light, both are to be practiced as foundations (5:70, 72), and the "People of the Gospel" are to judge by the Gospel (5:51).

Qur'anic evidence from this period shows that Muhammad was to be addressed differently than others (24:68), those wishing to see him were to ask for permission (33:53) and to pay their alms beforehand (58:13). Muhammad is said to have been a good example of a believer (33:21), and the claim is made that God and His angels pray for Muhammad (33:56). It appears that Muhammad was accused of having divided the spoils of war unjustly (9:58), and some of the Ansar were no doubt discouraged when they saw the spoils of the Banu Nadir and Hunayn divided among the others (cf. the admonition of 59:9). Muhammad was commanded not to obey either unbelievers or hypocrites (33:47), and for a time he was allowed to marry many women (33:49f). He was later forbidden to increase the number of his wives (33:52). Muhammad's earlier and later sins are said to have been forgiven (48:2), and he was commanded to pray for forgiveness (110:1f). The Sechinah is said to have been sent down on Muhammad (48:26; 9:26).

Notes:

[1] Guillaume, *Muhammad*, pp. 661 f; Ibn Sa`d, *Classes*, vol. 2, 1, p. 59; Wellhausen, Medina, pp. 151 f.

[2] Guillaume, *Muhammad*, pp. 666 f; Ibn Sa`d, *Classes*, vol. 2, 1, pp. 60 f; Wellhausen, *Medina*, pp. 224 f.

[3] Wellhausen, *Medina*, p. 153, gives 40 Ansar.

[4] Of the Banu Sulaym.

[5] Guillaume, *Muhammad*, pp. 433 f; Ibn Sa`d, *Classes*, vol. 2, 1, pp. 61 f; Tabari, *History*, vol. 7, pp. 151 f; Wellhausen, *Medina*, pp. 153 f; *Sahih Bukhari*, vol. 5, pp. 286 f.

[6] Ibn Sa`d, *Classes*, vol. 2, 1, pp. 64 f; Tabari, *History*, vol. 7, p. 156; Wellhausen, *Medina*, p. 155; *Sahih Bukhari*, vol. 5, pp. 287 f. Cf. Nöldeke and Schwally, *GQ*, vol. 1, pp. 246 f.

[7] Ibn Sa`d gives "10," Tabari gives "6," and Waqidi (Wellhausen) gives "7" or "10."

[8] Guillaume, *Muhammad*, pp. 426 f; Ibn Sa`d, *Classes*, vol. 2, 1, pp. 66 f; Tabari, *History*, vol. 7, 143 f; Wellhausen, *Medina*, pp. 156 f. In the last of these references, Waqidi also gives a tradition whereby the Muslims were originally sent out to spy on the Quraysh on the road to Najd, but were ambushed; cf. *Sahih Bukhari*, vol. 5, pp. 283 f.

[9] Owing to the various reasons given for this seige in Islamic traditions, some Western scholars believe that this accusation was simply invented in order to justify driving this tribe out of Medina; Buhl, *Muhammad*, p. 265, n. 12.

[10] *Sunan Abu Dawud*, vol. 2, p. 743. Cf. Wellhausen, *Medina*, p. 165. For more information on the expulsion of the Banu Nadir, see Guillaume, *Muhammad*, pp. 437 f; Ibn Sa`d, *Classes*, vol. 2, 1, pp. 68 f; Tabari, *History*, vol. 7, pp. 156 f; Wellhausen, *Medina*, pp. 160 f.

[11] Buhl, *Muhammad*, pp. 267 f: The wine of the Qurayza was spilled out in the year 5 AH. Buhl thinks that this prohibition may have been based at least partially on the practices of other ascetic Arabs.

[12] Cf. Wellhausen, *Medina*, pp. 166 f; *Sahih Bukhari*, vol. 6, pp. 377 f; Nöldeke and Schwally, *GQ*, vol. 1, p. 206.

[13] Cf. *Sahih Bukhari*, vol. 6, p. 378.

[14] Cf. Ibid., vol. 6, p. 379.

[15] Speyer, *Erzählungen*, p. 460.

[16] Tabari, *History*, vol. 7, p. 150.

[17] Ibid., vol. 7, p. 167.

[18] At Uhud Abu Sufyan is said to have challenged the Muslims to a battle at Badr a month later. Western scholars, however, think this to be inaccurate, since Dhu'l-Qa`da (the 45th month) was one of the months in which fighting was forbidden by the pagan Arabs. It is thought that Muhammad simply

wanted to have the Muslims be able to trade at the market in Badr; Buhl, *Muhammad*, p. 269.

[19] Guillaume, *Muhammad*, pp. 447 f; Ibn Sa`d, *Classes*, vol. 2, 1, pp. 71 f; Tabari, *History*, vol. 7, pp. 165 f; Wellhausen, *Medina*, pp. 167 f.

[20] Ibn Hisham - after the battle of the ditch, 5 AH; Ibn Sa`d - Ramadan, 6 AH; Tabari - 3 AH; Waqidi - the end of 4 AH. There are also discrepancies in location.

[21] Guillaume, *Muhammad*, pp. 482 f; Ibn Sa`d, *Classes*, vol. 2, 1, pp. 112 f; Tabari, *History*, vol. 7, pp. 99 f; Wellhausen, *Medina*, pp. 170 f. Cf. *Sahih Bukhari*, vol. 5, pp. 250 f.

[22] Ibn Sa`d - or 700; Waqidi - or 700, or 800.

[23] Guillaume, *Muhammad*, pp. 445 f; Ibn Sa`d, *Classes*, vol. 2, 1, pp. 74 f; Tabari, *History*, vol. 7, pp. 161 f; Wellhausen, *Medina*, 172 f.

[24] Waqidi also gives another tradition, whereby Muhammad is said to have wanted to possess Dumat al-Jandal (which is near Syria) and thus frighten the Byzantines; Wellhausen, *Medina*, pp. 174 f.

[25] Guillaume, *Muhammad*, p. 449; Ibn Sa`d, *Classes*, vol, 2, 1, p. 76; Wellhausen, *Medina*, pp. 174 f.

[26] After the blood money was already paid for Hashim b. Subaba's death, his brother killed the assailant and escaped to the Quraysh. Following the victory at Mecca, Muhammad had the man executed; Wellhausen, *Medina*, p. 176.

[27] According to one tradition, Juwayriya, whose original name was Barra, had already been ransomed by her father before Muhammad wanted to marry her; Wellhausen, *Medina*, p. 178.

[28] Ibn Hisham - 100 families; Ibn Sa`d - all or 40 families; Waqidi - 100 or 40 families.

[29] I.e. Onanism; *Sahih Bukhari*, vol. 5, p. 317; vol. 7, p. 103; vol. 8, p. 391; *Sahih Muslim*, vol. 2, pp. 732 f.

[30] Guillaume, *Muhammad*, pp. 490 f; Ibn Sa`d, *Classes*, vol. 2, 1, pp. 77 f; Wellhausen, *Medina*, pp. 175 f.

[31] Wellhausen, *Medina*, p. 181. Cf. Nöldeke and Schwally, *GQ*, vol. 1, p. 209.

[32] Wellhausen, *Medina*, p. 178. Cf. Buhl, *Muhammad*, p. 280.

[33] Cf. *Sahih Bukhari*, vol. 6, pp. 88, 103; vol. 7, p. 68; *Sahih Muslim*, vol. 1, p. 201.

[34] Although Waqidi gives one tradition, in which `Abdullah b. Ubayy is said to have been punished also, the silence of other traditions (which generally attempt to cast `Abdullah in a bad light) in this respect would seem to indicate that he was not punished with the others.

[35] Guillaume, *Muhammad*, pp. 493 f; Ibn Sa`d, *Classes*, vol. 2, 1, pp. 79 f; Wellhausen, *Medina*, pp. 184 f. Sahih Bukhari, vol. 6, pp. 248 f; *Sahih Muslim*, vol. 4, pp. 1450 f.

[36] See the references in n. 35, above.

[37] *Sahih Bukhari*, vol. 5, pp. 326 f.

[38] See p. 127, n. 197.

[39] See p. 252, below.

[40] Rudolph, *Koran*, p. 324, n. 10.

[41] Ibid., p. 325, n. 13.

[42] See p. 195, above.

[43] See Appendix F, p. 416.

[44] Nöldeke and Schwally, *GQ*, vol. 2, p. 97. Cf. Al-Kindi in *ECMD*, p. 457.

[45] Al-Kindi in *ECMD*, p. 457; Suyuti, *El-Itkan*, vol. 2, p. 66.

[46] *Sahih Bukhari*, vol. 8, pp. 536 f; *Sahih Muslim*, vol. 3, p. 912. Cf. Nöldeke and Schwally, *GQ*, vol. 1, pp. 248 f.

[47] *Sahih Bukhari*, vol. 9, pp. 212 f; *Sunan Abu Dawud*, vol. 3, p. 1231; Suyuti, *El-Itkan*, vol. 2, pp. 68 f.

[48] Suyuti, *El-Itkan*, vol. 2, p. 66.

[49] Nöldeke and Schwally, *GQ*, vol. 1, p. 249.

[50] *Sahih Bukhari*, vol. 8, pp. 526, 528 f; *Sahih Muslim*, vol. 3, pp. 912 f.

[51] See "The Book of Laws of Diverse Countries" in *Ante-Nicene Fathers*, vol. 8, p. 731.

[52] *Sahih Bukhari*, vol. 8, p. 527.

[53] *Sahih Bukhari*, vol. 8, pp. 544 f; *Sahih Muslim*, vol. 3, pp. 911 f.

[54] Aws b. Assamit is said to have divorced his wife Hawla (or Huwayla) using a heathen statement of divorce (cf 58:2), later he regretted his decision, and evidently had his case brought to Muhammad; Nöldeke and Schwally, *GQ*, vol. 1, p. 212.

[55] Ibid. Cf. Rudolph, *Koran*, p. 498, n. 7.

[56] See Appendix F, p. 416.

[57] Waqidi - or 10 day-long siege.

[58] Sa`d b. Mu`adh, see p. 253, below. For more information on the battle of the ditch, see: Guillaume, *Muhammad*, pp. 450 f; Ibn Sa`d, *Classes*, vol. 2, 1, pp. 80 f; Wellhausen, *Medina*, pp. 190 f.

[59] Wellhausen, *Medina*, p. 210.

[60] (Tabari, *Ta'rikh*, 1460f); *Sahih Bukhari*, vol. 6, p. 294; Andrae, *Mohammed*, pp. 153 f; Watt, *Muhammad*, pp. 156 f; *SEI*, p. 653. This subject was also used by early Christian polemicists; cf. *ECMD*, pp. 93, 142, 432. Muhammad's marriage to Zaynab is also said by some to have taken place prior to the raid on the Banu Mustaliq, because of the roles played by her and her sister in the matter of `A'isha; Nöldeke and Schwally, *GQ*, vol. 1, p. 207.

[61] Waqidi gives one tradition by which the Jews are said to have returned the arrow attacks of the Muslims.

[62] Wellhausen, *Medina*, p. 216.

[63] Ibn Hisham - or 800-900; Waqidi - or 750.

[64] Wellhausen, *Medina*, p. 217.

[65] Waqidi - some say she was married to Muhammad and wore the veil. Some say her name was Rayhana b. Zayd.

[66] Guillaume, *Muhammad*, pp. 461 f; Ibn Sa`d, *Classes*, vol. 2, 1,   pp. 91 f; Wellhausen, *Medina*, pp. 210 f.

[67] Nöldeke and Schwally, *GQ*, vol. 1, pp. 206 f.

[68] See Margoliouth, "Additions", *JRAS*, (1939), pp. 60 f, for a discussion of a borrowing from Ethiopic in v. 19.

[69] *Sahih Bukhari*, vol. 6, p. 291.

[70] Nöldeke and Schwally, *GQ*, vol. 1, p. 207, discredit the following

traditions as being (trans.): "anecdotic embellished narratives" which do not explain the context in which these verses were revealed: *Sahih Bukhari*, vol. 6, pp. 292 f; vol. 7, pp. 136 f; *Sahih Muslim*, vol. 2, pp. 761 f.

[71] *Sahih Bukhari*, vol. 6, p. 294. Cf. Nöldeke and Schwally, *GQ*, vol. 1, p. 207.

[72] According to a canonical tradition, everyone used to call Zayd b. Haritha "Zayd b. Muhammad" before the revelation of these verses; *Sahih Bukhari*, vol. 6, p. 290.

[73] `A'isha is said to have remarked that Muhammad's Lord was quick to grant Muhammad's desires: *Sahih Bukhari*, vol. 6, p. 295.

[74] Nöldeke and Schwally, *GQ*, vol. 1, p. 208.

[75] This verse is said to have been revealed in connection with Muhammad's marriage to Zaynab bt. Jahsh, and `Umar is again said to have influenced its revelation; *Sahih Bukhari*, vol. 6, pp. 296 f.

[76] Although some Muslims recognize the possible problems of the normal meaning of "yusalluna" with respect to Islamic Monotheistic theology (cf. *Sahih Bukhari*, vol. 6, pp. 302 f; *ECMD*, p. 322), a number of official Turkish translations of the Qur'an present this verse as meaning that God and His angels pray for Muhammad; cf. the translations of Ö. Bilmen, T. Kochyigit and S. Atesh.

[77] Cf. the references given by Nöldeke and Schwally, *GQ*, vol. 1, p. 255, n. 4.

[78] Waqidi - in the 55th month after the Hijra.

[79] Guillaume, *Muhammad*, p. 662; Ibn Sa`d, *Classes*, vol. 2, 1, p. 96; Wellhausen, *Medina*, p. 226.

[80] Or the 55th month; Wellhausen, *Medina*, p. 227.

[81] See p. 245, above. Guillaume, *Muhammad*, p. 485 f; Ibn Sa`d, *Classes*, vol. 2, 1, p. 97; Wellhausen, *Medina*, pp. 226 f.

[82] Waqidi - four.

[83] Waqidi and Ibn Sa`d - or 700.

[84] Guillaume, *Muhammad*, pp. 486 f; Ibn Sa`d, *Classes*, vol. 2, 1, pp. 99 f; Wellhausen, *Medina*, 227 f.

[85] Ibn Sa`d, *Classes*, vol. 2, 1, pp. 104 f; Wellhausen, *Medina*, p. 232.

[86] Ibn Sa`d, *Classes*, vol. 2, 1, pp. 105 f; Wellhausen, *Medina*, pp. 232 f.

[87] Ibn Sa`d also gives another version, by which the Muslims are said to have attacked and captured a man, who became a Muslims and was set free. Ibn Sa`d, *Classes*, vol. 2, 1, p. 106; Wellhausen, *Medina*, p. 233.

[88] Ibn Sa`d, *Classes*, vol. 2, 1, p. 106.

[89] See p. 203, above. Ibn Sa`d, *Classes*, vol. 2, 1, p. 107; Wellhausen, *Medina*, pp. 233 f.

[90] Ibn Sa`d, *Classes*, vol. 2, 1, p. 108; Wellhausen, *Medina*, p. 234.

[91] Ibn Sa`d, *Classes*, vol. 2, 1, pp. 108 f; Wellhausen, *Medina*, pp. 234 f.

[92] Guillaume, *Muhammad*, p. 664; Ibn Sa`d, *Classes*, vol. 2, 1, p. 109; Wellhausen, *Medina*, p. 236.

[93] Muhammad had allegedly instructed them not to kill any women and children. The "jizya" is a sort of tribute, which Muslims required (primarily) of their Jewish and Christian subjects. Owing to the various versions of the

accounts, Buhl (*Muhammad*, p. 279) thinks it more probable that no one converted at Dumat al-Jandal in this incident, but that they all agreed to pay the "jizya."

[94] Wellhausen, *Medina*, p. 237, gives "al-Asya` b. `Amr."

[95] Ibn Sa`d, *Classes*, vol. 2, 1, p. 110; Wellhausen, *Medina*, pp. 236 f.

[96] Ibn Sa`d, *Classes*, vol. 2, 1, pp. 110 f; Wellhausen, *Medina*, pp. 237 f.

[97] Guillaume, *Muhammad*, pp. 664 f; Ibn Sa`d, *Classes*, vol. 2, 1, pp. 111 f; Wellhausen, *Medina*, pp. 238 f.

[98] Guillaume, *Muhammad*, pp. 664 f; Ibn Sa`d, *Classes*, vol. 2, pp. 113 f; Wellhausen, *Medina*, pp. 239 f.

[99] The traditions in *Sahih Bukhari* (vol. 1, p. 148; vol. 5, p. 354, vol. 6, pp. 106 f) state that the shepherd was simply killed. Ibn Hisham claims that they killed the shepherd and stuck thorns in his eyes. Waqidi gives that the shepherd was killed in the cruellest manner, and Ibn Sa`d maintains that the shepherd had his hands and feet cut off, and thorns were stuck in his eyes and tongue. The progressive modifications of the narrative in this matter, by which the atrocities done to Muhammad's shepherd become more and more graphic, seem to aim at justifying Muhammad's torture of the `Urayna.

[100] *Sahih Bukhari* (vol. 1, p. 148, vol. 5, p. 354) gives traditions by which Muhammad burned out their eyes with iron. Waqidi gives a tradition in which it is said that Muhammad did not gouge out their eyes.

[101] Guillaume, *Muhammad*, pp. 677 f; Ibn Sa`d, *Classes*, vol. 2, 1, p. 114; Wellhausen, *Medina*, pp. 240 f.

[102] The would-be assassin became a Muslim.

[103] Ibn Sa`d, *Classes*, vol. 2, 1, pp. 115 f; Tabari, *History*, vol. 7, pp. 147 f.

[104] Nöldeke and Schwally, *GQ*, vol. 1, p. 213, state that the vv. 1-24, 43-56, 60-65 and 67-75 are Meccan, but later concede that the vv. 51-52 were probably Medinan.

[105] Ibid., vol. 1, p. 214.

[106] See p. 91, above.

[107] See p. 75, n. 192, above.

[108] Jeffery, *Vocabulary*, p. 84.

[109] Or South Arabic; Ibid., p. 200.

[110] See Appendix F, p. 416.

[111] Ibn Hisham - 700 or 1400; Waqidi and Ibn Sa`d - 1600, 1400, or 1525. Many of the Arab nomads refused to join the Muslims (Qur'an 48:10f, 15f) on this occasion; see Buhl, *Muhammad*, pp. 285 f; *SEI*, p. 401.

[112] An abbreviated version of the pilgimage; see *SEI*, pp. 604 f.

[113] Armed with only the weapons of travellers and sheathed swords.

[114] Guillaume, *Muhammad*, pp. 499 f; Ibn Sa`d, *Classes*, vol. 2, 1, pp. 117 f; Wellhausen, *Medina*, pp. 241 f.

[115] See n. 111, above.

[116] See n. 111, above.

[117] Nöldeke and Schwally, *GQ*, vol. 1, pp. 215 f.

[118] Guillaume, *Muhammad*, p. 653; Ibn Sa`d, *Classes*, vol. 1, 2, pp. 304 f.

[119] Waqidi - or the equivalent of the 73rd month.

[120] Waqidi - 10 or 17 Muslims; Ibn Sa`d - or 17 Muslims.

[121] Guillaume, *Muhammad*, p. 516; Ibn Sa`d, *Classes*, vol. 2, 1, pp. 131 f;
Wellhausen, *Medina*, pp. 280 f. Muhammad is said to have been affected by
the poison (*Sahih Bukhari*, vol. 3, pp. 474 f; *Sahih Muslim*, vol. 3, p. 1194),
and even claimed to be dying from the effects of the poison at his death some
years later (Guillaume, *Muhammad*, p. 516; Ibn Sa`d, *Classes*, vol. 2, 2, pp.
249 f; *Sahih Bukhari*, vol. 5, p. 509). Bishr is said to have died one year later
from the effects of the poison; Ibn Sa`d, *Classes*, vol. 2, 2, p. 252. The Chris-
tian polemicist al-Kindi refers to this incident in his famous *Apology*; see
ECMD, pp. 441 f.

[122] Ibn Hisham - Muhammad let her live. Cf. *Sahih Bukhari*, vol. 7,
p. 449; *Sunan Abu Dawud*, vol. 3, pp. 1262 f.

[123] It is claimed that the Jews broke the terms of their surrender, and
Muhammad then seized their property and women.

[124] In the battle at Khaybar, which in some aspects resembled an active
seige, the Muslims are said to have suffered from hunger. Cf. *Sahih Bukhari*,
vol. 5, pp. 372 f. One tradition claims that Mut`a was also forbidden; *Sahih
Bukhari*, vol. 5, p. 372.

[125] Guillaume, *Muhammad*, pp. 516 f; Ibn Sa`d, *Classes*, vol. 2, 1,
pp. 144 f; Wellhausen, *Medina*, pp. 278 f; 291 f. Cf. *Sahih Bukhari*, vol. 5,
pp. 369 f.

[126] Wellhausen, *Medina*, p. 281. For more information on the battle of
Khaybar, see Guillaume, *Muhammad*, pp. 510 f; Ibn Sa`d, *Classes*, vol. 2, 1,
pp. 131 f; Wellhausen, *Medina*, pp. 264 f.

[127] Waqidi also gives another version in a tradition which says that
Muhammad sent Muhayyisa b. Ma`sud to Fadak to call the Jews there to
Islam. When the Jews heard of the plight of some of the Jews at Khaybar, they
then agreed to the same terms; Wellhausen, *Medina*, p. 291.

[128] See p. 246, above.

[129] Cf. e.g. *Sahih Bukhari*, vol. 5, pp. 381 f. For more information on the terms made with the Jews of Fadak, see Guillaume, *Muhammad*, p. 523; Wellhausen, *Medina*, p. 291.

[130] Guillaume, *Muhammad*, pp. 526 f; Ibn Sa`d, *Classes*, vol. 2, 1, p. 134.

[131] Ibn Sa`d, *Classes*, vol. 1, 1, p. 240.

[132] Rudolph, *Koran*, p. 463, n. 12.

[133] See Andrae, *Muhammad*, p. 89.

[134] See Appendix F, p. 416.

[135] Ibn Sa`d, *Classes*, vol. 1, 1, pp. 151 f. Cf. Buhl, *Muhammad*, p. 297; Watt, *Muhammad*, p. 195.

[136] Cf. Qur'an 66; (Ibn Sa`d, *Tabaqat*, vol. 8, pp. 134 f, 154 f [from Buhl]) Nöldeke and Schwally, *GQ*, vol. 1, p. 217; Buhl, *Muhammad*, p. 297, n. 93; *EI²*, s.v. "Mariya." Nöldeke and Schwally show that the contradictory stories given in most Islamic traditions are later innovations; cf. e.g. *Sahih Bukhari*, vol. 3, pp. 387 f; vol. 7, pp. 140 f.

[137] *Sahih Bukhari*, vol. 6, p. 408 f.

[138] Cf. *Sahih Bukhari*, vol. 6, p. 410.

[139] See Appendix D, p. 389.

[140] See Appendix D, p. 389.

[141] Wellhausen, *Medina*, pp. 292 f. Cf. *Sahih Bukhari*, vol. 3, p. 559.

[142] Guillaume, *Muhammad*, p. 660; Ibn Sa`d, *Classes*, vol. 2, 1, p. 146; Wellhausen, *Medina*, p. 297.

[143] Ibn Sa`d, *Classes*, vol. 2, 1, pp. 146 f; Tabari, *History*, vol. 9, pp. 1 f; Wellhausen, *Medina*, p. 297.

[144] Guillaume, *Muhammad*, p. 660; Ibn Sa`d, *Classes*, vol. 2, 1, pp. 147 f; Wellhausen, *Medina*, pp. 297 f.

[145] Ibn Sa`d, *Classes*, vol. 2, 1, pp. 148 f; Wellhausen, *Medina*, p. 298.

[146] Ibn Sa`d, *Classes*, vol. 2, 1, pp. 149 f; Wellhausen, *Medina*, pp. 298 f.

[147] Guillaume, *Muhammad*, 531; Ibn Sa`d, *Classes*, vol. 2, 1, p. 152; Wellhausen, *Medina*, p. 303.

[148] Guillaume, *Muhammad*, pp. 530 f; Ibn Sa`d, *Classes*, vol. 2, 1, pp. 150 f; Wellhausen, *Medina*, 300 f.

[149] Ibn Sa`d, *Classes*, vol. 2, 1, p. 153; Wellhausen, *Medina*, p. 303.

[150] Guillaume, *Muhammad*, pp. 484 f; Wellhausen, *Medina*, pp. 303 f.

[151] Guillaume, *Muhammad*, pp. 660 f; Ibn Sa`d, *Classes*, vol. 2, 1, pp. 154 f; Wellhausen, *Medina*, pp. 307 f.

[152] See p. 263, above.

[153] Ibn Sa`d, *Classes*, vol. 2, 1, pp. 156 f.

[154] Waqidi - each man received 15 camels or 150 sheep as his share of the booty.

[155] Ibn Sa`d, *Classes*, vol. 2, 1, pp. 157 f; Wellhausen, *Medina*, pp. 308 f.

[156] Ibn Sa`d, *Classes*, vol. 2, 1, p. 158; Wellhausen, *Medina*, p. 308.

[157] Ibn Hisham - 200,000 men.

[158] Although the lists of those killed (as given in Ibn Hisham and Waqidi) show only eight to thirteen dead. For more information on this expedition, see Guillaume, *Muhammad*, pp. 531 f, Ibn Sa`d, *Classes*, vol. 2, 1, pp. 158 f; Wellhausen, *Medina*, pp. 309 f. A tradition in *Sahih Bukhari* (vol. 5, p. 393) claims that the Muslims won this battle.

[159] Guillaume, *Muhammad*, pp. 668 f; Ibn Sa`d, *Classes*, vol. 2, 1, pp. 162 f; Wellhausen, *Medina*, pp. 315 f.

[160] Guillaume, *Muhammad*, p. 673; Ibn Sa`d, Classes, vol. 2, 1, p. 163; Wellhausen, Medina, pp. 317 f.

[161] Ibn Sa`d - 2000 sheep.

[162] Guillaume, *Muhammad*, pp. 671 f; Ibn Sa`d, *Classes*, vol. 2, 1, pp. 163 f; Wellhausen, *Medina*, pp. 318 f.

[163] See p. 141, above.

[164] Nöldeke and Schwally, *GQ*, vol. 1, p. 218.

[165] Ibid., vol. 1, p. 219.

[166] Guillaume, *Muhammad*, pp. 540 f; Ibn Sa`d, *Classes*, vol. 2, 1, pp. 165 f; Wellhausen, *Medina*, pp. 319 f.

[167] Those killed were Ibn Khatal, al-Huwayrith b. Nuqaydh, Miqyas b. Saba and the woman singer Sara. `Ikrima b. Abu Jahl and Hind bt. `Uqba are reported to have become Muslims.

[168] Ibn Abu Sarh is said to have changed some of the wording in the Qur'an as he wrote what Muhammad was dictating; Wellhausen, *Medina*, p. 345. See also p. 98, n. 229, above.

[169] Waqidi - Muhammad is also said to have commanded `Umar to wash away Abraham's picture, after the latter had failed to do so at first. Some canonical traditions state that Ishmael was also portrayed in this picture;

Sahih Bukhari, vol. 2, pp. 392 f; vol. 4, pp. 365 f; vol. 5, p. 406; *Sunan Abu Dawud*, vol. 2, p. 538.

[170] A picture of Mary is mentioned in *Sahih Bukhari*, vol. 4, p. 365, and al-Araqi (cf. Guillaume, *Muhammad*, p. 552) is said to mention that a picture of Jesus was also there. The pictures of Mary and Jesus are reported to have still been seen in the Ka'ba as late as 683 AD; Guillaume, *Islam*, p. 14.

[171] Ibn Sa'd, *Classes*, vol. 2, 1, p. 167.

[172] Ibid., vol 2, 1, pp. 170 f; *Sahih Bukhari*, vol. 5, pp. 399 f.

[173] See p. 200, above. For more information on the conquest of Mecca, see the references in n. 166, above.

[174] See Nöldeke and Schwally, *GQ* vol. 1, p. 220. Cf. *Sahih Bukhari*, vol. 5, pp. 409 f.

[175] See p. 10, n. 35, above.

[176] Guillaume, *Muhammad*, pp. 565 f; Ibn Sa'd, *Classes*, vol. 2, 1, p. 180; Wellhausen, *Medina*, p. 351.

[177] See p. 9, n. 35, above.

[178] Ibn Sa'd, *Classes*, vol. 2, 1, pp. 180 f; Wellhausen, *Medina*, p. 350.

[179] See p. 10, n. 35, above.

[180] Ibn Sa'd, *Classes*, vol. 2, 1, p. 181; Wellhausen, *Medina*, p. 350.

[181] It is said that 30 men had been killed. Waqidi also gives another tradition, by which the Banu Jadhima is said to have accepted Islam after Khalid's attack. For more information on this expedition, see Guillaume, *Muhammad*, pp. 561 f; Ibn Sa'd, *Classes*, vol. 2, 1, pp. 182 f; Wellhausen, *Medina*, pp. 351 f.

[182] Waqidi in Wellhausen, *Medina*, p. 356.

[183] See p. 3, n. 33, above, for more on this pagan Arab ritual.

[184] Ibn Hisham in Guillaume, *Muhammad*, pp. 569 f.

[185] Wellhausen, *Medina*, p. 359.

[186] Ibid., p. 361.

[187] See p. 268, below.

[188] Cf. Qur'an 9:60; Buhl, *Muhammad*, p. 314; and Andrae, *Mohammed*, p. 78, who describes this as being "a type of bribery."

[189] *Sahih Bukhari*, vol. 5, pp. 432 f.

[190] They are said to have been given the choice of receiving their posses-sions, or families again. They chose the latter.

[191] Guillaume, *Muhammad*, pp. 566 f; Ibn Sa`d, *Classes*, vol. 2, 1, pp. 185 f; Tabari, *History*, vol. 9, pp. 1 f; Wellhausen, *Medina*, pp. 354 f.

[192] See *EI²*, s.v. "Dhu'l-Khaffayn."

[193] Ibn Sa`d, *Classes*, vol. 2, 1, pp. 194 f; Wellhausen, *Medina*, p. 368.

[194] Ibn Hisham - 17 or 20 days; Waqidi - 15, 18 or 19 days; Ibn Sa`d - 18 days; Tabari - 20 days.

[195] The Banu Thaqif then asked Muhammad why he was destroying the vineyards, since the vineyards would belong to him anyway if the Muslims were to win.

[196] It is quite likely that the Muslims wanted to learn of any other ways to enter the fortress; see Khaybar, p. 260, above.

[197] Guillaume, *Muhammad*, pp. 587 f; Ibn Sa`d, *Classes*, vol. 2, 1, pp. 195 f; Tabari, *History*, vol. 9, pp. 20 f; Wellhausen, Medina, pp. 368 f.

[198] See p. 267, above. Guillaume, *Muhammad*, p. 597; Tabari, *History*, vol. 9, pp. 26 f; Wellhausen *Medina*, pp. 373 f.

[199] Ibn Sa`d, *Classes*, vol. 1, 1, pp. 151 f; Tabari, *History*, vol. 9, p. 39.

[200] Tabari, *History*, vol. 9, p. 38.

[201] He was now an ally of the Muslims, and is also mentioned as having been at al-Ta'if and al-Ji`rana with the Muslims.

[202] Guillaume, *Muhammad*, pp. 628 f; Ibn Sa`d, *Classes*, vol. 2, 1, pp. 198 f; Tabari, *History*, vol. 9, p. 67; Wellhausen, *Medina*, pp. 385 f; *Sahih Bukhari*, vol. 5, pp. 459 f.

[203] Ibn Sa`d, *Classes*, vol. 2, 1, pp. 199 f; Wellhausen, *Medina*, p. 387.

[204] See n. 203, above. Cf. Nöldeke and Schwally, *GQ*, vol. 1, pp. 220 f.

[205] Cf. p. 264, n. 151, above.

[206] Ibn Sa`d, *Classes*, vol. 2, 1, pp. 200 f; Wellhausen, *Medina*, p. 387.

[207] Ibn Sa`d, *Classes*, vol. 2, 1, p. 201; Wellhausen, *Muhammad*, p. 388.

[208] Waqidi- The Muslims attacked and drove them away. Guillaume, *Muhammad*, p. 677; Ibn Sa`d, *Classes*, vol. 2, 1, pp. 201 f; Wellhausen, *Medina*, pp. 388 f.

[209] Ibn Sa`d, *Classes*, vol. 2, 1, pp. 202 f; Tabari, *History*, vol. 9, pp. 62 f.

[210] Ibn Sa`d, *Classes*, vol. 2, 1, p. 203.

[211] About 80 in number; they were excused by Muhammad.

[212] About 83 in number; they were not excused by Muhammad.

[213] Wellhausen, *Medina*, p. 404, has (trans.): "800 slaves."

[214] Guillaume, *Muhammad*, pp. 607 f; Ibn Sa`d, *Classes*, vol. 2, 1, pp. 205 f; Tabari, *History*, vol. 9, pp. 58 f; Wellhausen, *Medina*, pp. 403 f.

[215] Buhl points out that Islamic traditions claim this expedition took place in Rajab, which would have been October. After briefly summarizing the views of earlier Western scholars on this issue, Buhl argues (cf. Qur'an 9:82) in favor of a late summer dating; *Muhammad*, p. 322, n. 12.

[216] Guillaume, *Muhammad*, pp. 602 f; Ibn Sa`d, *Classes*, vol. 2, 1, pp. 203 f; Tabari, *History*, vol. 9, pp. 47 f; Wellhausen, *Medina*, pp. 390 f.

[217] Guillaume, *Muhammad*, pp. 609 f; Tabari, *History*, vol. 9, pp. 60 f; Wellhausen, *Medina*, pp. 410 f.

[218] See p. 268, above.

[219] Guillaume, *Muhammad*, p. 614; Tabari, *History*, vol. 9, p. 38; Wellhausen, *Medina*, p. 381.

[220] After it was already in the grave.

[221] *Sahih Bukhari*, vol. 7, pp. 461 f.

[222] Ibid., vol. 2, pp. 202, 242.

[223] Ibid., vol. 5, p. 510; vol. 7, pp. 423, 429 f, 433; *Sahih Muslim*, vol. 3, pp. 1195 f.

[224] *Sahih Bukhari*, vol. 7, p. 429.

[225] *Sahih Bukhari*, vol. 2, pp. 201 f; vol. 4, 156; vol. 6, pp. 153 f; and most of the *Sira* traditions (see n. 225, below for references).

[226] Guillaume, *Muhammad*, p. 623; Tabari, *History*, vol. 9, p. 73; Wellhausen, *Medina*, pp. 414 f. As a possible motive for Muhammad's actions with respect to `Abdullah b. Ubayy, cf. Guillaume, *Muhammad*, p. 235, where Muhammad is reported to have said that the death of someone else was unfortunate, because the Jews and hypocrites would then say: "If he (Muhammad) were a prophet, his companion would not die."

[227] See p. 204, above. Cf. also Nöldeke and Schwally, *GQ*, vol. 2, p. 80; Watt and Bell, *Introduction*, p. 60.

[228] Tabari, *History*, vol. 9, pp. 78 f. Cf. Nöldeke and Schwally, *GQ*, vol. 1, p. 222.

[229] See Appendix D, p. 390.

[230] See p. 275, below.

[231] See n. 188, above.

[232] Nabtal b. Harith is reported to have made this accusation, in that Muhammad is said to have believed all he heard from others; see Guillaume, *Muhammad*, p. 622 and p. 108, above.

[233] Ibn `Umar is quoted as having said that since Muslims were afraid that something might be revealed about them, they did not speak casually with their wives in Muhammad's presence, but began to do so after his death; *Sahih Bukhari*, vol. 7, p. 81.

[234] Rudolph, *Koran*, p. 193, n. 36.

[235] See p. 271, above.

[236] See the references for Tabuk in n. 215, above.

[237] For a description of similar Christian doctrines, see p. 52, n. 183, above, Andrae, *Ursprung*, p. 181; *Mohammed*, p. 86. For similar Jewish teachings, see Cook, *Muhammad*, pp. 78 f, 92.

[238] See p. 270, above.

[239] See p. 112, n. 33, above.

[240] See Guillaume, *Muhammad*, pp. 610 f.

[241] *Sahih Bukhari*, vol. 6, p. 480. Cf. Nöldeke and Schwally, *GQ*, vol. 1, p. 226; vol. 2, p. 14.

[242] Jeffery, *Vocabulary*, pp. 214 f.

[243] See Appendix F, p. 416.

[244] Guillaume, *Muhammad*, pp. 617 f; Ibn Sa`d, *Classes*, vol. 2, 1, pp. 208 f; Tabari, *History*, pp. 77 f; Wellhausen, *Medina*, pp. 416 f.

[245] Tabari, *History*, vol. 9, p. 78 f. Cf. *Sahih Bukhari*, vol. 6, p. 147.

[246] Ibn Sa`d, *Classes*, vol. 2, 1, p. 209.

[247] Or the 111th month.

[248] Guillaume, *Muhammad*, pp. 645 f; Tabari, *History*, vol. 9, pp. 89 f.

[249] Tabari, *History*, vol. 9, pp. 89 f.

[250] Guillaume, *Muhammad*, p. 678; Ibn Sa`d, *Classes*, vol. 2, 1, pp. 209 f; Wellhausen, *Medina*, pp. 417 f.

[251] Guillaume, *Muhammad*, pp. 634 f; Ibn Sa`d, *Classes*, vol. 1, 2, pp. 345 f; Tabari, *History*, vol. 9, pp. 76 f, 85 f.

[252] See pp. 4, 311; *SEI*, p. 416; *EI²*, s.v. "Musaylima."

[253] *SEI*, p. 49; *EI²*, s.v. "al-Aswad."

[254] *SEI*, pp. 595 f.

[255] Guillaume, *Muhammad*, pp. 648 f; Tabari, *History*, vol. 9, pp. 164 f.

[256] Some maintain that this correspondence occurred after Muhammad's farewell pilgrimage; Guillaume, *Muhammad*, p. 649; Tabari, *History*, vol. 9, pp. 106 f.

[257] Nöldeke and Schwally, *GQ*, vol. 1, pp. 227 f.

[258] This verse was said to have been revealed during Muhammad's farewell pilgrimage in 10 AH; *Sahih Bukhari*, vol. 6, p. 103; *Sahih Muslim*, vol. 4, p. 1551.

[259] See Appendix D, p. 390.

[260] See p. 257, above.

[261] Cf. *ECMD*, p. 451.

[262] And not the Qur'an.

[263] Cf. *Sahih Bukhari*, vol. 6, p. 102; *ECMD*, p. 499.

[264] This remark is similar to statements made concerning Muhammad; cf. Qur'an 21:3, 7f; 25:8f, 22.

[265] See p. 3, n. 32, above.

[266] *Sahih Bukhari*, vol. 9, p. 290; *Sahih Muslim*, vol. 4, p. 1257.

[267] See p. 177, n. 148.

[268] See Appendix D, p. 390.

[269] It may have been intended that Muslims celebrate this feast, not because of Jesus' resurrection, but because of this distorted version of the Eucharist.

[270] See Appendix D, p. 390.

[271] Jeffery, *Vocabulary*, p. 135.

[272] Ibid., p. 165.

[273] Ibid., pp. 255 f.

[274] See Appendix F, pp. 416 f.

[275] Ibrahim was said to have been 16 (Ibn Sa`d, *Classes*, vol. 1, 1, pp. 158 f) or 18 months old (Ibid., p. 162). He is also said to have died in Rabi` I, 10 AH, i.e. the 109th month (Ibid., p. 163). A solar eclipse occurred (cf. *Sahih Bukhari*, vol. 2, p. 84; vol. 8, p. 140) on the 27th of January, 632 AD (115th month); Buhl, *Muhammad*, p. 316, n. 145.

[276] Guillaume, *Muhammad*, pp. 649 f; Ibn Sa`d, *Classes*, vol. 2, 1, pp. 213 f; Tabari, *History*, vol. 9, pp. 109 f; Wellhausen, *Medina*, pp. 421 f.

[277] His father Zayd b. Haritha was killed at Mu'ta; see p. 264, above. Many of the Muslims are said to have been dissatisfied with Muhammad's appointment of Usama, who was only 19 years old at the time.

[278] Guillaume, *Muhammad*, pp. 652, 678; Ibn Sa`d, *Classes*, vol. 2, 1, pp. 235 f; Tabari, *History*, vol. 9, pp. 163 f; Wellhausen, *Medina*, pp. 433 f.

[279] Ibn Sa`d, *Classes*, vol. 2, 2, p. 289; Tabari, *History*, vol. 9, p. 170.

[280] Guillaume, *Muhammad*, p. 680; Ibn Sa`d, *Classes*, vol. 2, pp. 292 f; Tabari, *History*, vol. 9, pp. 177 f.

[281] Ibn Sa`d, *Classes*, vol. 2, 2, pp. 261 f; *Sahih Bukhari*, vol. 5, p. 510; vol. 7, pp. 423, 433; *Sahih Muslim*, vol. 3, pp. 1195 f.

[282] Ibn Sa`d, *Classes*, vol. 2, 2, pp. 261 f; *Sahih Bukhari*, vol. 5, p. 511.

[283] See p. 128, n. 208, above. Cf. Ibn Sa`d, *Classes*, vol. 2, 2, pp. 298 f.

[284] Ibn Sa`d, *Classes*, vol. 2, 2, pp. 299 f; *Sahih Bukhari*, vol. 1, p. 255; vol. 2, p. 232; vol. 4, p. 439; vol. 5, p. 516; *Sahih Muslim*, vol. 1, pp. 268 f.

[285] Ibn Sa`d, *Classes*, vol. 2, 2, pp. 301 f; Tabari, *History*, vol. 9, pp. 174 f; *Sahih Bukhari*, vol. 7, p. 389; vol. 9, p. 346; *Sahih Muslim*, vol. 3, p. 870. In another tradition (Ibn Sa`d, *Classes*, vol. 2, 2, p. 303) `Ali is said to have written what Muhammad dictated about prayers, "zakat" and slaves.

[286] Ibn Sa`d, *Classes*, vol. 2, 2, pp. 308 f; *Sahih Bukhari*, vol. 8, p. 201; *Sahih Muslim*, vol. 4, p. 1306.

[287] Ibn Sa`d, *Classes*, vol. 2, 2, pp. 310 f.

[288] Muhammad was thus said to have been a martyr (Ibn Sa`d, *Classes*, vol. 2, 2, p. 252); see n. 121, above.

[289] Or on Ali's lap; Ibn Sa`d, *Classes*, vol. 2, 2, pp. 327 f.

[290] Ibn Sa`d, *Classes*, vol. 2, 2, pp. 329 f.

[291] Guillaume, *Muhammad*, pp. 682 f; Ibn Sa`d, *Classes*, vol. 2, 2, pp. 332 f; Tabari, History, vol. 9, p. 184.

[292] Ibn Sa`d, *Classes*, vol. 2, 2, p. 339. Cf. Nöldeke and Schwally, *GQ*, vol. 2, p. 83, n. 1; *ECMD*, pp. x, 444.

[293] Guillaume, *Muhammad*, p. 683; Ibn Sa`d, *Classes*, vol. 2, 2, pp. 333 f; Tabari, *History*, vol. 9, pp. 184 f. Some Western scholars, in finding it hard to believe that `Umar could have forgotten such a verse, maintain that this verse

and others similar to it were added to the Qur'an after Muhammad's death; cf. Nöldeke and Schwally, *GQ*, vol. 2, pp. 82 f.

[294] They waited until his abdomen had swollen (Ibn Sa`d, *Classes*, vol. 2, 2, p. 338) and his nails had turned green (Ibid., p. 342). Cf. *ECMD*, p. 528, n. 48.

[295] Cf. Guillaume, *Muhammad*, p. 688; Tabari, *History*, vol. 9, p. 203 for `A'isha's remarks about this.

[296] Or Tuesday; Ibn Sa`d, *Classes*, vol. 2, 2, pp. 341, 380 f. On Tuesday, or three days after his death; Tabari, *History*, vol. 9, p. 202. In the middle of the night Wednesday; Guillaume, *Muhammad*, p. 688; Tabari, *History*, vol. 9, p. 204

[297] Guillaume, *Muhammad*, p. 688: Ibn Sa`d, *Classes*, vol. 2, 2, p. 380; Tabari, *History*, vol. 9, p. 209.

[298] Ibn Sa`d, *Classes*, vol. 2, 2, pp. 364 f.

[299] Or 60 or 65 years old; Ibn Sa`d, *Classes*, vol. 2, 2, pp. 383 f; Tabari, *History*, vol. 9, p. 206.

[300] Guillaume, *Muhammad*, pp. 678 f; Ibn Sa`d, *Classes*, vol. 2, 2, pp. 239 f; Tabari, *History*, vol. 9, pp. 162 f; Wellhausen, *Medina*, p. 281.

[301] Wellhausen, *Medina*, p. 417.

[302] Ibid., p. 427.

[303] See nn. 108, 242 and 271, above.

[304] See n. 272, above.

[305] See, nn. 109, 273.

[306] Islamic hadith claim that Muhammad knew Ethiopic; see p. 136, n. 306, above.

[307] See p. 202, above.

[308] See p. 257, above.

[309] See p. 263, above.

[310] See pp. 265 f , above.

[311] See p. 275, above.

[312] Cf. Wellhausen, *Medina*, p. 281.

[313] Later Islamic traditions incredibly depict many of the pagans, Jews and Christians who were attacked as having planned offensives against Muhammad. Typically, however, the Islamic reports often show that the Muslims seized the livestock of those they came across, even after they were unable to find any of the alleged enemy forces.

[314] See p. 246, above.

[315] See p. 252, above.

[316] See p. 262, above.

[317] See p. 270, above.

The Qur'an

Islamic traditions fairly consistently agree with one another in showing that at the time of Muhammad's death, the Qur'an had not been collected into a single volume. There is one hadith, however, which indicates that while Muhammad was still living, Zayd b. Thabit (with others) followed Muhammad's orders in collecting verses of the Qur'an (revealed at various times) into specific suras.[1]

Some Islamic traditions claim that a major collection of the Qur'an was carried out (in about 11-12 AH)[2] during the caliphate of Abu Bakr. Accordingly, `Umar is said to have informed Abu Bakr of the number of Qur'an reciters who had been killed in the battle of Yamama (against Musaylima) and suggested that the Qur'an be collected before most of it be lost. After asking `Umar how he was to accomplish something even Muhammad had not, Abu Bakr appointed one of Muhammad's former secretaries, the Ansar Zayd b. Thabit, to collect the Qur'an. Zayd is then said to have begun collecting verses of the Qur'an from notes, stones, palm stalks, shoulder bones, rib bones, pieces of leather, small boards and the memories of men. Zayd is only said to have been able to find Qur'an 9:129f with Khuzayma or Abu Khuzayma, and he then added these verses to the end of the that sura. This manuscript of the Qur'an was then passed from Abu Bakr to `Umar to Hafsa (`Umar's daughter), who had been the wife of Muhammad.[3] (There are also other versions of traditions about this collection of the Qur'an.)[4]

Western scholars have shown that this and similar traditions contain serious flaws: Islamic sources report that Muslim soldiers seem to have known little of the Qur'an,[5] and also only two Muslims listed among the casualties at Yamama seem to have been Qur'an reciters[6] - One Western scholar thinks that the period of Abu Bakr's reign was too short to have seen this work through and justifiably argues that `Umar may have actually begun the project in his caliphate[7] - Although the fear of most of the Qur'an being lost with its reciters is given as the reason for beginning its collection, Zayd is shown as having relied primarily on written sources[8] - The statement that this "collected" Qur'an codex was given to Abu Bakr then `Umar and then Hafsa seems to indicate that it was considered to be private, rather than public property.[9]

Islamic traditions also maintain that at least two witnesses were required for Zayd to add any verse to this collection.[10] `Umar is said to have brought Zayd the famous verse about stoning for adulterers, but this verse appears to have been rejected because he did not have a second witness for it.[11]

Strangely enough, at the time of Muhammad's death the only Muslims who are said to have possessed the entire Qur'an were all Ansars, and not of the Quraysh.[12] Muhammad is reported to have said that the Qur'an be learned from four people, who are generally given as: Ibn Mas`ud, Ubayy b. Ka`b, Salim, and Mu'adh b. Jabal.[13]

It appears that a number of personal codices of the Qur'an came into public use rather early on,[14] even though practically nothing is known of either their origins, or of how well they corresponded with the alleged codex that Zayd compiled and edited for Abu Bakr.[15] Two of the Qur'an codices, which appear to have become fairly well known were those of Ibn Mas`ud[16] and Ubayy b. Ka`b.[17] With respect to `Uthman's edition of the Qur'an, the codex of Ibn Mas`ud is said to have had quite a few variants,[18] and the suras 1, 113 and 114 are said to have been missing from it.[19] The Qur'an manuscript of Ubayy b. Ka`b also seems to have varied from both the `Uthmanic text and Ibn Mas`ud's,[20] and it is known to have contained two extra suras.[21]

The next collection of the Qur'an is said to have taken place during the caliphate of `Uthman in about 30 AH.[22] The Muslims of Damascus and Iraq are said to have recited the Qur'an differently from each other when they were fighting to conquer Armenia and Azerbaijan. Hudhayfa b. al-Yaman is said to have noticed this and asked `Uthman to take action to correct the problem. `Uthman is then said to have sent for the codex of Hafsa, and appointed Zayd b. Thabit, `Abdullah b. al-Zubayr, Sa`id b. al-`As and `Abdulrahman b. Harith to copy the codex. In case of differences of opinion on the text, it was to be written in the dialect of the Quraysh. It is said that Zayd was only able to find Qur'an 33:23 with Khuzayma. Hafsa's manuscript was then reportedly returned to her, and `Uthman sent copies out to other provinces (cities) commanding that all other Qur'an codices be destroyed.[23] (There are also other versions of traditions concerning this collection.)[24]

Even other hadith hint that there was some disunity about which version of the Qur'an was to be recited in early Islam,[25] and it appears that the Qur'an probably was collected and standardized in the time of `Uthman's caliphate.[26] Problems with this tradition, however, are that the instructions about using the dialect of the Quraysh do not seem to have been accurate,[27] the Qur'an codex of Hafsa was later destroyed by Marwan,[28] and discrepancies between the `Uthmanic text and the codices of Hafsa and Zayd are given in later Islamic works.[29]

Some of the pre-`Uthmanic Qur'an codices seem to have escaped the systematic destruction ordered by `Uthman, and copies based on the manuscripts of Ibn Mas`ud[30] and Ubayy b. Ka`b[31] were reportedly seen centuries later. Various Islamic traditions claim that many verses which once existed were no longer found in the text standardized under `Uthman,[32] and some hadith contend that whole suras had disappeared from the Qur'an.[33] Although some problems may have been solved by `Uthman's standardization, others were not, as even his text of the Qur'an is said to have contained errors.[34]

As the earliest extant manuscripts of the Qur'an clearly show,[35] the old texts were deficient of vowel pointings and diacritical marks (so some characters represented more than one consonant).[36] In Arabic, a purely consonantal text not only means that some verbs could have been read as either actives or passives, but in the absence of diacritical marks, masculine or feminine readings could have also been made.[37] Thus, those who read the oldest texts of the Qur'an *should* have first been made familiar with the text from oral sources.

Most traditions seem to agree that `Uthman had four copies of the standardized text of the Qur'an made.[38] It is reported that one was kept at Medina, and the others were sent to Mecca, Syria and Kufa.[39] Nevertheless, owing apparently to the ambiguities of the early Arabic scripts, a number of variant readings began to evolve in the cities of Medina, Mecca, Damascus, Kufa and Basra.[40]

In about the beginning of the 8th century AD, al-Hajjaj b. Yusuf, a governor in Iraq, is said to have tried to make the text of the Qur'an more uniform by more or less introducing the usage of diacritical marks and vowel pointing.[41] However, these improvements were neither immediate nor universal, since such additions to Qur'an codices can be shown to have been gradual.[42]

In the 9th century AD, Ibn Mujahid seems to have tried to further standardize the text of the Qur'an by dictating that only the readings of seven 2nd century AH scholars[43] were (essentially) orthodox.[44] The punishment incurred by those who continued to use the old readings of the Qur'an, even in Ibn Mujahid's day, was severe.[45]

Structurally, the usage of the "basmala" in the text of the Qur'an is thought to date from Muhammad,[46] and the mysterious letters preceding some suras may also date from him.[47] The present order of the suras in the Qur'an may have been determined in 'Uthman's day,[48] but the sura titles still do not seem to have been standard even as late as the 10th century AD.[49] The division of the Qur'an into sets of five or ten verses may date from the early 8th century,[50] and the division of the text into sevenths (for control purposes) seems to have been introduced by al-Hajjaj.[51] Most of the old Qur'an codices found in museums today are in Kufic script,[52] which is thought to date from about 790 AD.[53] The oldest scripts for the Qur'an are said to be Ma'il or Mashq.[54]

Later Islamic scholars worked on constructing chronological sura orderings,[55] they tried to research the etymologies of foreign vocabulary in the Qur'an,[56] and attempted to discover the meanings of strange words in the text.[57] Some traditions also list the number of verses,[58] words[59] and letters[60] of the Qur'an.

In the 1930's a group of Western scholars was working towards publishing the first critical edition of the text of the Qur'an.[61] However, after many setbacks, the project was more or less discontinued.[62]

Notes:

[1] Suyuti, *El-Itkan*, vol. 1, p. 137. Another tradition in this same reference states that when Muhammad died, all the verses of the Qur'an had been written, but the Qur'an had not been collected, and the suras had not been arranged.

[2] Nöldeke and Schwally, *GQ*, vol. 2, p. 12.

[3] *Sahih Bukhari*, vol. 6, pp. 477 f; vol. 9, pp. 228 f; Dodge, *Fihrist*, vol. 1, pp. 47 f; Suyuti, *El-Itkan*, vol. 1, pp. 137 f; Nöldeke and Schwally, *GQ*, vol. 2, pp. 11 f; Watt and Bell, *Introduction*, pp. 40 f; Watt, *Religionen*, pp. 176 f.

[4] See Nöldeke and Schwally, *GQ*, vol. 2, pp. 15 f. Another set of traditions, by which `Ali is said to have collected the Qur'an after the death of Muhammad (e.g. Ibn Sa`d, vol. 2, 2, pp. 435 f), is generally viewed as being the innovation of later Islamic traditionists; Schwally, *GQ*, vol. 2, pp. 8 f.

[5] Schwally, *GQ*, vol. 2, pp. 7 f, who also references Caetani, mentions some of these (trans. and condensed): After battle near Qadisiya `Umar instructed Sa`d b. Waqqas to divide the remainder of the spoils among the bearers [transmitters] of the Qur'an. When `Amr b. Ma`dikarib was asked about his knowledge of the Qur'an, he replied: "I converted to Islam in Yemen, but I was always in battles later and therefore did not have time to memorize the Qur'an." When Bishr b. Rabi`a (from Ta`if) was asked, he only recited the basmala. In the battle of Yamama, when one leader named the Ansar "the people of the Cow [Qur'an 2] sura," a soldier of the Tayyi' said that he had not memorized any verse of that sura. Aws b. Khalid, an esteemed person among the Tayyi', was beaten to death by a commissioner of the Caliph `Umar, because he could not recite any part of the Qur'an.

[6] Ibid., vol. 2, p. 20; cf. Watt and Bell, *Introduction*, p. 41, n. 3.

[7] Schwally shows that Abu Bakr died about 15 months after the battle of Yamama; Nöldeke and Schwally, *GQ*, vol. 2, p. 19; cf. Suyuti, *El-Itkan*, vol. 1, p. 139; Watt and Bell, *Introduction*, p. 41.

[8] Ibid., p. 21. Watt and Bell, *Introduction*, p. 41. Suyuti, *El-Itkan*, vol. 1, pp. 143 f, shows a tradition in which the claim is made that the collection of the Qur'an in the reign of Abu Bakr was based on oral sources, whereas the collection in the time of `Uthman was made using written sources. The last two verses of Qur'an 9 are said to have been received from Khuzayma in written form; Suyuti, *El-Itkan*, vol. 1, p. 140. See also n. 1, above.

[9] Nöldeke and Schwally, *GQ*, vol. 2, pp. 19, 21. Cf. Watt and Bell, *Introduction*, p. 41.

[10] Suyuti, *El-Itkan*, vol. 1, pp. 139 f.

[11] However, Ubayy b. Ka`b is also reported to have claimed that the verse on stoning used to be found in Qur'an 33; Suyuti, *El-Itkan*, vol. 2, p. 66. See pp. 250 f, for more about this verse. Cf. Watt and Bell, *Introduction*, p. 41.

[12] *Sahih Muslim*, vol. 4, p. 1313; Ibn Sa`d, *Classes*, vol. 2, 2, pp. 457 f. This last source claims that Ibn Mas`ud had only learned 90 suras up until the time of Muhammad's death.

[13] Cf. *Sahih Bukhari*, vol. 5, pp. 70 f; *Sahih Muslim*, vol. 4, p. 1312; Suyuti, *El-Itkan*, p. 167.

[14] See Jeffery, *Materials*, pp. 14 f.

[15] See Ibid., pp. 212 f, for information on Hafsa's codex, and the same reference, pp. 223 f, about Zayd b. Thabit's personal Qur'an codex. Based on the data given, these codices did not correspond very well with each other.

[16] For biographical information see: *Sahih Bukhari*, vol. 5, pp. 71 f; *Sahih Muslim*, vol. 4, pp. 1311 f; Ibn Sa`d, *Classes*, vol. 2, 2, pp. 441 f; Nöldeke and Schwally, *GQ*, vol. 2, p. 28.

[17] For biographical information see: *Sahih Bukhari*, vol. 5, pp. 96 f; *Sahih Muslim*, vol. 4, pp. 1313 f; Ibn Sa`d, *Classes*, vol. 2, 2, pp. 440 f; Nöldeke and Schwally, *GQ*, vol. 2, p. 28.

[18] See Jeffery, *Materials*, pp. 20 f; Schwally, *GQ*, vol. 2, pp. 39 f; Bergsträsser, *GQ*, vol. 3, pp. 60 f; Dodge, *Fihrist*, vol. 1, pp. 53 f. Cf. Watt and Bell, *Introduction*, pp. 45 f.

[19] *Sahih Bukhari*, vol. 6, p. 472; Suyuti, *El-Itkan*, vol. 1, pp. 153, 188; Jeffery, *Materials*, p. 21.

[20] See Jeffery, *Materials*, pp. 114 f; Schwally, *GQ*, vol. 2, pp. 30 f; Bergsträsser, *GQ*, vol. 3, pp. 83 f; Dodge, *Fihrist*, vol. 1, pp. 58 f.

[21] Suyuti, *El-Itkan*, vol. 1, pp. 153 f; Jeffery, *Materials*, pp. 180 f; Schwally, *GQ*, vol. 2, pp. 34 f.

[22] Schwally, *GQ*, vol. 2, p. 49.*Sahih Bukhari*, vol. 6, pp. 477 f; vol. 9, pp. 228 f; Dodge, *Fihrist*, vol. 1, pp. 47 f; Suyuti, *El-Itkan*, vol. 1, pp. 137 f; Nöldeke and Schwally, *GQ*, vol. 2, pp. 11 f; Watt and Bell, *Introduction*, pp. 40 f; Watt, *Religionen*, pp. 176 f.

[23] *Sahih Bukhari*, vol. 6, pp. 478 f; Dodge, *Fihrist*, vol. 1, pp. 48 f; Suyuti, *El-Itkan*, vol. 1, pp. 141 f; Nöldeke and Schwally, *GQ*, vol. 2, pp. 47 f; Watt and Bell, *Introduction*, pp. 42 f; Watt, *Religionen*, pp. 178 f.

[24] Cf. Nöldeke and Schwally, *GQ*, vol. 2, pp. 50 f.

[25] Cf. *Sahih Bukhari*, vol. 4, p. 521; vol. 9, p. 345.

[26] Nöldeke and Schwally, *GQ*, vol. 2, pp. 49 f; Watt, *Religionen*, p. 179.

[27] Nöldeke and Schwally, *GQ*, vol. 2, pp. 57 f; *EI²*, s.v. "Kur'an," p. 405. Cf. Nöldeke, "Qur'an," p. 24.

[28] Marwan was afraid that some would later be in doubt (about the text of the Qur'an). Jeffery, *Materials*, pp. 212 f; Watt and Bell, *Introduction*, p. 43; Watt, *Religionen*, p. 179.

[29] See n. 15, above.

[30] Dodge, *Fihrist*, vol. 1, pp. 53 f.

[31] Ibid., vol. 1, pp. 58 f.

[32] See Nöldeke and Schwally, *GQ*, vol. 2, pp. 234 f, for general discussions on Islamic traditions which allegedly give the texts of some missing passages. See also Suyuti, *El-Itkan*, vol. 2, pp. 65 f, for a tradition in which 'A'isha claims that Qur'an 33 contained 200 verses when Muhammad was still living, but that it only had as many as at present (?) after 'Uthman's edition was made. In another hadith (Ibid., vol. 2, p. 66) a man tells Ubayy b. Ka'b that Qur'an 33 has 72 or 73 verses, and Ubayy replies that this sura used to contain the verse about stoning (for adulterers) and was once as long as Qur'an 2 (286 verses).

[33] See *Sahih Muslim*, vol. 2, pp. 500 f. Cf. *Sahih Bukhari*, vol. 8, pp. 296 f. A hadith in Suyuti, *El-Itkan*, vol. 2, p. 65, quotes Ibn 'Umar as having said that no one was to claim he possessed the entire Qur'an, since much of it was gone. See also the references to n. 21, above.

[34] 'Uthman himself is reported to have found fallacious expressions in the completed manuscripts he had standardized and is quoted as having said that nothing should be changed as the Arabs would correct everything with their tongues. This tradition and others showing a number of alleged mistakes which were made in transcribing 'Uthman's standardized text of the Qur'an are given by Bergsträsser in *GQ*, vol. 3, pp. 1 f. Ubayy b. Ka'b is reported to have made some minor corrections to 'Uthman's text; Suyuti, *El-Itkan*, vol. 1, p. 509. Cf.

the text discrepancies of the `Uthmanic text of the Qur'an in *GQ*, vol. 3, pp. 26 f, and the Lewis Palimpsest of the Qur'an, as given in *GQ*, vol. 3, pp. 53 f, 97 f.

[35] See the photographic plates after p. 274 in *GQ*, vol. 3; and also the photograph in Campbell, *Qur'an*, p. 125.

[36] Bergsträsser, *GQ*, vol. 3, pp. 251 f; cf. Nöldeke, "Qur'an", p. 26; Watt and Bell, *Introduction*, pp. 47 f; Watt, *Religionen*, p. 182; *EI²*, s.v. "Kur'an," pp. 408 f.

[37] See Campbell, *Qur'an*, pp. 126 f; *EI²*, s.v. "Kur'an," p. 408.

[38] Suyuti, *El-Itkan*, vol. 1, pp. 143 f. He also gives a tradition whereby seven copies were said to have been made.

[39] Jeffery, *Materials*, p. 8. Cf. Al-Kindi in *ECMD*, p. 457; Nöldeke, "Qur'an," p. 23.

[40] Bergsträsser, *GQ*, vol. 3, pp. 9 f; *EI²*, s.v. "Kur'an," p. 408. In the first reference a listing of various readings is given.

[41] See Jeffery in *ECMD*, p. 116, n. 56. Al-Kindi, (*ECMD*, p. 458) claims that al-Hajjaj made a standard text of the Qur'an and had copies made and sent them to Egypt, Syria, Medina, Mecca, Kufa and Basra. Al-Kindi states that al-Hajjaj then destroyed all the other Qur'an codices available to him. Al-Hajjaj is well known for having despised the Qur'an text of Ibn Mas`ud; *Sunan Abu Dawud*, vol. 3, p. 1303.

[42] Watt and Bell, *Introduction*, p. 48.

[43] For listings of their names, see Bergsträsser, *GQ*, vol. 3, pp. 160 f; Jeffery, *Materials*, p. 1, n. 4; Watt and Bell, *Introduction*, p. 49; Watt, *Religionen*, p. 183; *EI²*, s.v. "Kur'an," p. 409.

[44] Dodge, *Fihrist*, vol. 1, p. 70; Bergsträsser, *GQ*, vol. 3, pp. 116 f; Jeffery, *Materials*, p. 1; Watt and Bell, *Introduction*, pp. 48 f; Watt, *Religionen*, p. 183; *EI²*, s.v. "Kur'an," pp. 408 f. See also p. 325, below.

[45] For a short biography of Ibn Shanabudh and some of the old readings used by him, see: Dodge, *Fihrist*, vol. 1, pp. 70 f. Cf. Jeffery, *Materials*, p. 1; Watt and Bell, *Introduction*, p. 49; *EI²*, s.v. "Kur'an," pp. 408 f.

[46] Nöldeke and Schwally, *GQ*, vol. 2, pp. 79 f; Watt and Bell, *Introduction*, p. 60.

[47] This view is somewhat speculative, however. See: Nöldeke and Schwally, *GQ*, vol. 2, pp. 68 f; Watt and Bell *Introduction*, pp. 61 f.

[48] Nöldeke and Schwally, *GQ*, vol. 2, pp. 63 f.

[49] The sura listings given in Dodge, *Fihrist*, vol. 1, pp. 49 f, are indicative of this.

[50] Bergstrasser, *GQ*, vol. 3, p. 258.

[51] Ibid., vol. 3, pp. 260 f; Jeffery in *ECMD*, p. 116, n. 56.

[52] Bergstrasser, *GQ*, vol. 3, p. 251.

[53] In an unpublished paper, J.H. Smith cites Lings and Safadi, *The Qur'an, A Catalogue... of Qur'an Manuscripts*, (1976), pp. 12 f, 17.

[54] In an unpublished papaer, J.H. Smith references Lings and Safadi, *The Qur'an, A Catalogue... of Qur'an Manuscripts*, p. 11 and Gilchrist, *Jam al-Qur'an*, pp. 144 f.

[55] Dodge, *Fihrist*, vol. 1, pp 49 f; Suyuti, *El-Itkan*, vol. 1, pp. 3 f.

[56] Suyuti, *El-Itkan*, vol. 1, 365 f. Cf. Margoliouth, "Additions," *JRAS*, (1939), p. 53.

[57] Suyuti, *El-Itkan*, vol. 1, pp. 273 f, 307 f.

[58] Ibid., vol. 1, pp. 157 f.

[59] Ibid., vol. 1, 164, gives traditions showing the Qur'an to contain 77934, 77437 or 77277 words. Dodge, *Fihrist*, vol. 1, p. 62 has a tradition stating that the Qur'an had 77439 words.

[60] Suyuti, *El-Itkan*, p. 157, gives a tradition which claims there are 323,671 letters in the Qur'an. Dodge, *Fihrist*, vol. 1, p. 63, presents hadith stating that there are 323,015 or 321,530 letters in the Qur'an. Suyuti, *El-Itkan*, p. 165, gives a hadith quoting `Umar as having said that the Qur'an contained 1,027,000 letters (including what had allegedly been abrogated).

[61] *GQ*, vol. 3, p. 274; Jeffery, *Materials*, pp. vii f. Some of the preliminary works for this project were *GQ*, vol. 3, (1938); Jeffery's *Materials*, (1937) and Spitaler's "Die Verszählung des Koran", (1935).

[62] See Jeffery's comments in his *The Qur'an as Scripture*, p. 103.

Islamic Tradition

As opposed to the evidence available on the development of the Qur'an, there are almost no sources describing the evolution of traditions after Muhammad's death.[1]

It appears that Qur'anic insufficiencies[2] led Muslims to begin collecting and classifying an enormous amount of hadith. Although there intially appears to have been a great interest in the traditional battle accounts of early Islam,[3] the need for certain doctrinal hadith gradually made itself felt.

Perhaps one of the earliest developments of Islamic doctrine in the hadith can be traced with respect to the "shahada," (or short creed) in which a Muslim bears witness to the uniqueness of Allah and the divine messengership of Muhammad. Archaeologically, Muhammad's name has not been found in any datable religious or official formulations much earlier than 690 AD,[4] and the verb for bearing witness only seems to appear in archaeological finds from the period of the `Abbasids.[5] Nevertheless, one would expect that a Monotheistic creed was used by Muslims at first, such as those which can be found in the Qur'an (e.g. sura 112) or implied in hadith.[6] Muhammad's name was certainly added to such formulations later, since it does not appear in any of the Qur'anic "creeds," but rather, in some canonical traditions.[7]

The doctrine of the famous "five pillars" of Islam,[8] as well as the institution of the five daily prayers,[9] are also enjoined in traditions, but not in the Qur'an.

Technically, each Islamic tradition is supposed to be accompanied by the names of its transmitters, an "isnad," back to an original source. Although it appears that the first few generations of Islamic scholars did not usually keep "isnads,"[10] their usage became very important when the collections of canonical traditions were being compiled. Thus, a great number of isnads were no doubt tampered with or invented altogether, and the standard Islamic practice of basing the reliability of a tradition simply on the "soundness" of its "isnad" has often caused difficulties.[11]

In the 3rd Islamic century, the first collections of the canonical hadith seem to have been compiled by the Sunnis,[12] and the collections of the Shiites appear to have followed about a century later.[13]

Indeed, many traditions in their present forms are tainted with the political overtones of early Islam, so that the evident biases in favor of Abu Bakr, `Umar, `Uthman, `Ali or the `Abbasids (Ibn `Abbas) imply that their various claims to the caliphate were somehow justified.

Even in the case of Muhammad, traditions seem to have been invented to support his claims to prophethood. Whereas the Qur'an shows that Muhammad did not have "signs" or miracles to confirm his ministry, a number of traditions were obviously developed to depict him as a performer of miracles.[14] Muhammad is also not referred to in the Qur'an as being a future intercessor for his followers, but quite a few later hadith present him as an intercessor for Muslims at the Judgment.[15]

Conversely, however, some later (i.e. post-traditional) Muslim theologians became rather successful in establishing and propagating doctrines which are in direct opposition to the Qur'an. The Qur'an and hadith show, for example, that Muhammad had sins and was commanded to pray for forgiveness (cf. e.g., 47:21), but later Islamic theologians declared that Muhammad was sinless.[16] Moreover, the Qur'an (93:7)[17] canonical hadith[18] and *Sira* traditions[19] show that Muhammad had probably been a pagan earlier, but dissatisfied Muslim theologians decreed that he had never been a polytheist.[20]

Some traditions claim that Muhammad also made prophecies, and although such hadith about specific persons seem to have been influenced by later Islamic political issues, others do appear to have been relatively old. In one example, Muhammad is reported to have said that "the Hour" (or end of the world) would come shortly after his death.[21] When Muhammad was asked about this on other occasions, he reportedly replied that no one would be living 100 years after his death.[22] Although this provision of a time period is somewhat out of keeping with the testimony of the Qur'an (cf. 36:48), the later modifications made to this hadith[23] (some of which claim that Muhammad had only said that none of his peers would be alive 100 years from then)[24] indicate that this tradition must really date from the first 100 years of Islam. Another hadith claims that Muhammad had said that when the then-reigning Byzantine emperor died, there would be no emperor after him.[25] But since Heraclius was indeed succeeded (by many generations of Byzantine emperors), this tradition must have at least predated Heraclius' death, which was in 641 AD. Other prophecies of Muhammad are also given in the canonical traditions.[26]

Unfortunately, however, many of Islamic traditions have proven themselves to be so unreliable[27] that more than a few Western scholars have considered practically all of them to be later fabrications.[28]

Indeed, even in cases where Islamic scholars could not have helped but known that the traditions they were using were not accurate, some appear to have thought a greater good would come by propogating them. One example of this is a famous tradition in which `Umar is said to have brought Hisham b. Hakim to Muhammad because Hisham had been reciting Qur'an 25 differently than he (`Umar) had learned it. Muhammad then reportedly listened to both recite the passage in dispute, replied that both versions were correct and said that the Qur'an had been revealed in seven different "letters" (modes, ways).[29] Although some Muslim scholars later determined that Muhammad's reply could not have meant seven dialects,[30] many evidently had problems with trying to figure out exactly what was meant by the term for "letters."[31] Whatever differences may have been involved though, it is almost certain that `Uthman's standardization made them uniform.[32] Nevertheless, the gradual evolution of various readings for his text seems to have introduced new discrepancies, and Ibn Mujahid (d. 935 AD) then used this tradition as a justification for the declaration that only seven readings of `Uthman's text were legitmate.[33]

Although there are Islamic hadith to discourage Muslims from consulting the People of the Book in religious questions, other hadith do exist which carry on the tradition of either borrowing from the structure of a Bible passage or of even modifying Biblical expressions and then claiming them for Islam.[34] Perhaps the epitome of this process can be seen in a tradition which has Muhammad recite an altered version of the Lord's Prayer.[35]

Notes:

[1] Guillaume, *Traditions*, p. 19, doubts a tradition given by Muir, in which 'Umar II (d. 720 AD) is said to have ordered the collection of hadith.

[2] The Qur'an can hardly be used as a historical document as the Bible can be and is (e.g. by archaeologists). Moreover, although the Qur'an mentions prayer and ablution, for instance, it does not describe exactly how these are to be performed. See also p. 15, above.

[3] See p. 15, above.

[4] Nevo, "Prehistory," *JSAI*, 17 (1994), pp. 109 f.

[5] Ibid., pp. 117 f.

[6] *Sahih Muslim*, vol. 1, p. 19.

[7] *Sahih Bukhari*, vol. 1, p. 17; *Sahih Muslim*, vol. 1, pp. 11 f.

[8] *Sahih Bukhari*, vol. 1, p. 17; *Sahih Muslim*, vol. 1, pp. 9 f.

[9] See p. 41, above.

[10] See p. 15, above.

[11] Schwally, *GQ*, vol. 2, p. 146; Juynboll, *Authenticity*, p. 139: "... only if the content of a tradition with a sound *isnad* was in flagrant contradiction to the Qur'an, it was rejected; if the content could in any way be interpreted so that it harmonized with the Qur'an and other traditions, it was left alone." Jeffery, *Materials*, p. viii, (in speaking of the "isnads" used by Ibn Abu Dawud in *Kitab al-Masahif*): "The assistance of Muslim savants in this matter was not very helpful for we could not overcome the principle that every *isnad* that led to a statement at variance with orthodoxy was ipso facto condemned."

[12] There are six collections of canonical hadith for the Sunnis, which are often referred to by the names of their editors: Bukhari (d. 870 AD), Muslim (d. 875 AD), Abu Dawud (d. 888 AD), al-Tirmidhi (d. 892 AD), al-Nasa'i (d. 915), and Ibn Maja (d. 886 AD); as shown in *SEI*, p. 119.

[13] The Shiites also have six collections of canonical hadith, the earliest of which is the *al-Kafi* of Muhammad b. Ya`qub (d. 939 AD). The basic difference between the Sunni and Shiite collections is that the Shiites place more value on the traditions of `Ali and those who thought he should have been the first caliph after Muhammad's death; *SEI*, p. 120.

[14] See *ECMD*, p. 724.

[15] Ibid., p. 722.

[16] Ibid., p. 723.

[17] The pagan oaths at the beginning of many of the earliest suras of the Qur'an also imply this.

[18] See the traditional commentary to Qur'an 74:1-5 in *Sahih Bukhari*, vol. 6, pp. 452 f.

[19] See e.g. pp. 26 and 28, above.

[20] Cf. *ECMD*, pp. 723 f.

[21] *Sahih Bukhari*, vol. 8, pp. 337 f.

[22] *Sahih Muslim*, vol. 4, p. 1348 (6162, 6165)

[23] Ibid.

[24] *Sahih Bukhari*, vol. 1, pp. 87, 315.

[25] *Sahih Bukhari*, vol. 4, pp. 166, 524; *Sahih Muslim*, vol. 4, p. 1509.

[26] *Sahih Muslim*, vol. 4, pp. 1506 f.

[27] See Crone, *Trade*, pp. 217 f, 224 f.

[28] Schwally's views as given here (*GQ*, vol. 2, p. 146) are shared by others (cf. Watt in Tabari, *History*, vol. 6, pp. xvii f), who reject not just juristic hadith, but also almost the whole body of Islamic tradition (trans.): "Thereby (it) should not be denied that in the wilderness of error and lies trustworthy traditions could be found. However, from the outset, and until proven to the contrary, every juristic hadith is to be considered (a) forgery."

[29] *Sahih Bukhari*, vol. 3, p. 355, vol. 6, pp. 482 f; *Sahih Muslim*, vol. 2, pp. 389 f.

[30] 'Umar and Hashim were from the same tribe; Suyuti, *El-Itkan*, vol. 1, p. 112; cf. Nöldeke and Schwally, *GQ*, vol. 1, p. 51.

[31] Suyuti, *El-Itkan*, vol. 1, pp. 114 f, gives 35 different interpretations for what this word may have meant.

[32] That was supposedly the purpose for having made the standardization in the first place. Cf. Ibid., p. 143.

[33] Watt and Bell, *Introduction*, pp. 48 f; Watt, *Religionen*, p. 183; *EI²*, s.v. "Kur'an," pp. 408 f.

[34]

Ps. 103:2a	*Sahih Bukhari*, vol. 8, p. 252	
Is. 42:1-7	*Sahih Bukhari*, vol. 3, p. 189	
	vol. 4, p. 345	
Mt. 6:3	*Sahih Bukhari*, vol. 2, p. 287	
Mt. 20:1-16	*Sahih Bukhari*, vol. 1, p. 311	
	vol. 4, p. 441	
Mt. 25:42-26	*Sahih Muslim*, vol. 4, p. 1363	
Lk. 23:34a (!)	*Sahih Bukhari*, vol. 9, p. 49	
Jn. 17:17b	*Sahih Bukhari*, vol. 9, p. 359	

[35] *Sunan Abu Dawud*, vol. 3, p. 1091; cf. *SEI*, p. 169.

APPENDIX A
SIRA TRADITIONS on the LIFE OF MUHAMMAD
from Ibn Hisham - Ibn Sa`d - Al-Tabari - Waqidi

H - Ibn Hisham, first the page numbers for *The Life of Muhammad*, ed. and trans. Guillaume, are given, followed by the page numbers for the edition of Wüstenfeld (as shown by Guillaume). The reference NL is for *New Light on the Life of Muhammad*, ed. and trans. Guillaume. The page numbers from this work are followed by the references for the manuscript Guillaume used.

S - Ibn Sa`d, the page numbers for *Kitab al-Tabaqat al-Kabir*, ed. and trans. Haq, are given, followed by the page numbers for the edition of Sachau, et al. (as given by Haq).

T - Al-Tabari, the first page numbers given are those for *The History of al-Tabari*, ed. and trans. Yar-Shater, et al. These are followed by the page numbers for the edition of de Goeje, et al. (as given by the translation, Buhl in *Muhammad* and the text itself).

W - Al-Waqidi, the first page numbers are for the abridged edition *Muhammad in Medina*, trans. Wellhausen, followed by references for the manuscript he used. The numbers directly below these references correspond to the volume and page numbers in *Kitab al-Maghazi*, ed. Jones.

Event	H	S(I,1)	T (VI)	W
Genealogy of Muhammad	3	50(28)	38f(1113f)	
The story of `Abdullah b. `Abdu'l-Muttalib's marriage to Amina and the story about the soothsayer	68f(100f)	101f(58f)	6(1078f)	
The pregnancy of Amina	106f(60f)			
`Abdullah dies		69(102)	107f(61f)	

	H	S(I,1)	T(VI)	W
Birth of Muhammad (p. 25)	69(102)	109f(62f) 170f(96f)		
`Abdu'l-Muttalib takes the baby Muhammad to the Ka`ba	70(103)		(999)	
Milk miracles	70f(104f)	121(69f) 171f(97f)		
Two men (angels) remove a black clot from Muhammad's heart and replace the heart in his chest	72(106)	123(70) 170f(96f)	63(1143) 75(1155)	
Amina dies	73(107)	128f(73f)		
`Abdu'l-Muttalib dies	73f(108f)	131(75)		
Muhammad in the custody of Abu Talib	79(114f)	132f(75f)		
The story of Bahira	79f(115f)	132(75f) 174f(99f)	44f(1123f)	
Muhammad grazed goats as other prophets		140f(79f)		
Muhammad was protected from pagan practices;	NL 20(21b)		46f(1126f)	
The battle of al-Fijar	82(119)	141f(80f)		
The oath of al-Fudul		144(82f)		
The second journey to Syria	82(119f)	145(82f)	47f(1127f)	
Muhammad's marriage to Khadija	82f(120)	147f(84f)	48f(1128f)	
Their children	83(121)	150f(85)	48f(1128)	

	H	S(I,1)	T(VI)	W
The rebuilding of the Ka`ba (p. 27)	84f(122f)	164f(93f)	51f(1130f)	
The Hums	87f(126f)			
Stones and trees greeted Muhammad		179(102)	63(1143)	
Tree miracles		195f(112f)		
The talking wolf		198(114)		
Questions of the Jews		200(115f)		
Soothsayers	90f(130f)		65(1144f)	
Speaking calves	93(134)	180(102f)	66(1145)	
Speaking camel			66(1146)	
Fortune-teller		172f(97f)		
The Jewish prophecies	93f(134f)			
Other Jewish prophecies		181f(103f)		

	H	S (I,2)	T(VI)	W
Confused version Is. 42:1-7 applied to Muhammad	NL 32(44b)	422f(87f)		
Christian prophecies	103f(149f)	426(89)		

	H	S (I,1)	T(VI)	W
Salman's testimony	95f(137f)			
The four non-poly-theists	98f(143f)			

Muhammad, the Qur'an and Islam

	H	S(I,1)	T(VI)	W
After sacrificing to idols, Muhammad is warned by Zayd b.'Amr b. Nufayl	NL 27(38b-) cf. SB 5:106 cf. NL 28			
Muhammad's calling (p. 39)	104f(150f)	219f(126f) 224f(129f)		
Qur'an 96	106(152f)	226f(130f)	68(1147) 70f(1149f)	
Waraqa b. Naufal	107(153f)	225f(130)	68(1148) 72(1151)	
Muhammad suffered from the evil eye before and after first revelation	NL 27(38b-)			
Muhammad during revelation		227(131f)		
Qur'an 68		69(1148)		
Qur'an 74		69(1148)	73(1153f)	
Qur'an 93		69(1148)		
Qur'an 74:5			76(1156)	
Khadija is first to believe	111(155f)		76f(1156)	
Gabriel shows shows Muhammad ablution and ritual prayers	112(158)		77(1157)	

	H	S(I,1)	T(VI)	W
First prayers were toward the Ka`ba	NL 31(43b)	81(1161)		
`Ali first male to believe **(p. 42)**	114(159f)	80f(1159f)		

	H	S(I,1)	T(VI)	W
Abu Bakr first male to believe			84f(1165f)	
Zayd b. Haritha first male believer			86(1167)	
`Ali first, Zayd second, Abu Bakr third	NL 32(43b)			
Muhammad secretly for three years		230(132)	88(1169)	
Abu Lahab and Qur'an 111	159f(231)	231(133)	89(1170)	
Excrement is thrown in front of Muhammad's door		232(134)		
The Quraysh come to Abu Talib	118f(167f)	233f(134f)	93(1174)	
The first Muslims sat around the Ka`ba		233(134)		
Miracles with food			89f(1172f)	
Abu Bakr	115f(162f)			
Muhammad and his followers prayed in glens	118(166)			

	H	S(I,1)	T(VI)	W
Muhammad called a kahin, possessed or a poet	121(171) 135f(191)		101(1185)	
Muhammad kisses circumambulates the black stone	131(183)		101(1185)	
Abu Bakr protects Muhammad	131(184)		102(1186)	
Hamza becomes a Muslim (p. 51)	131f(184f)		103f(1187f)	
The Quraysh try to dissuade Muhammad	133f(187f)		106f(1191)	
Muhammad is accused of being taught by al-Rahman in al-Yamama	134(189)			
Al-Nadr b. al-Harith	136(191)			
Muhammad is said to tell the fairy tales of the ancients (Q 68:15)	136(192)			
Al-Nadr goes to the Jews.Three questions to ask Muhammad: the young men who disappeared, the traveller who reached East and West, what is spirit?	136(192)			

	H	S(I,1)	T(VI)	W
Muhammad's answer is late. Q 18: the seven sleepers, Dhu'l-Qarnayn, spirit is by command	137f(194f)			
Muhammad's answer about al-Rahman in al-Yamama	140(200)			
Ibn Mas`ud is first to recite the Qur'an in public	141f(202f)		104f(1188f)	
Arabs disbelieve the resurrection	143(204) 165(238f)			
Persecutions of the lower class Muslims	143f(205f)			
Abu Bakr trades for Bilal and sets him free; he also buys others' freedom, incl. a slave girl of `Umar	144(205)			
The first hijra to Abyssinia	146f(208f)	235f(136f)	98f(1180f)	
The Quraysh send for them	150f(217f)			
`Umar becomes a Muslim **(p. 82)**	155f(224f)			
Muslims pray at the Ka`ba	155(224)			
A wine dealer in Mecca	157(228)			

	H	S(I,1)	T(VI)	W
Muhammad prayed facing Syria	157f(228)			
The Satanic verses	NL 38f(56b)	237f(137f)	107f(1192f)	
The boycott (p. 91)	159f(230f) NL 34f(49a-)	240f(139)	105f(1189f)	
Those from Abyssinia reach the outskirts of Mecca before finding out the verses were revoked	167f(241f) NL 39(56b-)	238(138f)		
The persecution of Muslims	161f(233f)			
`Ali worked for a Jew in Mecca temporarily	NL 43(62a)			
Al-Nadr accuses Muhammad again (Q 83:13)	162f(235)			
`Abdullah speaks words similar to Q 9:30	163(236f)			
Protectors	169f(243f)			
Boycott ended	172f(247f)	242(140)	112f(1196f)	
Al-Tufayl accepts Islam	175f(252f)			
Muhammad wrestles with Rukana; a tree comes and returns at Muhammad's command	178f(259) NL 57(86b-)			
Second hijra to Abyssinia		239f(138f)		

	H	S(I,1)	T(IX)	W
`Ubaydullah b. Jahsh became a Christian and died in Abyssinia	527f(784)	240(139)	133(1772)	
Some return to Arabia after the hijra to Medina		240f(139f)		
Abu Talib's death	136f(77f)			

	H	S(I,1)	T(VI)	W
Deaths of Abu Talib and Khadija	191f(277f)	244(142)	115(1199)	
Muhammad goes to al-Ta'if (p. 97)	192f(279f)	243f(141f)	115f(1200)	
Muhammad speaks with the Christian slave `Addas of Nineveh	193(280f)		117(1201)	
Youth throw stones at Muhammad	244f(142)			
Muhammad recites Q 72 to the jinn at Nakhla	193f(281f)	245(142)	118(1202f)	
Muhammad returns to Mecca		245(142)	118f(1202f)	
Some Christians accept Islam	179(259)			
Muhammad slept around the Ka`ba; the night journey; ascension to Heaven.	181f(263f) NL 58(92b)	246f(142f)	78f(1157f)	
Jabr and Q 16:105	180(260)			
Q 108 & Q 6:8,10	180f(260f)			
The mockers	187(271f) NL 56(85b-)			

	H	S(I,1)	T(VI)	W
Muhammad preaches to the Arab tribes	194f(282f)	249f(145f)	120f(1204f)	
Some of the Khazraj become Muslims	197f(286f)	250f(145f)	124f(1209f)	
First pledge of `Aqaba **(p. 141)**	198f(288f)	254f(147f)	126f(1211f)	
The prayers in Medina	199f(290f)	252(146)		
Second pledge of `Aqaba	201f(293f)	255f(148f)	130f(1217f)	
Command to fight	212f(313f)		139(1227)	
Hijra to Medina	213f(314f)	261f(152f)	139f(1227f)	
Muhammad's hijra	221f(323f)	263f(153f)	140f(1229f)	

--- 1 AH --

	H	S (I,2)	T (VII)	W
First Friday prayers in Medina held in a wadi of the Banu Salim	228(335)		1f(1256f)	
Muhammad's first message	230f(340f)		2f(1257f)	
Mosque built in Medina	228(337)	280f(2f)	5(1259f)	
The constitution governing Muslims, Medinans and Jews	231f(341f)			
Bonding of emigrants and helpers	234f(344f)	278f(1f)		
Abu Umama dies	235(346)		5f(1260f)	
Call to prayer established	235(346f)	290f(7f)		

	H	S(I,2)	T(VII)	W
Abu Qays b. Abu Anas	236f(348f)			
Muhammad's marriage to `A'isha **(p. 188)**			6f(1261f)	
Jewish adversity	239f(351f)			
`Abdullah b. Salam becomes a Muslim	240f(353f)			
Mukhariq	241(354)			
The charge of Nabtal b. al-Harith (Q 9:61)	243(362)			
Jews laugh at Muslim's religion after hearing narrations	246(362)			
Jews expelled from the mosque	247(363)			
Qur'an 2	247f(363f)			
Finhas the rabbi in a Jewish school	263(388f)			
Rifa`a the Jew reviles Islam	264(390)			
Stoning for adulterers	266f(393f)			
Christians from Najran	270f(401f)			
`Abdullah b. Ubayy	277f(411f)			179f(93b-)
Births in Medina			9(1263f)	
Illnesses in Medina	279(413f)			

	H	S (II,1)	T (VII)	W
Raid of Hamza	283f(419f)	2f(2)	10(1265) 13(1267f)	33(6a-) I:9f

	H	S(II,1)	T(VII)	W
Raid of `Ubayda b. al-Harith	281(416f)	3f(2f)	10f(1265) 12f(1267)	33(6b) I:10
Raid of Sa`d b. Abu Waqqas	286(422f)	4(3)	11(1265f)	33f(6b-) I:11
--- 2 AH --				
Raid on Waddan	281(416)	4f(3)	11f(1266f) 15(1279)	34(7a) I:11f
Raid on Buwat	285(421)	5f(3f)	13(1268) 15(1270f)	34(7b) I:12
Raid on Safawan	286(423)	6(4)	14(1270) 16(1271)	34(7a) I:12
Raid on al-`Ushayra	285f(421f)	6f(4f)	13f(1268f) 16(1271)	34(7a) I:12f
`Ali marries Fatima			18(1273) 92(1367)	
`Ali as Abu Turab	286(422)	7(5)	16f(1271f)	
Raid on Nakhla (p. 201)	286f(423f)	7f(5)	18f(1273f) 21f(1277f)	34f(7a-) I:13f
Muhammad's rebuke (Q 2:214)	287f(425)		20(1275f)	

	H	S (I,2)	T (VII)	W
Change of the qibla	289(427)	283(3f)	24f(1279f)	
Mosque at Quba		287(5f)		
The fast		293(8)	25f(1281)	
The fitra		293f(8f)		
The sacrifice		293f(8f)	87f(1362)	

	H	S(II,1)	T(VII)	W
Badr (p. 202)	289f(427f)	9f(6f)	26f(1281f)	37f(4b-) I:19f
Return to Medina	309(459)		64f(1334f)	71f(29b-)
The prisoners	311f(462f)		69f(1341f)	75f(31b-)
Murder of `Asma bt. Marwan	675f(995f)	30f(18)		90f(42a-)
Murder of Abu `Afak	675(995)	31(19)		91f(42b-)
Abu'l-As b. al-Rabi` becomes Muslim	316f(469f)		76f(1350f)	
`Umayr b. Wahb becomes a Muslim	318f(471f)		78f(1352f)	
Qur'an 8	321f(476f)			
The Banu Qaynuqa (p. 205)	363f(545f)	32f(19f)	85f(1359f)	92f(43b-) I:177f
`Id al-Adha			87f(1362)	
Raid of al-Sawiq	361f(543f)	33f(20)	89(1364f)	94(44a-) I:181f

--- 3 AH ---

	H	S(II,1)	T(VII)	W
Raid to al-Kudr	360(540)	34f(21)	88f(1363f)	94f(44b) I:181f
Murder of Ka`b b. al-Ashraf	364f(548f)	35f(21f)	94f(1368f)	95f(44b-) I:184f
Raid to Dhu Amarr	362(544)	39f(23f)	93(1367f)	99f(46b-) I:193f
Raid on al-Furu`	362(544)	41(24)	88(1362) 93(1368)	100(47a) I:196
Raid on al-Qarada	364(547f)	41f(24f)	98f(1374f)	100f(47b-) I:197f

	H	S(II,1)	T(VII)	W
Muhayyisa b. Mas`ud 369(553f)				
Muhammad marries Hafsa			105(1383)	
Uhud **(p. 210)**	370f(555f)	42f(25f)	105f(1383f)	101f(47b-) I:199f
Hamra al-Asad	390(589f)	57f(34f)	138f(1427f)	149f(77b-) I:334f
		--- 4 AH --		
Raid on Qatan **(p. 245)**	661f(975)	59(35)		151f(79a-) I:340f
Murder of Sufyan b. Khalid	666f(981f)	60f(35f)		224f(122b-) II:531f
Bi'r Ma`una	433f(648f)	61f(36f)	151f(1441f)	153f(80b-) I:346f
Al-Raji`	426f(638f)	66f(39f)	143f(1431f)	156f(82a-) I:354f
Banu Nadir **(p. 246)**	437f(652f)	68f(40f)	156f(1448f)	160f(84b-) I:363f
Badr al-Maw`id	447f(666f)	71f(42f)	165f(1457f)	167f(89a-) I:384f
Murder of Abu Rafi`	482f(714f)	112f(66)	99f(1375f)	170f(90b-) I:391f
		--- 5 AH --		
Raid on Dhat al-Riqa **(p. 247)**	445f(661f)	74f(43f)	161f(1453f)	172f(91b-) I:395f
Muhammad marries Zaynab bt. Khuzayma			150(1441)	
Muhammad marries Umm Salama			167(1460)	152(80a)

	H	S(II,1)	T(VII)	W
Raid on Dumat al-Jandal	449(668)	76(44f)	(1463)	174f(99a) I:402f
Al-Muraysi`	490f(725f)	77f(45f)	(1511f)	175f(99a-) I:404f
`A'isha	493f(731f)	79f(46f)	(1517f)	184f(96a-) II:426f
The ditch **(p. 251)**	450f(669f)	80f(47f)	(1467f)	190f(101b-) II:440f
Muhammad marries Zaynab bt. Jahsh			(1460f)	
Banu Qurayza **(p. 252)**	461f(684f)	91f(53f)	(1485f)	210f(114a-) II:496f
--- 6 AH --				
Raid on al-Qurata	662(975)	96(56)		226(123a) II:534
Banu Lihyan	485f(718f)	97(56f)	(1500)	226f(123a-) II:535f
Al-Ghaba	486f(719f)	99f(58f)	(1500f)	227f(123b-) II:537f
Raid to al-Ghamr		104f(61)		232(126b) II:550
Raid to Dhu'l-Qassa of Ibn Maslama		105f(61f)		232f(126b-) II:551f
Raid to Dhu'l-Qassa of Ibn al-Jarrah		106(62)		233(127a) II:552
Raid on al-Jamum		106(62)		II:553
Raid on al-`Is		107(63)		233f(127a-) II:553

	H	S(II,1)	T(VII)	W
Raid on al-Taraf		108(63)		234(127b) II:555
Raid on Hisma		108f(63)		234f(127b-) II:555f
Raid on Wadi al-Qura	664(979)	109(64)	(1556f)	236(128b) II:560
Raid of Ibn `Awf on Dumat al-Jandal		110(64f)	(1556)	236f(128b-) II:560f
Raid on Fadak (p. 257)		110f(65)		237f(129a-) II:562f
Raid on the Banu Fazara and murder of Umm Qirfa	664f(979f)	111f(65f)	(1557)	238f(129b-) II:564
Killing of Usayr b. Rizam	665f(980f)	113f(66f)		239f(130a-) II:566f
Vengence on some of the `Urayna	677f(999)	114(67f)	(1559)	240f(130b-) II:571
Murder attempt on Abu Sufyan b. Harb		115f(68)	147f(1437f)	
Al-Hudaybiya	499f(740f)	117f(69f)	(1528f)	241f(131a-) II:571f

	H	S(I,2)	T(VII)	W
Muhammad sends out messengers	653(972)	304ff(15f)	(1559f)	

--- 7 AH --

	H	S(II,1)	T(VII)	W
Khaybar (p. 260)	510f(755f)	131f(77f)	(1575)	264f(144b-) II:644f

	H	S(II,1)	T(VII)	W
The poisoned meat and Bishr b. al-Bara	516(764f)	143f(83f)	(1583f)	280f(154a-) II:678f
Muhammad marries Safiya	516f(766)	144f(84)		291f(161a)
Treaty of Fadak	523(776f)			291(160b)
Return of emigrants from Abyssinia (p. 261)	526f(782f)	134(78)		

	H	S(I,1)	T(VII)	W
Muhammad marries Umm Habiba; she returns from Abyssinia with others		240(139)	(1570)	
Maryam and Sirin			(1591)	

	H	S(II, 1)	T(VII)	W
Turaba	660(973)	146(85)	(1591)	297(164a) II:722

	H	S(II,1)	T(IX)	W
Raid on the Najd		146f(85f)	1f(1654f)	297(164a) II:722
Raid on Fadak	660(973)	147f(86)	(1592)	297f(164b) II:723
Raid on the Banu b. Tha'laba		148f(86)	(1593)	298(165a-) `Abd II:726
Raid to Yaman and Jamar		149f(87)		298ff(165b-) II:727f
`Umra al-Qadiyya	530f(788f)	150f(87f)	(1594)	300f(167a-) II:731f
Muhammad marries Maymuna bt. al-Harith	531(790)	152(88)	(1595)	303(168a)

	H	S((II,1)	T(IX)	W
Raid on the Banu Sulaym		153(89)	(1597)	303(168a-) II:741
--- 8 AH --				
`Amr al-`As and Khalid b. Walid become Muslims	484f(716f)		(1601f)	303f(168b-) II:741f
Raid on al-Kadid **(p. 264)**	660f(974f)	154f(89f)	(1597f)	307f(170a-) II:750
Another raid on Fadak		156f(91f)		
Raid on al-Siyyi		157f(92)	(1601)	308f(171a) II:753
Raid to Dhat Atla		158(92)	(1601)	308(170b) II:752
Raid on Mu'ta	531f(791f)	158f(92f)	(1615)	309f(171a-) II:755f
Raid to Dhat al-Salasil	668f(984f)	162f(94f)	(1604)	315f(174a-) II:769f
Raid of al-Khabt	673(992)	163(95)	(1605)	317f(175a-) II:784
Raid on al-Ghaba	671f(989f)	163f(95f)	(1607)	318f(176a-) II:788f
Al-Fath; the conquest of Mecca **(p. 265)**	540f(802f)	165f(96f)	(1618f)	319f(176b-) II:790f
Raid against al-`Uzza	565f(839f)	180(105)		351(196b) III:873
Raid against Suwa`		180f(105f)	(1649)	350(196a)
Raid against Manat		181(106)	(1649)	

	H	S(II,1)	T(IX)	W
Raid on the Banu Jadhima	561f(833f)	182f(106f)	(1649)	351f(197a-) III:875f
Hunayn	566f(840f)	185f(108f)	1f(1654f)	354f(199a-) III:885f
Raid against Dhu'l-Khaffayn		194f(113f)		368(207b)
Al-Ta'if (p. 268)	587f(869f)	195f(114f)	20f(1669f)	368f(207b-) III:922f
Al-Ji`rana	597(886f)		26f(1674f)	373f(211-) III:949f

	H	S(I,1)	T(IX)	W
Ibrahim b. Muhammad		151f(86f)	39(1686)	

--- 9 AH --

	H	S(II,1)	T(IX)	W
Banu Tamim	628f(933f)	198f(116f)	67(1710)	385f(218b-)
Taxes of the Banu Mustaliq		199f(116)		387(220a)
Raid on Khath`am		200f(117)		387(220a) III:981
Raid on al-Zujj		201(117)		388(220b) III:982
Raid against Abyssinians	677(998)	201f(117f)		388f(220b) III:983
Raid against al-Fuls		202f(118)	62f(1706f)	389f(220b-) III:984f
Raid on al-Jinab		203(118)		
Tabuk	602f(893f)	203f(118f)	47f(1692f)	390f(222a-) III:1060

	H	S(II,1)	T(IX)	W
Ukaydir b. `Abdulmalik	607f(903)	205f(119f)	58f(1702)	403f(230a-)
Mosque of opposition	609f(906f)		60f(1704f)	410f(234a-)
The Thaqif accept Islam **(p. 271)**	614(914f)	38(1685)		381f(215b-)
`Abdullah b. Ubayy	623(927)		73(1717)	414f(237a-)
Hajj under Abu Bakr	617f(919f)	208f(121f)	77f(1720f)	416f(241a-) III:1076

--- 10 AH --

	H	S(II,1)	T(IX)	W
Raid on the Banu `Abdulmadan		209(122)		
Raid on the Banu al-Harith	645f(958f)		82f(1724f)	
Raid on Yemen	678(999)	209f(122)	89f(1731f)	417f(241b-) III:1079

	H	S(I,2)	T(IX)	W
Various deputations	634f(943f)	345f(38f)	76f(1720f) 85f(1727f)	

	H	S(II,1)	T(IX)	W
The liars	648(964)		164f(1795f)	
Farewell pilgrimage **(p. 279)**	649f(966f)	213f(123f)	109f(1751f)	421f(243b-) III:1088

--- 11 AH --

	H	S(II,1)	T(IX)	W
2nd raid on Mu'ta	652(970)	235f(136f)	163f(1794f)	433f(249b-) III:1117f
Muhammad's illness and death	678f(1000f)	239f(1f)	162f(1793f) (1584)	281(154b-) II:679

APPENDIX B
SURA ORDERINGS OF THE QUR'AN

The order in which the suras of the Qur'an were revealed has been a subject of great interest for Eastern as well as Western scholars, in that it is essential to tracing the development of Islam. In general, the lists of suras are divided into two main groups: those revealed in Mecca and those revealed in Medina. Seven different orderings are given below in column form. The letters represent the following listings:

D : This sura ordering is given by Suyuti (*El-Itkan*, vol. 1, p. 5) from the book *Fadaylu'l-Qur'an* by Ibn Durays (d. 906). The isnad begins with Ibn `Abbas.

I : The sura ordering is given by Suyuti (*El-Itkan*, vol. 1, p. 4) from the *Dalaylu'l-Nubuwa* of al-Bayhaqi (d. 1066 AD). The isnad begins with Husayn b. Hasan and `Ikrima and is also transmitted through Muhammad b. Ishaq.

F : This sura ordering is given in the *Fihrist* of Ibn al-Nadim (d. 995) in which the list of Nöldeke and Schwally, *GQ* (p. 61) was compared with the translation of Dodge (pp. 49 ff.) and Flügel's edition of the *Fihrist* (pp. 25 ff.). The isnad begins with Muhammad b. Nu`man.

A : This ordering is based on the Qur'an codex of Ibn `Abbas as related in the "Muqaddima" of the *Tafsir* of al-Shahrastani (d. 1153). This listing was provided by al-Zandjani, who in turn is quoted by Jeffery in *Materials*, p. 194.

J : This ordering is based on the Qur'an codex of Ja`far b. al-Sadiq as given in the "Muqaddima" of al-Shahrastani (d. 1153). This listing was provided by al-Zandjani, who is in turn quoted by Jeffery in *Materials*, p. 330.

N : The ordering based on the work of Theodor Nöldeke in *GQ* (originally published in 1860) as given in the edition of Schwally, pp. xi-xii.

B : The sura ordering of Régis Blachère as given in *Le Coran* (1957), pp. 12-18, which was originally published in 1949-50.

	D	I	F	A	J	N	B
Meccan	96	96	96	96	96	96	96 [1-5]
	68[1]	68[2]	68	68	68	74	74 [1-7]
	73	73	73	93	73	111	106
	74	74	74	73	74	106	93
	111	111	111	74	111	108	94
	81	81	81	1	81	104	103
	87	87	87	111	87	107	91
	92	92	94	81	92	102	107
	89	89	103	87	89	105	86
	93	93	89	92	93	92	95
	94	94	93	89	94	90	99
	103	103	92	94	103	94	101
	100	100	100	55	100	93	100
	108	108	108	103	108	97	92
	102	107	102	108	102	86	82
	107	109	107	102	107	91	87
	109	105	109[3]	107	109	80	80
	105	113	105	105	105	68	81
	113	114	112	109	113	87	84
	114	112	113	112	114	95	79

D	I	F	A	J	N	B
112	53	114	53	112	103	88
53	80	53	80	53	85	52
80	97	80	97	80	73	56
97	91	97	91	97	101	69
91	85	91	85	91	99	77
85	95	85	95	85	82	78
95	106	95	106	95	81	75
106	101	106	101	106	53	55
101	75	101	75	101	84	97
75	104	75	104	75	100	53
104	77	104	77	104	79	102
77	90	77	50	77	77	96 [6-19]
50	50	50	90	50	78	70
90	86	90	86	90	88	73
86	54	55	54	86	89	76
54	38	72	38	54	75	83
38	72	36	7	38	83	74 [8-55]
7	36	7	72	7	69	111
36	25	25	36	72	51	108
25	35	35	25	36	52	104
35	20	19	35	25	56	90
19	56	20	19	35	70	105
20	26	56	20	19	55	89
56	27	26	26	20	112	85 [4]
26	28	27	27	56	109	112
27	17	28	28	26	113	109
28	11	17	17	27	114	1
17	12	11	10	28	1	113
10	15	12	11	17	54	114
11	6	10	12	10	37	51

D	I	F	A	J	N	B
12	37	15	15	11	71	54
15	31	37	6	12	76	68
6	34	31	37	15	44	37
37	39	23	31	6	50	71
31	40	34	34	37	20	44
34	93	21	39	31	26	50
39	41	39	40	34	15	20
40	42	40	41	39	19	26
41	43	41	42	40	38	15
42	45	42	43	41	36	19
43	46	43	44	42	43	38
44	51	44	45	43	72	36
45	88	45	46	44	67	43
46	18	46	51	45	23	72
51	16	51	88	46	21	67
88	71	88	18	51	25	23
18	14	18	16	88	17	21
16	21	6	71	18	27	25
71	23	16	14	16	18	27
14	32	71	21	71	32	18
21	52	14	23	14	41	32
23	67	32	13	21	45	41
32	69	52	52	23	16	45
52	70	67	67	32	30	17
67	78	69	69	52	11	16
69	79	70	70	67	14	30
70	84	78	78	69	12	11
78	35	79	79	70	40	14
82	30	82	82	78	28	12
84	29	84	84	79	39	40

	D	I	F	A	J	N	B
	30		30	30	82	29	28
	29		29	29	84	31	39
	83		83	83	30	42	29
			54		29	10	31
			86		83	34	42
						35	10
						7	34
						46	35
						6	7
						13	46
							6
							13
Medinan	2	83	2	2	2	2	2
	8	2	8	8	8	98	98
	3	3	7	3	3	64	64
	33	8	3	59	33	62	62
	60	33	60	33	60	8	8
	4	5	4	24	4	47	47
	99	60	99	60	99	3	3
	57	4	57	48	57	61	61
	47	99	47	4	47	57	57
	13	57	13	99	13	4	4
	55	47	76	22	55	65	65
	76	13	65	57	76	59	59
	65	55	98	47	65	33	33
	98	65	59	76	98	63	63
	59	98	110	65	59	24	24

[5] Nöldeke and Schwally, *GQ*, p. 61, give sura 90 at this position (which then presents sura 90 twice in the listing). The Arabic and the translation of Dodge (p. 52) show sura 69 at this position.

D	I	F	A	J	N	B
110	59	24	98	110	58	58
24	110	22	62	24	22	22
22	24	63	32	22	48	48
63	22	58	63	63	66	66
58	63	49	58	58	60	60
49	58	66	49	49	110	110
66	49	62	66	66	49	49
62	66	64	64	61	9	9
64	61	61	61	62	5	5
61	62	48	5	64		
48	64	5	9	48		
5	48	9[8]	110	9		
9[6]	9[7]		56	5[9]		
			100			
			113			
			114			

[1] Suyuti, *El-Itkan*, p. 5, leaves off sura 68, whereas Sell, *Development*, p. 203 shows sura 68 as being listed in this order by Suyuti.

[2] Suyuti, *El-Itkan*, p. 4 lists sura 24 here; it should no doubt be sura 68.

[3] Nöldeke and Schwally, *GQ*, p. 61, appear to have accidently left out sura 109 in their quotation of the *Fihrist*; both Flügel's edition (vol. 1, p. 25) and the translation of Dodge (vol. 1, p. 50) show this sura at this position.

[4] Welch in *EI²*, s.v. "Kur'an," p. 416, apparently overlooked this sura, which is listed in this position by Blachère. Welch (Ibid.) also shows 74 (7-55), but Blachère gives 74 (8-55), as presented above.

[5] Nöldeke and Schwally, *GQ*, p. 61, give sura 90 at this position (which then presents sura 90 twice in the listing). The Arabic and the translation of Dodge (p. 52) show sura 69 at this position.

[6] The suras 1, 72 and 79 are missing in this listing.

[7] The suras 1, 7, 10, 19, 44, 76, 82 and 102 are missing in this listing, and sura 35 appears twice.

[8] The suras 1, 33 and 38 are missing; the sura 7 appears twice.

[9] The suras 1 and 47 are missing; the sura 54 is listed twice.

QUR'AN DATING SYSTEMS AND INDICATORS
(Generalized)

Muslim:
(taken from Suyuti, *El-Itkan*, vol. 1, pp. 1-26)

      Mecca: Generally addresses to "O people" (except for suras 2, 3 and 13) or "O children of Adam."
               Suras mentioning the names of past peoples tribes
               Suras with the mysterious letters (except for sura 2)
               Suras containing the stories of Adam and Iblis (except for sura 2)
               Suras containing the narrations of the prophets
               Suras containing "sajda" verses

      Medina: Generally addresses to "O believers" or "hypocrites"
               Suras with regulations

Muslims also used traditions accounts of sura orderings and also recognized that some verses revealed in Mecca had been inserted into Medinan suras and vice versa. Some scholars even said that some verses were revealed in Mecca, but "completed" in Medina.

Nöldeke - Schwally:
(taken from *Geschichte des Qorans*, vol. 1, pp. xi, 143, 170-172)

      Mecca I: Suras containing heathen oaths

Mecca II: Suras containing "Rahman".
Mecca III: Suras with a more developed prose

Medina: Suras containing addresses to Believers, Jews and
hypocrites.
Suras regulating rituals or laws.

Nöldeke relied heavily on Islamic sources and methods together with Western methods of critical analysis. He also examined the literary style (including rhyme schemes) and theological content of the Qur'an in giving his own sura ordering.

Bell:
(taken from *The Qur'an Translated*, pp. vi-vii)

Aya :   "Signs" period with exhortations to worship God.
Qur'an: Period of the last years in Mecca and first two years in
Medina, when the "Qur'an" was recited.
Book: Period after 2 AH, when a "Book" was being compiled.

Bell's system is based on only three words in the Qur'anic vocabulary. He presumes the Qur'an to have been revealed in the form of verses which were later compiled somewhat haphazardly, especially in the Medinan suras. He builds on the research of those before him, but uses far fewer indicators than were available at the time. Bell saw very few suras as having been revealed as a unit, and so did not construct his own sura ordering.

EI² - Welch
(s.v. "al-Kur'an," pp. 414-425):

Welch gives other characteristics of the literary form and style of the Qur'an, and these can also be used in dating the various passages:

Oaths, "Sign" passages, "Say" passages, Punishment stories,
Prophet stories, Regulations, Last Judgment, Addresses, etc.

APPENDIX C
QUR'ANIC TIME CHART
Based on the sura orderings of Nöldeke

(H) = Hebrew	(A) = Aramaic	(S) = Syriac
(E) = Ethiopian	(G) = Greek	(M) = Muhammad
(Med.) = Medina		

Sura:	Group:	Names:	Terms:
96	Mecca I		zabaniyya (S)
74			rujz (S)
111			
106			House (Ka`ba)
108			sacrifice (nhr)
			"we"
104	I		
107			
102			
105			
92			
90	I		believe (amn)
94			
93			
97			spirit (rwh)
86			
91	I	Thamud	
80			
68 (N)			Muslim
			study (A)
			resurrection (S)

Sura:	Group:	Names:	Terms:
87		Abraham, Moses	
95	I		Mt. Sinai (S)
103	I		
85		Pharoah	Qur'an (S)
			story (hadith)
73			"zakat"
			prayer (S)
			messenger
			(for Muhammad)
101			fire (E)
99			
82	I		
81		Satan	cursed (E)
53		Noah	
84			
100			
79	I		
77			
78		"Rahman" (Mecca II)	Jahannam (E)
88			
89		`Ad	Iram
75	I		
83			`Illiyun (H)
			tasnim (M)
			sijjin (M)
69			
51			
52			"say"

Sura:	Group:	Names:	Terms:
56	I		
70			
55			
112			
109			
113			
114			
1	I		
54	II	Lot	zabur (script.)
37		Aaron, Elias, Isaac, Jonah, Baal	yaqtin (H) prophet (A) - Isaac
71	II		
76			
44 (HM)		Israel	
50 (Q)			
20 (TH)		Adam, Iblis, Samaritan,	manna (S) crucify basket (E)
26 (TSM) II		Hud, Salih, Shu`ayb	
15 (ALR)			mathani (A?)
19 (KHY`S)		Idris, Ismail, Jacob, Jesus, John, Mary, Zacharias	fast
38 (S)		David, Dhu al-Kifl, Job, Solomon	milla (S)
36 (YS)			
43 (HM) II			prophet (for Muhammad)
72			masjid
67			
23			burhan (E)

Sura:	Group:	Names:	Terms:
21		Gog, Magog	Zabur (Psalms)
			sijill (SG)
			furqan (S)
25			
17			
27 (TS)		Queen of Sheba	
18	II	Alexander the Great	Al-Raqim (S)
32 (ALM) III			
41 (HM) III			
45 (HM)			
16		Holy Spirit (qds)	Jews (hwd)
			hanif (S) (Med.)
			idol (E)
30 (ALM)			
11 (ALR)			Judi (AS)
			sura (S)
14 (ALR) III			
12 (ALR)		Joseph	cattle (AS)
			cup (E)
40 (HM)		Haman, Korah	
28 (TSM)			
39			Islam
29 (ALM) III			hypocrite (E)(Med.)
31 (ALM)		Luqman	
42 (HM SQ)			
10 (ALR)			qibla (Jews)
34			

Sura:	Group:	Names:	Terms:
35	III		
7 (ALMS)			Al-A`raf (E)
			hitta (HA)
			Sabbath (A)
46 (HM)			
6		Azar	swine (A)
13 (ALMR)			
2 (ALM)	Medina	Gabriel, Michael,	ark of C. (E)
		Harut, Marut, Saul,	Christians
		Goliath	Jews (yhd)
			Sabeans (A?)
			Shechina (HS)
			baptism (S)
			asbat (HS)
98			
64			
62			
8			
47	Medina		
3 (ALM)		Imran, Masih	Hawariyun (E)
			rabbani (S)
			qurban
			Gospel (E)
			Torah (H) (7:156)
			`azzara (H) "
			ribbiyun (S)
61			
57			
4			Jibt (E)
			hub (S)

Sura:	Group:	Names:	Terms:
65	Medina		
59			
33			
63			
24			
58	Medina		
22			church (S)
			monastery (E)
			bahima (H)
48			
66			
60			
110	Medina		
49			
9		Ezra	
5			dhakka (HA)
			suht (S)
			ma'ida (E)

APPENDIX D
QUR'ANIC NARRATIVES

105   The elephant.

The judgment narrative of the elephant is based upon the campaign of Abraha, the Abyssinian viceroy of Yemen, against Mecca after 540 AD. The goal of Abraha's army, which included an elephant, was to destroy the Ka`ba. See Guillaume, *Muhammad*, pp. 21 f.

68:17f   The owners of the garden who did not say "If God will."

Andrae in *Ursprung*, p. 133 shows this and other Qur'anic garden judgment parables to be related to a narrative of the Syrian church, whereby a powerful atheist who troubled the poor, widows and orphans is warned of God's judgment; after not repenting, his house burns down one night with many of his possessions; the man becomes ill and dies within ten days; his vineyards and orchards are destroyed in two years time; his family loses everything, including their slaves (*Anecdota Syriaca*, II, 39 f, as quoted by Andrae)

87:19   Scrolls of Abraham and Moses mentioned.

Geiger in *WMJA*, p. 120 states that the Jewish cabalistic Sepher Yezirah mentions Abraham as having written books, and this opinion is also shared by Nöldeke-Schwally, *GQ*, p. 17, n. 2 and others. In the late apocrypha, books are also ascribed to Abraham; see *Apokalypsen*, pp. 29 f.

85:4f   The comrades of the pit.

Although Geiger (*WMJA*, p. 189) and others following him think this to be a reference to Dan. 3:8 f, it is more probable that the Muslim authorities (cf. Guillaume, *Muhammad*, pp. 14, 17) are correct in seeing an allusion to the executions of Christians performed by Dhu Nuwas in Yemen in 523 AD. Cf. Nöldeke-Schwally, *GQ*, p. 97 f, n. 3; Andrae, *Ursprung*, pp. 10 f; Speyer, *Erzählungen*, p. 424.

85:18   Pharoah is mentioned.

The word was known to be a title, probably came from the Syriac and was most likely not used in Arabic before Muhammad's time; Jeffery, *Vocabulary*, p. 225.

84:7f   Those who receive books in the right or left hands at Judgment.

Ahrens in "Christliches," *ZDMG*, vol. 84, p. 55, believes this to have come from Christian sources and cites Baumstark, who thought Muhammad probably saw something to this effect in a Christian picture.

79:16   Moses' calling in the valley of Tuwa.

Islamic scholars and Qur'an translators usually identify the "valley of Tuwa" as being in the vicinity of Mount Sinai, but then are at a loss for being able to say which valley was meant. From the context (cf. Qur'an 20: 12 also) it is clear that Muhammad supposed Moses to have been in a valley when he was called to go to Egypt (cf. Ex. 3:1f). The word "Tuwa" appears to be related to "tawa" = "to roll" or "fold" (Kassis, *Concordance*, pp. 1245 f), and as such would be a rough equivalent of "Gilgal" near Jericho (Jos. 5:9) in whose vicinity Joshua was commanded to remove his shoes (Jos. 5:15). Some early Qur'an commentators also seem to agree that "Tuwa" must have the meaning of "folding" (or "doubling") as a tradition from Hasan says Tuwa was in Palestine and was so named for having been "twice holy," and Bishr b. 'Ubayd said that Tuwa was in Ayla and was thus named for having been "twice blessed," see Suyuti, *El-Itkan*, vol. 2, p. 370. Ibn 'Abbas seems to have thought "Tuwa" came from "to go around" as he said the valley was named Tuwa because Moses got lost there with his family at night and then saw the fire; see *Sahih Bukhari*, vol. 6, p. 231, Suyuti, *El-Itkan*, vol. 2, p. 370. If "Tuwa" really is related to the verb "to go around," then it would appear that Mount Seir was meant, cf. Deut. 2:1f.

In any event, neither Muslims nor Western scholars are sure where the "valley of Tuwa" is (cf. Horovitz, *Untersuchungen*, p. 125), and it is quite likely that Muhammad confused it with some other well-known Biblical place.

37:81f Abraham rebukes his father and people for idolatry, and is to be thrown into a furnace of fire.

Geiger, *WMJA*, pp. 121 f, gives Midrash Rabbah Genesis, parag. 17 as the source for this narration.

37:101f Abraham attempts to sacrifice son.

Speyer in *Erzählungen*, p. 164 shows that the narration of Pirke Rabbi Eliezer, 31 portrays Abraham as having received the commandment via a dream. Speyer also believes the son's willingness comes from Jewish sources (Midrash Tanhuma wayyera), which information was later used by Christians (I Clement 31, ed. Lightfoot). Cf. Gen. 22:2f. See also the comments on 37:112.

37:112 Isaac is Abraham's son.

Although the Qur'anic word for Isaac appears to have entered Arabic before Muhammad's time from the Christian-Palestinian dialect of Syriac (Horovitz, *Untersuchungen*, p. 90); it has been suggested that Muhammad got this information from Christian sources; see Ahrens, "Christliches," *ZDMG*, vol. 84, p. 176. The idea expressed by some, e.g. Speyer, *Erzählungen*, p. 164, that Ishmael must have been meant by Muhammad in 37:110f, since Isaac is first mentioned in v. 112, is doubtful, not only because the name Ishmael first appears later in the sura orderings (of Nöldeke), but also because Muhammad obviously did not know that Ishmael was Abraham's son until much later (cf. 19:50f; 11:72f; 29:26; 6:84f). This question was disputed among early Islamic authorities; see Tabari, *History*, vol. 2, pp. 82-90.

37:120   Aaron is mentioned with Moses.

The Qur'anic name for Aaron probably comes from the Christian-Palestinian dialect of Syriac, and pre-dates Muhammad (Jeffery, *Vocabulary*, pp. 283 f). Cf. Ex. 4:29.

37:123f Elias is mentioned with respect
to the challenge against Baal.

Jeffery believes that both of the Arabic names for Elias (Jeffery, *Vocabulary*, p. 67 f.) and Baal (Ibid., p. 81) probably come from Syriac and both pre-date Islam. Horovitz, *Untersuchungen* holds that Muhammad most likely heard the names from Ethiopians, and Ahrens, "Christliches," *ZDMG*, vol. 84, p. 38 maintains with Horovitz that both probably came from the Ethiopian Bible translation. The vast majority of scholars think that Muhammad received this narration from Christians. Cf. I Kings 18:21.

37:135 An old woman was not saved
with Lot.

The Arabic name for Lot, mentioned in Qur'an 54:33 perhaps for the first time, probably comes from Syriac and does not appear to have pre-dated Muhammad in Arabic (*Vocabulary*, p. 254 f). The peculiarity that Lot's wife is here described as simply being an old woman, suggests that Muhammad did not know who she was up until this time. Cf. Gen. 19:26.

37:139f Jonah would still be in the fish
if he had not praised God, he was
ill, God caused a gourd to grow
over him, he was sent to more than
100,000, who believed and were
allowed to live.

The Arabic name for Jonah came either from Syriac or Ethiopian, and thus from Christians; see Jeffery, *Vocabulary*, pp. 295 f. In 37:146, however, the non-Arabic word يقطين is thought to have come from the Hebrew for "gourd." Jeffery thinks that the form was garbled by Muhammad; cf. *Vocabulary*, p. 292. Cf. Jonah 1-4.

71:20f Noah mentions the names of gods worshipped in Muhammad's time.

This anachronism is due to Muhammad himself. See: *Sahih Bukhari*, vol. 6, p. 414; Nöldeke, "The Qur'an", p. 9; Speyer, *Erzählungen*, p. 101.

20:74 Pharaoh threatens the punishment of crucifixion in the time of Moses.

This appears to be an anachronism of Muhammad, since crucifixion was known to the Jews through the Romans, who had in turn taken it from Carthage; *Lexikon zur Bibel*, p. 812.

20:87f The Samaritan was a deceiver of Israel against Moses.

Speyer in *Erzählungen*, pp. 329 f. shows that Geiger thought Muhammad may have confused the angel Samael with "Samaritan" (*WMJA*, p. 163), but that this is improbable. Goldziher, along with the Muslim scholars, thought that the Samaritans are actually meant in this passage, cf. 20:97 where as a punishment the Samaritan is to say: "do not touch," *SEI*, p. 502. Speyer (*Erzählungen*, p. 330 f.) suggests that through Christian influence Muhammad may have meant Satan in the person of Zimri (Num. 25:14); this is also not very convincing though. A Jewish tradition (Midrash Tanhuma ki tissa) cited by Speyer (*Erzählungen*, p. 324) shows that magicians took part in making the golden calf, which according to Pirke Rabbi Eliezer, 45 and in harmony with 20:90, lowed. Al-Samiri essentially takes the place of the magicians in these traditions, and the only Samaritan magician known in the Bible is Simon (Acts 8:9f). Chrysostum, in his 18th homily on Acts (vol. 11, pp. 115 f; Eerdmans ed.) contrasts the miracles of Moses with the magic of Simon. The (apparently Ebionite) Recognitions of Clementine (book 3 ch. 56) compares Simon with the Egyptian magicians who resisted Moses (*Ante-Nicene Fathers*, vol. 8, p. 129), and in The Acts of Peter and Paul, Simon is also likened to Jannes and

Jambres (Ibid, p. 482.). It may well have been that through the influence of such parallels Muhammad confused the time periods and then transferred Jewish teachings about the Samaritans to a single person.

20:115f Iblis refuses to bow before Adam.

Although this story is well known from Jewish tradition (cf. Ginzberg, *Legends*, vol. 1, pp. 62 f), it is generally thought that this story came to Muhammad from Christian sources. The reasons for this are that the word for Satan used here "Iblis" appears to be from the Greek διάβολος and that the angels are commanded to bow down to Adam. Horovitz, *Untersuchungen*, p. 87, gives Iblis as having come into Arabic through Aramaic influence, since the "di" would have been deleted as in the case of other Aramaic borrowings from Greek. Geiger, *WMJA*, p. 202, n. to p. 98) shows that Zunz thought even the bowing before Adam was Jewish, but the source he gives for this is from the 11th century. Grünbaum, *Neue Beiträge*, pp. 57, 60 gives the Syrian parallels and states that Muhammad's source must have been Christian rather than Jewish. Cf. Geiger, *WMJA*, pp. 98 f.; Speyer, *Erzählungen*, pp. 54 f.; Guillaume, in *Legacy*, p. 139; Rosenblatt, "Hadith," *MW*, vol. 35, p. 240.

20:115f Satan deceives Adam and his wife.

It is generally thought that this passage also came to Muhammad through Christian influence, even though much of the material used in this passage is common to both Judaism and Christianity. Cf. Speyer, *Erzählungen*, pp. 66 f; Grünbaum, *Neue Beiträge*, pp. 57 f. 26:28 Pharoah claims to be God. Geiger, in *WMJA*, p. 157, shows this notion to be based on Midrash Rabbah Exodus, parag. 5.

26:123f Hud was an Arabian prophet who was a brother of the `Ad.

`Ad is mentioned in the pre-Islamic Arabic works of the poets al-Afwa al-Audi (c. 570 AD.) and `Adi b. Zayd (587 AD.); see Margoliouth, *Relations*, p. 73. Although the origins of the person of Hud are cloaked in uncertainty, the name does appear in pre-Islamic Arabic; see Horovitz, *Untersuchungen*, pp. 149 f.

The word comes from the same Arabic root as the word for "Jew"; cf. *SEI*, p. 140.

26:144f Salih was an Arabian prophet who was a brother of the Thamud.

Although the name Thamud was known and used by the pre-Islamic poets al-Afwa al-Audi (c. 570 AD) and `Adi b. Zayd (580 AD), see Margoliouth, *Relations*, p. 73, Horovitz (*Untersuchungen*, p. 123) believes that Salih was an invention of Muhammad. Cf. *SEI*, pp. 499 f.

26:176f Shu`ayb was a prophet (who was a brother of the Midianites; cf. 11:85f)

Horovitz, *Untersuchungen*, pp. 119 f., states that the name is unknown in pre-Islamic Arabic, and cannot be identified with any prophet from any other source. Simply based on the mention of "Midian" in this verse, later Islamic scholars identify him with Jethro the priest of Midian (Ex. 3:1). Horovitz (Ibid.) notes, however, that the name Shu`ayb does not appear in the later Qur'anic account of Mose's flight to and stay in Midian (28:21f), where Muhammad should have used it, if Jethro had been meant. Cf. *SEI*, p. 544.

15:60 Lot's wife was not to be saved.

There are both Jewish and Syrian Christian sources which portray the wife of Lot as being evil. See Speyer, *Erzählungen*, pp. 157 f; Grünbaum, *Neue Beiträge*, pp. 134, 145; *SEI*, p. 290 f. Cf. Gen. 19:26.

19:1f Zacharias could not speak for three nights (days) after receiving the promise of John's birth.

Origin unknown; but probably a misunderstanding on Muhammad's part. The Bible shows Zacharias as being unable to speak for approximately the duration of Elizabeth's pregnancy; cf. Lk. 1:20, 64.

19:7f John was the son of Zacharias; peace is wished for him on the day of his birth, death and resurrection.

For the possible origins of the blessing (19:15), which is essentially the same as the one for Jesus (19:34), see *SEI*, p. 490. Cf. Lk. 1:67f.

19:16f Mary has a book which is named after her; the birth of Jesus is related.

The book referred to may be the Gospel of the book of Mary, which was used by several early sects; see *Lost Books*, pp. 17 f; *Ante-Nicene Fathers*, vol. 8, pp. 384 f. 19:16 For Mary's withdrawal from her relatives; cf. the Prot-evangelion 9:23 in *Lost Books*; *Ante-Nicene Fathers*, vol. 8, p. 364, (Prot. 12); where Mary is said to have left Elizabeth to hide herself from the house of Israel (lest her pregnancy be known).

19:19 Jesus was pure.

Cf. Gospel of the book of Mary 7:20 in *Lost Books*; *Ante-Nicene Fathers*, vol. 8, pp. 386 f (Mary 9).

19:23f Mary gives birth to Jesus under a date palm.

Cf. Pseudo-Matthew 20, where on the journey to Egypt, it is the child Jesus who commands a palm tree to bend down its branches and give fruit to His mother, who was sitting under the tree. Afterwards Jesus commands the tree to open a spring of water from its roots, from which they, their cattle and beasts drank. (*Ante-Nicene Fathers*, vol. 8, pp. 376-377). In order to explain this Qur'an passage, Tabari, (*History*, vol. 4, p. 114) seems to have corrupted the Pseudo-Matthew account (as Muhammad may have done before him), so that Mary gives birth to Jesus on the way to Egypt.

19:28f   Mary is accused of immorality

Cf. Pseudo-Matthew 12, in which both Mary and Joseph are depicted as having been arrested and brought to the Temple. After both give their testimonies, they both drink the water of drinking (cf. Numbers 5:11f, where only the wife drinks the water) to see who was not telling the truth. In the end, both are cleared of any guilt, and Mary is recognized as being a virgin with child.

19:29   Mary is said to have been of "sister of Aaron."

An apparent mistake of Muhammad, whereby Mary the mother of Jesus was also thought to be Miriam the sister of Moses and Aaron. Speyer, *Erzählungen*, p. 243, cites Aphrahat (Homily 21, ch. 10) as an example of how Muhammad may have erred: "One Maryam stood on the bank of the river, as Moses floated on the water; and a Maryam bore Jesus, after the angel Gabriel had given her the promise." (cf. *The Nicene and Post-Nicene Fathers*, vol. 13, p. 396.) One of Ephraem the Syrian's *Hymns on the Nativity* reads: "The Virgin bare today the Adam that was Head over the Heavens. The staff of Aaron, it budded, and the dry wood yielded fruit." (See *Nicene and Post-Nicene Fathers*, vol. 13, Hymn 1, p. 223.

19:31   Jesus speaks from the cradle.

This appears to have come from the Infancy Gospel 1:2 (*Lost Books*), which was used by some early sects. The text of what Jesus is reported to have said (cf. Qur'an 19:31f with Infancy 1:3) seems to have been radically changed by Muhammad; cf. *Ante-Nicene Fathers*, vol. 8, p. 405.

19:43f   Abraham's father an idolater.

Geiger shows that the original source for this was Judaism; Midrash Rabbah Genesis, parag. 17 (*WMJA*, p. 122; cf. Ginzberg, *Legends*, vol. 1, pp. 195 f). However, this may also have reached Muhammad through Christians acquainted with the Jewish story.

**19:50 Isaac and Jacob were given to
Abraham (as sons); both were
prophets.**

Apparently an error of Muhammad, as Jacob was Abraham's grandson. That
both were prophets is clear from the Bible; Gen. 27:27-29, 39-40; 48:19;
49:1-27.

**19:55 Ishmael had a book named after
himself.**

It seems that this was an error of Muhammad.

**19:57 Idris is a prophet who had a book
named for himself.**

Since Idris is most probably to be identified with the cook Andreas in the
Syrian Alexander the Great legend (Horovitz, *Untersuchungen*, p. 88; Tabari,
History, vol. 3, pp. 2 f., n. 11, *SEI*, p. 158), this description appears to have
been due to a misunderstanding on Muhammad's part.

**38:17f Mountains and birds were subjected
to David.**

Cf. Ps. 148:7-10; Speyer, *Erzählungen*, p. 381.

**38:19f David's decision between the man with
99 sheep and the man with one is related,
David repents.**

This narration is a distortion of II Sam. 12:1-5, in which the Qur'an has this be
said of two who brought their case to David. The immediate source is unknown. Speyer, *Erzählungen*, pp. 378 f. thinks that the 99 and one sheep is
perhaps from Mt. 18:12; and maintains that Muhammad's source must have
been Christian, as David's form of repentance (38:23) "to fall down, bow and
repent" is alien to the liturgy of the Day of Atonement in post-Talmudic
Judaism. Cf. Tabari, *History*, vol. 3, pp. 145 f.

38:30f Solomon's love of horses.

Cf. I Kgs. 10.26f; Deut. 17:16. Muslim commentators understand this passage to show that Solomon's love for horses caused him to neglect his evening prayers; cf. *SEI*, p. 550; Rudolph, *Koran*, pp. 411 f.

38:33 A form on Solomon's throne.

Geiger, *WMJA*, p. 185, gives Gattin 68 as a similar Jewish tradition for this. Solomon's power over the spirits and demons, who helped him build the temple are also well attested to in Jewish traditions; Sanhedrin 20b, Midrash Rabbah Genesis, parag. 11, etc. (*Koran*, p. 412, n. 17); the Second Targum to Esther 1:2 (Geiger, *WMJA*, p. 182). Cf. Speyer, *Erzählungen*, pp. 386 f; Tabari, *History*, vol. 3, pp. 170 f.

38:34 Solomon repented and asked for a kingdom unlike any other.

Speyer, *Erzählungen*, pp. 383 f. shows that Solomon's prayer of I Kings 3:6f has been corrupted so that he asks for a kingdom rather than for wisdom. Speyer holds that the the idea of "kingdom" in this passage seems to be Christian.

38:35f The wind and jinn served Solomon.

Geiger, *WMJA*, p. 182, gives the Targum to Esther 1:2 as the ultimate source for the demons having served Solomon. Horovitz, *Untersuchungen*, pp. 117 f, shows that the pre-Islamic poets wrote of this, and that Muhammad might have gotten his information from them. Cf. the notes to Qur'an 38:33, above.

38:43 Job was to strike with a bundle of rushes to keep an oath.

This appears to have been a misunderstanding of Job 2:8-10, for which Muslim Qur'an exegetes later invented a story to better fit the general confusion of this passage; cf. Tabari, *History*, vol. 2, p. 140; SEI, p. 26.

38:48 Dhu'l Kifl is mentioned.

The identification of Dhu'l Kifl is as yet uncertain. Based on Islamic tradition Geiger, in *WMJA*, pp. 192 f, sees a parallel to the person of the Biblical Obadiah. Cf. I Kings 18:4.

36:12f Parable of the envoys and the city.

It has been suggested that this narration is based on the Syrian legend of the martyr Agabus (Acts 11:28; 21:10); cf. Rudolph *Koran*, p. 398, n. 5; Tabari, *History*, vol. 4, pp. 167 f. This view is however disputed in *EI²* (s.v. "Habib al-Nadjdjar") on the grounds that the place of martyrdom is not given in the legend. Another possibility is the Acts of Andrew and Matthias, together with the Acts of Peter and Andrew (*The Ante-Nicene Fathers*, vol. 8, pp. 517 f and 526 f, respectively), which were said to have been used by Gnostics, Man-ichaeans and others (Ibid. p. 356). An additional point in favor of these sources is that the "city" described in these documents is said to have been located in Ethiopia (Ibid. p. 356).

21:68f Abraham is delivered from furnace of fire.

Geiger, in *WMJA*, pp. 122 f, gives Midrash Rabbah Genesis, parag. 17 as the Jewish source. Speyer, *Erzählungen*, pp. 142 f. adds among others Pesahim 118a, and shows that this tradition was also known in Christian circles; the Syrian church even dedicated January 25th to the remembrance of Abraham being saved from the furnace of fire. Cf. Ginzberg, *Legends*, vol. 1, pp. 198 f; Grünbaum, *Neue Beiträge*, pp. 90 f.

21:78f David and Solomon decide about the retribution for those whose fields were entered by stray sheep.

This narration does not have any direct support from Jewish or Christian sources; however, in that the Jewish Law does make provision for such a case (cf. Ex. 22:5), one would suspect Jewish influence.

21:80 David was taught to make coats of mail.

Speyer, *Erzählungen*, thinks this may have come from Sanhedrin 93b, from I Sam. 25:13 through Sanhedrin 36a, or that even an unknown Jewish armorer may have been meant. Moed Katan, 16b, states that "David made himself hard as steel" (*Ency. Jud.*, vol. 5, p. 1327) and this might also have been a possible source. Muhammad probably received his information for this from the pre-Islamic Arab poets; Horovitz, *Untersuchungen*, pp. 109, 118. Cf. Tabari, *History*, vol 3, p. 143, n. 746.

21:96 Gog and Magog are mentioned.

Horovitz, in *Untersuchungen*, pp. 150 f, believes that although the Arabic for Magog could also be from the Hebrew, the name must have come from the Syriac. The reasons for this are that in the Qur'an Gog and Magog are associated with the end times (cf. also Rev. 20:8) and they moreover appear in the adapted Alexander the Great legend, which is known to have come from Syrian sources. As in many other cases, it appears that Muhammad then invented the Arabic word for Gog to make it rhyme with the word for Magog. Cf. Jeffery, *Vocabulary*, pp. 288f.

17:103 Moses given nine signs.

Horovitz, in *Untersuchungen*, p. 20, n.1, maintains that the number "nine" was used instead of the Biblical "ten," because Muhammad often preferred to use numbers which are one short of a round number. However, Speyer, *Erzählungen*, pp. 278 f., thinks that Muhammad was only speaking inexactly; cf. Midrash Rabbah Numbers (12,5), where the plagues are divided into nine and one.

27:16 David and Solomon were taught the speech of birds.

Speyer, *Erzählungen*, p. 384, gives (Jerusalem) Sotah 9, 24b, the second Targum to Esther and the Syriac Apocalypse of Baruch as references. Cf. I Kings 4:33; Ginzberg, *Legends*, vol. 4, p. 142; *SEI*, p. 55.

27:17f   An ant spoke and Solomon understands.

Geiger, *WMJA*, p. 186, recognizes the relationship to Prov. 6:6f and Hullin 57b; on which Speyer, *Erzählungen*, pp. 401 f elaborates. Cf. Prov. 30:25; Ginzberg, *Legends*, vol. 6, p. 163.

> ### 27:20f   Solomon and the Queen of Sheba exchange messages by a bird, with which Solomon speaks. The Queen of Sheba surrenders to God after seeing Solomon's palace, which is panelled with glass; she thinks the floors are water and exposes her legs.

Geiger, *WMJA*, pp. 183 f, shows that the Qur'anic version of this narration parallels that of the second Targum to Esther (1:3). Cf. Speyer, *Erzählungen*, pp. 390 f; Ginzberg, *Legends*, vol. 4, pp. 142 f. A 14th century source shows that the Abyssinian kings at Axum claimed to have been the descendants of one of the sons of Solomon and the Queen of Sheba (*Encyclopedia of the Early Church*, s.v. "Ethiopia," p. 291; *Ency. Jud.*, s.v. "Ethiopia," p. 943); however, it is not clear as to whether this tradition predates the Qur'an.

18:8f   The Seven Sleepers.

This narration is based on the Christian legend of the seven sleepers, in which seven Christians, who were fleeing the persecution of the Emperor Decius, escaped to a cave near Ephesus, where they slept for about 196 years; Rudolph, *Koran*, p. 271, n. 2; cf. also Ibid., p. 273, n. 11; *SEI*, 45. The legend is thought to have come to Muhammad through Syrian sources; in which al-Raqim (in southern Palestine) is used instead of Ephesus; Horovitz, *Untersuchungen*, p. 95. The time discrepancy is also thought by Horovitz (p. 20, n. 2) to have been an innovation of Muhammad, who gives 309 years instead of 196 (or 377). Andrae, *Ursprung*, pp. 158 f, shows that Nestorian theologian Babai the Great (c. 580 AD) used the legend of the seven sleepers to explain that church's doctrine of "death-sleep."

18:31f   Parable of two men with gardens.

Andrae, *Ursprung*, p. 133, thinks this narration is related to the Syrian parable found in *Anecdota Syriaca*, vol. 2, pp. 39 f. See comments to Qur'an 68:17f above.

18:43   Parable of water.

Cf. Ps. 90:5-6; Is. 55:9-10.

18:59f   Moses and his servant meet a prophet, they journey together.

Geiger, in *WMJA*, p. 203, n. to p. 168, (citing Zunz) shows that this narration is similar to Jewish legends about Rabbi Joshua ben Levi. Nöldeke-Schwally, *GQ*, p. 142, note, think that the parallels to Rabbi Joshua are remote, but also see a weak relation to the Syrian legend about Alexander the Great. Horovitz, *Untersuchungen*, pp. 141 f, elaborates on this idea, maintaining that Moses was somehow confused with Alexander and perhaps with R. Joshua ben Levi as well. Horovitz also shows that the Qur'anic narration also shares a resemblance to the Gilgamesh epic, in which the mountain Masu, may have led someone to substitute "Musa." Horovitz shows that the Qur'anic narrative is similar to a homily of Jacob of Sarug. In any event, the later Islamic legends about al-Khidr also reinforce the idea that the Qur'anic version of this story is a conglomeration of various Middle Eastern narrations. Cf. *SEI*, pp. 232 f.

18:82f   Alexander goes to where the sun sets and sees it set in a muddy spring. He prays to Allah. Alexander goes so far to the East that he meets a people who were not protected from the sun, and who could hardly understand a word. Alexander built a barrier of iron to keep Gog and Magog from entering the land.

This Qur'anic narrative is based on the Syrian Alexander the Great legend, which appears to have been written in 515-516 AD. (cf. Nöldeke-Schwally,

GQ, pp. 140 f., n. 5; Horovitz, *Untersuchungen*, pp. 111 f) and whose pre-Islamic version is only known from Nestorian sources; see Andrae, *Ursprung*, p. 197. It is moreover obvious that Muhammad made some modifications of his own (e.g. 18:85-86, 94, 97f, cf. Nicetas of Byzantium, *ECMD*, p. x.). Cf. Dan. 8:20f; *SEI*, pp. 76, 176, 637.

11:44f   One of Noah's sons drowned.

This idea seems to be alien to Jewish and Christian sources. Geiger, *WMJA*, p. 109, thinks that Canaan was probably meant, and this is the position taken by Islamic scholars also; cf. Tabari, *History*, vol. 1, p. 368. It is also possible that the following lines of the first Nisibene Hymn by Ephraem the Syrian (*Nicene and Post-Nicene Fathers*, vol. 13, p. 167, Carm. Nisib. I, 4) were misunderstood: "... Noah overcame the waves of lust, which had drowned in his generation the sons of Seth."

11:46   The ark rested on al-Judi.

Horovitz, *Untersuchungen*, pp. 107 f, as most after him, cites Nöldeke in the opinion that Muhammad actually meant a mountain in Arabia. Horovitz (Ibid.) thinks Muhammad may have done this just to make it local to Arabia. However, this notion may have originally come from some Jewish and Christian sources, which, contrary to the Biblical account, but in harmony with Babylonian tradition, maintain that the ark rested on the Gordyene (Qardu) Mountains in Mesopotamia. Later Islamic scholars then presumably found the Jewish and Christian sources, and held that the Gordyene Mountains were meant in this passage. See Gen. 8:4; Speyer, *Erzählungen*, p. 107; Jeffery, *Vocabulary*, pp. 106 f.

12:4f   Story of Joseph is related.

Geiger, in *WMJA* and Speyer, in *Erzählungen* show the heavy dependency of the Qur'anic narration on Jewish tradition:

12:24   Joseph would have sinned, but he saw a vision.

Geiger, p. 140: cf. Sotah 36b.

12:26f   Was Joseph's shirt torn from the front or back?

Geiger, p. 142: cf. Sefer ha-Yashar.

12:28f   [Potiphar] justifies Joseph.

Speyer, p. 204: cf. Midrash Rabbah Genesis, parag. 87, 10.

12:30   Egyptian women shame [Potiphar]'s wife.

Speyer, p. 205: cf. Midrash Yalkut Genesis, parag. 146.

12:31f   Egyptian women cut their hands on seeing how handsome Joseph is.

Geiger, p. 140: cf. Sefer ha-Yashar; see also Speyer, p. 205 f.

12:50f   [Potiphar]'s wife admits her guilt after Joseph is brought out of prison.

Speyer, p. 210 f: Ephraem's homily on Gen. 41 (*Opp.* vol. 1, 93C f).

12:67   Jacob tells his sons to enter through many gates and not just one.

Geiger, p. 145: cf. Midrash Rabbah Genesis, parag. 92.

12:69   Joseph secretly told his brother [Benjamin] who he was.

Geiger, p. 146: cf. Sefer ha-Yashar.

12:77   He stole and thus his brother stole.

Geiger, p. 145: cf. Midrash Rabbah Genesis, parag. 92, 8: "A thief the son of a [female] thief" was apparently distorted to the Qur'anic. See Speyer, p. 216.

12:86,97 Jacob knows Joseph lives.

Geiger, p. 145 f: Midrash Tanhuma (Midrash Yalkut, 143).

12:100   Joseph welcomes his parents to Egypt.

Geiger, p. 147, thinks this to be an error on Muhammad's part, based on the fulfillment of his dream (12:101); Speyer, p. 221, also believes this to be an invention of Muhammad.

For the original Joseph narrative, see Gen. 37f. For more materials on the Qur'anic account: cf. Ginzberg, *Legends*, vol. 2, pp. 3 f.; Guillaume, in *Legacy*, pp. 146 f.; *SEI*, pp. 646 f.

40:25   Moses was sent to Pharaoh, Haman and Korah.

Geiger, *WMJA*, p. 153, shows that Korah is depicted as having been the head administrator of Pharoah's household in Midrash Rabbah Numbers, parag. 14. Horovitz,*Untersuchungen*, p. 149, thinks that Muhammad's error of making Haman contemporary with Korah may have come from Jewish sources, e.g. Midrash Rabbah Numbers (22:6), where Haman is named alongside of Korah as having been a rich man.

40:38f   Haman was to build a tower for Pharaoh to go up to God.

An apparent error of Muhammad, where Biblical narration of the tower of Babel (Gen. 11:1f) has been placed in the time of Moses with Haman. Margoliouth ("Additions," *JRAS*, (1939), pp. 58 f) connects Pharaoh's name with the Arabic verb "fr`" and maintains that the word usually translated as "rope" or "road" (v. 38), came from Ethiopic and actually means "watchtower."

28:8   Moses was adopted by Pharaoh's wife.

An apparent error of Muhammad. Cf. Geiger, *WMJA*, p. 153, Horovitz, *Untersuchungen*, p. 86; Ex. 2:10. The Qur'anic accounts also have the same Pharaoh reign from the time of Moses' birth until his return to Egypt, whereas one Pharaoh died while Moses was in Midian (Ex. 2:23) and Moses was 80 years old when he came before the other Pharaoh (Ex. 7:7).

28:14f   Moses kills and asks for forgiveness.

Geiger, *WMJA*, pp. 154 f, presents this notion as being alien to Judaism (cf. Midrash Rabbah Exodus, parag. 5); Speyer, *Erzählungen*, pp. 246 f, agrees with Geiger and shows that Jewish tradition rather tries to absolve Moses from guilt in this matter. Speyer thinks that the source was Christian, but it is also possible that this was simply a modification of Muhammad based on the Qur'anic doctrine of repentance. Cf. Ex. 2:12f for the Biblical account.

28:27   Moses served 8-10 years for his wife.

Muhammad obviously confused the narrative of Jacob (Gen. 29:18f) with that of Moses (Ex. 2:21) and distorted the number of years.

28:76f   Korah was wealthy, envied by Moses' people, swallowed by the earth, he was not a believer.

Speyer, in *Erzählungen*, pp. 342 f, cites Jewish traditions which portray Korah as wealthy: Pesahim 119a, Sanhedrin 110a, (Jerusalem) Nedarim, 9, 4, 26b. Speyer also references Sanhedrin 108a as showing that Korah had no part in either this world or the one to come. Cf. Num. 16: 1f; *SEI*, p. 415.

29:13 Noah was 950 years old at the time of the flood.

As Noah is said to have lived for a total of 950 years in the Biblical account (Gen. 9:28f), Geiger, *WMJA*, p. 109, is no doubt correct in believing this to be an error of Muhammad. Cf. Speyer, *Erzählungen*, p. 109.

31:12 Luqman told his son not to ascribe partners to God.

Horovitz, *Untersuchungen*, pp. 132 f. shows Luqman to have been an Arab wise man who was known in the pre-Islamic poetry of al-A`sha and Zabban b. Sayyar. Cf. *SEI*, p. 289 f.

10:87 Moses and his brother are told to make houses a qibla for prayer and proclaiming the good news to believers in Egypt.

Practically all of the research concerning this verse has centered on the word "qibla" (direction of prayer); cf. Nöldeke-Schwally, *GQ*, p. 176, note; Speyer, *Erzählungen*, pp. 285 f. However, what was probably meant were synagogues, which were usually built facing Jerusalem and were places of prayer and instruction. One would suspect a Jewish source here, which anachronistically not only attempted to make the institution of synagogues date from Moses' time; cf. Acts 15:21; Josephus, *Apion* 2:175; Targum Pseudo-Jonathan to Ex. 18:20; Midrash Yalkut Exodus 408 (from *Ency. Jud.*, vol. 15, p. 580), but from even before the exodus from Egypt.

10:90 Pharaoh repents, becomes a Muslim and is saved from the closing sea.

Geiger, *WMJA*, p. 160 gives Pirke Rabbi Eliezer, 43; Midrash to Ps. 106; Midrash Yalkut 238 as the Jewish sources for Pharoah's repentance, cf. also Speyer, *Erzählungen*, pp. 290 f. The idea that Pharaoh became a Muslim was an innovation of Muhammad, similar to the Qur'anic claims that many other Biblical characters were allegedly Muslims; cf. e.g. Qur'an 3:60.

10:98　The people of Jonah believed.

Cf. Jonah 3:10. See Tabari, *History*, vol. 4, p. 160, where the phrase "people of Jonah," may have caused the Muslim scholars to think Jonah was originally from Nineveh.

34:14f　The two gardens and a flood in Saba' (Sheba).

Andrae, *Ursprung*, p. 133, thinks this was also based on the Syrian garden parable (*Anecdota Syriaca*, vol. 3, pp. 39 f.). However, others maintain that this actually refers to the dam breaks of Ma'rib, which occurred in 456, 549 and c. 570 AD (Rudolph, *Koran*, p. 388, n. 10; cf. Watt and Bell, *Introduction*, p. 7). Horovitz, *Untersuchungen*, pp. 115 f, also shows that among the pre-Islamic Arab poets al-A`sha speaks of the dam in Saba'.

7:105　Moses performs the miracle of the leprous hand in front of Pharoah.

Speyer, in *Erzählungen*, p. 265, gives Pirke Rabbi Eliezer, 48 as the Jewish source for this.

7:139f　Moses requests to see God, but God doesn't allow this; destroys a mountain instead.

Speyer, *Erzählungen*, pp. 341 f, believes that the destruction of the mountain is a corruption of a Talmudic legend, in which Moses threatened to let the mountain fall on the people, because they refused to accept the Torah; cf. Avodah Zarah 2b; Shabbat 88a.

7:163f　Fish which would only come on the Sabbath.

Speyer, *Erzählungen*, p. 314, thinks that Muhammad probably confused various Jewish traditions in this narration; cf. Kiddushin 72a; Shabbat 118a.

7:166   The Sabbath violators who were turned into apes.

Speyer, *Erzählungen*, p. 313, holds that Muhammad probably confused traditions related to the Sabbath with Sanhedrin 109a, where the workers on the tower of Babel said they wanted to fight against God and were then turned into apes, spirits, male and female demons. Cf. *SEI*, p. 415.

7:170   The mountain which was shaken over the children of Israel.

Geiger, *WMJA*, p. 161, gives Avodah Zarah 2b as the source for this.

6:74   Abraham's father was Azar.

It appears that Muhammad mistook the name of Abraham's servant Eliezer (Gen. 15:2) for that of his father Terah (Gen. 11:26f). For an interpretive history of research regarding the origin of the name, see Jeffery, *Vocabulary*, pp. 53 f.

6:75f   Abraham rejects the stars, moon and sun as possible gods.

This material is based on the Midrash Rabbah Genesis parag. 17, Nedarim 32a and Josephus, *Antiquities*, 1,7,1; see Rudolph, *Koran*, p. 143, n. 29. Cf. Grünbaum, *Neue Beiträge*, p. 131; Ginzberg, *Legends*, vol. 5, p. 210, nn. 15-16; *SEI*, p. 154.

2:63f   Moses and the cow.

Speyer, *Erzählungen*, pp. 345 f. shows that Muhammad confused several Old Testament passages here, includung Ex. 12:1f; Num. 19:2f and Dt. 21:2f. Cf. Geiger, *WMJA*, pp. 168 f.

2:92   Gabriel is mentioned with Michael.

Following Dan. 8:16 and 10:13, where the names first appear, Jewish and

Christian apocryphal literature abounds with passages in which the names are mentioned together. Both of the names seem to have come from the Syriac, and the Arabic name for Gabriel does not appear to pre-date Muhammad; cf. Jeffery, *Vocabulary*, pp. 100 f, 275 f.

2:96   Solomon was not an unbeliever.

Speyer, *Erzählungen*, p. 389, shows as a Jewish source Shabbat 56b, which states: "Whoever says that Solomon has sinned, he errs..."

2:96   Harut and Marut are two angels in Babylon.

Horovitz, *Untersuchungen*, pp. 146 f. shows that Lagarde and Littmann thought these to be the Haurvatat and Ameretat of the Avesta, whereas Wensinck, based on Muhammad's tendency to make rhymed pairs of names whereby only one of the pairs is traditional, held that "Marut" may be based on the Syriac (="power"). The only close similarity to Jewish or Christians sources may be found in the apocyrphal Enoch 7:1, where unnamed angels are said to teach humans magic. Cf. Speyer, *Erzählungen*, pp. 388 f.; Jeffery, *Vocabulary*, pp. 282 f.; Margoliouth, "Additions," *JRAS*, (1939),   p. 61; *SEI*, pp. 134 f.

2:118   Abraham was an "imam" and not an idolater.

Speyer, *Erzählungen*, p. 130, believes that the mention of Abraham as an "imam," in the sense of "religious leader" for humanity goes back to Gen. 12:3. Jewish legends which attempt to absolve Abraham of charges that he may have been an idolater before believing on God, can be found in Nedarim 32 (see *SEI*, p. 154). Cf. Ginzberg, *Legends*, vol. 1, pp. 188 f.

2:119f   Abraham and Ishmael to purify Allah's house [the Ka`ba].

That Muhammad regarded the Ka`ba as "Allah's house" can be inferred from even the earliest of the Qur'an's suras (106:3), however, the idea connecting

Abraham and Ishmael with the Ka`ba are Medinan, and not Meccan as one should expect. Whereas in Mecca Muhammad was not aware that Abraham and Ishmael were even related (Cf. Qur'an 19:50; 11:72f; 29:26; 6:83f; Bell, *Origins*, p. 129; Horovitz, *Untersuchungen*, p. 91; Speyer, *Erzählungen*, p. 170; etc.), the Qur'anic legend of Abraham is forged in Medina. Although Nöldeke and Schwally, (*GQ*, p. 147, n. 3) suggest that this idea may have come from Arab Jews or Christians (or just Arabized Jews; cf. *SEI*, p. 399; Crone, *Trade*, p. 190, n. 104), the negative reactions of the Jews and Christians and Muhammad's conciously making a break with them in 2:129-140 show that the idea could not have come from them. Moreover, the change of the qibla (2:136f), which Muhammad essentially justifies by introducing Abraham and Ishmael as the builders of the Ka`ba, also shows that this notion must have been original with Muhammad; the Jews prayed facing Jerusalem and Christians in the East prayed facing eastwards. There can be little doubt that the inspiration for Muhammad's idea was found in the Abraham - Moriah - Temple teaching of the Jews (cf. Gen. 22:2 - II Chr. 3:1 - Josephus, Antiquities, I, 13, 2.)

2:248   Saul was made king by a prophet.

Cf. I Sam. 10:1f. Horovitz, Untersuchungen, p. 123, holds with Geiger (*WMJA*, p. 179) that the Arabic form comes from "to be tall" (cf. I Sam. 9:2). Horovitz (Ibid., p. 106) also thinks that since the name rhymes with the Arabic for Goliath (and Muhammad was inclined to making such pairs), this form was also due to Muhammad.

2:250f   Saul's soldiers are tested by a river as they advance toward Goliath.

Muhammad obviously confused the narration of Gideon, cf. Judges 7:4f, with that of Saul. It is highly probable that this narrative was composed after the battle of Badr, in that about 950 Meccans are said to have been defeated by just more than 300 Muslims. Even later Muslim authorities, in allusions to the Muslim victory at Badr, deliberately confuse the story of Saul with Gideon, where the latter defeated a numerically superior foe (the Midianites) with only 300 soldiers; cf. *Sahih Bukhari*, vol. 5, pp. 201 f; Ibn Sa`d, *Classes*, vol. 2, 1, pp. 19 f; Tabari, *History*, vol. 7, p. 39. The additional reference to David killing Goliath (Qur'an 2:252) could have also been an allusion to the battle of Badr.

2:260   He [Nimrod] who argued with Abraham.

Geiger, *WMJA*, pp. 121 f., gives Midrash Rabbah Genesis, parag. 17 as a Jewish source, but this midrash really only relates how Abraham was thrown into the fiery furnace. Speyer, *Erzählungen*, pp. 140 f., maintains that the Qur'anic narration, whereby Abraham demands that Nimrod make the sun rise in the West, parallels Sanhedrin 91b, in which Antoninus asks the prince Yahuda why the sun sets in the West. Speyer (Ibid.) shows Tanna d. be Elijahu Zuta to be the nearest to the Qur'anic narration and holds that although this midrash is not that old, it must have been based on earlier oral tradition; cf. Ginzberg, *Legends*, vol. 5, p. 218, n. 50.

2:261   He who was made to die 100 years.

Horovitz, in *Untersuchungen*, p. 40, following Schreiner, shows that this narration is based upon Taanit 23a, in which Honi, who falls asleep for 70 years, wakes up to find, among other things, the corpse of his donkey. Cf. Speyer, *Erzählungen*. p. 425; Rudolph, *Koran*, p. 68, n. 141. Margoliouth ("Additions," *JRAS*, (1939), p. 54) suspects a Hebraism in v. 261.

2:262   Abraham asks for a proof of the Resurrection, and is told to cut up four birds, which will brought to life when he calls them.

Geiger, *WMJA*, p. 125, thinks this to be reminiscent of Gen. 15:9f, but shows the Qur'anic account to be alien to Judaism. This story was most likely an innovation of Muhammad.

16:113f   The city and the apostle from their midst.

Muhammad's own experiences with regard to the city of Mecca rather clearly seem to have been meant in this parable.

3:30f   Mary is the daughter of `Imran and came under the care of Zacharias.

Muhammad obviously confused Mary the mother of Jesus with Miriam the sister of Moses, and thus thought that Amram, the father of Miriam and Moses, was the father of Mary; cf. *SEI*, pp. 328 f. The story about Zacharias and Mary seems to have been based on the Protevangelium; cf. Protevangelion 7:1f (*Lost Books*). The Qur'anic account in 3:32, where Zacharias is always said to have found that Mary had food in her chamber, also follows the account of Protevangelion 8:2, in which it is said an angel brought her food.

3:37f   The annunciation is related.

Cf. Protevangelion 9:9f; Infancy Gospel 1:2f; John 1:1, 14. The matter of 3:39 is related in Protevangelion 8:6f and the Gospel of the book of Mary 5:16-6:1 in *Lost Books*.

3:43   Jesus was to make clay birds live.

Cf. Infancy Gospel 15:6; Gospel of Thomas 1:4-8 in *Lost Books*.

3:48f   Allah said He would allow Jesus to die and then would take Him to Heaven.

Source uncertain. Taken literally, this idea is contrary to contemporary Islamic views regarding Jesus' death. Islamic theologians generally attempt to resolve this by saying that such verses (cf. 19:34) will be fulfilled after Jesus' second coming (cf. *Sahih Bukhari*, vol. 3, p. 233; *Sahih Muslim*, vol. 4, p. 1517). Another interesting, but lesser-known view relative to this verse can be found in a tradition transmitted through Ibn Ishaq (Tabari, *History*, vol. 3, p. 122), in which God is said to have permitted Jesus to die at three o'clock in the afternoon.

61:6   Jesus said "Ahmad" would come.

Nöldeke-Schwally, *GQ*, p. 9, n. 1, have shown rather conclusively that this notion had to have been an innovation of Muhammad. Later Islamic efforts at trying to connect this with the New Testament passages regarding the Paraclete of John 14-16 (cf. *ECMD*, s.v. "Paraclete" index), not only aim at trying to make Muhammad a "Biblical" prophet, but also are part of the Islamic apologetic of the Qur'an.

4:156   The Jews did not kill Jesus, but it seemed so to them.

Cf. Gnostic Acts of John 98-100 (*Apokryphen*, pp. 169 f). See the comments to Qur'an 3:48f, above.

4:162   God spoke directly to Moses.

Cf. Ex. 33:11; Dt. 5:4; 34:10; Speyer, *Erzählungen*, pp. 299 f.

4:169   Jesus is a Word and a Spirit from God.

For His being the Word of God, see John 1:1,14. For the notion of Him being the Spirit of God, see Gnostic Acts of John, 98 (*Apokryphen*, pp. 169 f). This verse was used frequently by early Christian polemicists as a Qur'anic source in favor of Jesus' divinity, see *ECMD*, s.v. "4:169" p. 748.

66:10   Noah's and Lot's wives went to Hell.

Jewish and Christian sources only know that Lot's wife was killed; cf. Gen. 19:26. Islamic tradition (*Sahih Bukhari*, vol. 6, p. 408) shows that in Qur'an 66:1-5 Hafsa and ʿAʾisha are referred to and threatened with divorce from Muhammad (v. 5). The "pairs" of women in vv. 10-12 were doubtless used by Muhammad as examples of unbelievers and believers for Hafsa and ʿAʾisha to learn from. The idea that Noah's and Lot's wives went to Hell was most likely an innnovation of Muhammad. In v. 11 Pharaoh's wife prayed to be saved from him. In v. 12 the Spirit was breathed into Mary. See comments to 66:10, above. An interesting hadith (*Sahih Bukhari*, vol. 5, p. 75) reports that Mary and Pharoah's wife attained perfection, and `A'isha is praised as being superior to other women.

9:30   The Jews are said to accept Ezra as God's Son.

Although there is no evidence that any Jews ever held this view, Speyer, *Erzählungen*, p. 413, shows that IV Ezra 14:9 depicts Ezra as having been translated and sitting with God's Son, and he also cites Rießler in mentioning the Apocalypse of Ezra (1:7), in which God's Son was sent to bring the soul of Ezra to heaven. (Cf. *Apokalypsen*, p. 116).

5:30f   The two sons of Adam [Cain and Abel].

Geiger, in *WMJA*, pp. 101 f. demonstrates that this narration is based on Rabbi Pirke Eliezer, 21, in which a raven inspires Adam and Eve (not Cain as in the Qur'an) to bury Abel. Geiger (Ibid.) also shows that 5:35 is based on Sanhedrin 4,5.

5:112f   Jesus has a table come down from Heaven which was to become feast for His disciples and those to come.

It is generally recognized that Muhammad misunderstood the Eucharist in this passage; cf. Nöldeke, "Qur'an", p. 10; Bell, *Origins*, p. 136; *SEI*, p. 174. However, see p. 306, n. 269, above.

5:116f   Jesus denies having said that He and Mary were to be accepted as two gods alongside of Allah.

Andrae, *Ursprung*, p. 205, thinks that Monophysite Abyssinians, who he believes made Mary the heiress to Isis, probably led Muhammad to think that the Trinity was composed of Father - Son - Mary. Cf. Ahrens, "Christliches," *ZDMG*, vol. 84, p. 173.

APPENDIX E
QUR'ANIC PROPHETS & PERSONS
(in approximate order of appearance)

Islamic historians were not only hampered by their disrepect for Biblical sources, but also in that they had to find stories which conformed to the narratives in the Qur'an. It is clear that the first generation of Islamic scholars often had no idea who was meant, and that later Muslim authorities frequently found suitable accounts in Jewish legends, which are frequently far afield of the Biblical accounts. The information from the Qur'an and the traditions from Bukhari (d. 870 AD), Muslim (d. 875 AD), Tabari (d. 923 AD) and Suyuti (d. 1505 AD) show how Islamic knowledge about the prophets and people in the Qur'an developed.

SB - *Sahih Bukhari*, ed. and trans. Muhammad Muhsin Khan
SM - *Sahih Muslim*, ed. and trans. Abdul Hamid Siddiqi
Tabari - *The History of al-Tabari*, ed. Ehsan Yar-Shater
Suyuti - *El-Itkan fi Ulumi'l Kur'an*, ed. and trans. Sakip Yildiz and
     Hüseyin Avni Chelik

For non-Qur'anic works, the first number in parentheses gives the volume number, the second number is the page number.

Abraham - (Ibrahim) The name is not Arabic, its derivation is uncertain, but it must have come from Jews or Christians; it was probably changed from Abraham to Ibrahim to conform with the Arabic forms of Ismail and Israel. (*Vocabulary*, pp. 44 f). QUR'AN: The scroll of Abraham is mentioned (87:19). Abraham preaches Montheism (37:84). Abraham attempts to sacrifice his son (37:101f). Abraham is delivered from a furnace of fire (21:68-69). His father was an idolater (19:43f). Isaac and Jacob were given to Abraham [as sons] (19:50). Abraham was an "imam," and not an idolater (16:121). He is told Lot's city will be destroyed and pleads for him (29:30f). Abraham's father was named Azar (6:74). Abraham and Ishmael were commanded to purify Allah's house of prayer, i.e. Ka`ba (2:119). Abraham was neither Jew nor Christian (3:60). God made Abraham His friend (4:124) HADITH: He was the best of creation (SM 4:1262). He is mentioned as God's

Friend and as having sinned (SM 1:127-9). He lied about Sarah by saying she was his sister to the king of a village (SB 3:230). He lied three times (SB 4:368). He was circumcised at age 80 (SB 4:368). He brings Hagar and Ishmael to the Ka`ba and prays facing it, he later returns to build the House with Ishmael (SB 4:372). He saw in a dream that he was to offer his son (SB 9:99). He was Jacob's father (SM 4:1267). He was tall and resembled Muhammad in appearance (SB 4:367). He will meet his father Azar (SB 4:365) and be the first to be clothed on the day of Resurrection (SB 8:349). He was mentioned in a prayer of Muhammad (SB 8:245). He was seen on the seventh level of heaven during the night journey (SM 1:100). His picture was found in the Ka`ba (SB 4:365). TABARI: He sold idols for his father (2:52). He desecrated an idol and was to be burned to death by Nimrod (2:55f). He has Ishmael divorce his first wife (2:75). He proclaimed the Hajj (2:78). He taught the (Muslim) rituals of prayer and the Hajj (2:81). He tried to sacrifice Isaac (2:90) or Ishmael (2:92). He was buried in Sarah's tomb in Hebron and died at 200 or 175 (2:130). SUYUTI: He was born 2000 years after Adam, was circumcised at 120 years old and died at 200 or 175 years old (2:358-9).

Moses - (Musa) The name is not Arabic; its derivation is uncertain, but does not seem to predate Muhammad (*Vocabulary*, pp. 274 f.) QUR'AN: The scroll of Moses is mentioned (87:19). Moses was accused of coming to drive the Egyptians out of the land (20:59,66). Moses preaches Monotheism (26:23). Moses was given nine signs and Pharaoh says Moses is bewitched (17:103). Moses and his servant meet a prophet and they journey together (18:59f). Moses was thrown into a river (28:6). He was adopted by Pharaoh's wife (28:8). Moses kills and asks for forgiveness (28:14f). He served 8-10 years for his wife (28:27). He requests to see God, but God does not allow this and destroys a mountain instead (7:139f). Moses and the calf (2:63f). God spoke directly to Moses (4:162). HADITH: He killed a man without God's permission (SM 1:127-9). Ibn `Abbas guesses Moses fulfilled the longer (10 year) term to marry one of two daughters (SB 3:525). Ashura commemorates the victory of Moses over Pharaoh (SB 6:211). He screened himself while bathing, was accused of having a hernia or defect, the stone runs away with his clothes, which he beats with his clothes when he overtakes it (SB 1:169). Moses said he was the most learned of the people (SB 1:90). He had troubles dividing spoil, but was patient (SB 5:437). He was tall, had brown curly hair

(SB 4:303) and rode a red camel (SB 4:367). He slaps the angel who has come to take his life (SB 2:236). His following is numerous (SB 4:44) During Muhammad's night journey, Moses is seen praying in his grave (SM 1:1266) and on the sixth level of heaven, where he also encourages Muhammad to request that the number of daily prayers be reduced (from 50 to 5) (SM 1:100). Muhammad was not to be given superiorty over Moses by his followers (SB 4:410). As Aaron was to Moses, so `Ali is to Muhammad (SB 5:46). Muhammad once coughed when saying his name while reciting Q 23:45 (SM 1: 246). Nauf al-Bikali does not believe the Moses of Q 18 to be the prophet Moses; Nauf is called an enemy of God (SB 6:211). TABARI: He and Israel returned to settle in Egypt after the exodus (3:10). He met a prophet (al-Khidr) after re-settlement in Egypt (3:10). He was a year younger than Aaron (3:33). He was taken up to God on a horse and stayed 40 days (3:72). Moses was accused of killing Aaron (3:86). SUYUTI: Moses is described as being the son of `Imran the son of Yashkur the son of Fahas the son of Levi the son of Jacob. He lived 120 years and a physical description of him is given (2:361).

Pharaoh - (Fir`aun) The word is not Arabic and probably from Syriac; it was known to be a title. Since it does not appear in the story of Joseph (Qur'an 12) it may not have been known prior to Muhammad (*Vocabulary,* p. 225). QUR-'AN: Pharaoh used the punishment of crucifixion (20:74). Pharaoh considered himself to be God (26:28). Pharaoh and his people are destroyed because they accused Moses and Aaron of lying (23:50). Pharaoh tried to scare the Israelites out of the land [of Egypt] (17:105). Pharaoh's wife adopts Moses (28:8). Moses appears before Pharaoh and Haman (28:29f). Pharaoh repents, becomes a Muslim and is saved from the closing sea (10:90f). Pharaoh's wife prayed to be saved from him (66:11). HADITH: His wife Asiya is mentioned as one of the three women who had attained perfection (SB 7:244). TABARI: His name was al-Walid b. Mus`ab (3:31). He married an Israelite woman named Asiya, who adopted Moses (3:32). His horses were deceived to follow Israel into the sea (3:64f) SUYUTI: ---.

Satan - (Shaytan) The word is probably not of Arabic origin, but rather owing to Christian influence; it predates Muhammad (*Vocabulary* pp. 187 f). QUR'AN: The Qur'an is not the word of a stoned Satan (81:25). Satan deceives Adam and his wife (20:118 developed later in 7:19f) and says he will lead (Adam) to the tree of Eternity (20:118). HADITH: He touched all humans at birth except for Mary and Jesus (SB 4:324). Gabriel took the part of Satan from Muhammad's heart (when he was a child), washed his heart in Zamzam and placed it back in his body (SM 1:103). Satan never appears in Muhammad's form (SM 4:1225). He takes to flight when the Adhan and Iqama are read (SB 1:336). Satan weeps when the verse of sajda (prostration) is recited and performed (SM 1:48). He runs away from houses where Q 2 is read (SM 1:377). He ties three knots in the head (hair) of the sleeping (SB 2:134). He stays in the upper part of the nose at night (SB 4:328). He relieves himself in the ears of those who sleep through the morning prayers (SB 2:135). Yawning is from Satan (SB 4:325). He is on the loose at night, but he cannot open closed doors, sealed waterskins or vessels (SM 3:1113). Satan eats the food dropped at a meal (SM 3:1121). The bell is an instrument of Satan (SM 3:1163). Muslim fought Muslim at Uhud because Satan had tricked them (SB 4:325). Satan always takes another route when he sees 'Umar (SB 4:328). Satan has given up hope of being worshipped in Arabia, so he tries to instigate dissension (SM 4:1471). His head will appear from the east (SB 4:321). TABARI: Many references. SUYUTI: Many references.

Noah - (Nuh) The name is not Arabic, probably from Syriac and predates Muhammad (*Vocabulary* p. 282). QUR'AN: Noah is accused of lying, cries to his Lord for help and the flood is sent (54:9f). Noah is a preacher of forgiveness (71:4,9). Noah describes rain as a blessing (71:10f). Noah's people rebelled against him (71:20). Noah mentions the names of gods worshipped in Muhammad's time (71:22f). Noah prays that no unbelievers be left upon the earth (71:27). Noah preaches Monotheism (26:108). The vilest follow Noah (26:111). One of Noah's sons drowned (11:44f). Noah was 950 years old before the flood (29:13) Noah's wife went to Hell (66:10). HADITH: He is mentioned as having cursed the earth in his day (SM 1:1279). TABARI: He worked on the ark 400 years (1:356). In the presence of his disciples, Jesus resurrected Noah's son Ham and asked him questions (1:357). Noah was even commanded to take trees with him on the ark; at least 13 people and Satan were in the ark (1:360). Og b. Anak, who was 800 cubits tall, survived the flood (1:361). Adam's corpse was in the ark; the Ka'ba was not submerged in the Flood (1:362). According to some there were 80 people in the ark (1:364).

SUYUTI: Some say he is Idris and lived 20 generations later than Adam. He was a prophet at 40, lived 950 years of which 60 were after the flood. He was born 126 years after Adam's death. Noah was the oldest prophet (2:357-8).

Lot - (Lut) The name is not Arabic, probably from Syriac and does not predate Islam (*Vocabulary*, p. 255). QUR'AN: An old woman was not saved with Lot (37:134). Lot preached Monotheism (26:163). Lot's wife was not to be saved (15:59f). Lot's people want to drive him from the land (27:57). He offered his two daughters to the people (11:80). Lot believed Abraham (29:25). Lot's wife was sent to Hell (66:10) HADITH: --- TABARI: Is the son of Haran the son of Terah (2:111) SUYUTI: He is the son of Haran the son of Azar, or according to another, he is the son of Abraham's brother's son (2:360).

Aaron - (Harun) The name is not Arabic, probably from a Christian-Palestinian dialect of Syriac and predates Muhammad (*Vocabulary*, pp. 283-4). QUR'AN: He is mentioned with Moses (37:120). Mary is said to have been of "sister of Aaron" (19:29). Moses and his brother Aaron were sent to Pharaoh (23: 47f). HADITH: As Aaron was to Moses, so `Ali is to Muhammad (SB 5:46). Muhammad once coughed when reciting Aaron's name in Q 23:45 (SM 1:246). It is said that the brother of Mary was different from Miriam's brother (SM 4:1169). Aaron was seen on the fifth level of heaven during the night journey (SM 1:100). TABARI: He died in an illusion of a house on a mountain top (3: 75) and according to some, rose from the dead and cleared Moses from the accusations that Moses had murdered him (3:88). SUYUTI: He is the brother of Moses, some say by his mother, some by his father. He died before Moses and was one year older than him. He was the son of `Imran. Aaron means "beloved" in Hebrew ["enlightened"]. A physical description of him is given (2:361).

Isaac - (Ishaq) The name is not Arabic, probably came from Christian sources and is said to predate Islam, there is no evidence of this though (*Vocabulary*, p. 60). QUR'AN: Isaac is Abraham's son (37:112). He was a prophet (19:50). HADITH: --TABARI: He was to be sacrificed by Abraham

(2:90). He lived to be 160 (2:147). SUYUTI: He was 14 years younger than Ishmael. He died at 180 and his name means "to laugh much" ["laughter"] (2:359).

Elias - (Ilyas) The name is not Arabic, is probably from Syriac (or Ethiopic) and predates Islam (*Vocabulary*, pp. 67-8). QUR'AN: Elias is mentioned with respect to the challenge against Baal (37:123f). HADITH: --- TABARI: Rain was held back three years because of his prayer (3:123). He was taken away on a fiery horse (3:125). SUYUTI: According to Ibn Ishaq, Ilyas is the son of Yasin the son of Fenhas the son of Ayzar the son of Aaron whose brother was Moses b. `Imran. Another says he was a grandson of Yusha (Joshua ?). Another says he lived as long as al-Khadir and would live until the Judgment. Another says he is Idris (2:363).

Baal - (Ba`l) The name is not Arabic, probably from the Syriac (or Ethiopic) and predates Muhammad (*Vocabulary*, p. 81). QUR'AN: Baal is mentioned (37:123f). HADITH: --- TABARI: Was an idol worshipped in the time of Elijah (3:123). SUYUTI: It is said this was a woman's name which was worshipped (2:367).

Jonah - (Yunus) The name is not Arabic, probably came from Christians and is said to predate Islam, although the evidence is doubtful (*Vocabulary*, pp. 295-6). QUR'AN: Jonah would still be in the fish if he had not praised God, he was ill, God caused a gourd to grow over him, he was sent to more than 100,000 people, who believed and were allowed to live (37:139f). The people of Jonah believed (10:98f). HADITH: None is to say he is better than Jonah the son of Matta (SB 4:413). TABARI: He is placed after Jesus in time, and is said to have been from Nineveh (4:160). Others said he was told to go to Nineveh by Gabriel and the whale brought him to Nineveh via the Tigris (4:161). Some say a tree and a goat witness that a shepherd had seen Jonah and thus many believed in him (4:164). SUYUTI: He is the son of Matta. According to one, his mother had this name, another says Matta must have been his father's name. One says he lived in the times of the Iranian kings. Some say he lived in the belly of a fish for 40 days, another says 7 days, another says 3 days. Another says he was swallowed in the morning and spit out after sunset (times given as Islamic prayer times) (2:362-3).

Adam - (Adam) The name is not Arabic, as the Arabs can give no worthy explanation as to its meaning; it probably came from Hebrew and predates Muhammad (*Vocabulary*, pp. 50-1). QUR'AN: Satan does not bow to Adam; Adam and his wife are deceived by Satan (20:114f). This theme is more developed in 7:10f. HADITH: He was 60 cubits tall (SB 4:342). He was not responsible for his sin, as this was his pre-determined fate (SB 4:410). Adam's son was the first murderer (SB 3:900). Adam was seen on the first level of heaven during Muhammad's night journey (SM 1:100) TABARI: Angels used to eat of the forbidden tree and live eternally (1:277). Adam was driven out of Paradise, was forgiven and died on Fridays (1:282). Adam was in Paradise 500 years and was cast down to earth in India (1:290). Eve was cast down to earth in Mecca (1:292). Adam's height was reduced to 60 cubits, he was sent to Mecca, where he circumambulated the House (1:293). The Ka`ba was white in Adam's time (1:297). The House was a jewel or pearl sent down from heaven (1:302). SUYUTI: His name is Arabic, or Hebrew meaning "soil" ["man"]. He lived 960 or 1000 years (2:357).

Iblis - (Iblis) The name is not Arabic, probably comes from the Greek and does not predate Muhammad (*Vocabulary* pp. 47-8). QUR'AN: Iblis refuses to bow before Adam (20:114f) HADITH: --TABARI: Many references. SUYUTI: Ibn `Abbas: Iblis was a jinn whose first name was Azazel. According to some his first name was Haris, which means Azazel.

Samaritan - (al-Samiri) The name is not Arabic, probably comes from the Hebrew (Midrash ?) and probably does not predate Muhammad (*Vocabulary*, pp. 158-9). QUR'AN: The Samaritan was a deceiver of Israel against Moses (20:87f). HADITH: --TABARI: His name was Musa b. Zafar (3:76). The golden calf, which could bellow and walk was made so from the dust the Samaritan gathered from the hoof (print) of Gabriel's horse (3:72) SUYUTI: ---.

Hud - (Hud) The name is Arabic, his identity is disputed; the root of the name means to be of Jewish faith (*SEI*, p. 140). QUR'AN: Hud was an Arabian prophet who was the brother of the 'Ad (26:123f). Hud preached Monotheism (26:126). HADITH: --TABARI: He preached the oneness of God to the `Ad (2:29), who were in turn destroyed for not believing him (2:39f). He is said to be Aber (Heber ?) b. Arpachshad b. Shem b. Noah. According to others he is the son of Abdullah b. Rabah b. Hafaz b. Uz b. Iram b. Shem b. Noah (2:28). SUYUTI: He was the one who most resembled Adam and was strong (2:369).

Salih - (Salih) The name is Arabic; he was a prophet sent to the Thamud (*SEI*, p. 499) QUR'AN: Salih preached Monotheism (26:144). Salih was an Arabian prophet who was a brother of the Thamud (11:64). HADITH: --- TABARI: He was b. 'Ubayd b. Arif b. Masikh b. 'Ubayd b. Khadir b. Thamud b. Gether b. Aram b. Shem b. Noah, or according to others: b. Arif b. Ka-mashij b. Iram b. Thamud b. Gether b. Aram b. Shem b. Noah (2:49). Salih prayed for a sign from God; a she-camel was given, which was later hamstrung by the Thamud, who were then destroyed for this sin (2:40f) SUYUTI: He was the son of 'Ubayd b. Khayir b. Samud b. Khayir b. Shem b. Noah. A physical description of him is given. He lived 40 years and was a prophet between Noah and Abraham. According to another he was the son of 'Ubayd b. Khazar b. Samud b. 'Ad b. Uz b. Aram b. Shem b. Noah, and died at 58 in Mecca (2:360).

Shu'ayb - (Shu'ayb) The name is Arabic; he was a prophet sent to the Aika, he was later than Hud and Salih (*SEI*, p. 544) QUR'AN: Shu'ayb preached Monotheism (26:179). Shu'ayb was a prophet who was a brother of the Midianites (11:85) HADITH: --TABARI: He was Moses' father-in-law Jethro (3:31). He was sent as a prophet to the Midianites and "the masters of the thorn bush" (2:145). His people were punished for cutting dirhams (2:147). SUYUTI: Some say his name was Ibn Mikyal. According to one, his name was Ibn Mikyal b. Yashjan b. Levi b. Yacob. Another writes he was Shu'ayb b. Mikyal b. Yashjan b. Madyan b. Abraham al-Khalil. He was a prophet sent to the peoples of Madyan and Aika as an apostle; he prayed much. In his old age, he lost his sight. Some say no other prophet was sent to two peoples aside from Shu'ayb (2:360-1).

Zacharias - (Zakariyya) The name is not Arabic, probably comes from Syriac and is not found in pre-Islamic literature (*Vocabulary*, p. 151). QUR-'AN: Zacharias could not speak for three nights (days) after receiving the promise of John's birth (19:1f). Zacharias asks for an heir for himself and the house of Jacob (19:5). Mary is taken care of by Zacharias (3:30f). HADITH:

He was a carpenter (SM 4:1267). TABARI: He was accused of making Mary pregnant, he fled, was enclosed in a tree and sawed up by the Jews (4:120). SUYUTI: He was from the lineage of Solomon b. David. He was martyred after his son. He was (either) 92, 99 or 120 years old when his son was born. His name is Persian (2:363).

John [the Baptist]- (Yahya) The name is not Arabic. probably comes from Syriac and seems to predate Muhammad (*Vocabulary* p. 290). QUR'AN: John was the son of Zacharias; similar to Jesus peace is wished for him on the day of his birth, death and resurrection (19:7f) HADITH: He is seen with Jesus on the second level of Heaven during Muhammad's night journey (SM 1:100). TABARI: He was born 6 months before Jesus and was killed before the latter's ascension (4:102). Some say Nebuchadnezzar attacked Israel because the Jews had killed John (4:54); the verions of Ibn `Abbas (4:103) and Ibn Mas`ud (4:104), which are the oldest, propagate this view. A version approximating the Biblical accounts is also given later (4:108). SUYUTI: He is the son of Zacharias, according to the Qur'an he is the first to be named Yahya. He was born 6 months before Jesus and was proclaimed by prophecy at a young age. He was martyred by torture. God punished his murderer by sending Bukht Nasar [Nebuchadnezzar] and his army to attack him. Some think his name was Arabic, others do not (2:363-4).

Mary - (Maryam) The name is not Arabic, probably comes from the Syriac and does not predate Muhammad (*Vocabulary*, p. 262). QUR'AN: Mary has a book which is named after her; the birth of Jesus is related (19:16f). Mary is the daughter of `Imran and came under the care of Zacharias (3:30f). The Qur'anic annunciation is related (3:37f). The Spirit was breathed into Mary (66:12). HADITH: She and Jesus were not touched by Satan at birth as all other humans are (SB 3:324). She was the best of women in her lifetime (SB 5:103) and was one of three women to attain perfection (SB 5:75). A picture of her was found in the Ka`ba (SB 3:365). TABARI: She gave birth to Jesus at 13 and died at 50 (4:102). She was the sister of Elizabeth and was looked after by Zacharias (4:103). She was of Solomon's lineage (4:103), but another says of Aaron's (4:120). She and her relative Joseph (a carpenter) served in the temple (4:113). SUYUTI: No other woman's name is mentioned in the Qur'an. "Maryam" means "servant" in Hebrew ["fat, thick, strong"] (2:367).

Jesus - (`Isa) The name is not Arabic (from Aramaic?). This form does not predate Muhammad and might have been made so to rhyme with Musa (*Vocabulary*, pp. 218 f). QUR'AN: Jesus was pure (19:19). He speaks from the cradle (19:31). Jesus and Mary were made a sign (23:52). Jesus was the Messiah (3:40). God said He would allow Jesus to die and then would take Him to Heaven (3:48). The Jews did not kill Jesus, but it seemed so to them (4:156). Jesus is a Word and a Spirit from God (4:169). Jesus said "Ahmad" would come (61:6). Jesus was sent to confirm the Torah and was given the Gospel (5:50). God speaks to Jesus at the Judgment; Jesus made a clay bird live, healed the blind and lepers; raised the dead (5:109f). Jesus has a table come down from Heaven which was to become a feast for His disciples and those who followed (5:112f). Jesus denies having said that He and Mary were to be accepted as two gods alongside of Allah (5:116f). HADITH: He and Mary were not touched by Satan at birth as all other humans (SB 4:324). He is a "pious slave" (SB 4:436). He is God's slave, Apostle, Word and Spirit (SB 4:429). He was of medium height, "moderate complexion" with reddish-white "lank" hair (SB 4:303). Muhammad tells of a prophet who after being beaten with blood running down his face said "Forgive my people, as they do not know" (SB 9:49) [from the crucifixion; Lk. 23:34] There were 600 years between Jesus and Muhammad (SB 5:194). There was no prophet between Jesus and Muhammad (SM 4:1260). Muhammad is the closest to Jesus of all people (SB 4:434). Muhammad is not to be praised by his followers as Jesus is by the Christians (SB 4:435). Jesus is worshipped as God's Son by the Christians (SB 9:395). Muhammad sees Jesus near the Ka`ba in a dream (SB 9:106). Jesus sees a man stealing, but drops the accusation when the other swears by God that he did not steal (SB 4:434). Muhammad once coughed when reciting Jesus' name in Q 23:52 (SM 1:246). He who first believed in Jesus, but then in Muhammad will receive a double reward (SB 4:435). Jesus is to descend on the mosque in Damascus (SM 4:1516). He is to return to earth as a judge, who will break all crosses, kill swine and abolish the "jizya" (tax) (SB 3:233). He will judge by the Qur'anic law, and not that of the Gospel (SB 4:437). Although all other prophets have sins, including Muhammad,

Jesus will mention none for Himself during the Judgment (SB 6:198). He was seen on the second level of Heaven with John (the Baptist) during Muhammad's night journey (SM 1:100). TABARI: He lived 32 years before His ascension (4:102). When He was born all the idols on earth fell over (4:120). He solved a theft in while in Egypt and turned water into wine at age 12 (4:117). He spoke of His impending death to His disciples, but He was raised up to God and another died in His place (4:122, 125). Ibn Ishaq: Jesus died (4:122). SUYUTI: He was born without father. Mary was 10 or 15 years old, and was pregnant with Him (according to scholars) 1 hour, 3 hours, 6 months, 8 months or 9 months. He was 33 at His ascension. Some hadith say He will return, kill Dajjal, marry, have children, perform the Hajj, live 7 years and be buried next to Muhammad. Physical description from Bukhari is given. There were only two prophets with two names: Jesus (Jesus, Messiah) and Muhammad (Muhammad, Ahmad) (2:364).

Jacob - (Ya`qub) The name is not Arabic and comes from either the Hebrew or Syriac; it predates Muhammad (*Vocabulary*, p. 291). QUR'AN: Issac and Jacob were given to Abraham [as sons]; both were prophets (19:50). HADITH: He was Abraham's son and Joseph's father (SM 4:1267). TABARI: Some say he settled in Anatolia (2:137). SUYUTI: He lived 147 years.

**Ishmael - (Isma`il)** The name is not Arabic and probably comes from a Christian-Palestinian dialect of Syriac; it predates Muhammad (*Vocabulary*, pp. 63-4). QUR'AN: Ishmael is commanded to purify the house of prayer, i.e. Ka`ba, with Abraham (2:119). Ishmael had a book named after himself (19:55). HADITH: He drank from the spring Zamzam, where he and his mother Hagar were left by Abraham, he later helped Abraham build the House (SB 4:372). He was a great archer (SB 4:97). Ishmael's picture was in the Ka`ba (SB 4:366). TABARI: He was to be sacrificed by Abraham (2:92). He divorced his first wife (2:75). He was sent as a prophet to the Amalekites and the Yemenites (2:132). SUYUTI: He was Abraham's oldest son (2:359).

Idris - The name is not Arabic, probably came from a Christian-Palestinian dialect of Syriac; it is thought to come from "Andreas" (the cook of Alexander the Great in the Syrian Alexander legend) (*Vocabulary*, p. 52).

QUR'AN: Idris is a prophet who had a book named for himself (19:57)
HADITH: He is seen on the fourth level of heaven during Muhammad's night
journey (SM 1:100). TABARI: He was Cain's son (1:337). According to some
he died at age 365 (1:346). [As al-Khidr he drank from the River of Life and
became eternal (3:2)]. SUYUTI: He is said to have preceded Noah and was
the first to give prophecy. Some say he was Noah's father, a physical description is given on weak evidence. He was taken (translated) at 350 years. There
were 100 years between him and Noah (2:358).

David - (Dawud) The name is not Arabic, probably comes from the Aramaic
and predates Muhammad (*Vocabulary*, p. 128). QUR'AN: David's decision
between the man with 99 sheep and the man with one is related, David repents
(38:16f). David and Solomon decide about the retribution for those whose
fields were entered by stray sheep; the mountains and birds were subjected to
David (21:78f). Iron was made soft for David to make coats of mail (21:80,
34:10). David killed Goliath (2:252). HADITH: He prayed for one third of the
night and fasted on every other day (SB 2:129). David fasted half of the year
(SB 3:110). He recited the entire Zabur [Psalms] as his animals were being
saddled (SB 4:416). Two women had children, a wolf took the child of one,
and the two women argued about which had been taken. They come to David,
who decides to give the "living" child to the oldest woman; they then go to
Solomon, who decides to cut the child in two with a knife, and then gives the
child to the woman who said it belonged to the other (SB 4:637). TABARI:
He had at least 12 brothers (3:135). He was chosen to fight Goliath by having
a horn of oil placed over his head, which overflowed and annointed him
(3:136). A physical description is given (3:140). He would spend one day with
the people, one in worship and one with his 99 wives (3:144). A parable of 99
ewes and 1 ewe is told David by two angels after Uriah had been killed
(3:145). The rebellion of Absalom (3:149). David began building the Temple
(3:150f). David lived to be 100 or 77 (3:151). SUYUTI: He was the son of
`Isa [Joshua] b. Avbad b. Baar b. Solomon b. Yashun b. Uma b. Yarab b.
Ram b. Hadran b. Faris b. Yahuda [Judah] b. Jacob. According to Tirmidhi he
was the most worshipful prophet. A physical description is given. He died at
100 years, reigned 40 years and had 12 sons (2:361-2).

Solomon - (Sulayman) The name is not Arabic, comes from Syriac (speaking Christians) and predates Muhammad (*Vocabulary*, p. 178). QUR'AN: Solomon is shown to have loved horses (38:30f). Solomon asked for a kingdom unlike any other (38:34). David and Solomon decide about the retribution for those whose fields have been entered by stray sheep (21:78f). Solomon and David were taught the speech of birds; an ant spoke and Solomon understands; Solomon and the Queen of Sheba exchange messages by a bird, with which Solomon speaks (27:20f). Solomon was not an unbeliever (2:96). HADITH: He wanted to have many sons who would fight for God, so he slept with 100, 70 or 90 women, but these gave birth to but a "half man," if he had said "inshallah" Solomon's intent would have been realized (SB 4:56, 421). Two women had children, a wolf took the child of one, and the two women argued about which had been taken. They come to David, who decides to give the "living" child to the oldest woman; they then go to Solomon, who decides to cut the child in two with a knife, and then gives the child to the woman who said it belonged to the other (SB 4:637). TABARI: He was a man of war, with an army of humans, jinn, wild animals and birds (3:153f). He travelled seated on his throne, which was then driven by the wind (3:157). Solomon answers the riddles of the Queen of Sheba (3:159f). Ibn `Abbas - Solomon marries her (3:163). A wife of Solomon worships an image of her father (3:167). Solomon is punished 40 days, after a devil steals his signet ring (3:169). Solomon's ring and kingdom are restored (3:170). SUYUTI: Physical description is given. He was given wisdom although he was young. Ibn `Abbas: Two believers ruled the world - Solomon and Alexander the Great. Two unbelievers ruled the world - Nimrod and Buhtu Nasr [Nebuchadnezzar]. Solomon was ruler at 13 and began to build the Temple in the 4th year of his reign. He died at 53 years (2:362).

Job - (Ayyub) The name is not Arabic, probably comes from the Syriac and predates Muhammad (*Vocabulary*, p. 73). QUR'AN: Job was to strike with a bundle of rushes to keep an oath (38:43). HADITH: Golden locusts used to cover Job as he was bathing (SB 1:169). TABARI: He was thought to have been a (Syrian) Byzantine (2:140). He was b. Maws b. Razih b. Esau b. Isaac b. Abraham; or b. Maws b. Raghwil (2:140). His wife was one of Jacob's daughters (2:140). His trials are mentioned (2:141f) He was set on fire by Iblis (2:142). According to some he was thought to have stayed on a dung heap for

7 years (2:142). He lived at the time of Jacob (2:143). He lived to be 93 (2:143). SUYUTI: If it is true that he is of the Israelites, it is known his father was Abyad. One says he was the son of Mus b. Ravh b. Is b. Isaac. Another says his mother was Lot's daughter, his father was one who believed in Abraham. He must have lived before Moses. One says he lived after Shu`ayb, another says after Solomon. At 70 he was ill for 7 years; some say this lasted 3 or 13 years. One said he lived 93 years (2:362).

Dhu'l-Kifl - The name is Arabic, but the person is unknown. Suggestions include Joshua, Elijah, Zacharias, a Bishr (*SEI*, p. 76) or Ezekiel (Kassis, p. 637). QUR'AN: He is mentioned (38:48 and 21:85) HADITH: --- TABARI: As Dhu'l-Kifl he is said to have been Bishr b. Job, who lived to be 75 and died in Syria (2:143). SUYUTI: Some say he was Job's son, another says Bishr b. Job was sent as a prophet and named Dhu'l-Kifl. He preached Monotheism and died at 75 years. He spent his entire life in Damascus. Another says he was Elijah or Joshua b. Nun or the Zacharias of Q 3:37. He was surety for him whom God gave the double of works, or the one who made al-Yasa his representative. He fasted during the day and prayed at night, or prayed the ritual prayer 100 times a day, or his name is al-Yasa and the other name was Dhu'l-Kifl (2:362).

Gog and Magog - (Yajuj wa Majuj) The names are not Arabic, probably came from Syriac and probably do predate Muhammad (*Vocabulary*, p. 288). QUR'AN: They are mentioned (21:96). Alexander the Great built a barrier to keep Gog and Magog from entering the land (18:93f). HADITH: Their peoples will be sent to Hell (SM 1:143). TABARI: Are cousins of the Turks (2:11). They are east of the Turks (2:16). SUYUTI: They are considered to be the names for tribes (2:367).

Sheba (the Queen of) - (Saba) The name probably comes from Arabic-Jewish or Christian sources; it predates Muhammad (*Vocabulary*, p. 160.) QUR'AN: The Queen of Sheba and Solomon exchange messages by a bird (27:20f). She surrenders to God after seeing Solomon's palace, which is panelled with glass; she thinks the floors are water and exposes her legs (27:45). HADITH: --- TABARI: Her name was Bilqis, Yalmaqah bt. al-

Yashrah, or bt. Ayli Sharh, or bt. Dhi Sharh, etc. (3:156). Her riddles to
Solomon are mentioned (3:159f). She had unshaven legs (3:162). Ibn `Abbas:
She married Solomon (3:163). Ibn Ishaq - She married the king of Hamdan
(3:164). SUYUTI: ---.

Alexander - (Dhu'l-Qarnayn) The name is Arabic and is based on a Syrian
(the Great) legend (*SEI*, p. 76). QUR'AN: He goes to where the sun sets and
sees it set in a muddy spring (18:84). He goes far to the east and meets a
people who can hardly understand a word (18:92). He is commanded to build
a wall between Allah and Gog with Magog, which he does (18:93f). Alexander prays to Allah (18:84f). HADITH: --- TABARI: He marched to "the dark
area near the North Pole" and to the "area of the southern sun" (4:94). SU-
YUTI: According to one, Dhu'l-Qarnayn was an angel (2:365). He is Alexander, according to others. Dhu'l-Qarnayn was thought to be someone else
(2:373).

Joseph - (Yusuf) The name is not Arabic, probably comes from the Jews and
seems to predate Muhammad (*Vocabulary*, p. 295). QUR'AN: The Qur'anic
story of Joseph is related (12:4f). HADITH: He stayed in prison for a long
time (SB 4:386). There was a famine of 7 years in his time (SB 2:64). He is
the most righteous among the people (SB 4:366). Woman Muslims were
described as being the companions of Joseph (SB 1:367). He was seen on the
third level of heaven during Muhammad's night journey (SM 1:100). TA-
BARI: Some say he was born after Leah's death (2:135). Joseph was later
married to Potiphar's widow (2:166). Joseph was 97 when he saw Jacob again
(2:183). Joseph died at 120 (2:183). The Torah says he lived to be 110
(2:185) SUYUTI: He was the son of Ishaq b. Abraham. He was in the well at
12 and reunited with his father at 80, he died at 120. According to some, the
Joseph in Q 40:36 is Joseph b. Efraim b. Joseph b. Jacob. The Jacob in Q 19:6
is thought to be Jacob b. Mathan. The wife of Zacharias, the daughter of
`Imran b. Mathan, is Mary's sister, so it is strange to think of him as Jacob b.
Isaac b. Abraham. Two scholars thought that the Joseph in Q 40:36 was a jinn,
who had been sent as an apostle of God (2:359).

Haman - (Haman) The name is not Arabic and is probably came from the
Jews (through rabbinic legends) (*Vocabulary*, p. 284). QUR'AN Moses was

sent to Pharaoh, Haman and Korah (40:25). Haman was to build a tower for Pharaoh to go up to God (28:38). HADITH: - -- TABARI: Haman pursued the Israelites with Pharaoh (3:64). SUYUTI: He was an unbeliever (2:367).

Korah - (Qarun) The name is not Arabic, probably came from the Jews (through rabbinic legends); it rhymes with Harun (Aaron) (*Vocabulary*, p. 231). QUR'AN: Moses was sent to Pharaoh, Haman and Korah (40:25). Korah was wealthy, envied by Moses' people, swallowed by the earth and was not a believer (28:76f). HADITH: --- TABARI: He was the son of Izhar (3:99). His treasure keys were carried by 40 or 60 mules (3:101). He paid off a prostitute and accused Moses of committing adultery (3:105). SUYUTI: Ibn `Abbas: He was the son of Yahser. Yahser is the son of Moses' uncle (2:367).

Luqman - (Luqman) The name is Arabic; he is a personage from pagan Arabia (*SEI*, p. 289). QUR'AN: He told his son not to ascribe partners to God (31:12). HADITH: --- TABARI: He was the master of `Ad (2:34). SUYUTI: Although some say he was a prophet, most scholars follow Ibn `Abbas in saying he was an Abyssinian slave who was a carpenter (2:366).

Azar - (Azar) The name is not Arabic, came from the Hebrew; Muhammad confused Eleazar (Abraham's servant) with Terah (Abraham's father) (*Vocabulary*, p. 55). QUR'AN: He was Abraham's father (6:74). HADITH: He will be seen by his son Abraham on the day of Resurrection and then be transformed into an animal which will be thrown into Hell (SB 4:365). TABARI: He made idols to sell (2:52) SUYUTI: He was an unbeliever; the father of Abraham. Azar was Terah's nickname. Some say Abraham's father was Terah, (and that) Azar was the name of an idol (2: 367).

Gabriel - (Jibril) The name is not Arabic, probably came from Syriac and probably does not predate Muhammad (*Vocabulary*, pp. 10 f). QUR'AN: He is mentioned with Michael (2:92). HADITH: He escorts Muhammad to Heaven during the night journey (SM 1:100). He recited the Qur'an to Muhammad in seven different ways (SB 4:294). He had 600 wings (SB 4:301). His genuine size covered the horizon (SB 4:301). He and other angels do not enter houses where there are dogs or pictures (SM 3:1157). He offers `A'isha greetings, which she returns, but she cannot see him as Muhammad does (SB 4:1302). He met with Muhammad each Ramadan, at which time Muhammad recited the Qur'an to him (for verification) (SM 4:1241). He recited the Qur'an with Muhammad once or twice yearly, twice in Muhammad's last year, for which reason Muhammad thinks his death is impending (SM 4:1307). TA-BARI: Many references. SUYUTI: He is an angel whose name along with the angels', means "God's servant" according to some (including Ibn `Abbas) [Heb. "God is mighty"] (2:365).

Michael - (Mikal) The name is not Arabic, probably came from the Syriac and predates Muhammad (*Vocabulary*, pp. 275-6). QUR'AN: He is mentioned with Gabriel (2:92). HADITH: --- TABARI: Many references. SU-YUTI: He is an angel, whose name, according to Ibn `Abbas, means "humble worshipper," [Heb. "who is like God? "] because the "el" at the end of each word means "one who serves God." Another says "el" in Hebrew means God (2:367).

Harut and Marut - (Harut wa Marut) The names are not Arabic and probably came from Aramaic (*Vocabulary*, pp. 282 f). QUR'AN: They are two angels in Babil (2:96). HADITH: --- TABARI: --- SUYUTI: According to `Ali, both are the names of angels in Heaven (2:365).

Saul - (Talut) The name is not Arabic, probably came from Hebrew, and was corrupted by Muhammad; it rhymes with Jalut (Goliath) (*Vocabulary*, p. 204). QUR'AN: Saul was made king by a prophet (2:248). His soldiers are tested by a river as they advance toward Goliath (2:250f). HADITH: --- TABARI: He tried to kill David (2:137). He killed many scholars (2:137f). Some say that the prophet who was resurrected to tell Saul he had been forgiven was Joshua, others say it was Elisha "b. Akhtub" (3:139). SUYUTI: ---.

Goliath - (Jalut) The name is not Arabic, came from Hebrew, was introduced by Muhammad and rhymes with Talut (Saul) (*Vocabulary*, p. 97). QUR'AN: He was an enemy of Saul and was killed by David (2:250f). HADITH: --- TABARI: He was the king of the Amalekites (3:129). David's shot pierced through his head and killed others behind him (3:137). SUYUTI: He was an unbeliever (2:367).

Amram - (`Imran) The name is not Arabic, probably came from the Syriac and was known before Muhammad (*Vocabulary*, p. 217). QUR'AN: He is the father of Mary (3:30f). HADITH: --- TABARI: His wife was Jochebed or Anahid (3:30). He lived to be 136 (3:31). SUYUTI: According to one, he is not Mary's father, but Moses' (2:359) He is the father of Mary, Moses' father or Mary's brother Aaron. According to a hadith in *Sahih Muslim*, he (Aaron) is not the brother of Moses (i.e. this Aaron is another Aaron) (2:366).

Messiah - (Masih) The word is not Arabic, probably came from the Syriac and predates Muhammad (*Vocabulary*, p. 266) QUR'AN: "Masih" is mentioned 11 times in the Qur'an. See entry for "Jesus" above. HADITH: see Jesus. TABARI: see Jesus. SUYUTI: The word means "true." According to one it does not come from "flat-footed," but from "one who heals the ill by touching," "beautiful" or "wandering on earth." [Heb. "anointed"] (2:372).

Ezra - (`Uzayr) The word is not Arabic, but probably comes from the Hebrew. The form is probably owing to an error on the part of Muhammad (*Vocabulary*, p. 214) QUR'AN: The Jews are said to accept him as God's Son (9:30). HADITH: The Jews admit to believing Ezra is God's Son at the Judgment (SB 9:395). TABARI: The Torah had been destroyed and Ezra was enlightened to write it out from memory; he also taught the people. The Jews later believed he was God's Son (4:64-5) SUYUTI: One says he was a righteous servant; another says he was a prophet (2:366).

APPENDIX F
QUR'ANIC VERSE SOURCES

Almost all of the Qur'anic similarities to other works given here are remote and frequently have only a phrase (or at times a single word) in common. Qur'anic verse locations which are not preceded by numbers were sourced by the author, numbers not accompanied by letters cite the page numbers to Karl Ahrens' article "Christliches im Qoran," *ZDMG*, 84 (1930), who also used W. Rudolph's *Die Abhängigkeit des Qorans von Judentum u. Christentum*, Stuttgart, 1922. Numbers accompanied with letters give the page numbers of the following reference works:

A - Andrae, *Ursprung*
B - Bell, *Origins*
G - Geiger, *WMJA*
K - *Koran*, ed. K. Rudolph
N - Nöldeke, "Qur'an"
S - Speyer, *Erzählungen*

Mecca I

180	Q 96:1	- cf. Is. 40:6
171	Q 74:4	- cf. Rev. 7:16
	Q 74:5	- cf. Mt. 3:7
	Q 74:6	- cf. Lk. 6:30, 35
	Q 74:7	- cf. Ja. 5:7
S-458	Q 107:4f	- cf. Mt. 6:5
A-130	Q 102:1f	- cf. Carm. Nisib. 74:97-98 (Ephraem)
161	Q 90:10	- cf. Mt. 7:13-14
180	Q 90:12f	- cf. Is. 58:6-7
165	Q 90:18	- cf. Mt. 25:41
182	Q 97:3	- cf. Ps. 84:10
171	Q 68:16	- cf. Rev. 9:4
	Q 87:13	- cf. Mk. 9:48; Is. 66:24
	Q 95:2	- cf. Testament of Ephraem the Syrian
	Q 101:5f	- cf. IV Ezra (Apokalypse, p. 144) A-69
171	Q 99:1	- cf. Rev. 6:12-14

	Q 82:1 - cf. Rev. 6:14
A- 65	Q 81:2 - cf. Rev. 6:13
171	Q 81:10 - cf. Rev. 20:12
S-457	Q 53:39 - cf. Gal. 6:5
S-445	Q 53:45 - cf. I Sa. 2:6
S-460	Q 53:45 - cf. Jewish Tefillah
S-442	Q 53:46 - cf. Gen. 1:27
A-153	Q 96:18 - cf. Op. Syr. III, 237, etc. (Ephraem)
171	Q 100:1f - cf. Rev. 6:1-8
54	Q 79:6f - cf. Op. Gr. I,52 etc. (Ephraem)
A-142	Q 77:46 - cf. Lk. 12:19-20
	Q 78:18 - cf. Mt. 24:31
	Q 89:28f - cf. Mt. 25:21,23
S-446	Q 83:1f - cf. Amo. 8:4; Dt. 25:13f
K-533	Q 74:30 - prob. Gnostic source
A-148	Q 69:23 - cf. Op. Syr. III, 583 (Ephraem)
	Q 51:57 - cf. Ps. 50:12
G- 66	Q 56:52 - cf. Sukkah 32
A- 66	Q 70:8 - cf. II Pet. 3:12
181	Q 1:5 - cf. Ps. 27:11 N-10
K-479	Q 53:25 - cf. Rev. 1:8; Is. 44:6
184	Q 73:20 - cf. Pro. 19:17

Mecca II	
54	Q 54:50 - cf. I Cor. 15:52
162	Q 37:22f - cf. Mt. 13:41f
171	Q 37:57 - cf. Rev. 2:11
S-458	Q 76:13 - cf. Rev. 7:16
179	Q 50:2 - cf. Dt. 18:15
184	Q 50:29 - cf. Pro. 30:15f G-67
K-294	Q 20:96f - cf. Sanhedrin 67b
S-445	Q 20:105f - cf. Is. 2:12-15; 40:4
184	Q 20:109 - cf. Ps. 139:5-6
G- 66	Q 15:44 - cf. Sotah 10; Sohar 2
184	Q 38:8 - cf. Ps. 135:7
169	Q 38:40 - cf. Ja. 5:11
S-446	Q 36:38 - cf. Ecc. 1:5
G-72	Q 36:65 - cf. Hagigah 16; Taanit 11.

181	Q 36:82 - cf. Ps. 33:9
	Q 43:37 - cf. Ps. 103:12
	Q 43:39 - cf. Ex. 4:11
165	Q 43:66 - cf. Mk. 13:36
165	Q 43:85 - cf. Mt. 24:36
G- 63	Q 67:3 - cf. Hagigah 12,2
	Q 23:10 - cf. Ja. 2:5
	Q 23:11 - cf. Mt. 25:34
	Q 23:64 - cf. I Cor. 10:13
170	Q 23:98 - cf. Rom. 12:21
S-455	Q 21:48 - cf. Mt. 17:20 etc.
182	Q 21:105 = Ps. 37:29 N-10, S-440
178	Q 21:108 - cf. Dt. 6:4
171	Q 25:28 - cf. Rev. 12:10
169	Q 25:46 - cf. I Pet. 2:25
160	Q 25:64 - cf. Mt. 5:5
S-458	Q 25:64 - cf. Avot 4,15
170	Q 17:16 - cf. Gal. 6:5
	Q 17:23 - cf. Ex. 20:3
	Q 17:23 - cf. Ex. 20:5; Dt. 6:13
	Q 17:23 - cf. Ex. 20:12
	Q 17:31 - cf. Dt. 15:7-8
	Q 17:34 - cf. Ex. 20:14
	Q 17:35 - cf. Ex. 20:13
	Q 17:36 - cf. Dt. 24:17
	Q 17:37 - cf. Lev. 19:35-36
	Q 17:40 - cf. Prov. 6:16
181	Q 17:46 - cf. Ps. 19:2-4
171	Q 17:46 - cf. Rev. 5:13; Ps. 103:20-22
S-454	Q 17:46 - cf. Carm. Nisib. 48:119 (Ephraem)
170	Q 17:47f - cf. II Cor. 3:13f
	Q 17:48 - cf. Is. 6:9-10
183	Q 17:68f - cf. Ps. 107:23-28 G- 87
	Q 17:110 - cf. Berakhot 31,1
S-443	Q 17:111 - cf. Dt. 32:3
171	Q 27:84 - cf. Rev. 13:11
168	Q 18:23 - cf. Ja. 4:13, 15

166	Q 18:31f - * Lk. 12:16-21; B-114
182	Q 18:43 - cf. Ps. 90:5-6; Is. 55:9-10
S-458	Q 18:44 - cf. Avot 6,9
	Q 18:55 - cf. Is. 6:10
	Q 18:109 - cf. Jn. 21:25

Mecca III

	Q 32:4 - cf. Ps. 90:4; II Pet. 3:8
G- 72	Q 41:18f - cf. Hagigah 16; Taanit 11
184	Q 41:46 - cf. Pro. 9:12 181
	Q 45:12 - cf. Ps. 8:6-8
182	Q 16:10 = Ps. 104:13
182	Q 16:11 = Ps. 104:14f
182	Q 16:12 = Ps. 104:19
182	Q 16:15 = Ps. 104:5
182	Q 16:18 = Ps. 104:24
	Q 16:23 - cf. Dt. 6:4
168	Q 16:25 - cf. Ja. 4:6 (Prov. 3:34)
161	Q 16:81 - cf. Mt. 10:29
A- 69	Q 16:91 - cf. Avodah Zarah 2a-3b
	Q 16:93 - cf. Dt. 29:9-12
G- 64	Q 11:9 - cf. Rashi on Gen. 1:2
	Q 14:1 - cf. Acts 26:18
	Q 14:5 - cf. Acts 26:18
171	Q 14:19 - cf. Rev. 21:1; Is. 65:17 S-454
181	Q 14:21 - cf. Ps. 1:4
180	Q 14:29f - cf. Ps. 1:3 etc.
S-458	Q 14:29f - cf. Avot 3,22
S-460	Q 40:1f - cf. Jewish Tefillah
184	Q 40:7 - cf. Sir. 18:13
184	Q 40:10 - cf. Sir. 12:6
178	Q 40:82 - cf. Dt. 4:38 etc.
169	Q 28:60 - cf. I Jn. 2:17
	Q 39:9 - cf. Gal. 6:5
S-458	Q 39:30 - cf. Avot 2,13-14
K-420	Q 39:49 - prob. Zoroastrian source
163	Q 39:63 - cf. Mt. 16:19 etc.

179	Q 39:67 - cf. Is. 34:4; 40:12
S-446	Q 39:68 - cf. Dan. 7:10
S-456	Q 39:68 - cf. I Cor. 15:52
S-459	Q 39:74 - cf. Sanhedrin 10,1
170	Q 29:33 - cf. Rom. 1:18
162	Q 29:42 - cf. Mt. 13:11
160	Q 29:60 - cf. Mt. 6:26
G- 88	Q 31:13 - cf. Yevamot 4,10
167	Q 42:16 - cf. Jn. 5:25
171	Q 42:19 - cf. Gal. 6:8
S-460	Q 42:24 - cf. Jewish Tefillah
160	Q 42:38 - cf. Mt. 5:9
183	Q 42:48 - cf. Ps. 115:3
S-445	Q 10:19 - cf. Is. 44:10, etc.
S-445	Q 10:62 - cf. Is. 40:15
170	Q 34:30f - cf. I Cor. 8:10-13
161	Q 34:46 - cf. Mt. 10:8
S-456	Q 34:46 - cf. Avot 1,3
179	Q 35:1 - cf. Is. 6:2
	Q 35:19 - cf. Gal. 6:5
183	Q 35:44 - cf. Ps. 130:3
S-442	Q 7:23f - cf. Gen. 3:17
168	Q 7:32 - cf. Ac. 17:26
164	Q 7:38 - cf. Mt. 19:24 etc.
170	Q 7:42 - cf. Gal. 3:13
S-453	Q 7:44 - cf. Lk. 16:26
166	Q 7:48 - cf. Lk. 16:24, 26 N-10
162	Q 7:56 - cf. Mt. 13:3-8
S-442	Q 7:125 - cf. Ex. 14:13-14; Ps. 37:9 S-447
S-442	Q 7:142 - cf. Dt. 27:8
S-447	Q 7:155 - cf. Ps. 145:9
162	Q 7:178 - cf. Mt. 13:15; Ps. 115:5-7
183	Q 7:194 - cf. Ps. 115:5-7
G- 90	Q 46:14 - cf. Avot 5,21
166	Q 46:19 - cf. Lk. 16:25 N-10
180	Q 6:1 - cf. Is. 45:7
179	Q 6:33 - cf. I Sa. 8:7

S-446	Q 6:52 - cf. Pro. 7:15; Hos. 5:15
168	Q 6:54 - cf. Ac. 17:30f
S-452	Q 6:54 - cf. apoc. Mission Sermon of Peter
S-454	Q 6:59 - cf. Mt. 10:29
S-452	Q 6:109 - cf. Lk. 16:27-31
166	Q 6:111 - cf. Lk. 16:31
170	Q 6:153 - cf. I Cor. 10:13
168	Q 6:159 - cf. Ja. 2:17

Medina

181	Q 2:14 - cf. Ps. 2:4
S-460	Q 2:28 - cf. Jewish Tefillah (Qedussa)
179	Q 2:28 - cf. Is. 6:3
164	Q 2:41 - cf. Mt. 23:3
182	Q 2:45 - cf. Ps. 49:8; Gal. 6:5
S-447	Q 2:55 - cf. Ps. 100:4
168	Q 2:59 - cf. Ac. 10:35
164	Q 2:69 - cf. Mt. 19:8
167	Q 2:73 - cf. Jn. 7:49
168	Q 2:82 - cf. Ac. 7:51
S-443	Q 2:87 - cf. Dt. 5:24
S-459	Q 2:96 - cf. Sanhedrin 10,2
G-138	Q 2:127 - cf. Midr. Rabba Gen. parag. 98, etc.
S-444	Q 2:182 - cf. Is. 55:6; 58:2,9
G- 87	Q 2:183 - cf. Berakhot 1,2
160	Q 2:224 - cf. Mt. 5:34
160	Q 2:226 - cf. Mt. 6:1
S-443	Q 2:233 - cf. Dt. 24:16
G- 85	Q 2:240 - cf. Berakhot 4,5
S-443	Q 2:256 - cf. Dt. 29:18
184	Q 2:256 - cf. I Ch. 29:11
183	Q 2:256 - cf. Ps. 121:4
S-444	Q 2:256 - cf. Is. 40:28
180	Q 2:256 - cf. Is. 66:1
169	Q 2:258 - cf. I Pet. 2:9
162	Q 2:263 - cf. Mt. 13:8; Gen 41:7
S-447	Q 2:266 - cf. Mt. 6:1
162	Q 2:266f- cf. Mt. 13:5-8

160	Q 2:273 - cf. Mt. 6:4
S-444	Q 2:275 - cf. Mt. 6:4; Is. 40:29-31
S-451	Q 2:286 - cf. I Cor. 10:13
171	Q 16:115 - cf. I Tim. 4:2-4
S-454	Q 16:127 - cf. Mt. 5:38-39; Berakhot 9,5
165	Q 62:5 - cf. Mt. 23:4
S-461	Q 62:5 - cf. Traditional Jewish proverb
170	Q 8:24 - cf. I Jn. 3:20 178
	Q 8:67 - cf. Lev. 26:8
	Q 47:16 - cf. Secrets of Enoch 8:6; Apoc. Paul 23
166	Q 3:25 - cf. Lk. 1:52; I Sam. 2:6-7
	Q 3:32 - cf. Protevangelion 8:2
	Q 3:39 - cf. Protevangelion 8:6f
160	Q 3:43 - cf. Mt. 6:19, 25
161	Q 3:43 - cf. Mt. 11:5
180	Q 3:46 - cf. Mal. 3:16
170	Q 3:58 - cf. Gal. 3:16f
164	Q 3:68 - cf. Mt. 18:23-34
163	Q 3:85 - cf. Mt. 16:26
S-451	Q 3:92 - cf. I Clem. 52:1
171	Q 3:98 - cf. Eph. 2:14
165	Q 3:120f- * Mt. 26:53
184	Q 3:129 - cf. Ps. 130:4
171	Q 3:141 - cf. I Tim. 4:8
S-444	Q 3:153 - cf. Is. 42:1-7
S-443	Q 3:158 - cf. Dt. 18:15
179	Q 3:179 - cf. Lev. 9:24 (I K. 18:38)
160	Q 3:180 - cf. Mt. 5:12
S-451	Q 3:182 - cf. Mt. 16:28 (poet Nabiga 27,28)
178	Q 3:188 - cf. Dt. 6:7
178	Q 3:191 - cf. Num. 23:10 G-89
164	Q 3:194 - cf. Mt. 19:29
180	Q 57:3 - cf. Is. 44:6; 48:12 (Rev. 1:17; 22:13)
165	Q 57:13 - cf. Mt. 25:1-13
169	Q 57:28 - cf. I Jn. 1:7; Is. 2:5 S-445
K- 96	Q 4:3 - cf. Yevamot, 44a, 4-1, etc.
164	Q 4:11 - cf. Mt. 23:14

	Q 4:27 - cf. Lev. 18:6-18
G- 86	Q 4:46 - cf. Berakhot 31,2
G- 86	Q 4:46 - cf. Berakhot 3,4
G- 90	Q 4:87 - cf. Bava Kama 92
S-458	Q 4:88 - cf. Avot 1,15
G- 86	Q 4:102 - cf. Berakhot 4,4
168	Q 4:124 - cf. Ja. 2:23; II Chron. 20:7
S-447	Q 4:139 - cf. Ps. 1:1
160	Q 4:141 - cf. Mt. 6:5
S-444	Q 4:154 - cf. Lev. 26:41; Jer. 9:25
K-115	Q 4:156 - cf. Gnostic Acts of John 98-100
170	Q 4:158 - cf. Gal. 3:19
S-460	Q 59:23f - cf. Jewish Tefillah
	Q 24:22 - cf. Mt. 6:15
S-460	Q 24:24 - cf. Hagigah 14a
G- 88	Q 24:31 - cf. Lev. 18:6-18
169	Q 24:35 - cf. I Jn. 1:5
S-460	Q 24:36f - cf. Jewish Tefillah (Qedussa)
S-455	Q 24:39f - cf. II Pet. 2:17
163	Q 58:8 - cf. Mt. 18:20
S-459	Q 58:8 - cf. Avot 3,7
S-445	Q 22:38 - cf. Is. 1:11; Jer. 6:20, etc.
169	Q 22:46 - cf. II Pet. 3:8
165	Q 48:29 - cf. Mk. 4:26f
161	Q 9:24 - cf. Mt. 10:37 (34)
168	Q 9:34f - cf. Ja. 5:3
S-458	Q 9:38 - cf. Avot 4,17
164	Q 9:81 - cf. Mt. 18:21-22
161	Q 9:110 - cf. Mt. 7:24-26
178	Q 5:4 - cf. Lev. 17:15
G- 86	Q 5:8 - cf. Berakhot 15a, 46
S-452	Q 5:40 - cf. Mt. 16:26
178	Q 5:21 - cf. Dt. 14:1
N- 10	Q 5:35 - cf. Sanhedrin 4,5
178	Q 5:49 - cf. Lev. 24:19-20; Ex. 21:23-25
178	Q 5:69 - cf. Num. 11:23; Is. 59:1
S-447	Q 5:82 - * Ps. 109

S-452   Q 5:82 - * Mt. 23
S-443   Q 5:91 - cf. Lev. 5:11
S-443   Q 5:91 - cf. Dt. 23:24
S-452   Q 5:112f- cf. I Cor. 10:21; Ac. 10:11f

BIBLIOGRAPHY

Ahrens, Karl. "Christliches im Qoran," *ZDMG*, vol. 84 (1930), pp. 15-68, 148-190.

Andrae, Tor. *Der Ursprung des Islams und das Christentum.* Uppsala: Almqvist & Wikells Boktryckeri, 1926.

_____. *Mohammed: the Man and His Faith.* Trans. Theophil Menzel. New York: Harper & Brothers, repr. 1960.

The Ante-Nicene Fathers. Ed. Philip Schaff. Grand Rapids: Wm. B. Eerdmans Publishing Co., repr. 1983.

Apokalypsen. Ed. Rosel Termolen. Augsburg: Pattloch Verlag, 1990.

Bell, Richard. *A Commentary on the Qur'an.* Eds. C.E. Bosworth and M.E.J. Richardson. Manchester: University of Manchester, 1991.

_____. *The Origin of Islam in its Christian Environment.* London: Frank Cass & Co. Ltd., repr. 1968.

Buhl, Frants. *Das Leben Muhammad.* Trans. H.H. Shaeder. Darmstadt: Wissenschaftliche Buchgesellschaft, repr. 1961.

Campbell, William. *The Qur'an and the Bible in the Light of History and Science.* Upper Darby, PA: Middle East Resources, 1986, repr. 1992.

Charles, R.H. *The Book of Enoch.* London: SPCK, 1966.

The Early Christian-Muslim Dialogue. Ed. N.A. Newman. Hatfield, PA: Interdisciplinary Biblical Research Institute, 1993.

Cook, Michael. *Muhammad.* Oxford: Oxford University Press, 1983.

Le Coran. Trans. Régis Blachère. Paris: G. P. Maisonneuve, 1957.

Crone, Patricia. *Meccan Trade and the Rise of Islam*. Princeton: Princeton University Press, 1987.

Encyclopedia of the Early Church. Ed. Angelo di Berardino, Trans. Adrian Wolford. New York: Oxford University Press, 1992.

Encyclopaedia of Islam. 2nd ed. Leiden: E.J. Brill, 1960-.

Encyclopaedia Judaica. Jerusalem: Keter Publishing House, Ltd., 1972.

Enzyklopädie des Islam. Leiden: E.J. Brill, 1927.

Geiger, Abraham. *Was hat Mohammed aus dem Judenthume Aufgenommen?*. Leipzig: Verlag von M.W. Kaufmann, repr. 1902.

Ginzberg, Louis. *The Legends of the Jews*. Philadelphia: Jewish Publication Society, 1909-1936.

_____. *Legends of the Bible*. Philadelphia: Jewish Publication Society, condensation of above work.

Grünbaum, Max. *Neue Beiträge zur semitischen Sagenkunde*. Leiden: E.J. Brill, 1893.

Guillaume, Alfred. "The Influence of Judaism on Islam," *The Legacy of Israel*. Oxford: Clarendon Press, 1928, pp. 129-171.

_____. *Islam*. Baltimore: Penguin Books, repr. 1964.

_____. *New Light on the Life of Muhammad*. Manchester: Manchester University Press, 1960.

_____. *The Traditions of Islam*. Beirut: Khayats, repr. 1966.

Horovitz, Josef. *Koranische Untersuchungen*. Berlin: Walter de Gruyter & Co., 1926.

Ibn Ishaq, Muhammad. *The Life of Muhammad*. Trans. A. Guillaume. Karachi: Oxford University Press, 1955.

Ibn al-Nadim. *Fihrist*. Ed. G. Flügel. Leipzig: Verlag F.C.W. Vogel, 1871-1872.

_____. *The Fihrist of al-Nadim*. Trans. and ed. B. Dodge. New York: Columbia University Press, 1970.

Ibn Sa`d, Muhammad. *Ibn Saad*. Eds. E. Sachau, et al. Leiden: E.J. Brill, 1904-.

_____. *Kitab al-Tabaqat al-Kabir*. Trans. S.M. Haq. New Delhi: Kitab Bhavan, 1972.

Jeffery, Arthur. *Foreign Vocabulary of the Qur'an*, Baroda: Oriental Institute, 1938.

_____. *Materials for the History of the Text of the Qur'an*, New York: AMS Press, repr. 1975.

Josephus, Flavius. *The Works of Josephus*, Trans. William Whiston. Peabody: Hendrickson Publishers, repr. 1989.

Juynboll, G. H. A. *The Authenticity of the Tradition Literature: Discussions in Modern Egypt*. Leiden: E.J. Brill, 1969.

Kassis, Hanna E. *A Concordance of the Qur'an*, Berkeley: University of California Press, 1983.

Der Koran. Trans. Max Henning. Eds. Ernst Werner and Kurt Rudolph, Wiesbaden: VMA Verlag, n.d.

The Koran Interpreted. Trans. A.J. Arberry. New York: Macmillan, 1955, repr. 1986.

The Meaning of the Glorious Koran. Trans. M.M. Pickthall. repr. New York: The New American Library, 1953, repr. 1961.

Kur'an-i Kerim. Trans. Ö.N. Bilmen. Ankara: Akchagh, 1962

Kur'an-i Kerim. Trans. A. Gölpinarli. Istanbul: Yükselen Matbaasi, 1958.

Lexikon zur Bibel. Ed. Fritz Rienecker. Wuppertal: R. Brockhaus Verlag, 1960, repr. 1991.

Lightfoot, J.B. *The Apostolic Fathers*. Grand Rapids: Baker Book House, repr. 1983.

The Lost Books of the Bible and The Forgotten Books of Eden, Eds. Frank Crane, et al. World Bible Publishers Inc., 1926, repr. n.d.

Margoliouth, D.S. *The Relations Between the Arabs and Israelites Prior to the Rise of Islam*. London: 1924.

_____, "Some Additions to Professor Jeffery's *Foreign Vocabulary of the Qur'an*," *JRAS*, (1939), pp. 53-61.

Neutestamentliche Apokryphen. Ed. Wilhelm Schneemelcher. Tübingen: J.C.B. Mohr, 1990.

Nevo, Yehuda D. "Towards a Prehistory of Islam," *Jerusalem Studies in Arabic and Islam*. Jerusalem: Hebrew University of Jerusalem, 1994, pp. 108-127.

The Nicene and Post-Nicene Fathers. Ed. Philip Schaff. Grand Rapids: Wm. B. Eerdmans Publishing Co., repr. 1983.

Nöldeke, Theodor; Schwally, Friedrich; Bergsträsser, G., and Pretzl, O. *Geschichte des Qorans*. Hildesheim: Georg Olms Verlagsbuchhandlung, repr. 1961.

Nöldeke, Theodor. *"The Qur'an: An Introductory Essay"*, ed. N.A. Newman. Hatfield, PA: Interdisciplinary Biblical Research Institute, 1992.

The Oxford Dictionary of the Christian Church. Eds. F.L. Cross and E.A. Livingstone. Oxford: Oxford University Press, 1983.

The Holy Qur'an. Trans. A.Y. Ali. New York: Hafner Publishing Co., 1946.

The Qur'an: Translated with a critical re-arrangement of the Surahs, Trans. Richard Bell. Edinburgh: T. & T. Clark, 1937, repr. 1960.

Rosenblatt, Samuel. "Rabbinic Legends in Hadith," *The Moslem World*, vol. 35 (1945), pp. 237-252.

Sahih Bukhari, Trans. Muhammad Muhsin Khan. Chicago: Kazi Publications, 1976.

Sahih Muslim, Trans. Abdul Hamid Siddiqi. Lahore: Sh. Muhammad Ashraf Publishers, 1976.

Sell, Canon. *The Historical Development of the Qur'an*, Madras: 1898, repr. Chicago: People International, n.d.

Sezgin, Fuat. *Geschichte des arabischen Schrifttums*, Leiden: E.J. Brill, 1967-.

Shahid, Irfan. *Byzantium and the Arabs in the Fifth Century*, Washington: Dumbarton Oaks Research Library, 1989.

Shorter Encyclopaedia of Islam. Eds. H.A.R. Gibb and J.H. Kramers. Leiden: E.J. Brill, 1974.

Speyer, Heinrich. *Die biblischen Erzählungen im Qoran*. Darmstadt: Wissenschaftliche Buchgesellschaft, 1931, repr. 1961.

The Standard Jewish Encyclopedia. Jerusalem: Massadah Publishing Co., 1958.

Sunan Abu Dawud, Trans. Ahmad Hasan. Lahore: Sh. Muhammad Ashraf Publishers, 1984.

Suyuti, Jalaladdin. *El-Itkan fi Ulumi'l Kur'an*. Trans. Sakip Yildiz and Hüseyin Avni Chelik. Istanbul: Hikmet Neshriyat, 1987.

Al-Tabari, Abu Ja'far Muhammad ibn Jarir. *Annales*. Ed. M.J. de Goeje. Leiden: E.J. Brill, 1881-1882.

————. *The History of al-Tabari*. Ed. Ehsan Yar-Shater. New York: State University of New York, 1987-.

————. *Taberi Tefsiri*. (abridged) Eds. M.A. al-Sabuni and S.A. Riza. Trans. M. Keskin. Istanbul: Shule Yayinlari, n.d.

————. *Tarih-i Taberi* Trans. unknown. Istanbul: Elif Ofset Tesisleri, repr. 1982-1983.

Der Babylonischen Talmud. (Abridged). Ed. Reinhold Mayer. Munich: Wilhelm Goldmann Verlag, 1963.

Wansbrough, John. *Quranic Studies, etc*. London: Oxford University Press, 1977.

Al-Waqidi, Muhammad b. ʿUmar. *Muhammad in Medina: Kitab al-Maghazi*. (abridged) Ed. and Trans. Julius Wellhausen. Berlin: Druck und Verlag von G. Reimer, 1882.

————. *Kitab al-Maghazi*. Ed. Marsden Jones. London: Oxford University Press, 1966.

Watt, Montgomery W. *Muhammad: Prophet and Statesman*. London: Oxford University Press, 1961.

————. *Die Religion der Menschheit: Der Islam*. Trans. S. Höfer. vol. 25.1. Stuttgart: Verlag W. Kohlhammer GmbH, 1980.

_____ and Bell, Richard. *Introduction to the Qur'an.* Edinburgh: University Press, 1970, repr. 1994.

Wellhausen, Julius. *Reste arabischen Heidentums*, Berlin: Walter de Gruyter & Co., repr. 1961.

Würthwein, Ernst. *The Text of the Old Testament.* Trans. E.F. Rhode. Grand Rapids: William B. Eerdmans Publishing Co., 1979.